Alfresco 3
Records Management

Comply with regulations and secure your organization's records with Alfresco Records Management

Dick Weisinger

[PACKT] open source*
PUBLISHING   community experience distilled

BIRMINGHAM - MUMBAI

Alfresco 3 Records Management

Copyright © 2011 Packt Publishing

First published: January 2011

Production Reference: 1110111

Published by Packt Publishing Ltd.
32 Lincoln Road
Olton
Birmingham, B27 6PA, UK.

ISBN 978-1-849514-36-1

www.packtpub.com

Cover Image by Asher Wishkerman (a.wishkerman@mpic.de)

Credits

Author
Dick Weisinger

Reviewer
Sherwin John Calleja-Tragura

Acquisition Editor
Steven Wilding

Development Editors
Rakesh Shejwal

Swapna Verlekar

Technical Editor
Dayan Hyames

Copy Editor
Leonard D'Silva

Indexers
Tejal Daruwale

Rekha Nair

Editorial Team Leader
Aanchal Kumar

Project Team Leader
Priya Mukherji

Project Coordinator
Shubhanjan Chatterjee

Proofreaders
Jacqueline McGhee

Aaron Nash

Graphics
Nilesh R. Mohite

Production Coordinator
Adline Swetha Jesuthas

Cover Work
Adline Swetha Jesuthas

About the Author

Dick Weisinger is Vice President and Chief Technologist at Formtek, Inc. and has more than 20 years of experience in the area of Enterprise Content Management especially Content, Document, and Image Management. His career spans many projects and organizations and he has contributed to software solutions used for health care, finance, engineering, discrete manufacturing, and aerospace and defense applications. Dick is a regular contributor to the Formtek blog at `http://www.formtek.com/blog` on topics that include ECM, SaaS, Open Source, SOA, and New Technology.

Dick earned a Masters in Engineering Science in Operations Research from the University of California at Berkeley and a Masters in Engineering Science from the Johns Hopkins University. Dick is an AIIM-certified Records Management Specialist.

I would like to thank everyone who helped make this book a reality, including Rakesh Shejwal, the development editor; Shubhanjan Chatterjee, the project coordinator; Dayan Hyames, the technical editor, and Sherwin John Calleja-Tragura, the book's technical reviewer.

Special thanks to Dennis Scanlon and to team members at Formtek for providing support and the necessary time needed to work on this book, and also thanks to my wife and son for their support and understanding.

About the Reviewer

Sherwin John Calleja-Tragura is a Java Technical Consultant/Architect of Alibata Systems Incorporated (ASI), a software development and training team in Manila, Philippines. He is currently conducting corporate training on different object-oriented disciplines, especially Java/JEE-core and C++ courses. He also spearheads the technical team of the company's Ofbiz/Opentaps ERP and Alfresco Document Management projects. He is currently an EMC Documentum Proven Associate (E20-120).

Tragura started his career as a Computational Science faculty at the University of the Philippines-Los Banos where he took some units in MS Computer Science. He was a part-time PHP developer then.

I would like to thank my UPLB-FOREHA friends for their utmost support to my skill sets and talents. Likewise to Owen Estabillo who is always there through my ups-and-downs.

www.PacktPub.com

Support files, e-books, discount offers and more

You might want to visit www.PacktPub.com for support files and downloads related to your book.

Did you know that Packt offers e-book versions of every book published, with PDF and e-Pub files available? You can upgrade to the e-book version at www.PacktPub.com and as a print book customer, you are entitled to a discount on the e-book copy. Get in touch with us at service@packtpub.com for more details.

At www.PacktPub.com, you can also read a collection of free technical articles, sign up for a range of free newsletters and receive exclusive discounts and offers on Packt books and e-books.

http://PacktLib.PacktPub.com

Do you need instant solutions to your IT questions? PacktLib is Packt's online digital book library. Here, you can access, read and search across Packt's entire library of books.

Why Subscribe?
- Fully searchable across every book published by Packt
- Copy and paste, print and bookmark content
- On demand and accessible via web browser

Free Access for Packt account holders

If you have an account with Packt at www.PacktPub.com, you can use this to access PacktLib today and view nine entirely free books. Simply use your login credentials for immediate access.

Table of Contents

Preface

Alfresco Enterprise Content Management (ECM) software provides content-centric features in the areas of Document Management (DM), Web Content Management (WCM), and Microsoft SharePoint-like Collaboration. Alfresco is particularly strong in handling the storage of large amounts of content and in enabling collaboration. Alfresco software is licensed as either open source Community or with a fully-supported Enterprise license.

There has been incredible growth in the breadth of the capabilities of Alfresco software since the initial Alfresco software release in 2005. Much of that growth has been possible due to good software architectural decisions that Alfresco developers made early on. Those early decisions drove the development of a solid and extensible software foundation that has enabled new capabilities to be rapidly built out.

In late 2009, Alfresco introduced another new capability, an extension for Records Management that was not only compatible with, but also certified for, the Department of Defense (DoD) 5015.2 Records Management standard.

The announcement was notable, because firstly, the certification for 5015.2 is difficult to achieve. Only a few more than a dozen vendors out of an industry with vendors numbering in the hundreds have managed to be certified for 5015.2. Secondly, it was notable because Alfresco made the records software available as a free component in the open source community version of its software. Prior to that announcement, certified Records Management software was available for many tens, if not hundreds, of thousands of dollars.

The focus of this book is the Alfresco Records Management Module. To fully understand how Alfresco Records Management works, and why it works the way it does, it is necessary to also understand many of the basics of Records Management. This book tries to cover sufficient background in Records Management to bring users up to speed so that they can effectively set up a records program within their organization and then go about implementing the program using Alfresco Records Management.

As a result of the approach taken, the first chapter in the book is focused almost exclusively on Records Management without any specifics on the Alfresco implementation. After that, we dive down into great detail about how to set up, configure, and actually use Alfresco Records Management.

Dick Weisinger, the author of this book, is Vice President and Chief Technologist at Formtek, Inc. Formtek and provides Enterprise Content Management (ECM) software and services to its customers globally. Headquartered in the US, Formtek has partners and customers in the Americas, Asia, and Europe. Records Management and Alfresco software are some of Formtek's core capabilities.

 Additional information can be found about Formtek products and services at http://www.formtek.com.

What this book covers

Chapter 1, Records Management, describes the importance of Records Management and provides an overview of the general principles and the benefits that can be derived from implementing Records Management. Both Records Management standards, ISO 15489 and DoD 5015.2, are introduced.

Chapter 2, Getting Started with the Alfresco Records Management Module, narrows the discussion of Records Management to the Alfresco Records Management implementation. This chapter describes in detail how to install Alfresco Share with the Records Management Module, and then how to create the Alfresco Share Records Management site. In the latter part of this chapter, we discuss technical details of Alfresco webscripts and some of the underlying implementation of the Records Management dashlet.

Chapter 3, Introduction to the Alfresco Share Records Management Site, describes the basic framework of an Alfresco Share site, describing Share dashboards and collaboration features. The chapter also gives an overview of the File Plan and Records Search pages, which are unique to the Records Management site. At the end of this chapter, we examine some of the internal workings of Share site dashboards and the dashlets contained within them.

Chapter 4, Metadata and the Alfresco Content Model, introduces the Content Model structure used by Alfresco for defining document types and for specifying the metadata properties that are associated with document types. This chapter discusses in great detail how to define and extend document types and aspects of the Alfresco Content Model. Specifically the Records Management content models are looked at in detail.

Chapter 5, Creating the File Plan, describes best practices for developing a File Plan that uniquely fits the needs of your organization. We then see how to take the File Plan design and implement it within Alfresco. The chapter describes the mechanics of the File Plan implementation which involves creating the DoD 5015.2 foldering hierarchy of Series, Category, and Folder container. In the latter part of the chapter, we look at the internals of the File Plan page within the Records Management site. We note that this page is similar to and shares code with the Document Library page used by standard Share sites.

Chapter 6, Creating Disposition Schedules, describes how record retention and lifecycle information is defined within the disposition schedule. This chapter shows how a disposition schedule is created and applied at the Category level within the File Plan. The end of the chapter examines how the disposition page in the web client is constructed and interacts with the Alfresco repository using AJAX. We also see in detail how and where disposition information is stored within the repository.

Chapter 7, Filing Records, shows that methods other than the Alfresco Share web browser interface can be used to file records. The chapter describes how records can also be filed from an e-mail client, like Microsoft Outlook, or directly from the file system, using, for example, Windows Explorer in the Microsoft Windows operating system, or via FTP or batch loading programs. At the end of the chapter, we examine the low-level details of how files are uploaded and stored in the repository, and we also look at the internals of the upload form that allows multiple files to be selected for upload from the browser client.

Chapter 8, Managing Records, covers how to perform operations on records once the records have been filed into the File Plan. The operations discussed include copy, move, delete, the creation of links between records, and the viewing of a record's audit history. The latter part of the chapter discusses some of the internal implementation details of the built-in web preview capability.

Chapter 9, Following the Lifecycle of a Record, walks through the possible steps of the record lifecycle, typically from filing to destruction. The discussion includes record transfer and record accession, and describes how and why records might need to be frozen. The difference between the destruction and deletion of records is also described. The discussion on implementation internals looks at e-mail notifications and how background scheduled jobs automatically process steps of the record lifecycle.

Chapter 10, Searching Records and Running Audits, describes how to perform basic and complex searches for records in the File Plan, and how frequently used searches can be saved and later recalled and reused. The chapter describes the Audit Tool within the Records Management console and shows how reports can be run to audit actions and events that have occurred in the records system. At the end of the chapter, the internal implementation of the repository webscripts that are used to implement search and audit capabilities are discussed.

Chapter 11, Configuring Security and Permissions, explains how to create and modify users and groups that will have access to the Alfresco Share Records Management site. It describes how to create and modify Records Management roles and then how to assign permissions to those roles. The chapter also discusses how to set access rights for areas within the File Plan. The end of the chapter describes how webscripts are used to retrieve user, group, and role information from the repository.

Chapter 12, Configuring Records Management Parameters, discusses a number of useful administrative features that are available in the Records Management console. One of these tools allows the user to add custom metadata properties to extend the standard Alfresco Records Management content model. Other administrative tools are used to create custom events and to specify relationship types between records. In the implementation discussion for this chapter, we look in detail at how Alfresco implements dynamic metadata extensions to the content model.

Appendix A, Records Management Standards, discusses the ISO 15489 and DoD 5015.2 standards in greater detail than covered in *Chapter 1*.

Appendix B, The Records Content Model, shows the detailed structure of the content model for Records Management in Alfresco.

Appendix C, Records Management Terms, lists and defines commonly used terms used in Records Management.

You can download Appendices A, B, and C from https://www.packtpub.com/alfresco-3-records-management/book.

What you need for this book

The focus of this book is on the Alfresco Records Management module and requires only the following Alfresco software and Alfresco software stack elements:

- Alfresco 3.2r+ Software, Enterprise, or Community
- Alfresco 3.2r+ Records Management Module, Enterprise or Community

Alfresco offers stack-complete installation bundles on both Windows and Linux that include all elements of the stack needed for the software to run, like the database (MySQL) and application server (Tomcat).

More information is provided in *Chapter 2* where the software installation is discussed in detail.

Who this book is for

The primary target audience of this book includes individuals who will be implementing Records Management programs for their organizations. It will be particularly relevant to Records Managers, Business Analysts, and Software Developers.

Alfresco Share Developers will also be interested in some of the implementation details which are discussed here and which can be applied generally to other Alfresco Share development projects.

Alfresco Share is built on the Spring-Surf framework which extensively uses client and server-side Javascript and the FreeMarker templating language. At the end of many of the chapters are sections which are aimed at developers and which discuss the implementation details of Records Management within Alfresco Share. An understanding of Javascript, FreeMarker, and HTML would be useful when reading those sections of this book. Readers not interested in the details of the implementation should feel free to skip over those sections of the book.

No prior knowledge of Alfresco Share software is required to follow this book.

Conventions

In this book, you will find a number of styles of text that distinguish between different kinds of information. Here are some examples of these styles, and an explanation of their meaning.

Code words in text are shown as follows: "Objects of the type disposition action, or `rma:dispositionAction`, are being tracked."

A block of code is set as follows:

```
## Title
header.fileplan=File Plan
## Filters
label.transfers=Transfers
label.holds=Holds
```

Any command-line input or output is written as follows:

```
C:\>net config workstation
```

New terms and **important words** are shown in bold. Words that you see on the screen, in menus or dialog boxes for example, appear in the text like this: "We can click on **Next** and then on **Finish** to create the new e-mail account".

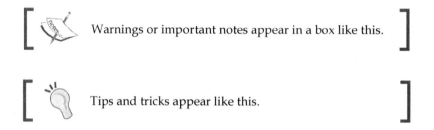

Warnings or important notes appear in a box like this.

Tips and tricks appear like this.

Reader feedback

Feedback from our readers is always welcome. Let us know what you think about this book—what you liked or may have disliked. Reader feedback is important for us to develop titles that you really get the most out of.

To send us general feedback, simply send an e-mail to feedback@packtpub.com, and mention the book title via the subject of your message.

If there is a book that you need and would like to see us publish, please send us a note in the **SUGGEST A TITLE** form on www.packtpub.com or e-mail us at suggest@packtpub.com.

If there is a topic that you have expertise in and you are interested in either writing or contributing to a book, see our author guide on www.packtpub.com/authors.

Customer support

Now that you are the proud owner of a Packt book, we have a number of things to help you to get the most from your purchase.

Downloading the example code for this book

You can download the example code files for all Packt books you have purchased from your account at `http://www.PacktPub.com`. If you purchased this book elsewhere, you can visit `http://www.PacktPub.com/support` and register to have the files e-mailed directly to you.

Errata

Although we have taken every care to ensure the accuracy of our content, mistakes do happen. If you find a mistake in one of our books—maybe a mistake in the text or the code—we would be grateful if you would report this to us. By doing so, you can save other readers from frustration and help us improve subsequent versions of this book. If you find any errata, please report them by visiting `http://www.packtpub.com/support`, selecting your book, clicking on the **errata submission form** link, and entering the details of your errata. Once your errata are verified, your submission will be accepted and the errata will be uploaded on our website, or added to any list of existing errata, under the Errata section of that title. Any existing errata can be viewed by selecting your title from `http://www.packtpub.com/support`.

Piracy

Piracy of copyright material on the Internet is an ongoing problem across all media. At Packt, we take the protection of our copyright and licenses very seriously. If you come across any illegal copies of our works, in any form, on the Internet, please provide us with the location address or website name immediately so that we can pursue a remedy.

Please contact us at `copyright@packtpub.com` with a link to the suspected pirated material.

We appreciate your help in protecting our authors, and our ability to bring you valuable content.

Questions

You can contact us at `questions@packtpub.com` if you are having a problem with any aspect of the book, and we will do our best to address it.

1
Records Management

In this first chapter, before getting into the specifics of the Alfresco implementation of Records Management, let's examine in detail exactly what records are and the reasons why Records Management is important for organizations of all sizes.

In this chapter, we will cover:

- What a record and Records Management are
- What we mean by a records lifecycle
- The difference between Document and Records Management
- The benefits of Records Management

What is a record?

Let's start with a definition of what a record is. The **ISO 15489** definition of a record is as follows:

> Records contain "information created, received, and maintained as evidence and information by an organization or person, in pursuance of legal obligations or in the transaction of business".

 ISO 15489 is an international standard issued by the International Organization for Standardization (ISO) that specifies high-level best practices around Records Management. Many more prescriptive Records Management standards draw heavily on the basic concepts described in ISO 15489, like the US Department of Defense's (DoD) 5015.2 specification and the European MoReq specification. More information about ISO 15489 and the DoD 5015.2 can be found in Appendix A (which is available for download from the Packt Publishing website).

The ISO 15489 standard distinguishes a record from an ordinary document with this definition:

> *A document is "recorded information or an object which can be treated as a unit".*

In short, records are a subset of all documents that enter or that have been created within an organization. Records are that group of documents which contain information about the actions, decisions, and operations that have occurred in the organization.

As a rule of thumb, if you can answer 'yes' to any of these questions, then the document being considered should be classified or declared as a record:

- Does it support or document a transaction?
- Does it provide information used in making a business decision?
- Does it document actions taken in response to an inquiry?
- Does it document the reasoning for creating or changing a policy?
- Does it document your business process?

It is useful to note that some things are generally not considered to be records. These include such things as copies of records made for your reference, document drafts that have not been published, notes that have not been shared with colleagues, and envelopes used for routing. The specific records maintained by any one organization will differ based on the nature of the organization. Examples of records include items such as facility blueprints, bank records, board minutes, contracts, correspondence, deeds for property owned, general ledgers, insurance policies, meeting minutes, organizational charts, patents and trademarks, payroll information, personnel folders, policy and procedures, research data, protocols, quarterly reports, and technical system documentation.

Records can be stored on paper, electronic files, e-mail, microfiche, audiotapes, videos, databases, photographs, and other media. Information in voice mail and instant messaging can also be considered as records. Even information exchanged with Social Media tools and software can be considered as records, such as information stored in microblogs (for example, Twitter tweets), content posted to social networking sites like Facebook and LinkedIn, blog posts, and wikis.

Electronic Records Management (ERM) systems often separate records into two categories—electronic and non-electronic or physical. Electronic records can be stored directly in the repository of the Records Management system and have the advantage of being quicker and easier to search and retrieve. Non-electronic records, like those stored on paper or microfilm, are not stored digitally, and must be tracked by their physical location.

What is Records Management?

The ISO-14589 definition for Records Management is as follows:

> *"Records Management is the field of management responsible for the efficient and systematic control of the creation, receipt, maintenance, use, and disposition of records, including the processes for capturing and maintaining evidence of and information about business activities and transactions in the form of records."*

While Records Management is a vital tool for companies to address governance, compliance, and retention requirements, the benefits of Records Management go beyond government regulations. For example, the use of Records Management improves a company's overall data management processes, particularly in the areas of data security and data access.

Electronic Records Management

Records Management systems that use software to automate the management of records are called **Electronic Records Management (ERM)** systems. This book discusses Alfresco, which is an example of an ERM system. ERM systems are not limited to managing only electronic records; non-electronic records can also be tracked with ERM systems.

Record lifecycles

A distinguishing feature of a record, compared to a document, is that every record has a lifecycle. When a record is initially filed and declared, the lifespan of the record is implicitly defined. That definition includes how long it will be usable, and at what point in time will it be either moved to permanent archival or destroyed. Best practice Records Management, as derived from the ISO 15489 definition of Records Management above, defines the following steps in the lifecycle of a record:

- Creation, receipt, and capture of a document
- Classification, filing, and declaration of the document as a record
- Maintenance, use, storage, and retrieval of the record
- Disposal of the record

Throughout the course of daily business transactions, documents are typically received, created electronically, or captured by scanners and then converted into electronic image files. Documents are then filed within the Records Management system and declared to be records.

Within the Records Management System, on a daily basis, records will be searched for and retrieved, viewed, and used, as needed. Ultimately, the life of the record comes to an end and it is routed through its final disposition step. Typically, some small number of records, because of their long-term historical importance, will be moved to a long-term archival location for preservation. But most other records will be destroyed in the final step of their disposition.

Much of the remainder of this book discusses the specifics about how the Alfresco ERM system manages records and each of these steps in the record lifecycle. We'll go over these steps in much greater detail in later chapters.

The following figure summarizes the lifecycle of a record:

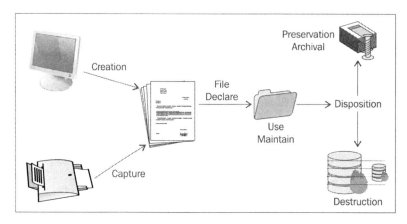

Until about 25 years ago, Records Management focused almost exclusively on the management of paper records. Microfilm and microfiche were occasionally used to store records, but the bulk of records were in paper. As offices were automated with desktop computers, electronic documents and records became more common. Today, most new documents created in offices are created electronically.

Electronic Records Management focuses primarily on the management of unstructured documents. While structured data has a rigid data structure, like the information stored in the schema fields of a database, unstructured data refers typically to documents that have been created without following a rigid data model. Because something unstructured is less predictable than something which has a structure, the management of unstructured data is a more complex problem. Document and Records Management systems were designed specifically for dealing with unstructured documents. AIIM found in a survey taken in mid-2009 that 70 percent of organizations have seen huge growth in the volume of the electronic records that they manage, while somewhat surprisingly, as many as 56 percent of organizations say that their volume of paper records are also continuing to increase, although not as quickly as their electronic records.

How does Records Management differ from Document Management?

If you already have a Document or Content Management System, you may wonder if that system can provide the same level of functionality and benefits that a Records Management System would provide. The two are similar, but Records Management offers unique capabilities not found in a standard Document or Content Management system.

The two types of systems are very closely related, but distinctly different. Document Management systems are typically deployed to enable departmental sharing of documents and to manage document revisions. Document Management systems often lack certain key functions that are needed to perform effective Records Management.

> Because of the close relationship between Document and Records Management, a number of vendors combine the two types of systems into one, namely, an Electronic Document and Records Management system (EDRMS). This is usually a good approach, since not all documents are records and often a document may need to be rewritten and versioned multiple times (document operations) before it is ultimately filed and declared as a record.

Records are really a special kind of document and often a record begins its 'life' as a standard document. At some point, the document gets declared to be a record and thereafter takes on the special behaviors of a record. The relationships and differences between documents and records are summarized in the following table:

	Document Management	**Records Management**
Stored Objects	A Document is stored information that contains structured and unstructured data. Documents are often associated with metadata; a set of properties or attributes that further describe or summarize document content.	Records are a special kind of document. Like documents, records can be structured or unstructured data. Records can also have metadata. Records contain information that is used for making business decisions. Lifecycle instructions get assigned to records that describe how long the record should be stored and how to dispose of the record at the end of the lifecycle.

	Document Management	Records Management
Static versus Dynamic	Documents can be very dynamic and support frequent revisions and updates.	Records are generally static and are not intended to be altered unless and until the lifecycle of the record indicates that they need to be superseded.
Object Security	Most Document Management systems have capabilities for security and privileges, but it isn't strictly required.	Records Management is very strict in specifying the security of records—who can declare and access records, and who can approve final record disposition.
Auditability	Document Management Systems provide audit capability to show the complete history of changes made by the authors of a document.	Auditability plays a key part in Records Management. This involves being able to see where records are in their lifecycle and who has accessed and modified them.
Management Software	Document Management software focuses on searching and retrieving document content. Document Management systems control the creation of document versions and support the locking of documents checked-out for revisions.	Record Management software is complementary to Document Management. Once a document is declared to be a record, the RM system will ensure that the record is not altered. Records are filed or categorized based on a file plan. Records are then disposed of at the end of the record's life, based on the record disposition schedule.
Workflow	Workflows direct how documents flow through the organization and how users within the organization act on the data contained in the document.	The record disposition schedules are the instructions for a record lifecycle and are a special kind of workflow that is associated with a record. Compared to document workflow, record workflow is typically much simpler, usually involving just a few steps.
Object Disposal	Document Management systems don't have strict requirements about when documents should be deleted and often no documents are ever deleted.	The destruction of records is usually regulated by laws. Federal agencies often transfer records to be permanently archived to NARA, the National Archives.

Benefits of Records Management

Records Management provides the following benefits to organizations:

- Legal compliance
- Accountability
- Preservation of assets
- Efficiency
- Preparedness
- Security
- Good business

Records Management is about complying with legal requirements

Records Management is an important support tool that enables organizations to comply with legal requirements. One of the most compelling reasons for adopting a Records Management system is to be able to produce evidence relative to litigation brought against an organization in a timely manner. Electronic Records Management can do just that. It can be used to quickly search and find the evidence that can help to either prove or disprove compliance with regulations or to supply information relevant to e-discovery requests.

Unfortunately, almost all companies will need to defend themselves against lawsuits at some point in time. It may seem hard to factor potential litigation into the **Return on Investment (ROI)** calculation for Records Management when there is no immediate litigation pending, but it is usually too late to implement a Records Management system once faced with a lawsuit.

Litigation can be extremely expensive. The average cost for defending a lawsuit in the United States exceeds $1.5 million per case and more than a quarter of that cost is IT-related. In 2009, 22 percent of all companies and 36 percent of companies valued at more than $1 billion had more than 20 lawsuits brought against them with only 27 percent of companies having no lawsuits.

Regulatory compliance

Regulatory compliance has continually been ranked as a very high priority for both business and IT. In the last decade, organizations have come under an increasing number of local, state, federal, and industry regulations. By some estimates, there are more than 8500 state and federal regulations in the United States that involve Records Management. The regulatory landscape is constantly changing with regulations being added, rewritten, or retired.

Non-compliance with these government regulations can result in severe penalties that include fines, customer and shareholder lawsuits, and negative publicity. In 2009, 34 percent of companies were involved in litigation due to regulatory proceedings brought against them.

Organizations are also often bound by compliance issues relative to internal business practices and corporate governance. Typically, any process, at some point, may need to be documented or audited to ensure that the correct operation falls in the realm of internal compliance. This might include, for example, documenting and enforcing standard operating procedures or documenting processes like those in accounts payable or with the steps of a hiring process. Corporate governance and compliance is relevant for any department within an organization like finance, engineering, IT, sales, and marketing.

Often, regulations don't specifically require the use of Records Management software for compliance, and Sarbanes-Oxley is one prominent example of this, but in order to cost-effectively satisfy the need for creating the audit trails requested by regulations, an automated system for Records Management almost becomes mandatory.

Authority Documents and compliance

Organizations are required to comply with numerous types of regulations, guidelines, policies, procedures, principles, and best practices. The documents in which the requirements for these many different types of compliance are written are called "Authority Documents".

It is not uncommon for certain types of records to fall under multiple authorities. Sometimes, even the policies suggested by two relevant Authority Documents will conflict. Typically, the conflict is with the length of the document retention period. In those cases, the longer of the two specified retention periods is typically used. But it is important to document the reasoning used in compiling the retention policies that you ultimately implement.

Without knowing what Authority Document requirements your organization is bound by, it isn't possible to fully set up and configure your Records Management System. You'll need to do some research. Exactly which Authority Documents your organization will need to comply with will depend on your type of business or operation. One of the first steps that you will need to do in setting up your Records Management system will be to find out which Authority Documents your business is affected by.

One group called the **Unified Compliance Foundation (UCF)** has compiled and cross-referenced requirements from most state and federal Authority Documents and mapped those requirements to different disciplines and industries. Their research is not free, but it can serve as a useful starting point when determining which Authority Documents are important for your organization.

Once you know which Authority Documents you are targeting to support your Records Management system, you will then need to map the requirements from those authorities back to the types of records that you will be storing. Many of the requirements from the Authority Documents will be realized by implementing them as steps of the disposition lifecycle schedule for the appropriately affected records.

E-discovery

In addition to regulatory compliance, Records Management is an important legal component of e-discovery. E-discovery is the process in civil and criminal litigation where electronic data is requested, searched, and produced for use as evidence.

There are similarities and even overlaps in the compliance and e-discovery processes. Often records are asked to be produced as evidence of regulatory compliance. Like compliance, failure to respond in a timely way to an e-discovery request can have significant consequences that include fines, monetary sanctions, and criminal penalties. In cases where records should have been preserved but which cannot be produced, the jury can be instructed that it is likely there was something bad to hide.

In December 2006, the **Federal Rules of Civil Procedure (FRCP)** were updated to consider electronic data as part of the discovery process. Basically, all of an organization's information is subject to e-discovery, unless it is "not reasonably accessible due to undue burden or cost". That includes all information that is stored in desktops, laptops, servers, and networked storage systems. The changes to the FRCP require that companies be able to access and search electronic information quickly in the event of litigation.

The following table summarizes some recent cases where significant fines were levied against companies because of lapses with the way e-discovery information was (or was not) produced. What stands out in these examples is that the organizations listed are some of the most venerable and sophisticated companies in the United States. It shows that no companies are immune from complying with e-discovery requests:

Organization	Reason for e-discovery fine	Fine and date
Morgan Stanley	E-mails created during a company merger were improperly deleted. Additional backup tapes found during the investigation were not later reported.	$1.58 billion fine May 2005 Later overturned, but not because of the e-discovery problems
UBS Warburg	E-mails were deleted in violation of a court order. Unable to produce backup tapes. Jury told that missing evidence may be a sign that something is being hidden.	$29.3 million April 2005
Lucent Technologies Inc.	Records produced for a Securities and Exchange Investigation were incomplete.	$25 million fine May 2004
Morgan Stanley	Failure to produce e-mail in a timely manner as part of a Securities and Exchange investigation.	$15 million fine May 2006
Banc of America Securities	Failure to produce e-mail in a timely manner and failure to preserve documents related to on-going litigation.	$10 million fine March 2004
Philip Morris USA (Altria Group)	Over two years, deleted all e-mails over 60 days old when under legal order to preserve documents related to on-going litigation.	$2.75 million fine July 2004
J. P. Morgan	Failure to produce e-mails requested by the Securities and Exchange commission related to stock analyst misconduct.	$2.1 million fine February 2005

Besides the fines that can be imposed for the inability to comply with e-discovery requests, the negative publicity that an organization receives from fumbles in responding can prove embarrassing to the organization. For example, in an investigation by the FTC of Countrywide, Bank of America's mortgage servicing unit, on risky lending practices and imposing misleading and excessive fees, the FTC chairman made the disparaging comment that was widely reported in the media that "the record-keeping of Countrywide was abysmal. Most frat houses have better record-keeping than Countrywide."

Often when an e-discovery request catches an organization totally unprepared, the organization is forced to respond reactively. A better and more pre-emptive approach is to be proactively prepared for any type of request that may come in. Being prepared allows you to reduce your risks and your ultimate costs. Having information and evidence in hand early on can give you time to review and understand your situation from the contents of the data. This allows you to be prepared for, and be able to appropriately defend yourself, if and when needed. A Records Management system can help you to be prepared.

Records Management is about ensuring accountability

Records Management is a powerful tool for providing accountability and transparency. Records contain the historical details and reasoning behind why certain policies and decisions were made. Records can prove that an organization acted responsibly and with good intent (or not).

But for records to be accepted, they must be trustworthy and believable. They must be accurate and complete. They must be verifiable. Good Records Management systems, practices, and processes are the vital elements that can ensure that records are trustworthy.

> *When speaking about accountability and transparency in government, Barak Obama declared that "The Government should be transparent. Transparency promotes accountability and provides information for citizens about what their Government is doing. Information maintained by the Federal Government is a national asset".*

But while accountability is something that is often spoken of relative to state and federal governments, accountability is a concept that is not limited to just governments. Governments are accountable to their citizens. Non-government organizations are accountable to their members, their employees, their customers, their communities, and their environments.

Accountability mandates that organizations keep accurate records that can later be reviewed, accessed, and analyzed by individuals inside the organization, and sometimes external to it.

Records Management is about preserving assets

At the heart of Records Management is the idea that records are retained and preserved to ensure that information is available for continued use and reuse. The required retention time for records varies widely. While the majority of records typically have only short-term value and are ultimately destroyed, most organizations also have a category of records, often representing a fairly large fraction of their total number, that need to be retained and preserved for long-term financial, historical, or cultural reasons. This category of records often needs special consideration to ensure that records will remain usable for long periods of time.

Electronic Records Management offers clear benefits over paper-based record systems. The process automation capabilities of ERM make the capturing and ingestion of record data fast and efficient. ERM records can be searched and we can retrieve orders of magnitude more quickly than with paper systems, and backups or copies of the electronic data can be made easily so that data can be safely stored in off-site locations. Because of these benefits, organizations are increasingly abandoning paper and turning towards the digital storage of their information.

While ERM can offer impressive benefits in terms of efficiencies and cost savings, digital assets themselves can be quite fragile, if not properly maintained. Two main areas of concern about preservation of digital assets are the long-term viability of the storage media and the data formats used to store the records.

Magnetic and Optical storage devices are surprisingly short-lived. Both types of media are subject to bit rot, the process where bits become corrupted because they lose their magnetic orientation, or the disk material itself breaks down. Hard drives, for example, have only a three to six-year lifespan expectancy. Magnetic tapes are expected to last ten to twenty years, and the lifespan of CD-ROMs and DVD-ROMs is in the range of 10 to 100 years.

Properly maintained, despite being extremely fragile, some paper has been able to last for thousands of years, and no doubt with the right amount of scientific research, proper attention, and careful handling, the lifespan of digital media could be extended to go beyond the current expected lengths. Both paper and disks tend to do better in cool, dark environments with low humidity. But it should be a given that the lifespan of storage devices will be relatively short.

As ERM systems have centralized storage, storage media degradation for ERM systems isn't really an issue. Because all data is stored centrally, rather than needing to examine and treat the storage media of each asset as a special case, the storage and management of all records can be treated holistically.

However, Records Management systems aren't static. As time passes, ERM systems will obviously evolve. Records Management systems will be upgraded, hopefully on a regular basis, and data and records will be migrated to newer storage hardware and improved ERM software. Data migrations performed in support of regular maintenance and upgrades won't always be trivial, but with careful planning, the work involved to migrate records to new software and hardware should be straightforward.

So from a data preservation level, the worry is not so great that records stored in actively maintained and regularly backed-up Records Management systems would somehow be lost because of degradation of storage media. The real worry is whether the format that digital assets are stored in can continue to be readable.

Data file formats change very rapidly. With some software products, every new release may involve changes to the format in which the data is stored. Without the proper software reader to read a digital asset, the stored data becomes, in effect, useless. A common solution to reduce the size of this problem is to limit or convert the formats of data being stored to a small set of stable core data types. This is an important problem to be aware of when designing and planning for a Records Management systems that requires long-term record preservation. This is one topic that we'll expand on in greater detail in *Chapter 4* relative to the Content Model, file content, and data types.

Records Management is about efficiency

Keeping records for a period past the necessary retention period results in inefficiencies. Storing expired documents simply takes up space and clogs up the Records Management system.

When records are kept longer than needed, those outdated records can be unnecessarily considered during the discovery process. When performing e-discovery key-word searches, outdated documents can be returned as possible search candidate matches, even though they are no longer relevant.

For example, consider an e-discovery request made to the chemical company DuPont. To respond to the request, the company found that it was necessary to review 75 million pages of text over a period of three years. At the end of the e-discovery, they realized that more than half of the documents they examined were outdated and past their retention period. If Records Management guidelines had been applied prior to the discovery, outdated documents would have been properly disposed of, and the discovery process could have been performed much more efficiently. That could have saved DuPont $12 million.

In this example, greater efficiency could have been achieved by eliminating obsolete records, thus minimizing the volumes of data examined during e-discovery. Eliminating obsolete records also reduces the legal risks that could result from obsolete content that may have been in those records.

Having a Records Management system in place prior to an e-discovery request can be an insurance policy that could ultimately save you many times over the cost of the system itself.

Records Management is about being prepared

Records Management is about being prepared, being prepared for the unexpected. No one can see the future, but disasters do happen, and unfortunately, on an all too regular basis.

On the morning of September 11, 2001, terrorists crashed airliners into each of the Twin Towers of the World Trade Center in New York City. The death toll that day was nearly 3000 people. The destruction was in the billions of dollars and the event seriously impacted the economy in New York City and affected the psyche of nearly every citizen in the United States. Lives and businesses were disrupted and changed.

One business directly affected by this disaster is the law firm of Sidley Austin Brown & Wood LLP (SAB&W), which occupied the fifth fourth to the fifty ninth floors of the North Tower. While 600 SAB&W employees worked in the Trade Center offices, the firm suffered only a single death that day. Unfortunately all physical assets at the location were lost.

Luckily SAB&W was prepared. The firm had a solid disaster recovery plan and within hours after the disaster, the plan was in full effect. By making use of vital records maintained offsite that included information about floor plans, personnel locations, procedures, clients, and vendors, the firm was able to spring into action. The vital records that they had access to included important insurance records. From these records, they were quickly able to determine that their total loss would be fully covered by their insurance and they were also able to quickly start the processing of their insurance payout.

Based on personnel records, an intensive search was immediately initiated to locate all employees from that location. A new office space of similar size was leased at another location in New York City hours after the event. Computers, networking equipment, and furniture were purchased.

Backup tapes kept in Chicago of e-mails and other data from the New York office were identified. Within three days, e-mail and voice mail were fully restored. On the fourth day, the document management system was available again and temporary office space was being set up. Somewhat unbelievably, within only one week, SAB&W was back up and running and in reasonable operational shape.

Unfortunately, most stories of disaster can't boast of such quick and successful recoveries. Consider what happened at Embry-Riddle Aeronautical University near Daytona Beach, Florida in late December, 2006. Four Christmas day tornadoes struck the area. With winds as strong as 159 mph, mobile homes were destroyed and apartment buildings in the area had their roofs torn off. Some of the worst damage from the tornadoes occurred at Embry-Riddle. The storm tossed one of the Embry-Riddle airplanes into the school's main administration building, Spruance Hall. The maintenance hangar, 50 of their 65 airplanes, and Spruance Hall were all destroyed. Total damage totaled $60 million.

Embry-Riddle's Spruance Hall housed the financial aid, the bursar, the president, and general administration offices. The day after the tornado, paper documents literally covered the campus grounds around the area. But in this case, unlike SAB&W, Embry-Riddle was not adequately prepared. They had no disaster or business continuity plan. The mentality had been that disasters are something remote and can never happen to us. But, unfortunately, when disasters do happen and you are not prepared, the results can be devastating.

Hurricane Katrina is another disaster that caught many unprepared with significantly worse consequences than that of Embry-Riddle. Katrina hit the Gulf Coast area in late August 2005 with torrential rains and flooding that caused widespread and serious damage. Katrina is considered to be one of the most catastrophic natural disasters in all of U.S. history. Damage was reported in Texas, Louisiana, Mississippi, and Alabama. Homes and businesses were destroyed, hundreds of lives were lost, and tens of thousands of lives were deeply disrupted.

The widespread loss and damage to documentation and records was a major tragedy of the Katrina disaster, and much of the damage was as a result of the heavy reliance on the use of paper records. It is another reminder that disasters like floods, fires, tornados, and hurricanes come with little warning and can bring about devastating results. The previous largest disaster prior to Katrina for losing historical documents happened in Florence, Italy in 1966 due to flooding.

In the case of Katrina, the loss or damage of records wasn't limited to individuals; institutions and government agencies were heavily affected too. Historical treaties and photographs were destroyed. Vital records of all kinds were affected by Katrina that included medical records, school records, law enforcement records, birth records, and marriage and driver's licenses.

After documents come into contact with water or moisture, it takes only 48 hours before mold starts growing, and after that, the deterioration of paper documents accelerates quickly. The flood waters in many areas hit by Katrina were several feet high, forcing many residents to evacuate and leave behind their belongings, only being allowed to come back into the area many days later. But by that time, for many documents that were damaged, it was too late.

Some buildings in New Orleans containing legal and vital records were bulldozed before the records could be removed. Emergency teams were initially told to discard damaged records to keep city residents safe from molds and other contaminants, a policy that was later retracted, but which resulted in the unnecessary loss of many valuable records.

The loss of legal documents in the Gulf region because of the Katrina disaster was stunning. One-third of the 5000 to 6000 lawyers in Louisiana lost all of their client files. The Louisiana state supreme court lost a significant number of their appellate files and evidence folders. Much of the problem resulted because records were often stored in basements or the lower levels of buildings. For example, court files in Mississippi and Louisiana were both stored in courthouse basements, and in both cases, many of the paper records were irrecoverably destroyed.

All told, an incredible number of records were simply lost. Many others, while damaged, were recoverable and needed to be painstakingly restored. But perhaps most frustrating was the fact that many of the documents that actually did survive the storm were inaccessible for weeks. For example, in New Orleans, the vital records office for Louisiana stored state birth certificates, death certificates, marriage licenses, and divorce papers. Most of the records at this location were paper and dated back over 100 years. But in the aftermath of the storm, the state records office was nearly shut down, being manned by only five percent of its normal staff, making records accessible only after very long waits.

Katrina hit medical records very hard too. Estimates are that tens of thousands and possibly millions of pages of healthcare records, files, and charts were lost in private-practice offices, clinics, and hospitals. More than one million people were separated from their healthcare records during the disaster, with many people forced to relocate to other parts of the country, and of those receiving treatment, many could not continue because the record of their diagnosis and treatment was lost.

Much of the damage from Katrina was as a direct result of the fact that most records were stored on paper. The Tulane Medical Center located in New Orleans presents an interesting contrast to most other New Orleans hospitals. The Tulane Medical Center maintained their medical diagnostic records electronically. Their electronic records included lab, radiology, cardiology, and nursing documentation. Because the data was stored electronically and not physically located in New Orleans, availability of this data was not affected at all because of the disaster.

Disasters are good teachers. After the event at Embry-Riddle, creating and maintaining a disaster recovery plan immediately became a top priority for the school. The school invested in Document Imaging and Records Management software, and after seeing firsthand what could happen when planning and preparation for worst-case scenarios aren't done, the faculty and staff of the university resolved that they did not want to see a repeat episode.

Similarly, less than one year after Katrina, officials, archivists, and records managers from nine Southeastern states affected by Katrina's destruction gathered to begin planning ways to be better prepared for future Katrina-scale disasters. A big deficiency noted in the emergency response to the disaster was the disconnection between archivists and state emergency planners. After meeting, the states resolved in the future to include state archives as part of any emergency response.

Whether they are man-made or natural, disasters happen. Preparation and planning are key for being able to successfully cope with disasters.

Records Management is about coming to grips with data volumes

The volume of data within organizations is growing at a phenomenal rate. In fact, **International Data Corporation (IDC)**, a research and analyst group, estimates that the volume of digital data is doubling every 18 months. And that growth is having a huge impact on organizational IT budgets. For example, if we assume that the average employee generates 10 gigabytes of data per year, and storage and backup costs are $5 per gigabyte, a company with 5000 employees would pay $1.25 million for five years of storage.

Consider the costs of e-discovery. "Midsize" lawsuits that involve e-discovery typically result in the processing of about 500 GB of data at a cost of $2.5 to $3.5 million. Lawyers and paralegal staff must review the content of the data, determine which documents are relevant, redact, or black-out parts of the documents considered private or company confidential, and finally, output the data into a common data file format like PDF that will be used for delivery to the requester.

The goal of Records Management is to allow organizations to cut back on what information must be retained. Organizations with no Records Management policies in place have no clear guidelines for what documents to save and what documents to discard. The end result is that these organizations typically save everything.

And we've seen, trying to save everything comes at a steep cost. Keeping records that should have been destroyed earlier means that more storage space is required. It means that backup times are longer. It means that data searches are slower because there is more information to search. It means that people's time gets wasted when irrelevant records turn up in search results. Records Management helps clear the clutter and bring greater efficiency.

Records Management isn't going to be able to put a stop to the general upward trend of creating and storing more information, but by strictly following Records Management retention schedules, organizations should be able to significantly reduce the volume of data that they do keep.

Records Management is about security

The security of records is an important issue and the responsibility of the Records Management system. This is one area where an Electronic Records Management system really shines when compared to manual methods for managing records.

A major advantage of ERM is that the application of security and access controls over electronic records and folders is much easier to implement and can be applied in a much more granular way than over physical folders and records.

Records stored on paper and other non-electronic media are very hard to tightly secure, especially when the requirements for access control become even moderately complex. Physical records require that filing cabinets and storage locations be appropriately secured. They typically need to be controlled and managed by trusted records librarians. Physical Records Management requires far greater day-to-day supervision by people and, because of that, is subject to many more points of potential security lapses than with an automated system.

That is not to say that the physical security of the computer hardware used to run the Records Management system is not important.

With ERM, access rights can be changed or revoked, as needed, protecting records from unauthorized users. The system is able to validate that the data managed is accurate and authentic. An ERM system can also provide an audit trail of all activities for all records and thus demonstrate compliance.

Records Management is about good business

Regulations usually contain detailed instructions about how records should be handled, but often the regulations don't actually mandate that a formal Records Management system be used. But really, what's the alternative?

Not having a Records Management program at all is a recipe for problems, if not disaster. Without a Records Management system in place, tracking down the records that document policies, procedures, transactions, and decisions of an organization becomes extremely difficult or next to impossible.

We've discussed how Records Management can enable important business benefits like accountability, compliance, efficiency, and security. Taken as a whole, these benefits are really the characteristics of doing good business. And at its very essence, that's what Records Management is all about.

Summary

Before getting into the details of how Alfresco implements Records Management, this first chapter presented an overview of general Records Management concepts and the benefits that can be achieved by using Records Management.

In this chapter, we covered:

- The meaning of a record and the lifecycle of a record
- The high penalties that could be imposed due to inadequate Records Management
- The difference between Document and Records Management
- The benefits of Records Management

We've seen that *records* are documents that have been used when making a business decision, a transaction, or a communication of a policy. A *Records Management* System manages the complete *lifecycle* of a record, from its *creation* and *declaration*, through its *retention period*, and ultimately to its final *disposition*, which typically is either permanent archival or destruction.

Software Applications that are designed to handle Records Management are called *Electronic Records Management* (ERM) systems. ERM systems can greatly speed and automate Records Management. They are especially well suited for managing large volumes of electronic data, like e-mail, which organizations now are forced to deal with.

Records Management helps organizations achieve *compliance* with financial regulations, audit requirements, and e-discovery requests. It enables *accountability* and *transparency* and ensures the *authenticity* and *trustworthiness* of the records being managed.

Despite ever-changing software and hardware technologies, a Records Management system preserves your records, which are important business *assets*, for either a short-term or potentially a very long-term, based on assigned retention schedules.

Records Management facilitates organizational *efficiencies*. Information can be found and shared more easily. Records Management removes unneeded or obsolete records, freeing up storage space.

Records Management supports risk management, keeping your organization *prepared*, for anything from an e-discovery request to disaster continuity.

Furthermore, Records Management *security* provides fine-grained access control rights for your data so that people have access to only the information that they are privileged to see.

The benefits of Records Management are many, but one of the most compelling reasons for implementing Records Management is that it's simply good business.

In the next chapter, we will start looking at Alfresco in detail. In that chapter, we will see how to install both Alfresco and the Records Management module.

2

Getting Started with the Alfresco Records Management Module

Before we get started with discussing the details of the Records Management software implementation, it is important to point out that the software implementation is only one element of a successful Records Management program. People, process, and culture often are as big, if not bigger, components than the software. With that in mind, let's now shift gears and begin our discussion of Alfresco Records Management software.

In this chapter, we will describe:

- How to acquire and install Alfresco Records Management software
- How to set up the Records Management site within Alfresco Share
- Some of the internal workings of Alfresco Share involved in creating the Records Management site

The Alfresco stack

Alfresco software was designed for enterprise, and as such, supports a variety of different stack elements. Supported **Alfresco stack** elements include some of the most widely used operating systems, relational databases, and application servers.

The core infrastructure of Alfresco is built on Java. This core provides the flexibility for the server to run on a variety of operating systems, like Microsoft Windows, Linux, Mac OS, and Sun Solaris. The use of Hibernate allows Alfresco to map objects and data from Java into almost any relational database. The databases that the Enterprise version of Alfresco software is certified to work with include Oracle, Microsoft SQL Server, MySQL, PostgresSQL, and DB2. Alfresco also runs on a variety of Application Servers that include Tomcat, JBoss, WebLogic, and WebSphere. Other relational databases and application servers may work as well, although they have not been explicitly tested and are also not supported.

 Details of which Alfresco stack elements are supported can be found on the Alfresco website: http://www.alfresco.com/services/ subscription/supported-platforms/3-x/.

Depending on the target deployment environment, different elements of the Alfresco stack may be favored over others. The exact configuration details for setting up the various stack element options is not discussed in this book. You can find ample discussion and details on the Alfresco wiki on how to configure, set up, and change the different stack elements. The version-specific installation and setup guides provided by Alfresco also contain very detailed information.

The example description and screenshots given in this chapter are based on the Windows operating system. The details may differ for other operating systems, but you will find that the basic steps are very similar. In later chapters, we'll be focusing on the details of the application itself, and as such, the descriptions and screens that we'll look at in those chapters will apply to any Alfresco installation, regardless of the specific stack elements that it is running on.

 Additional information on the internals of Alfresco software can be found on the Alfresco wiki at http://wiki.alfresco.com/ wiki/Main_Page.

Alfresco software

As a first step to getting Alfresco Records Management up and running, we need to first acquire the software. Whether you plan to use either the Enterprise or the Community version of Alfresco, you should note that the Records Management module was not available until late 2009. The Records Management module was first certified with the 3.2 release of Alfresco Share. The first Enterprise version of Alfresco that supported Records Management was version 3.2R, which was released in February 2010.

Make sure the software versions are compatible

It is important to note that there was an early version of Records Management that was built for the **Alfresco JSF-based Explorer client**. That version was not certified for DoD 5015.2 compliance and is no longer supported by Alfresco. In fact, the Alfresco Explorer version of Records Management is not compatible with the Share version of Records Management, and trying to use the two implementations together can result in corrupt data.

It is also important to make sure that the version of the Records Management module that you use matches the version of the base Alfresco Share software. For example, trying to use the Enterprise version of Records Management on a Community install of Alfresco will lead to problems, even if the version numbers are the same. The 3.3 Enterprise version of Records Management, as another example, is also not fully compatible with the 3.2R Enterprise version of Alfresco software.

Downloading the Alfresco software

The easiest way to get Alfresco Records Management up and running is by doing a fresh install of the latest available Alfresco software.

Alfresco Community

The Community version of Alfresco is a great place to get started. Especially if you are just interested in evaluating if Alfresco software meets your needs, and with no license fees to worry about, there's really nothing to lose in going this route.

Since **Alfresco Community** software is constantly in the "in development" state and is not as rigorously tested, it tends to not be as stable as the Enterprise version. But, in terms of the Records Management module for the 3.2+ version releases of the software, the Community implementation is feature-complete. This means that the same Records Management features in the Enterprise version are also found in the Community version.

The caveat with using the Community version is that support is only available from the Alfresco community, should you run across a problem. The Enterprise release also includes support from the Alfresco support team and may have bug fixes or patches not yet available for the community release. Also of note is the fact that there are other repository features beyond those of Records Management features, especially in the area of scalability, which are available only with the Enterprise release.

Building from source code

It is possible to get the most recent version of the Alfresco Community software by getting a snapshot copy of the source code from the publicly accessible Alfresco Subversion source code repository. A version of the software can be built from a snapshot of the source code taken from there. But unless you are anxiously waiting for a new Alfresco feature or bug fix and need to get your hands immediately on a build with that new code included as part of it, for most people, building from source is probably not the route to go.

Building from source code can be time consuming and error prone. The final software version that you build can often be very buggy or unstable due to code that has been checked-in prematurely or changes that might be in the process of being merged into the Community release, but which weren't completely checked-in at the time you updated your snapshot of the code base.

> If you do decide that you'd like to try to build Alfresco software from source code, details on how to get set up to do that can be found on the Alfresco wiki: http://wiki.alfresco.com/wiki/Alfresco_SVN_Development_Environment.

Download a Community version snapshot build

Builds of snapshots of the Alfresco Community source code are periodically taken and made available for download. Using a pre-built Community version of Alfresco software saves you much hassle and headaches from not having to do the build from scratch. While not thoroughly tested, the snapshot Community builds have been tested sufficiently so that they tend to be stable enough to see most of the functionality available for the release, although not everything may be working completely.

> Links to the most recent Alfresco Community version builds can be found on the Alfresco wiki: http://wiki.alfresco.com/wiki/Download_Community_Edition.

Alfresco Enterprise

The alternative to using Alfresco open source Community software is the Enterprise version of Alfresco. For most organizations, the fully certified Enterprise version of Alfresco software is the recommended choice. The Enterprise version of Alfresco software has been thoroughly tested and is fully supported.

Alfresco customers and partners have access to the most recent Enterprise software from the Alfresco Network site: `http://network.alfresco.com/`. Trial copies of **Alfresco Enterprise** software can be downloaded from the Alfresco site: `http://www.alfresco.com/try/`. Time-limited access to on-demand instances of Alfresco software are also available and are a great way to get a good understanding of how Alfresco software works.

Installing the base Alfresco software

Once you have access to Alfresco software, the easiest way to get started with Alfresco is to do a full installation of Alfresco on a Windows machine. With just a few steps, you can be up and running with this procedure. The full setup on Windows installs all components needed to run Alfresco in a self-contained way under a single directory with no dependencies on any other files outside of the installation directory.

Running the installer

One useful technique when performing full installs of Alfresco on Windows is to create a directory, like `c:\Alfresco`, and then install the new Alfresco software stack as a subdirectory in it. It is likely that we'll want to install other versions of Alfresco for testing and development purposes. All Alfresco installs can be kept side-by-side in this single directory. In that way, it is easy to find and then start and stop any of the installed versions of Alfresco, as needed.

It is also possible to install Alfresco as a service on Windows. In some situations, like for a Windows production system, this makes life easier and minimizes the number of DOS-based pop-up windows that you see when you start the Alfresco system. But for development and test scenarios, it is generally easier to not install Alfresco as a Windows service. The steps for installing Alfresco are as follows:

1. The Alfresco Enterprise version 3.3 full installation file for Windows is `Alfresco-Enterprise-3.3-Full-Setup.exe`. Download this file and run it to begin installation of Alfresco. Other installation options exist, but this one provides the complete stack of required software for Alfresco to run, and is perhaps the easiest and quickest way to get Alfresco installed on a Windows machine.

2. The first installation screen that you'll see is one that asks what you prefer as the language to be installed. The default language is **English**. After selecting the language, click on **OK**:

3. Respond **Yes** to the prompt to continue the installation of Alfresco:

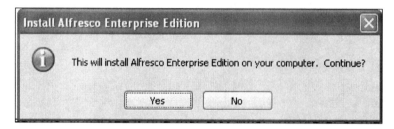

4. Click on **Next** on the first screen of the Alfresco installation **InstallJammer Wizard**:

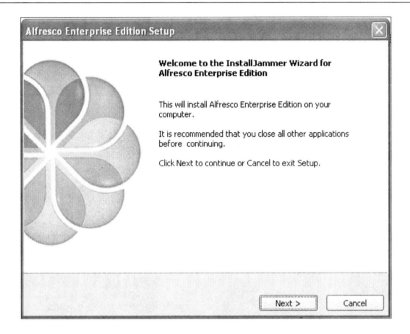

5. On the next screen, select the **Custom** install and then click on **Next.** The Alfresco installer does not include Records Management as part of the **Typical** install. You could still do a **Typical** install and then add the Records Management modules later, but it saves some time if you install the Records Management modules automatically as part of the wizard-driven installation:

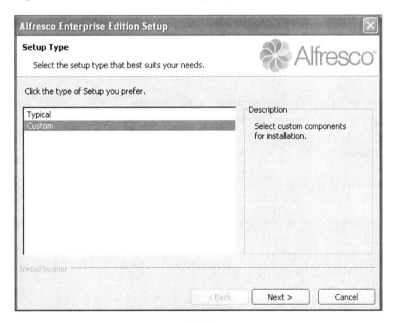

6. On the screen showing the custom components to install, make sure that **Records Management** is selected. Other components like **WCM** or the IBM **Quickr** integration may not be needed and can be left unchecked. Note that when using Records Management on the Enterprise version, an additional license specific to the Records Management module from Alfresco needs to be obtained. Click on **Next**:

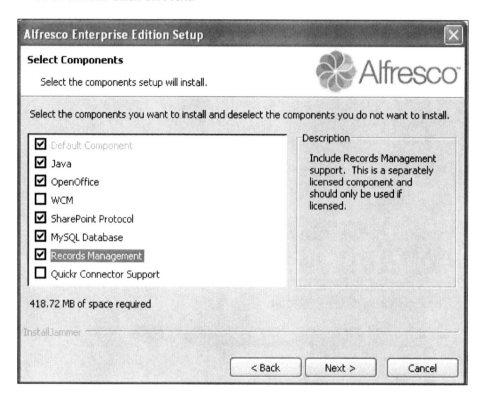

7. Next, select the location where this instance of Alfresco will be installed. In this example, we will be installing it in a directory called Ent33 under the Alfresco directory where we will keep all of our Alfresco full instance installations. Click on **Next** to start the installation of the files:

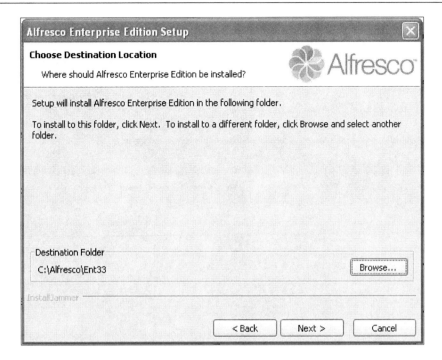

8. The installation wizard next summarizes the choices that we've made, prior to installing the files. Verify that this is correct, and then select **Next**:

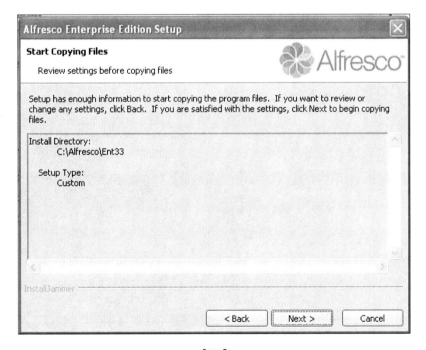

The installation of the Alfresco files then begins:

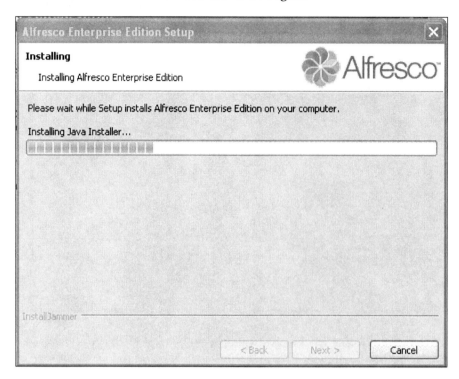

9. The next screen prompts you to enter the password for the user admin, the administrator of the Alfresco system. In this case, we enter **admin** as the password, which is the default value most commonly used for the Alfresco admin user. In a production environment, a more secure password should be selected. Click on **Next**:

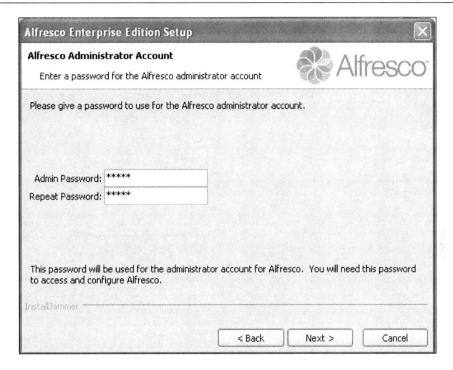

10. After doing that, if you had selected the **OpenOffice** option on the Custom install screen, it will start to install. **OpenOffice** may take a few minutes to install:

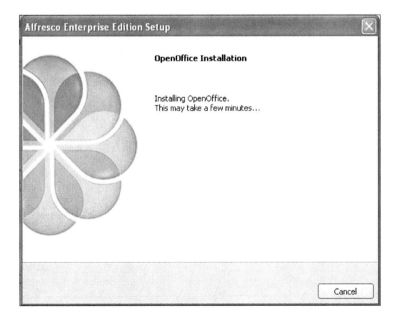

11. After that, a screen will ask if the **Records Management** module should be automatically installed at this part of the wizard installation. That's what we want, so we agree with this and click on **Next**:

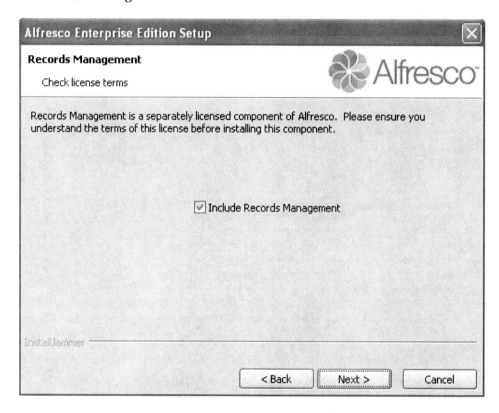

12. After doing that, success! We should see the final screen of the installation wizard indicating that the installation was successfully completed. Click on **Finish** and the installation is over:

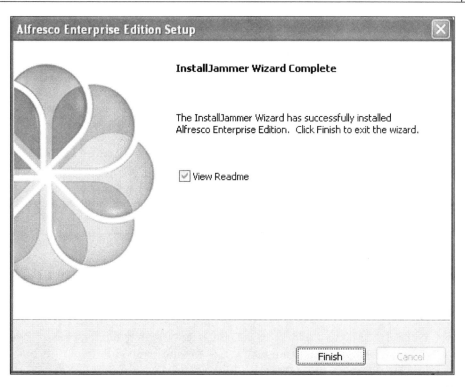

Congratulations on the successful installation of Alfresco software!

Installing Alfresco Records Management modules manually

In the last section, we took the easy route and installed a fresh copy of the full Alfresco Windows setup. But what if we already have a base instance of Alfresco installed that we wanted to add Records Management to? In that case, we need to install the two Alfresco Records Management modules manually into the existing instance.

We need to download the two **Records Management AMP files** separately. In Alfresco 3.3, these files are named `alfresco-dod5015-3.3.amp` and `alfresco-dod5015-share-3.3.amp`. The first of these files will be applied against the `alfresco.war` file, and the second will be applied against the `share.war` file. These two WAR files can be found in the `tomcat\webapps` directory.

The Alfresco and Share applications are distributed in the WAR (short for Web ARchive) file format.

A WAR file is a special kind of ZIP file that contains the Java classes, XML, HTML, property, and any other files needed to run a Web application. By dropping a single WAR file into the deployment folder of an application server like WebSphere, JBoss, or Tomcat, the web application contained in the WAR file can be installed. The application server will expand the folder structure and all files contained in the WAR the first time the application is started.

`alfresco.war` is the distribution WAR file that contains both the Alfresco Explorer client and also the services and other base components of the Alfresco repository.

`share.war` is the distribution WAR file for the Share application.

We need to make sure that the version of the base Alfresco install matches the version of the AMP files that we are about to apply. If not, it is necessary to run upgrade or patch files to bring the installation up to the right version.

Copy the file `alfresco-dod5015-3.3.amp` into the directory named `amps` at the top level of the Alfresco installation area. Copy the file `alfresco-dod5015-share-3.3.amp` into the directory named `amps-share`. If no directory named `amps-share` exists, create it parallel to the `amps` directory and add the Alfresco Share AMP file to it.

Then, in a Windows DOS Command window, navigate to the directory where the instance of Alfresco is installed and locate the Windows Batch file called `apply_amps.bat`. Before running the Batch file, note that running this will merge Records Management functionality into the `alfresco.war` and `share.war` files. On completion, the Batch file will delete the contents of the Alfresco and share folders where the previous versions of the WAR files existed. If you have made any customizations in either of these two folders, those customizations will be deleted.

To apply the Records Management AMP files, run the `apply_amps.bat` file from the command line, as shown below:

```
Microsoft Windows XP [Version 5.1.2600]
(C) Copyright 1985-2001 Microsoft Corp.

C:\Documents and Settings\Dick>cd \alfresco\ent33

C:\Alfresco\Ent33>apply_amps

This script will apply all the AMPs in C:\Alfresco\Ent33\amps to the
alfresco.war and share.war files in C:\Alfresco\Ent33\tomcat\webapps
```

```
Press control-c to stop this script . . .
Press any key to continue . . .
```

When instructed, follow the several messages where you will be prompted to press a key. After the AMPs are successfully applied to the `alfresco.war` and `share.war` files, you will see a message like the following where the time and date of the successful installs for the AMP files are indicated:

```
Module managment tool available commands:
-----------------------------------------------------------

install: Installs a AMP file(s) into an Alfresco WAR file, updates if an
older version is already installed.
usage:   install <AMPFileLocation> <WARFileLocation> [options]
valid options:
  -verbose    : enable verbose output
  -directory : indicates that the amp file location specified is a
    directory.
      All amp files found in the directory and its sub
        directories are installed.
  -force      : forces installation of AMP regardless of currently
    installed module version
  -preview    : previews installation of AMP without modifying WAR file
  -nobackup  : indicates that no backup should be made of the WAR

-----------------------------------------------------------

list:  Lists all the modules currently installed in an Alfresco WAR
file.
usage: list <WARFileLocation>

-----------------------------------------------------------

Module 'org_alfresco_module_dod5015' installed in
'C:\Alfresco\Ent33\tomcat\webapps\alfresco.war'
  -  Title:       DOD 5015 Records Management
  -  Version:     1.0
  -  Install Date: Mon Jul 26 21:12:41 PDT 2010
  -  Description:  Alfresco DOD 5015 Record Management Extension
Module 'org.alfresco.module.vti' installed in
'C:\Alfresco\Ent33\tomcat\webapps\alfresco.war'
  -  Title:       Vti
```

```
-  Version:       1.2
-  Install Date: Mon Jul 26 21:06:16 PDT 2010
-  Description:   Alfresco Vti Extension
Module management tool available commands:

------------------------------------------------------------

install: Installs a AMP file(s) into an Alfresco WAR file, updates if an
older version is already installed.

usage:  install <AMPFileLocation> <WARFileLocation> [options]

valid options:

  -verbose  : enable verbose output

  -directory : indicates that the amp file location specified is a
directory.

    All amp files found in the directory and its sub
    directories are installed.

  -force     : forces installation of AMP regardless of currently
    installed module version

  -preview   : previews installation of AMP without modifying WAR file

  -nobackup  : indicates that no backup should be made of the WAR

------------------------------------------------------------

list:  Lists all the modules currently installed in an Alfresco WAR
file.

usage: list <WARFileLocation>

------------------------------------------------------------

No modules are installed in this WAR file

No modules are installed in this WAR file.

About to clean out tomcat/webapps/alfresco directory and temporary
files...

Press any key to continue . . .
```

Starting the Alfresco Repository and Share application

Both the Alfresco base software and the Records Management should now be installed. Let's start up the application server and start looking at Share. In this case, Tomcat is the application server that we are using.

In Windows, we bring up a DOS command Window to start Alfresco. To do that, navigate to the top of the Alfresco installation area and run the DOS batch file alf_start.bat, as shown in the code below. Alfresco will start up and display some configuration settings. In this case, we are using a MySQL database that came bundled with the Windows full setup:

```
Microsoft Windows XP [Version 5.1.2600]

(C) Copyright 1985-2001 Microsoft Corp.


C:\Documents and Settings\Dick>cd \alfresco\ent34


C:\Alfresco\Ent33>alf_start

Starting MySQL...

Starting Tomcat...

Using CATALINA_BASE:    "C:\Alfresco\Ent34\tomcat"

Using CATALINA_HOME:    "C:\Alfresco\Ent34\tomcat"

Using CATALINA_TMPDIR:  "C:\Alfresco\Ent34\tomcat\temp"

Using JRE_HOME:         "C:\dev\Java6\jdk"

Using CLASSPATH:        "C:\Alfresco\Ent33\tomcat\bin\bootstrap.jar"
```

```
C:\Alfresco\Ent33>
```

Two additional windows are created on startup with this configuration—one is the Tomcat console window and the other is a window for MySQL. If you are running an operating system other than Windows, or if you are using a different database or application server, the behavior that you see on startup may differ. The Tomcat console is a useful place to look when testing and developing to catch or examine in more detail any errors that might be reported when we're running Alfresco.

If this is the first time that we've started the application server, after startup, we will see that there are two WAR files, one for the Alfresco Repository and the other for the Share application. Both should have been exploded or expanded to contain all the files that were bundled in the WAR files.

WAR files are basically ZIP files where the folders and files are stored in the same structure as they need to be located in when the application runs. The WAR files and their corresponding exploded directories can both be found under the tomcat\ webapps directory. The folders alfresco and share along with the tomcat\shared folder contain all the necessary Alfresco Repository and Share application files.

Once the application server is fully started, you should see a message on the application server console that says something like:

INFO: Server startup in 100093 ms

Starting Alfresco Share

The server is now up and running and we are ready to connect to the Alfresco Share application using a web browser. Alfresco Share is a team collaboration application built using a modern web interface. Project or topic-specific sites can be created within Share, and Share users can get access to the different sites within Share by becoming a site member by either invitation or by request. Members of a Share site can share documents and use collaboration tools like blogs, wikis, and calendars for tracking events.

We'll need to bring up a browser from a client machine running on the same network. Alfresco Share is certified to work with various versions of web browsers that include Firefox, Microsoft Internet Explorer, and Safari. Share also works fairly well with Google Chrome, although Chrome is not officially supported.

For testing and development, it is often convenient to connect to the Share application on the same machine where the server is running. This doesn't model a typical production environment, but will be sufficient for our purposes. To connect to the Share application running on the local server using the default configuration, use this URL: `http://localhost:8080/share`. Entering this URL into the browser location field brings up the login screen for Alfresco Share.

Share is the second generation of client applications built by Alfresco. The first Alfresco client is still available and is bundled as part of the `alfresco.war` file and can be accessed at the URL `http://localhost:8080/alfresco`. It is sometimes referred to as the Alfresco Explorer client. The Explorer client was written using an older Java UI technology called JSF (Java Server Faces), and it focused almost exclusively on interacting with the Alfresco repository. You'll notice the difference in the "look" between the two application technologies just by bringing up and comparing the login screens of the two clients:

We can now log in as the administrator for the application as the user admin. When we installed the application, we selected the password **admin**. Entering the **User Name** and **Password** on the login screen will give us access to the dashboard of Share.

The system administrator for Alfresco is, by default, user admin. User admin has administrative privileges both in the Share application and also within the Alfresco JSF client. The **User Name** and **Password** login credentials for user admin are identical for accessing both clients. A user created to access Share will also, by default, be able to access the JSF client, and users created in the JSF client will have access to Share:

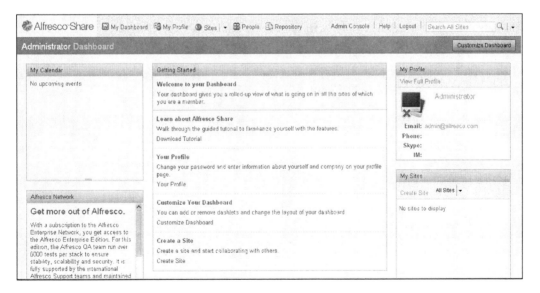

Share dashlets

The content that appears on the home dashboard page for Share is totally configurable. Dashlets are small applications that can independently interact with a service for preparing and presenting targeted information to the user. The dashlets that are available for display on the dashboard include the following:

My Profile: Picture and summary of the contact information from the user profile

Getting Started: Information and links to highlights of Alfresco Share for new or infrequent users

Alfresco Network: Text and links that describe how to get Enterprise Edition support from Alfresco and updates on news about Alfresco

My Calendar: A summary of upcoming events posted to the calendars of the sites that the user is a member of

My Tasks: A list of advanced workflow tasks assigned to the user

My Sites: A list of links to the Share sites that the user has either created or is a member of

My Site Activities: A summary of the recent actions that have occurred in the Share sites that the user is a member of

Documents I'm Editing: A list of documents that are currently checked out to the user from any of the Share site Document Libraries that the user belongs to

RSS Feed: A dashlet that can be configured to display any RSS feed. The default is the Alfresco site feed

CMIS Feed: Information and links about the CMIS (Content Management Interoperability Services) specification

Web View: A dashlet that can embed the display of the web page corresponding to any URL

My Workspaces: A list of Document Workspaces that you are a member of (SharePoint integration)

My Meeting Workspaces: A list of Meeting Workspaces that you are a member of (SharePoint integration)

Records Management: Provides links to install, access, and manage Records Management capabilities

Enabling the Records Management dashlet

Next, the Records Management dashlet needs to be added to the dashboard to enable the option for installing Records Management. To do that, click on the **Customize Dashboard** button towards the upper right.

On the screen to customize the dashlet, click on the **Add Dashlets** button. Then find the Records Management Console dashlet and drag it to one of the columns of your dashboard layout:

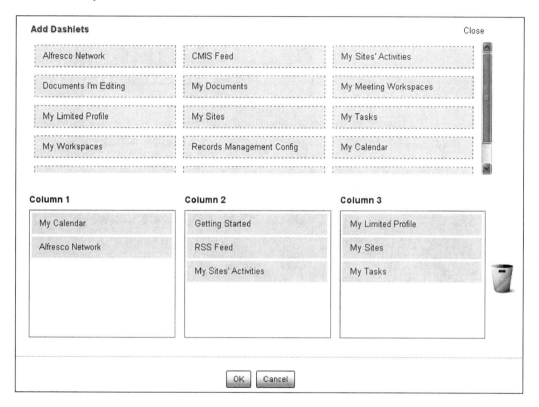

After doing that, we will see the Records Management dashlet displayed on the dashboard when we navigate back to the dashboard page. It will look something like this:

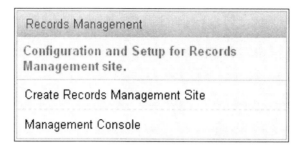

Adding the Records Management site

Within Share, we still need to install the Records Management site from which we can access the Records Management functionality. In version 3.x of Alfresco, only a single Records Management site is allowed. To install the site, click on the **Create Records Management Site** link on the dashlet.

You will see the message: **Creating Records Management Site. Please Wait**. After that, the Records Management site is installed and is available. The contents of the Records Management dashlet have been refreshed, and the dashlet will now appear as follows:

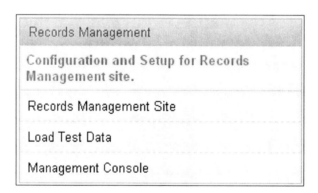

The **Creating Records Management Site** link that was displayed initially has been hidden and that link has been replaced with two new links: **Records Management Site** and **Load Test Data**. Details of the behind-the-scene mechanics of how this dashlet works when you click on the **Create Records Management Site** link are discussed at the end of this chapter.

If we refresh the dashboard page in the browser, we will also see that the **My Sites** dashlet on the dashboard updates to show that the Records Management site now exists and, by default, user admin is a member of it because that user created the site.

Designating the Records Management administrator

The Records Management site in Share now exists, but you will soon find that it isn't too useful just yet. At this point, no users, including the admin user, have sufficient privileges to create any data in the site.

In a later chapter, we will create Records Management users and assign privileges to them for the Records Management site. For now, we will work with just the admin user and designate user admin to also have administrator rights to the Records Management site. With those privileges, the admin user will be able to create elements of the File Plan, the hierarchical folder-like structure used for classifying and filing records, and have capabilities related to the configuration of the Records Management site.

Before going into the Share administration area, we need to work around one quirk of the Records Management installation. No Records Management groups have yet been created. The Records Manager groups and the assigned privileges for each group will happen automatically the first time someone tries to navigate to the Records Management site.

So, even though we don't have privileges to do anything in the Records Management site just yet, we bring up the Records Management site. We do that by clicking on the **Records Management Site** link on the dashlet. The Records Management groups will now be created.

To make a user admin a Records Management administrator, we next navigate to the Share administration area by clicking on the **Admin Console** link along the top of the Share dashboard. Click on the **Groups Tool** along the left navigation pane, and then click on the **Browse** button in the middle pane on the right:

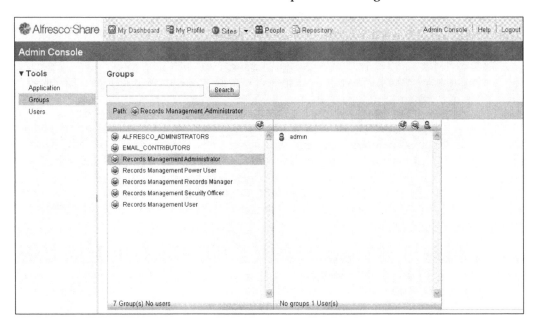

We can then see a list of all the available groups in Alfresco Share. Click on the **Records Management Administrator**. We need to add the user admin to this group. To do that, in the listbox to the right of the group list, click on the upper-right-most icon of a person, search for **admin**, and finally add that user to the group.

After completing this step, the Records Management module is installed and the Records Management site has been created and is available. However, at this point, the user admin is the only active user for the site.

How does it work?

Let's dig in a bit deeper to get a better understanding of how Records Management has been integrated into Alfresco Share. To do that, let's look in more detail at how the Records Management dashlet is built.

The Records Management AMP Files

The Alfresco Records Management application is deployed using two **AMP files**. An AMP file, or an Alfresco Module Package, is a bundled collection of files that together extend the Alfresco platform to provide a new set of related functionality.

Alfresco Records Management functionality is split across two AMP files. One of the AMP files is applied to the Alfresco WAR, extending basic Repository services, and the other AMP file is applied to the Share WAR, defining the Share Records Management site.

AMP files are ZIP files that are packaged and arranged in a folder structure that mirrors the directory structure of the WAR files that they are being deployed into. While we may be adding only Records Management, a single new Alfresco module, the files that make up the Records Management functionality are stored across many standard Alfresco Repository and Alfresco Share directories.

From a systems perspective, when trying to analyze Records Management internals or when trying to modify and customize Records Management behavior, Records Management files are spread across many directories and mixed with the files already in those directories. Because Records Management files are mixed together with non-Records Management files, once the Records Management module is installed, it can be hard when looking at the files in a directory to identify which files in that directory are specific to Records Management.

As a tip, it can be useful when troubleshooting functionality specific to Records Management to isolate only those files related to Records Management. That's easy to do. We can just unzip the AMP files into a directory outside the normal Alfresco structure and then use the files in this location when searching code. The directory structure of the unzipped AMP files mirrors the directory structure of the files that are active in the Share application. Searching across only the Records Management files, while not always foolproof, can make for a more efficient way of searching Alfresco source code, limiting ourselves to looking at only those files that are specific to the Records Management implementation.

The next screenshot shows the unzipped AMP folder hierarchy. We can see that there are many different directories where files for the Share Records Management AMP file are stored:

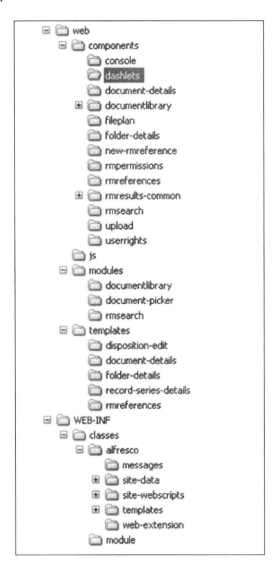

The Records Management Console dashlet

The Alfresco Records Management dashlet provides the starting point for installing the Records Management site and also provides an easily accessible link to an administration page that is specific to configuring and managing the Records Management site. The Records Management dashlet itself is an excellent example of how dashlets within Alfresco Share work.

Let's look briefly at the Records Management Dashlet to gain some insight into how dashlets work within Alfresco and also to understand how we can customize the Records Management dashlet to work differently.

The flow of Alfresco webscripts

In order to understand how Alfresco dashlets work, let's take a step back and look at the general flow of information in Alfresco webscripts. The flow that we'll now discuss is at the core of understanding how Alfresco Share dashlets, pages, and components work.

In the next diagram, we can see the flow of information in the Alfresco Webscript Framework. The Webscript Framework is basically Spring Surf, an Open Source framework for building web pages. The framework was first used to build the Alfresco Share application. Later, in cooperation with SpringSource, Alfresco donated the web framework technology to the Spring open source community using an Apache license.

Webscripts consist of files written using the scripting language, JavaScript, the templating language, FreeMarker, and XML to define and describe how the webscript will operate. Webscripts provide a lightweight framework for building complex interfaces and applications.

 The announcement of the formation of the open source Spring Surf project was jointly announced by Alfresco and SpringSource in December, 2009. The Spring Surf website is available at this URL: http://springsurf.org.

Spring Surf uses a design pattern found frequently in software architecture called Model-View-Controller (MVC). Alfresco webscripts follow the MVC design pattern. In the MVC pattern, a model or data package is built by a software element called the controller. The model data is then applied to a view template that can render the model data for display.

The advantage of MVC is that it cleanly allows business logic to be separated from the presentation or view logic. The MVC principle encourages developers to write code that is more reusable and modular.

Let's walk through the steps, as shown in the next diagram, to see the flow through the web framework from the initial HTTP request to the response. The steps are as follows:

1. An HTTP/HTTPS request is made by invoking a URI. The URI is associated with an application that processes the parameters of the URI and then handles where the request is to be sent next.

2. The request is dispatched to the Controller element in the Webscript Container, which matches the parameters of the request. This hand off to the Controller starts the MVC process. For some simple, basically static pages or components, it isn't necessary to have a controller element or model; in those cases, control is passed directly to the view in step 5. The Controller logic is typically written using JavaScript, but for more complex tasks, it is also possible to write the Controller as a Java bean that can get wired into the MVC framework.

3. The controller is tasked with building the model, which returns a set of named properties that are used by the view during rendering. To build the model, the controller will often need to call out to services to retrieve the data and sometimes also process or transform the data before entering it into the model.

4. The dispatcher next finds the view template that contains the markup instructions for how to render the information contained in the model. The controller then passes off the model data to the view.

5. The view consists of FreeMarker tags that specify the layout and instructions for rendering the information. Based on the requested format, the view constructs the formatted view. Typically, the view will format the information in HTML, JSON, or RSS, but almost any format is possible.

6. The formatted view information is finally returned in the response to the HTTP request.

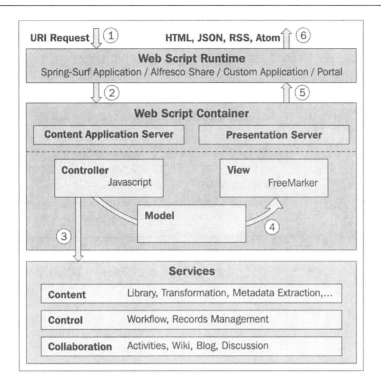

The flow of the Records Management webscript dashlet

Let's see now how the flow of the Records Management dashlet follows the Web Framework MVC pattern that we just discussed.

The Records Management dashlet files

To do that, let's first identify the files that make up the website dashlet. These files were bundled into the `Site-webscripts` directory of the Alfresco Share Records Management AMP. By navigating to the `tomcat\webapps\share\WEB-INF\ classes\alfresco\site-webscripts\org\alfresco\components\dashlets` directory, we'll find the files specific to the Records Management dashlet.

The following table lists the Records Management dashlet files with a brief description of their purpose:

Filename	Description
rma.get.desc.xml	The descriptor file for the dashlet. This file defines the name, description, and URL for the dashlet.
rma.get.js	This file contains the definition of a function for checking to see if the Records Management site has already been created or not. The script also executes the function, returning true or false.
rma.get.head.ftl	This file defines markup to include the client JavaScript file rma-dashlet.js on the page displaying the dashlet.
rma.get.html.ftl	This file provides the FreeMarker tags that define the layout and appearance of the dashlet.
rma.get.properties	This file defines the text shown on labels of the dashlet UI and also contains the text for messages that may be displayed. The text in this file is English, but localized versions of this file can be created for displaying text in different languages corresponding to different locales.

In addition to these files, the client-side JavaScript file referenced in rma.get.head. ftl is also involved in rendering the Records Management dashlet. This file is in the directory tomcat\webapps\share\components\dashlets:

Filename	Description
rma-dashlet.js	This client-side JavaScript file defines actions associated with clicking on some of the links displayed on the dashlet.

The Records Management dashlet files in the MVC Pattern

These files are used to construct the Records Management dashlet using the Web Framework MVC pattern as follows:

1. The dashboard has a reference to the URI for the Records Management dashlet. When it is called, it will look something like: http:// localhost:8080/share/page/components/dashlets/rma?htmlid=rmid.

2. The Web Framework runtime then processes the URL and tries to determine if a controller exists to initiate MVC processing for the dashlet. To do that, the framework identifies the file rma.get.desc.xml as the descriptor file for the dashlet.

3. `rma.get.js` is the controller file for the dashlet. Its name matches the file name signature of the descriptor file. This file is run and determines if the Records Management site is already installed into Alfresco Share. To do that, it calls into the Alfresco repository and queries for the existence of the site.

4. The model is then constructed by adding a single parameter into it called `sitefound`. If the Records Management site exists, the parameter is true, otherwise it is false.

5. The model data then gets dispatched to the view. The view is constructed with the files `rma.get.head.ftl`, `rma.get.html.ftl`, and `rma.get.properties`. The view generates the appropriate HTML for the display of the dashlet on the dashboard. `rma.get.head.ftl` adds an `<include>` tag into the `<head>` tag of the dashboard page for the client-side JavaScript file `rma-dashlet.js`.

6. The HTML data is returned in the response.

If we markup the previous diagram of the Web Framework MVC process with the names of the files that are involved, we can see something that looks like the following:

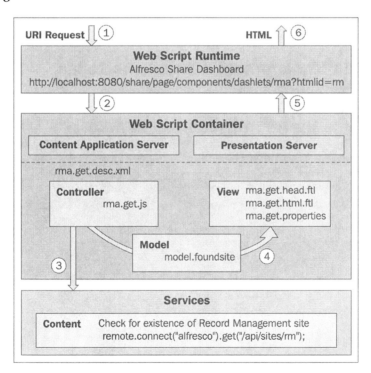

The Records Management descriptor file

When a user logs into Share, the dashboard page will collect the page layout and display all dashlets for the user. Each dashlet is referenced and displayed based on the URI defined in the descriptor file for the dashlet.

The descriptor file for the Records Management dashlet is the file `rma.get.desc.xml`. The contents of that file are as follows:

```
<webscript>
  <shortname>Records Management Config</shortname>
  <description>Records Management site configuration and helper
    component</description>
  <family>user-dashlet</family>
  <url>/components/dashlets/rma</url>
</webscript>
```

The descriptor for the dashlet webscript defines a `shortname` and a `description`. Webscripts are assigned a family, which is similar to a tag, and is used to group together webscripts of a similar type when browsing or searching for webscripts. The last parameter in this file defines a URL value for referencing the dashlet. The dashlet URL would expand to something like `http://localhost:8080/share/page/components/dashlets/rma?htmlid=rmid`.

The Records Management dashlet controller

When the Records Management dashlet is first invoked for display on the dashboard, the controller file is run. The controller populates the values for the properties of the model. If we examine the code in the controller file, we see a very simple model with only the property `foundsite`. `foundsite` is a Boolean flag that specifies whether or not the Records Management site has already been created.

The value for `foundsite` is determined by connecting with the Alfresco Content Repository and checking to see if a site called `rm`, the Records Management site, exists.

```
function main()
{
  // Check for RMA site existence
  var conn = remote.connect("alfresco");
  var res = conn.get("/api/sites/rm");
  if (res.status == 404)
  {
    // site does not exist yet
    model.foundsite = false;
  }
  else if (res.status == 200)
```

```
  {
    // site already exists
    model.foundsite = true;
  }
}
main();
```

The Records Management dashlet view

The model generated by the Controller is then passed to the view.

If we open the file `rma.get.html.ftl`, we can see the markup that specifies the layout for the dashlet UI. A lot of the file uses standard HTML tags, and FreeMarker tags are used to identify message labels and to hide or display links on the dashlet. The message labels that are referenced are defined in the properties file. Putting text into a properties file is considered a best practice that is used frequently in Java programming and which easily enables localization of text.

```
<script type="text/javascript">
  //<![CDATA[
    new
    Alfresco.dashlet.RMA("${args.htmlid}").setMessages(${messages});
//]]>
</script>
<div class="dashlet">
  <div class="title">${msg("label.title")}</div>
  <div class="body theme-color-1">
    <div class="detail-list-item-alt theme-bg-color-2 theme-color-2"
      style="padding: 0.5em;border-bottom: 1px solid #DDD6A0">
      <h4>${msg("label.summary")}</h4>
    </div>
    <div id="${args.htmlid}-display-site" class="detail-list-item"
      <#if !foundsite="">style="display:none"</#if>>
      <a href="${url.context}/page/site/rm/dashboard">
        ${msg("label.display-site")}</a>
    </div>
    <div id="${args.htmlid}-create-site" class="detail-list-item"
      <#if foundsite="">style="display:none"</#if>>
      <a id="${args.htmlid}-create-site-link"
        href="#">${msg("label.create-site")}</a>
    </div>
    <#if user.isAdmin="">
      <div id="${args.htmlid}-load-data" class="detail-list-item"
        <#if !foundsite="">style="display:none"</#if>>
```

```
        <a id="${args.htmlid}-load-data-link"
          href="#">${msg("label.load-test-data")}</a>
      </div>
    </#if>
    <div class="detail-list-item last-item">
      <a id="${args.htmlid}-role-report-link"
        href="${url.context}/page/console/rm-console/">
        ${msg("label.rm-console")}</a>
    </div>
  </div>
</div>
```

By looking up the string values in the `rma.get.properties` file, we can see the basic content that will be displayed in the dashlet.

Property file label	Text string value
`label.title`	Records Management
`label.summary`	Configuration and setup for the Records Management site
`label.display-site`	Create the Records Management site
`label.create-site`	The Records Management site
`label.load-test-data`	Load test data
`label.rm-console`	The Management console

The header file is also a great place to reference any custom stylesheets. But the Records Management dashlet is fairly simple. It conforms to the standard look of the Alfresco dashboard and does not use a custom stylesheet.

The Records Management dashlet URL

The dashlet lives in the context of the dashboard page, but it is interesting to see the URL for the dashlet render outside the context of the dashboard. If we do that, we can see something like the following screenshot. We can then look at the source code for the rendered page and can see that the HTML created for the dashlet lacks <head> and <body> tags and also doesn't contain a reference to the Records Management dashlet client-side JavaScript file. The dashlet also relies on the standard stylesheet for the dashboard page, so the rendering of it here is different than it would be on the dashboard page:

If we look at the source code of this page after being rendered in the browser, we can see how the messages are evaluated and used. The messages are passed in as an argument to the creation method for the client-side RMA dashlet object. All the dashlet labels and display strings have been evaluated too, like the title and link text:

```
<script type="text/javascript">//<![CDATA[
  new Alfresco.dashlet.RMA("rm").setMessages({"label.summary":
    "Configuration and Setup for Records Management site.",
    "label.load-test-data": "Load Test Data", "message.creating":
    "Creating Records Management Site please wait...", "label.rm-
    console": "Management Console", "message.create-fail": "Failed to
    create Records Management Site.", "message.importing": "Importing
    Records Management test data please wait...", "label.create-
    site": "Create Records Management Site", "label.user-role-
    report": "User Role Report", "message.import-fail": "Failed to
    import test data into Records Management Site.", "message.create-
    ok": "Records Management Site successfully created.",
    "label.display-site": "Records Management Site", "message.import-
    ok": "Records Management Site import successful.", "label.title":
    "Records Management"});
//]]></script>
<div class="dashlet">
  <div class="title">Records Management</div>
  <div class="body theme-color-1">
    <div class="detail-list-item-alt theme-bg-color-2 theme-color-
      2"
      style="padding: 0.5em;border-bottom: 1px solid #DDD6A0">
      <h4>Configuration and Setup for Records Management site.</h4>
    </div>
    <div id="rm-display-site" class="detail-list-item" >
      <a href="/share/page/site/rm/dashboard">Records Management
        Site</a>
    </div>
```

```
<div id="rm-create-site" class="detail-list-item"
  style="display:none">
  <a id="rm-create-site-link" href="#">Create Records
    Management Site</a>
</div>
<div id="rm-load-data" class="detail-list-item" >
  <a id="rm-load-data-link" href="#">Load Test Data</a>
</div>
<div class="detail-list-item last-item">
  <a id="rm-role-report-link"
    href="/share/page/console/rm-console/">Management
    Console</a>
</div>
  </div>
</div>
```

The Records Management console client-side JavaScript

In the HTML for the dashlet that we just looked at, some of the `<a>` tags referenced `"#"` as the target href link value. The `"#"` refers to the current HTML page. In these cases, the dashlets, instead of linking to a new URL from an `href` target value, are activated by click events, which call JavaScript methods.

For example, consider the following line from the evaluated HTML:

```
<a id="rm-create-site-link" href="#">Create Records Management Site</
a>
```

What is important here is the `id` for the `<a>` tag.

Recall that the dashlet file, `rma.get.head.ftl`, includes markup in the `<head>` tag for the dashboard HTML page to include the client-side JavaScript file `rma-dashlet.js`. If we look at the contents of that JavaScript file, we'll find the constructor for an RMA object:

```
Alfresco.dashlet.RMA = function RMA_constructor(htmlId)
{
  return Alfresco.dashlet.RMA.superclass.constructor.call(this,
    "Alfresco.dashlet.RMA", htmlId);
};
```

The constructor method is called from the script at the top of the file `rma.get.html.ftl` that we discussed above. The object `Alfresco.dashlet.RMA` that is created by the constructor extends from the `Alfresco.component.base` object. The RMA object is constructed using elements of the Yahoo! User Interface library or YUI.

Much of the Share JavaScript client code is written to use the YUI 2.0 library. YUI provides a set of utilities and controls for more easily creating rich browser-based applications. It uses techniques based on DOM scripting, DHTML, and AJAX. YUI uses the BSD license and is free to use. It is important to understand the basics of YUI in order to fully understand how many of the Alfresco Share JavaScript files work.

 More details of the Yahoo! User Interface library can be found here: `http://developer.yahoo.com/yui/2/`.

The skeleton of the object methods for the `Alfresco dashlet.RMA` object is as follows:

```
YAHOO.extend(Alfresco.dashlet.RMA, Alfresco.component.Base,
{
  /**
    * Fired by YUI when parent element is available for scripting
    * @method onReady
  */
  onReady: function RMA_onReady()
  {
  ...
  },
  /**
    * Create Site link click event handler
    *
    * @method onCreateSite
    * @param e {object} DomEvent
    * @param args {array} Event parameters (depends on event type)
  */
  onCreateSite: function RMA_onCreateSite(e, args)
  {
  ...
  },
  /**
    * Load Test Data link click event handler
    *
    * @method onLoadTestData
    * @param e {object} DomEvent
    * @param args {array} Event parameters (depends on event type)
  */
  onLoadTestData: function RMA_onLoadTestData(e, args)
  {
  ...
```

```
      },
      /**
       * User Role Report link click event handler
       *
       * @method onUserRoleReport
       * @param e {object} DomEvent
       * @param args {array} Event parameters (depends on event type)
      */
      onUserRoleReport: function RMA_onUserRoleReport(e, args)
      {
      ...
      }
   }
}
```

The `RMA_onReady` method defines the element IDs in the HTML that can trigger actions. In the dashlet HTML, we saw the element IDs for the `<a>` tags above: `rm-create-site-link`, `rm-load-data-link`, and `rm-report-link`. The element ID names were constructed by taking an HTML ID value that is passed in and appending a string to it. In our test, we used "`rm`" for the HTML ID. In general, the base HTML ID is a fairly long text string of various concatenated pieces of information that may look something like this: page_x002e_component-1-3_x002e_user_x007e_admin_x007e_dashboard-create-site:

```
onReady: function RMA_onReady()
{
  var me = this;

  this.widgets.feedbackMessage = null;

  // setup link events
  Event.on(this.id + "-create-site-link", "click",
    this.onCreateSite, null, this);
  Event.on(this.id + "-load-data-link", "click",
    this.onLoadTestData, null, this);
  Event.on(this.id + "-role-report-link", "click",
    this.onUserRoleReport, null, this);
}
```

We saw earlier in this chapter that one of the last steps in installing and creating the Records Management site is to click on the link **Create Records Management Site**. The event caused by clicking on the link caused the `onCreateSite` method action to be called:

```
onCreateSite: function RMA_onCreateSite(e, args)
{
  Event.stopEvent(e);

  if (this.widgets.feedbackMessage === null)
```

```
{
  this.widgets.feedbackMessage =
    Alfresco.util.PopupManager.displayMessage(
  {
    text: this.msg("message.creating"),
    spanClass: "wait",
    displayTime: 0
  });

  // call web-tier to perform site creation
  Alfresco.util.Ajax.request(
  {
    method: Alfresco.util.Ajax.GET,
    url: Alfresco.constants.URL_SERVICECONTEXT +
      "utils/create-rmsite?shortname=rm",
    successCallback:
    {
      fn: function()
      {
        this.widgets.feedbackMessage.destroy();
        Alfresco.util.PopupManager.displayMessage(
        {
          text: this.msg("message.create-ok")
        });

        // refresh UI appropriately
        Dom.setStyle(this.id + "-create-site",
          "display", "none");
        Dom.setStyle(this.id + "-display-site",
          "display", "block");
        Dom.setStyle(this.id + "-load-data", "display",
          "block");
        Alfresco.util.Anim.pulse(this.id + "-display-
          site");

  // reset feedback message - to allow another action if
   required
        this.widgets.feedbackMessage = null;
      },
      scope: this
    },
    failureCallback:
    {
      fn: function()
      {
```

```
                  this.widgets.feedbackMessage.destroy();
                  Alfresco.util.PopupManager.displayMessage(
                  {
                    text: this.msg("message.create-fail")
                  });

      // reset feedback message - to allow another action if
        required
                  this.widgets.feedbackMessage = null;
                },
               scope: this
             }
          });
      }
   }
```

The onCreateSite method first displays a message indicating that the Records Management site is being created. Next an AJAX call is made to create the Records Management site for Share on the server. If the site is created successfully, a pop-up message displays a success message, and the visibility of the links on the dashlet are adjusted, hiding the **Create Records Management Site** link, and now showing as available links for loading test data and for navigating to the newly created Records Management site. If the site fails to be created, a failure message will be displayed.

Creation of the Records Management site

We just saw how the onCreateSite method for the Alfresco dashlet.RMA object made an AJAX call to the server to create the Records Management site. The Share webscript that is referenced in the AJAX call is Alfresco.constants.URL_SERVICECONTEXT + "utils/create-rmsite?shortname=rm

This will evaluate to a URL that looks something like http://localhost:8080/share/service/utils/create-rmsite?shortname=rm. We can find that this URL is defined by the Records Management webscript create-rmsite that was installed into Share.

This AJAX call provides another example of the use of webscripting within Alfresco Share. The files for the create-rmsite webscript can be found in the directory tomcat\webapps\share\WEB-INF\classes\alfresco\site-webscripts\org\alfresco\utils. The files that define this webscript are as follows:

Filename	Description
`create-rmsite.get.desc.xml`	The descriptor file for the webscript. It includes text strings for the shortname and description. It also defines the URL reference to the webscript.
`create-rmsite.get.html.ftl`	This file contains the FreeMarker markup that is used to construct the HTML response to a call to the webscript.
`create-rmsite.get.properties`	This properties file contains the text strings used that are displayed in the response page for the webscript.
`create-rmsite.get.js`	This JavaScript file acts as the controller for the response to a call to the webscript.

Let's now look at the internals of the `create-rmsite` webscript to see how it builds the Records Management site. Here we can see the contents of the file `create-rmsite.get.desc.xml`:

```
<webscript>
  <shortname>Create RM Site</shortname>
  <description>
    Will create a new RM site in the repo and create the RM preset in
      the web-tier.
  </description>
  <url>/utils/create-rmsite?shortname={shortname}</url>
</webscript>
```

The `shortname` and `description` values are self-explanatory. The URL value is a location that the web framework dispatcher will check when it tries to match incoming URLs to be evaluated. In this case, we see that it is necessary to include the `shortname` parameter on the URL (which is different from the `shortname` used in the webscript XML). We saw that the site will be called with the `shortname` "rm" from the `onCreateSite` method discussed above.

Next, let's look at the controller JavaScript file for this webscript. The contents of the file `create-rmsite.get.js` are as follows:

```
function main()
{
  // Call the repo to create the site
  var siteJson =
  {
    shortName: args["shortname"],
    sitePreset: "rm-site-dashboard",
    title: msg.get("title.rmsite"),
    description: msg.get("description.rmsite")
  };
```

```
    var scriptRemoteConnector = remote.connect("alfresco"),
      repoResponse = scriptRemoteConnector.post("/api/sites",
        jsonUtils.toJSONString(siteJson), "application/json");
    if (repoResponse.status == 401)
    {
      status.setCode(repoResponse.status, "error.loggedOut");
      return;
    }
    else
    {
      var repoJSON = eval('(' + repoResponse + ')');

      // Check if we got a positive result
      if (repoJSON.shortName)
      {
        // Yes we did, now create the site in the webtier
        var tokens = new Array();
        tokens["siteid"] = repoJSON.shortName;
        sitedata.newPreset("rm-site-dashboard", tokens);

        model.success = true;
      }
      else if (repoJSON.status.code)
      {
        status.setCode(repoJSON.status.code, repoJSON.message);
        return;
      }
    }
  }
}

main();
```

Here the Controller posts back to the Alfresco Repository API to create the Records Management site, passing into the API method an object with parameters that define the new site. Some of the parameter values come from the string message data found in the properties file create-rmsite.get.properties:

```
title.rmsite=Records Management
description.rmsite=DoD 5015.02-STD Electronic Recordkeeping
```

If the site structure is successfully created in the repository, the Share root object sitedata is updated to now know about the new Records Management site available within Share. The controller populates the Boolean parameter success in the model and returns it for use in the view.

A complete description of `sitedata` and other root-scoped objects that are available with the Spring Surf web framework in Share can be found on the Alfresco wiki: `http://wiki.alfresco.com/wiki/Surf_Platform_-_Freemarker_Template_and_JavaScript_API`

Finally, the View component of the MVC process is invoked and has available to it the model from the Controller. The contents of the View file `create-rmsite.get.html.ftl` is as follows:

```
<#if success>
  Successfully created RM site '<a
    href="${url.context}/page/site/${args["shortname"]}/dashboard">
    ${args["shortname"]}</a>'.
</#if>
<#if code?exists><br>Error code: ${code}</#if>
<#if error?exists><br>Error: ${error}</#if>
```

Here, if the model returned success, the HTML markup returned will report success with a link to the dashboard page of the Records Management site. If an error occurred, an error code is reported.

In this "How does it work?" section and in similar sections in subsequent chapters, we try to get a look at how both Alfresco Share and the Records Management module work. As a user of the system, this information isn't mandatory to know, but the knowledge of system internals can be useful in troubleshooting, and also for understanding how and where customizations in the system are possible.

Alfresco provides a truly open system. All of the source code is readily available, and Alfresco promotes itself as a core around which content-based applications can be built.

The use of dashlets and webscripts provide an ideal starting point for users that want to customize Alfresco. The scripting and template languages used by webscripts make rapid iterative development possible, and dashlets typically only require a modest amount of code to write.

Web development within Share

That concludes our introduction to the internals of the Spring Surf web framework within the Alfresco Share application. In future chapters, we'll continue our discussion on 'How does it work?' and our understanding of the Alfresco MVC process will be applied to other components of the Records Management module. As we've seen, the architecture for Share is quite clean and that promotes rapid development.

Summary

In this chapter, we learned how to install Alfresco Records Management software. We covered the following topics:

- How to install the base Alfresco software and the Records Management modules
- How to add the Records Management console dashlet to the dashboard
- How to create the Records Management site
- How to create a Records Manager administrator

At the end of the chapter, in a 'How does it work?' section, we looked in detail at how the Records Management console dashlet in the Alfresco Share dashboard is constructed. In particular, we covered:

- The MVC design pattern as used by the Spring Surf web framework within Alfresco Share
- How Alfresco webscripts work
- How the Records Management dashlet works
- How the Records Management site is created internally

With Alfresco Records Management software now up and running, in the next chapter, we will begin looking at how to effectively configure Alfresco software to match our Records Management Program's requirements.

3
Introduction to the Alfresco Share Records Management Site

In the last chapter, we walked through the steps for installing and setting up a standard instance of Alfresco software with the Records Management module and then creating the Records Management Share site. In this chapter, we will spend some time familiarizing ourselves with the Alfresco Share environment and with some of the fundamentals of how to get started working within the Alfresco Records Management site.

Alfresco Share was built using elements of the Spring Surf web framework and the Alfresco Content Repository. While the Records Management site is no exception and while it follows a design pattern similar to that used by other sites within Share, there are also features of the Records Management site that make it distinctly different from standard Share sites, and we will highlight some of those similarities and differences here.

In this chapter, we will describe:

- How to customize the Share user and site dashboards
- The Records Management site dashboard
- Collaboration features available within Share and accessible from the Share Records Management site
- The Records Management File Plan and Records search pages
- How to control which users and groups have access to the Records Management site

We will also look at some of the internals of Alfresco Share and Records Management. In particular, we will look at:

- Share and Records Management configuration files
- How user and site dashboards are constructed and how their configuration data is persisted
- How to create a new Share theme

The Share environment

A good way to first start trying to understand how Records Management works within Alfresco is by getting an understanding of the overall structure and environment that it runs in, **Alfresco Share**. The Share Records Management site is built in a way that extends and reuses many elements of standard Share site functionality. Because of that, a good understanding of the basics of Alfresco Share can also provide a good foundation for learning how Records Management works.

But while there are similarities between standard Share sites and the Share Records Management site, there are also a number of differences. Compared to standard Share sites, Records Management is quite unique, and we will discuss the differences that exist between standard sites and the Records Management site.

A brief history of Alfresco Share

In early December 2007, Alfresco announced the broadening and repositioning of Alfresco software to include Social computing and collaboration capabilities. The announcement was a turning point for Alfresco product development. While Alfresco was only a couple of years old at the time, prior to that, product development had focused primarily on building the Alfresco content repository and the library services that are requisite for an enterprise content management system.

Alfresco Share as a social platform

After that announcement, Alfresco blog articles and press releases started referring to the Alfresco platform as the "Open source social computing platform for enterprise". While that name is a bit of a mouthful, the thinking behind it did strike a chord in a world that at the time was seeing phenomenal growth in the acceptance and use of **Social Media**.

The new positioning of Alfresco brought along with it new descriptions of the software that included phrases like "Enterprise 2.0 software" and "Web 2.0 user interface". To make good on this new positioning, Alfresco aggressively introduced integrations with **Social Networking** sites like **Facebook** and with wiki products like **MediaWiki** and **WordPress**.

Alfresco Share and the Alfresco 3 Labs release

The move towards including collaboration capabilities in Alfresco software preceded the actual introduction of Alfresco Share. It wasn't until nearly seven months later, near the end of July 2008, that Alfresco Share was announced. Share initially appeared in what was called the "Alfresco 3 Labs version" and was ultimately released in the enterprise version of Alfresco in October 2008.

The **Alfresco 3.0** release was very feature rich and included the introduction of the Surf development platform, the Alfresco Share application, and an implementation of Microsoft's SharePoint protocol. The SharePoint protocol implementation allowed the Alfresco repository to be accessed in the same way as a SharePoint repository by Microsoft Office applications.

Almost from the very beginning of Alfresco as a company, Alfresco team members identified EMC **Documentum** and Microsoft as their principle competitors in the **Enterprise Content Management** (ECM) market. The 3.0 release really focused on the identification of that competition. It became very clear that Alfresco was positioning itself with **Microsoft SharePoint** as its principle competitor.

Alfresco founder and CTO John Newton introduced Share as the "first open source alternative to Microsoft SharePoint", and noted that Alfresco's goal was to achieve interoperability and compatibility with Microsoft SharePoint. Undoubtedly, the product name "Share" was also selected to further emphasize the similarity of Alfresco with SharePoint. SharePoint was clearly in Alfresco's crosshairs.

Alfresco Share 3.X Post-Labs release

With each point release of the Alfresco 3.x series of releases, Alfresco Share has continued to evolve and to add features for better usability, expanded tools for administration, and improved capabilities for promoting collaboration.

In the Alfresco Share 3.x release, Web 2.0 tools and services became available that included a calendar, blogs, discussions, RSS feeds, and wikis. Alfresco added lightweight scripting APIs to enable **Rich Internet Application** (RIA) mash up applications with technologies like **Adobe Flex** and Alfresco's own Spring Surf framework. Additional integrations with applications and services like Drupal and iGoogle were also released.

New features added in the Alfresco 3.3 release of Share include:

- Document management—complete access to all core document management capabilities.

- Permission management—ability to assign permissions to folders and content within Share.

- Rules and Actions—access to the Alfresco Rules Engine developed for use with the Explorer client has been moved to Share. Rules that trigger on certain events can be created and configured via a rules wizard.

- Data lists—users can create multi-column lists to hold data like task or item lists and associate the lists with a Share site.

- Google-like search—support for Boolean operators, range searches, and search over metadata fields was added.

Use cases for Alfresco Share

Alfresco Share was designed to enable site-centric sharing of information. Sites within Share were designed to be the focal point for managing information and content related to a specific project or topic.

Team project sites

By far, the most common usage scenario for Alfresco share is for a site to be set up within Share that can serve as a portal for team members to share information and documents associated with a project. The site Document Library can identify those documents relevant to the project and the most current versions of documents. For many teams, the Document Library replaces the use of an unmanaged shared drive. Events and milestones for the project site can be tracked on the calendar, and members can share information in the discussion areas, blogs, and wiki pages.

Publishing sites

Publishing sites are very similar to team project sites, but publishing sites, instead of being project-focused, focus on a specific topic. Publishing sites can be set up for internal use by employees of an organization, usually on an intranet, or they can be made available for access to users that are located both internal and external to the organization. For example, the HR department might set up a site dedicated to providing information about company benefits, or the training department might make available training materials from the site, or a hardware maker might, for example, create a portal that included product information, community support via discussions, manuals, and downloadable software drivers.

Personal sites

While the idea may run counter to the idea of shared collaboration, Share sites can also be set up for the personal use of individual users. With a personal Share site, users can create their own personal dashboard, set up their personal calendar and tasks, and manage their personal documents. Parts of a personal site could be made public, if desired. For example, a user might publish a blog from their personal site that is accessible to the rest of the organization.

Records Management exists as a special kind of site within Share. The focus of the Records Management site is the Document Library, and to support the requirements of the DoD 5015.2 specification for managing records, the Document Library has been re-engineered to become the Records Management File Plan. It functions in a way that is significantly different from the standard Document Library.

The Records Management site is similar to the Project Team site because, typically, the primary members for the site are Records Management team members. But that isn't always true because often record keeping is decentralized, and users from all parts of the organization might be given some level of access and filing capabilities within the File Plan.

Alfresco Share and collaboration

Alfresco Share was conceived as an application that provides a central point for:

- Project-based collaboration
- Wikis
- Blogs
- Discussions
- Calendar
- Data lists
- Document Library

Share dashboards

The first screen that we see after logging into the Alfresco Share application, whether we are the administrator or a user, is the user **dashboard**. Each user is able to customize their home page dashboard by changing the overall layout and the content that appears within it.

The dashboard page is like the page of a portal. It consists of small panels that can be arranged in positions on a grid defined by the page layout template. Available page layouts range from a single column to four columns. Each of the panels on the page is called a dashlet and each dashlet usually corresponds to a small, fairly self-contained webscript that is able to calculate and render itself within the region of the dashlet. Dashlets are constrained to fill the width of the dashboard column and can be constructed to have either a fixed or variable height.

Dashlets can be placed in any of the layout columns, and dashlets fill a dashboard column, starting from the top in the order that they are assigned to it:

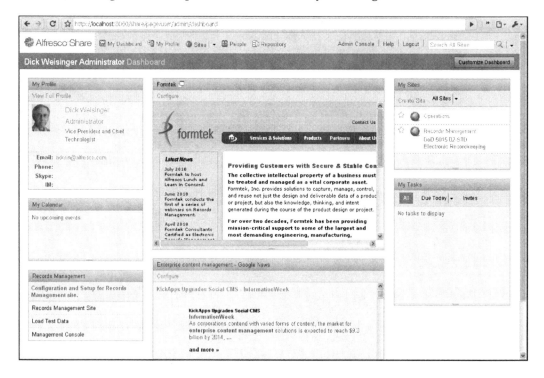

From the user dashboard, a **Customize Dashboard** button on the upper-right of the screen leads to a page where each user can customize his/her own dashboard. Alfresco then saves and thereafter uses that custom dashboard configuration:

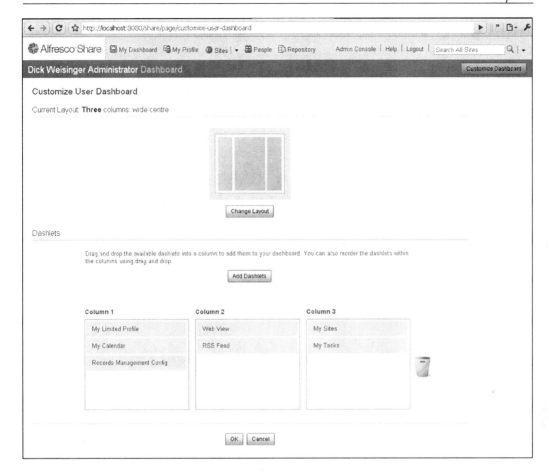

The **Customize User Dashboard** screen is divided in half vertically with the upper half used for specifying the overall dashboard layout, and the bottom half used for placing the dashlets in the screen layout.

Much of the user interface of Alfresco Share is built using the Yahoo! User Interface (YUI) library that allows the creation of user interfaces with very rich client-side interaction. This particular screen is a good example of the dynamic screens that can be built with the YUI library.

 More information about the YUI 2 library can be found at `http://developer.yahoo.com/yui/2/` and `http://yuilibrary.com/projects/yui2/`.

Changing the dashboard layout

On the layout specification area on top, clicking on the **Change Layout** button will expose additional layout graphics. Each graphic gives an indication of the number of and the relative widths and placements of the columns in the layout. Standard page layouts range from using a single column to four columns. There may be layouts with the same number of columns, but which differ by the width of the columns. In this way, the user can visually select the layout configuration for the dashboard.

Changing the placement of dashboard dashlets

On the bottom area of the customization screen, dashlets can be placed on the column grid of the selected layout. Note that the screen mockup doesn't show the relative heights of the individual dashlets, just the order in which the dashlets will be displayed.

Clicking on the **Add Dashlets** button will expose all dashlets that are available for display on the dashboard. Dashlets can be moved from one grid layout location to another by clicking on the dashlet and then dragging and dropping it into its new position.

Dashlets that have been placed and which you would like to remove from the layout can be dragged to either the trash icon or to the list of available dashlets.

After modifying the layout or changing the dashlet positioning, the new configuration can be saved by clicking on **OK**. After that, the newly configured dashboard will display. Your configuration changes for the dashboard are stored on the Alfresco server and will be recalled and used the next time that you access the dashboard page.

If, instead, you click on **Cancel**, any changes you made on the dashboard configuration page will be lost and the dashboard page will display with no modifications.

Changing site dashboards

In Alfresco Share, there are two types of dashboards: the **user dashboard** which displays as the top-level user home page, and **site dashboards** which display as the home page for each site. In the section above, we've looked in detail at the user dashboard.

The configuration for each type of dashboard is done identically to the way described previously, although the dashlets that are available differ depending on the dashboard type. But, in both cases, the mechanics of the configuration are done the same way.

Dashlets are built using webscripts. When a dashlet is defined, the dashlet family is specified as part of the dashlet description. Possible types of dashlet families are `user-dashlet`, `site-dashlet`, and `dashlet`. Type `dashlet` means that it can be used as either a user or site dashlet. The family setting determines which dashlets are available for a dashboard type.

Site pages

While the user dashboard page and the site dashboard page are very similar, site dashboards also include top navigation links to site pages. The user dashboard has no such navigation links. Standard sites for example, include by default, page links to the site wiki, the site blog, the document library, a calendar, a list of links, discussions, and data lists:

Configuring site page navigation

The page links available on a site can be configured. From the site dashboard page, on the upper right, select **Customize Site** from the **More** button menu. After doing that, the following screen for customizing the site pages is displayed:

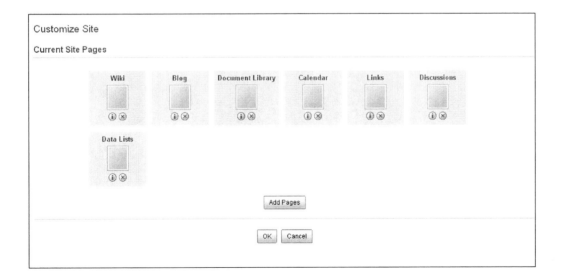

If there are additional pages that are not already included on the navigation bar, they can be added by first clicking on **Add Pages** and then selecting the new page or pages from a list of available ones. Pages can be deleted from the list by clicking on the **x** located on the lower middle right of each page graphic.

For a standard site, all available pages are included as part of the initial site configuration. In that case, because all pages have already been assigned to the site, no additional pages are available when **Add Pages** is clicked on. That isn't true for the Records Management site though.

For Records Management, two pages that are unique to the Records Management are assigned to the site by default: the **File Plan** and the **Records Search** pages. However none of the standard Share collaboration pages, like the calendar or blog, are installed.

The focus of the Records Management site was clearly to be on Records Management. Other capabilities were disabled by default so as not to steal attention from the Records Management features. But collaboration features can be useful in support of the Records Management process. They are available for use in the Records Management site; they just aren't exposed by default.

The screen for customizing the site pages for Records Management looks like the following screenshot:

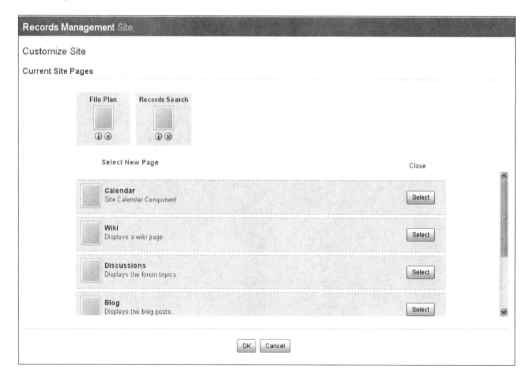

Collaboration pages can be added to the Records Management site, although the content associated with those pages will not be managed according to the Records Management File Plan. This means that if the blog page is added to the Records Management site, new blog entries will be associated with the Records Management site, but those blog entries will not be associated with the File Plan, and accordingly, will not be records and will not be associated with a disposition schedule.

Currently, there is much debate in the Records Management community about how to treat, or if even to treat as records, collaboration data created from applications like wikis, blogs, and discussions. Collaboration data is often very transient and undergoes frequent updates. As of yet, there is no clear consensus in the Records Management community as to exactly how Records Management principles can be best applied to manage collaboration data as records.

While collaboration data may not be managed as records within Alfresco, Alfresco can still be configured to log audit information for any type of data stored in the system, including collaboration data. Also, like all other data in the repository, collaboration data is text indexed and fully searchable.

Blogs, wiki, and discussion information associated with the Records Management site can be used to enhance the overall usability of Records Management. These tools can be used to explain and comment on the Records Management process and procedures.

Text written to collaboration pages like blogs, wikis, and discussions are fully searchable via the standard Alfresco site search, but content from these pages are not records and hence not included as part of the search set when using the Records Management site **Records Search**.

Share themes

The standard color scheme for Share makes use of sky-blue and lavender colors. It's a pleasant and fresh look for the application, but you may not like it, or you may have a different color scheme that you'd like to brand the application with.

Share provides a method for "skinning" the look of the application, which allows developers to make consistent broad changes to the look of the Share application. Color, font, and layout parameters for Share are controlled by the Share theme. Internally themes are defined via custom CSS files and images.

Five themes come as standard with Share. The standard themes available are called **Default**, **Green**, **Yellow**, **High Contrast**, and **Google Docs**. It is also very easy to create new themes too. Themes are assigned by an administrator and are applied to all pages of the Share application. There can only be a single theme that applies to all pages of the Share application.

Share themes can be changed and applied by using the **Application** tool within the Share administration console. You can get to the **Admin Console** from a link on the top of the Share page just to the left of the **Search** field.

Currently themes are the only optional configuration parameter in the **Application** tool. We might expect to see other application parameters made available for configuration within this tool too:

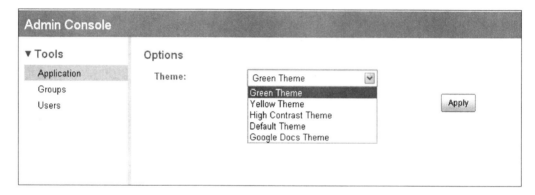

Share collaboration

As discussed above, Share offers a number of useful communication tools for engaging team members in project collaboration, and as just pointed out, all of these collaboration pages are also available for use in the Records Management site.

Collaboration tools

Out of the box, the following collaboration tools can be used with Share sites:

Wiki: A wiki is a tool for collaboratively creating web pages. Wikis are typically a collection of web pages, with each wiki page being written in the format of an entry, like that of a dictionary or encyclopedia, which is focused on providing a clear explanation of a topic or term. Generally, any user with access to a wiki is able to contribute to or collaborate on the content of any wiki page. A change log or history of all page changes is kept for each page of the wiki. The page history identifies the users that have made wiki page edits, when they made them, and what content was changed or added to the wiki page.

Blog: A blog is a web page that contains journal-like entries made by one person or a group of people. Blogs entries are often themed around a particular topic. Entries to the blog are posted in chronological order and are usually written in an editorial first-person format. Blog entries often contain commentary and opinion, description of events, and advice. Entries are often assigned tags or categorized so that entries on a common topic can be grouped or more easily searched. Unlike a wiki where any part of the content posted is available to be edited, blog entries, once written, are usually never edited, but can be commented on in a discussion thread that follows the original blog entry by readers of the blog posting.

Document Library: The document library is an area within each Share site where documents and files can be uploaded and made available for search, viewing, and download. The document library in Share has been enhanced significantly since the original release of Share 3.0. It now exposes most Alfresco repository capabilities in the Share user interface, like library services, preview, metadata editing, aspects, rules, and workflow.

Calendar: The calendar provides a convenient location to aggregate event and meeting notices that are relevant to members of the Share site. An integration with Microsoft SharePoint also allows meeting requests created in Outlook to automatically be sent to and registered on the site calendar.

Links: The links page provides a summary of URL links to web pages that are relevant or of interest to members of the Share site. Links added to the list can be titled and briefly described.

Discussions: The discussion page is a web page where users can start dialog threads with other site members around questions or topics of interest to the group.

Data Lists: Data lists are spreadsheet-like lists maintained as a simple webpage. A list consists of rows of data with each column containing a specific type of data attribute. Example data lists include contacts, events, issues, and locations.

Project-based collaboration data

The focus of Alfresco Share is to create sites for projects to centralize the location of all project data and project collaboration. The goal is to make a Share site the go-to location for finding all information pertinent to a project. Without a tool like Share, project communications typically take place via e-mails, and e-mails can quickly become scattered or lost. On a Share site, users can find the most current documentation and news about a project.

The Records Management site

The Records Management site can be accessed in a number of ways. The dashboard from the Share home page provides the following three links to the Records Management site:

- From the **Sites** drop-down menu on the upper-most Share navigation bar
- From the My Sites dashlet
- From the Records Management console dashlet

The site dashboard

As we have seen earlier, the Records Management site dashboard functions identically to the user dashboard. Like the user dashboard, the dashboard layout and the dashlet placement is totally configurable:

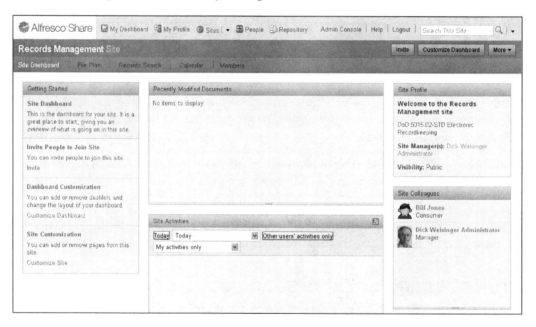

The File Plan

Clicking on the **File Plan** page link in the top navigation for the Records Management site brings up the File Plan page. The File Plan is really at the heart of Records Management. Let's look at this page in more detail to get an understanding of how to administer the File Plan:

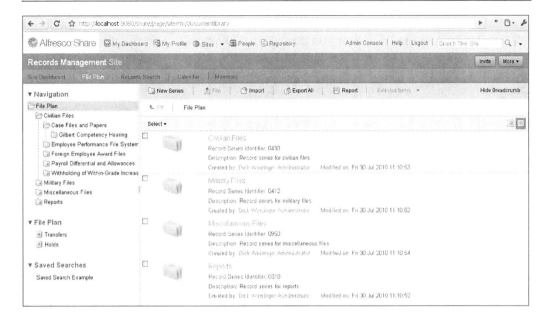

The File Plan toolbar

The **File Plan** toolbar is displayed as a banner of icons and actions at the top of the main column of the File Plan. There is much more to say about the records File Plan, but for now, consider the File Plan as the folder hierarchy used for organizing folders and records. Depending on the state of items in the File Plan window, some of the icons may not apply and may not be selectable.

If a toolbar item is not selectable, the item will be dimmed on the toolbar. Availability of items on the toolbar is also determined by the role of the user. If the user's role does not include an action or capability, the corresponding icon on the toolbar button will also be dimmed.

 After installing Records Management, no users, not even the administrative user who installed the site will have sufficient privileges to perform any actions within the File Plan. When testing and exploring the full capabilities of Alfresco Records Management, it is best to select a user that is a member of the Records Management administrator group.

New Containers: Standard File Plan container elements, like Series, Categories, or Folders can be created by clicking on the left-most icon action on the toolbar. For example, clicking on this button will launch a dialog that initiates the creation of a new container of the type indicated on the button label. Depending on the level that you are positioned at within the File Plan, the New Container toolbar item will be labeled one of **New Series**, **New Category**, or **New Folder**. The File Plan strictly follows the DoD 5015.2 convention for determining which type of container can be added to the current location in the File Plan. The DoD 5015.2 specifies a folder hierarchy of three levels, and the naming of those three levels is predefined: Series, Category, and Folder. The toolbar enforces this hierarchy and allows only the correct type of container to be created at a given level within the File Plan structure.

File: Clicking on the **File** button will launch a dialog that lets the user select the files to be uploaded to the current location in the File Plan. In the previous screenshot of the toolbar, we see that the ability to **File** is dimmed because we are positioned in a File Plan Series and records can only be filed under a folder, not directly into a Series.

Import: Clicking on the **Import** button will bring up a dialog that allows you to navigate to and select an **Alfresco Content Package** (ACP) file which contains the zipped structure and contents of an exported File Plan. After selecting the ACP file, the data from the file will be imported alongside the contents of the current File Plan data. An ACP file is a ZIP file with the files and folders in it stored in an expected structure.

Export All: Clicking on this button will export all metadata, content, and folder structure of the current Records Management File Plan into an ACP or ZIP file. The ACP file created by doing an export can later be used to import the same data into an Alfresco Records Management system using the previously described **Import** button.

Report: Clicking on the **Report** button will launch a pop up that displays a visual layout of the Records Management File Plan. The root of the diagram will be the folder within the File Plan that you were positioned at when the **Report** button was clicked on. A report of this type looks something like the following screenshot:

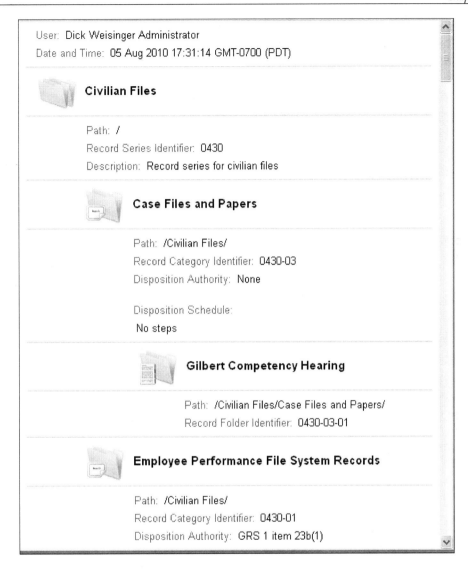

User: Dick Weisinger Administrator
Date and Time: 05 Aug 2010 17:31:14 GMT-0700 (PDT)

Civilian Files

Path: /
Record Series Identifier: 0430
Description: Record series for civilian files

Case Files and Papers

Path: /Civilian Files/
Record Category Identifier: 0430-03
Disposition Authority: None

Disposition Schedule:
  No steps

Gilbert Competency Hearing

Path: /Civilian Files/Case Files and Papers/
Record Folder Identifier: 0430-03-01

Employee Performance File System Records

Path: /Civilian Files/
Record Category Identifier: 0430-01
Disposition Authority: GRS 1 item 23b(1)

The size of the text and icons in the **Report** are visually pleasing, but the data displayed is somewhat verbose and there is little that can be done to customize the look of the report. For File Plans with large numbers of categories and records, this sort of output is simply not practical. If the report is being run over a large number of folders and records, it might be better to instead use the records search functionality. However, in that case, the search results won't visually depict the File Plan folder structure.

Selected Items: Clicking on the **Selected Items** button of the toolbar will display a drop-down menu of actions that can be run against the selected set of containers or records. This button is only active when some items of the current File Plan position have been first selected:

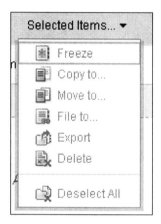

Left navigation panel

The left panel of the File Plan page contains a variety of shortcuts for quickly finding data within the File Plan. Uppermost in the panel is the **Navigation** tree. The tree view allows you to quickly navigate through the File Plan tree containers visually and see the relative placement of the containers:

▼ Navigation

📂 File Plan

   📂 Civilian Files

      📂 Case Files and Papers

         🗋 Gilbert Competency Hearing

      🗋 Employee Performance File System Records

      🗋 Foreign Employee Award Files

      🗋 Payroll Differential and Allowances

      🗋 Withholding of Within-Grade Increase (WGI) Records

   🗋 Hello

   🗋 Military Files

   🗋 Miscellaneous Files

   🗋 Reports

▼ File Plan

   ⊡ Transfers

   ⊡ Holds

▼ Saved Searches

   Saved Search Example

Below the Navigation tree on the left panel is a section called **File Plan**. There are two links located there: **Transfers** and **Holds**. Clicking on these links will bring up either a list of transfer or a list of hold groups.

At the bottom of the left panel is a list of all **Saved Searches**. **Saved Searches** are created within the **Records Search** area. Each search link here is a collection of search criteria that is remembered and applied via a single click, rather than having to re-enter the search criteria.

Records search

As of the Alfresco 3.3.1 release, Alfresco Share doesn't yet have the equivalent of the advanced search capabilities that are available in the Alfresco JSF Explorer web client. Advanced search capabilities aren't expected to be part of Alfresco Share until the 4.0 release:

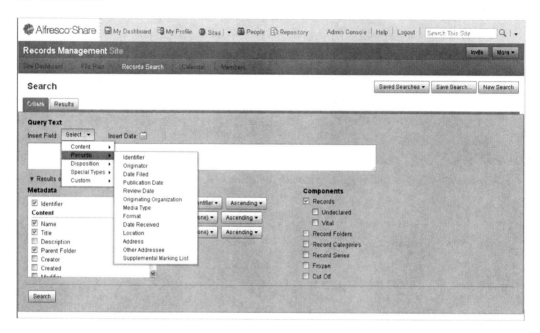

Records Management requirements, such as those in the DoD 5015.2 specification, are very demanding around being able to search for and identify records. Because standard search capabilities within Share weren't sufficient to meet those requirements, a special search tool called **Records Search** was created which was tuned for searching over records components of the File Plan.

It is likely that elements of the **Records Search** page of the Records Management site will be reused or reworked to be used as part of the planned future Alfresco Share advanced search capability.

Records Search consists of a page with two tabs: one to specify search criteria, and a second to show the search results. The query string is created using a syntax that Alfresco describes as Google-like in the way that full-text content and metadata search criteria are combined into a single query field.

Site members

Alfresco Share users are able to become members of any of the Share sites that are hosted by the single instance of Share running on the server. But before a user is able to access a Share site, they must first become a member of the site, and to become a member, the user must either be invited or, if the site is publicly available, they can explicitly choose to join it.

Administration of site members

By default, within each Share site, there is a navigation link called **Members** that is shown always as the right-most list of page links available for the site. From **Members**, the site administrator can search for and view profile information about site members, change the role assigned to them, or remove them from the site member list:

The site administrator is also able to invite Share users or groups to become members of the site. The process for doing this is initiated by clicking on the **Invite People** button of the site **Members** page. On this screen, the site administrator is able to find existing Share users or to enter information needed to contact people not yet users of the Share instance. Both types of people can be selected and invited by sending a system-generated e-mail.

From the invite screen, there are links to access a form for sending invitations to all users of a Share group and also to check on the status of invitations that have been previously sent.

If the Share site is public, then another route for a Share user to become a member of a site is to go to the user **Sites** page, available from a link at the very top of the page, and search for the name of the site that they wish to **Join**:

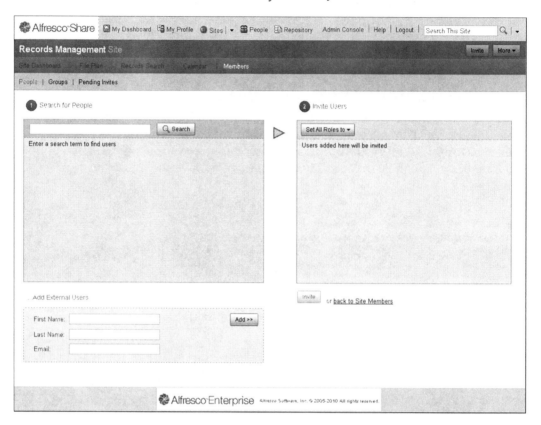

How does it work?

We've looked now at many of the default capabilities of Share. In the rest of this chapter, we will examine various ways in which Share can be configured.

Share configuration files

Alfresco developers were influenced early on by the Spring framework in the creation and architecture of the Alfresco software. The core Java code is based on Spring, and much of the Spring philosophy of flexibility and easy configurability was carried through to the creation of the Surf web framework and to other design aspects of the Alfresco platform.

Beginning with the 3.2 release of Alfresco, many repository configurations within Alfresco can be made without shutting down the entire Alfresco server. Alfresco was designed to work as a collection of independent subsystems, although the ability to use subsystems is available only as a feature of the Enterprise version of Alfresco. Alfresco subsystems can be administered using a JMX client, like JConsole. JConsole is available from the OpenJDK group. `http://openjdk.java.net/tools/svc/jconsole/`. Information about JMX and Alfresco subsystem configuration is available on the Alfresco wiki. `http://wiki.alfresco.com/wiki/JMX`

Repository property files

Alfresco Share is heavily dependent on the Alfresco repository for persisting web assets, files, and collaboration content stored within the document library. Much of the communication made from Share to the Alfresco repository is done via web service calls.

Because of Share's dependence on the repository, it's important to understand how the repository can be configured and monitored. When the repository starts up, it loads information specified in the repository system configuration files.

The system configuration files are loaded in the following order:

- `tomcat/webapps/alfresco/WEB-INF/classes/alfresco/repository.properties`
- `tomcat/webapps/alfresco/WEB-INF/classes/domain/hibernate-cfg.properties`
- All property files within the subfolders of `tomcat/webapps/alfresco/WEB-INF/classes/alfresco/subsystems`
- `tomcat/shared/classes/alfresco-global.properties`

The properties files were designed so that out of the box configuration settings can be overridden by the user with different values.

Since the file `alfresco-global.properties` is loaded last, the best practice is to centralize configuration property changes in this one file. This is the practice that Alfresco recommends, and by following this recommendation, configurations can be much more easily identified when it's time to upgrade the system, and the risk that configurations might get lost during upgrades is minimized.

If you use an Alfresco installation wizard, values of the file `alfresco-global.properties` are modified as the wizard runs. During installation, some of the properties set in the file relate to the location of where Alfresco content will be stored, the location of the Lucene full-text index information, database connection properties, paths to third-party software, database driver connect information, and hibernate properties.

Customizing bean files

In addition to property files, Alfresco can be configured by making changes to Spring-context bean files. All of these files have filenames that end with `context.xml`. Alfresco uses bean files for configuring both the base Alfresco repository and also the Share application.

Share bean configuration

The principle file for configuring Share is `share-config.xml`. This file is located in the `tomcat\webapps\share\WEB-INF\classes\alfresco` directory. It is used for configuration because it is referenced from the Spring-context bean file `slingshot-application-context.xml`, which can be found in that same directory.

Internally, much of the Alfresco Share source code still refers to **slingshot**, the product code name used for Share before the Share product was actually named.

Overrides to the standard settings in `share-config.xml` should be put in a file named `share-config-custom.xml`, which is placed in the tomcat\shared\classes\ alfresco\web-extension directory.

Client debug settings

Copy the following code from the file `share-config.xml` and place it into the file `share-config-custom.xml` with the value for the tag `<client-debug>` set to `true`. Doing this will put Share pages into debug mode as shown in the screenshot below:

```
<config replace="true">
  <flags>
    <!--
       Developer debugging setting to turn on DEBUG mode for client
       scripts in the browser
    -->
    <client-debug>true</client-debug>
```

```
<!--
   LOGGING can always be toggled at runtime when in DEBUG mode
      (Ctrl, Ctrl, Shift, Shift).
   This flag automatically activates logging on page load.
   -->
   <client-debug-autologging>false</client-debug-autologging>
 </flags>
</config>
```

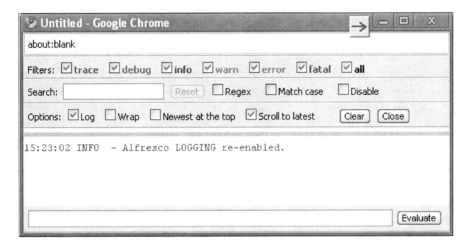

After making this change and restarting the server, bring up the client browser debugger and navigate to a page within Share. Then type the following four keys in sequence to bring up the JavaScript debug browser window at runtime: *Ctrl, Ctrl, Shift, Shift*. This won't work in Microsoft Internet Explorer. In that case, you can get the debug window to launch by appending the parameter `log=on` to the end of the page URL. For example, try using a URL of the following format:

`http://localhost:8080/share/page/user/admin/dashboard?log=on`

> For client-side browser debugging, Firebug with Firefox, Google Chrome, or Inspector with Safari are recommended browsers. The Alfresco JavaScript debugger uses Tim Down's log4javascript library. Detailed information and a tutorial can be found online at `http://log4javascript.org/docs/quickstart.html`.

Some logging will occur automatically into the debug window. You can modify existing JavaScript code or write new code that uses the client logging feature that will write messages to this window. The syntax of the logger is based on the methods available in the Java log4j logger. For example, the following methods are available within JavaScript code:

```
Alfresco.logger.debug();
Alfresco.logger.info();
Alfresco.logger.warn();
Alfresco.logger.error();
Alfresco.logger.fatal();
```

> Remember that if you do things like turn on debugging or increase the amount of information being written to the log file, it can seriously affect system performance. If you intend to use the system for production, the settings should be reverted to their original values when you have completed your experiments.

Available aspects list

The file `share-config.xml` also controls which aspects are available on the user interface to be applied to content objects. To override the standard list of aspects, the following code should be copied from `share-config.xml`, modified as appropriate, and then pasted into the file `share-config-custom.xml`:

```
<aspects>
    <!-- Aspects that a user can see -->
    <visible>
      <aspect name="cm:generalclassifiable" />
      <aspect name="cm:complianceable" />
      <aspect name="cm:dublincore" />
      <aspect name="cm:effectivity" />
      <aspect name="cm:summarizable" />
      <aspect name="cm:versionable" />
      <aspect name="cm:templatable" />
      <aspect name="cm:emailed" />
      <aspect name="emailserver:aliasable" />
      <aspect name="cm:taggable" />
      <aspect name="app:inlineeditable" />
    </visible>
  <!-- Aspects that a user can add. Same as "visible" if left empty
    -->
    <addable>
```

```
      </addable>
  <!-- Aspects that a user can remove. Same as "visible" if left
    empty -->
      <removeable>
      </removeable>
  </aspects>
```

Available content types

The file `share-config.xml` controls which content types are available from the user interface. To override the standard list, copy the following code, which defines the available content types, modify as appropriate, and paste into the file `share-config-custom.xml`:

```
<types>
  <type name="cm:content">
    <subtype name="cm:mysubtype" />
  </type>
  <type name="cm:folder">
  </type>
</types>
```

Later on, we will be creating new content types, based on the types of documents and records kept in your organization. This configuration makes the custom content types available through the Share user interface. In the example here, a new content type called `cm:mysubtype` is added to the content types available.

Access to the complete Alfresco repository from Share

Depending on the level of sophistication of the end user and also on the way in which you intend to use Share within your organization, the ability to expose all of the Alfresco repository from Share can either be a welcome capability or something that you may prefer to turn off.

The default behavior in Share is for access to the **Repository** to be available. In the long term, Alfresco plans to replace the JSF Explorer client with Share, so Share will ultimately need to be able to handle all the repository and library service capabilities that the Explorer client is now capable of doing.

The visibility of the **Repository** link is controlled by the `RepositoryLibrary` section of the file `share-config.xml`. It is possible to configure this behavior by making changes to the following XML block and adding it to the file `share-config-custom.xml`:

```
<config evaluator="string-compare" condition="RepositoryLibrary"
  replace="true">
<!--
  Whether the link to the Repository Library appears in the
    header component or not.
-->
<visible>true</visible>

<!--
  Root nodeRef for top-level folder.
-->
<root-node>alfresco://company/home</root-node>

<tree>
 <!--
Whether the folder Tree component should enumerate child folders or
  not.
This is a relatively expensive operation, so should be set to
  "false" for Repositories with broad folder structures.
 -->
 <evaluate-child-folders>false</evaluate-child-folders>

 <!--
Optionally limit the number of folders shown in treeview throughout
  Share.
 -->
 <maximum-folder-count>500</maximum-folder-count>
</tree>
</config>
```

To display or not to display the link is controlled by the `<visible>` tag. By changing this code block, it is also possible to set the root folder from where the repository navigation will start, and to configure properties for the display of the navigation tree:

Records Management configuration

There are also some Spring-context bean files specific to Records Management. These configuration files are located in the `tomcat\webapps\alfresco\WEB-INF\ classes\alfresco\module\org_alfresco_module_dod5015` directory.

In particular, the file `rm-job-context.xml` is of interest. This file defines two cron jobs that run at scheduled times in the background. One job sends e-mail notifications when the records become due for review. The other job checks records and updates them based on their lifecycle disposition instructions. The file defines the cron schedule for when these background jobs will be run:

Filename	Description
`rm-webscript-context.xml`	Beans for RM Rest API
`rm-action-context.xml`	The beans that implement RM actions
`rm-capabilities-context.xml`	The beans that implement RM capabilities
`rm-job-context.xml`	Sends out e-mail notifications for records that are due for review and background process to check and update record lifecycles
`rm-service-context.xml`	The Records Management service registry
`rm-public-services-security-context.xml`	The beans that the intercept method calls to the repository services to enforce security based on the currently authenticated user

Server log configuration file

The `log4j.properties` file for the Share application controls the level of detail of output written at the server to the Alfresco log file. Information being logged is specific to operations that occur in Share. The file is configured to allow very granular control over what type of information or debug information will be written. This file is located in the `tomcat\webapps\share\WEB-INF\classes` directory.

There is a companion parallel file, also called `log4j.properties`, located in the `tomcat\webapps\alfresco\WEB-INF\classes` directory. This file controls debugging information relative to Alfresco repository operations. Often, to get debug information printed about a repository operation that is initiated by a Share webscript accessing the repository, it is necessary to also configure the settings in this file.

Dashboards

The first page of Alfresco Share that a user sees after logging into Share is the dashboard. This is the user's home page. Dashboards show up in other parts of Share too. For example, the first page of each Share site is also a dashboard and is configured in a way that is identical to how the user home page dashboard is configured.

We've seen that the user can customize the layout of the home dashboard page and pick which of the dashlets will be available on that page. In a similar way, the owner of each Share site can configure the way that the site dashboard page will be presented to site members when they access the site.

Preset dashboard configurations

Both user dashboards and site dashboards have default layouts that are configured with default or preset dashlets. Preset dashboard settings are configured in the file `presets.xml` which is located in the directory `share\WEB-INF\classes\alfresco\site-data\presets`.

When we open the `presets.xml` file, we find that it consists of groups of `<preset>` tags. The overall structure of the file `presets.xml` can be seen here:

```xml
<?xml version='1.0' encoding='UTF-8'?>
<presets>
  <!-- Well known preset used to generate the default Collaboration
    Site dashboard -->
  <preset id="site-dashboard">
    ...
  </preset>
  <!-- Well known preset used to generate the default User dashboard
    -->
  <preset id="user-dashboard">
    ...
  </preset>
  <!-- Well known preset used to generate the default RM Site
    dashboard -->
  <preset id="rm-site-dashboard">
    ...
  </preset>
  <!-- Well known preset used to generate the Sharepoint protocol
    integration Site -->
  <preset id="document-workspace">
    ...
```

```
    </preset>
    <!-- Well known preset used to generate the Sharepoint protocol
      integration meeting Site -->
    <preset id="meeting-workspace">
      ...
    </preset>
  </presets>
```

The first three `<preset>` tag sections of the file define default configurations for site dashboards, user dashboards, and the dashboard for the Records Management site. Let's look now in detail at the structure of the data defined in the `<preset>` tag sections.

The preset IDs for the dashboards defined in this file correspond to the unique ID of a type of dashboard. For example, when a site is created, it is assigned the ID `site-dashboard`; when the Records Management site is created, the `rm-site-dashboard` ID is assigned; and when a user is created, the `user-dashboard` ID is assigned.

An example of when the ID is assigned to a dashboard element can be found in the file `webapps\share\WEB-INF\classes\alfresco\site-webscripts\org\alfresco\modules\create-site.get.js`. This JavaScript controller contains code that hardcodes the ID to be used with sites as `site-dashboard`:

```
    var sitePresets = [{id: "site-dashboard",
      name: msg.get("title.collaborationSite")}];
    model.sitePresets = sitePresets;
```

In a similar way, when the Records Management site is first created, the file `webapps\share\WEB-INF\classes\alfresco\site-webscripts\org\alfresco\utils\create-rmsite.get.js` defines the ID of the site to be `rm-site-dashboard`. Actually, we've already seen this in the previous chapter with the discussion of setting up the Records Management dashlet.

Preset dashboard layout

Each preset section in `presets.xml` contains a `<pages>` tag section that defines the parameters of the Spring Surf dashboard page. Here we see the preset page specification for a site dashboard, as configured in the `presets.xml` file:

```
    <pages>
      <page id="site/${siteid}/dashboard">
        <title>Collaboration Site Dashboard</title>
        <title-id>page.siteDashboard.title</title-id>
        <description>Collaboration site's dashboard page</description>
        <description-id>page.siteDashboard.description</description-id>
        <template-instance>dashboard-3-columns</template-instance>
```

```
          <authentication>user</authentication>
          <properties>
            <sitePages>[{"pageId":"wiki-page"}, {"pageId":"blog-postlist"},
              {"pageId":"documentlibrary"},
              {"pageId":"calendar"},{"pageId":"links"},
              {"pageId":"discussions-topiclist"},{"pageId":"data-
              lists"}]</sitePages>
          </properties>
       </page>
    </pages>
```

An important piece of configuration information defined here for the page is
the `template-instance`. In this example for the site dashboard, we can see that
it specifies, by default, to use the template called `dashboard-3-columns`. The
`template-instance` definition files can be found in the directory `webapps\share\`
`WEB-INF\classes\alfresco\site-data\template-instances`. That directory
also contains the other dashboard layouts that Share supports with no additional
customization. All five of the available dashboard `template-instance` layouts are
shown here:

dashboard-1-column.xml

dashboard-2-columns-wide-left.xml

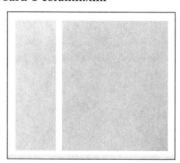

dashboard-2-columns-wide-right.xml

dashboard-3-columns.xml

dashboard-4-columns.xml

These five standard layout formats are referenced in the file `webapps\share\`
`WEB-INF\classes\alfresco\site-webscripts\org\alfresco\components\`
`dashboard\customized-layout.get.js`. Changing available layouts or adding
new ones can be done by modifying the list of layouts defined in this file. In the
Alfresco 3.3.1 release, available layout templates are hardcoded in a JavaScript array
as follows:

```
// Hardcoded templates until proper service exists
var layouts = [
  {templateId: "dashboard-1-column",  noOfColumns: 1, description:
   msg.get("msg.template-1-column")},
  {templateId: "dashboard-2-columns-wide-right", noOfColumns: 2,
    description: msg.get("msg.template-2-columns-wide-right")},
  {templateId: "dashboard-2-columns-wide-left",  noOfColumns: 2,
    description: msg.get("msg.template-2-columns-wide-left")},
  {templateId: "dashboard-3-columns", noOfColumns: 3, description:
    msg.get("msg.template-3-columns")},
  {templateId: "dashboard-4-columns", noOfColumns: 4, description:
    msg.get("msg.template-4-columns")}
];
```

Looking back again at the `page` tag of a preset definition in `presets.xml` for the site
dashboard, we also see that default site pages are defined. This information is stored
in the property `sitePages`. By default, a standard site will include pages for a wiki, a
blog, a document library, a calendar, a list of links, a discussions page, and a data list
page. These page links are visible across the top of the site as seen here:

Operations Site

Site Dashboard   Wiki   Blog   Document Library   Calendar   Links   Discussions   Data Lists   Members

The pages of the Records Management site are defined in the `presets.xml` file
as follows:

```
<pages>
  <page id="site/${siteid}/dashboard">
    <title>Records Management Site Dashboard</title>
    <title-id>page.rmSiteDashboard.title</title-id>
    <description>Records Management site's dashboard
      page</description>
    <description-id>page.rmSiteDashboard.description</description-id>
    <template-instance>dashboard-3-columns</template-instance>
    <authentication>user</authentication>
    <properties>
      <sitePages>[{"pageId":"documentlibrary"},
        {"pageId":"rmsearch"}]</sitePages>
          <pageMetadata>{"documentlibrary":{"titleId":"page.
rmDocumentLibrary.
  title", "descriptionId":"page.rmDocumentLibrary.description",
  "type":"dod5015"}}</pageMetadata>
    </properties>
  </page>
</pages>
```

As we can see from this file, by default, there are only two pre-configured site pages
for Records Management—the document library (or **File Plan**), and the **Records
Search** page. In the next image, we can see these page navigation links as they are
displayed across the top of the Records Management site:

Another thing to notice in the Spring Surf page description is that the text labels
for the dashboard page titles and description are defined. The `<title-id>` and the
`<description-id>` tags contain this information. The text strings referred to by
the values for these tags are stored in properties files. For example, text strings like
`page.rmSiteDashboard.title`, which is the default title for a site dashboard, can
be found in `webapps\share\WEB-INF\classes\alfresco\messages\slingshot.
properties`, and the strings for the Records Management site can be found in
`webapps\share\WEB-INF\classes\alfresco\messages\dod5015.properties`.

Preset dashboard dashlets

The `presets.xml` file also defines which dashlets are to be included on the dashboard layouts and where the dashlets will be positioned in the layout. In the `presets.xml` configuration file, the dashlet `region-id` positions are named based on their position in the layout. The convention is to name the `region-id` in the format `component-<column>-<row>`. For example, the region-id `component-2-1` refers to the first row position at the top of the second column.

The dashlets that appear on a dashboard are defined in the components section for the dashboard preset definition. For example, the components definition for the Records Management dashboard is defined as follows:

```
<components>
  <!-- title -->
  <component>
    <scope>page</scope>
    <region-id>title</region-id>
    <source-id>site/${siteid}/dashboard</source-id>
    <url>/components/title/collaboration-title</url>
  </component>
  <!-- navigation -->
  <component>
    <scope>page</scope>
    <region-id>navigation</region-id>
    <source-id>site/${siteid}/dashboard</source-id>
    <url>/components/navigation/collaboration-navigation</url>
  </component>
  <!-- dashboard components -->
  <component>
    <scope>page</scope>
    <region-id>component-1-1</region-id>
    <source-id>site/${siteid}/dashboard</source-id>
    <url>/components/dashlets/site-welcome</url>
  </component>
  <component>
    <scope>page</scope>
    <region-id>component-2-1</region-id>
    <source-id>site/${siteid}/dashboard</source-id>
    <url>/components/dashlets/docsummary</url>
    <properties>
      <dod5015>true</dod5015>
    </properties>
  </component>
  <component>
```

```
        <scope>page</scope>
        <region-id>component-2-2</region-id>
        <source-id>site/${siteid}/dashboard</source-id>
        <url>/components/dashlets/activityfeed</url>
      </component>
      <component>
        <scope>page</scope>
        <region-id>component-3-1</region-id>
        <source-id>site/${siteid}/dashboard</source-id>
        <url>/components/dashlets/site-profile</url>
      </component>
      <component>
        <scope>page</scope>
        <region-id>component-3-2</region-id>
        <source-id>site/${siteid}/dashboard</source-id>
        <url>/components/dashlets/colleagues</url>
      </component>
    </components>
```

First, the `title` and `navigation` components are defined for the page. After that, each of the preset dashlets for the dashboard is defined. The `URL` tag specifies the unique path identifier for the dashlet and the `region-id` defines the position on the dashboard where the dashlet will appear, using the convention for positioning that we just discussed. The next figure labels the dashlets by position and URL name on a screenshot of the preset Records Management site dashboard:

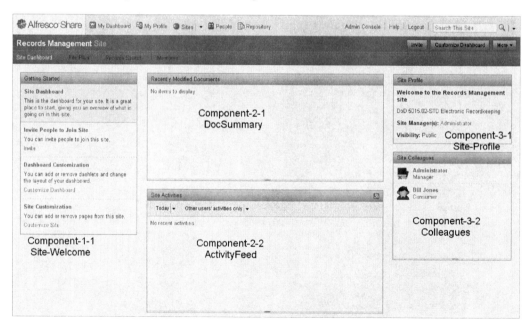

Modifying the preset dashboard configurations

The Alfresco architecture was designed in a way to provide for a high degree of configurability as we have seen. By modifying the `presets.xml` file, we can redefine the initial dashboard settings for both user and site dashboard pages. We have seen that both the layout of the dashboard and dashlets can be configured in this file.

But Alfresco best practice is not to directly modify Alfresco source files. Instead changes to standard configuration files should be stored in the extension and web-extension directories. Files placed in these directories override settings found in standard Alfresco files.

In the case of the `preset.xml` file, best practice would be to create a new file in the directory called `tomcat\shared\classes\alfresco\web-extension\site-data\presets\presets.xml`. We can in fact do that, and Alfresco will pick up our modified `presets.xml` file, but the changes we make may not be applied in the way that we intended.

Attempting to override the `presets.xml` file in this way, at least in the Alfresco Share 3.3.1 release, tries to aggregate all components for the dashboard that are defined in both the original file as well as the override file. Components from both, the standard `presets.xml` file and the new override file in the web-extensions area will be merged. New components that you define in the override file will display, but standard components will continue to display in the column where they were originally defined. Because of this, when overriding in this way, it isn't possible to remove any of the standard dashlet components. This behavior is a bug which may be corrected in a future version of Share.

So, if you wish to modify the preset configuration, the recommendation would be to create an override file and place it in the `web-extension\site-data\presets` area like we just discussed, restart the server, and then check your results. If the layout isn't what you expected, at least in the short term, until this behavior is changed, it is necessary to make changes directly to the standard Alfresco `presets.xml` file.

> Remember that when a dashboard is created for the first time, the configuration that it uses is based on dashboard settings found in `presets.xml`. The newly created dashboard configuration is then saved. Any changes made later to the `presets.xml` file will be applied only to newly created dashboards for users and sites. Dashboards that existed prior to changes in the `presets.xml` file will not be affected.

Persistence of dashboard configurations

We have just seen how initial dashboard layouts are defined by using the `presets.xml` file. Once the dashboard is created, and each time it is modified from the Alfresco Share user interface, the dashboard configuration is saved.

 Alfresco is in the middle of re-architecting Web Content Management (WCM) and the AVM storage area used by WCM. The goal is to ultimately unify the AVM content storage with the standard Alfresco repository storage. Because of that, in the future, there may be refactoring or changes made with the way that Alfresco Share persists data to the AVM store.

Using the Node Browser to find persisted dashboard data

The persisted dashboard configuration information is currently stored within the Alfresco storage area called AVM. We can use the Node Browser tool within the administration console of the Alfresco JSF Explorer client to see how the dashboard configuration information is persisted within Alfresco. The Node Browser feature is not yet available via the Share interface.

To access the Node Browser, open the Alfresco JSF client. For example, in a local installation, the Alfresco JSF explorer client can be accessed at:

```
http://localhost:8080/alfresco
```

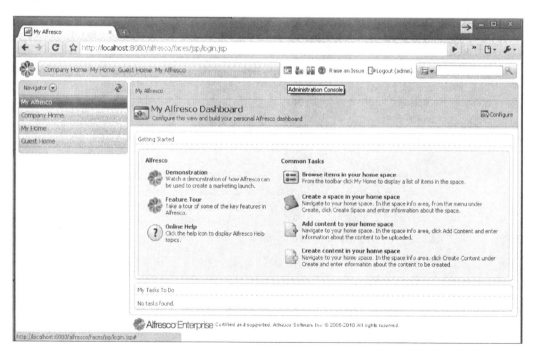

Log in as the administrator and then click on the **Administration Console**. From there, the Node Browser can be accessed:

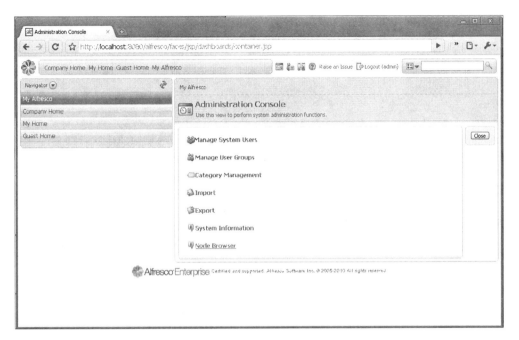

Within the Node Browser, click on the Store labeled `avm://sitestore`. This storage area is typically used for storing Web Content Management assets, but it is also used by Alfresco Share for storing application data. At the top level of the AVM Store, scroll down the page and you will see a list of the child nodes that exist at the root of the store:

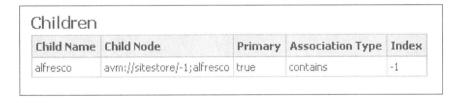

Next, click on the child node link labeled something like `avm://sitestore/-1;alfresco`. After navigating into this first child node, scroll down again to see the children of the new node:

At this point, we have navigated into the Alfresco Share **site-data** node. Under this node, Share site data is persisted. Again, navigate a level lower by clicking on the link for the child node named site-data. After doing that, at the level we are within the node hierarchy, we can again scroll down and find the children of this node. Here we can see the children containing additional site information for site **components** and site **pages**:

Children				
Child Name	**Child Node**	**Primary**	**Association Type**	**Index**
components	avm://sitestore/-1;alfresco;site-data;components	true	contains	-1
pages	avm://sitestore/-1;alfresco;site-data;pages	true	contains	-1

AVM Store Share component nodes

If we first look at the child nodes for the **components** node, we will see something like the following list of children. Here we recognize the components from the site and user dashboards:

Children

Child Name	Child Node
page.component-1-1.site~operations~dashboard.xml	avm://sitestore/-1;alfresco:site-data;components;page.component-1-1.site~operations~dashboard.xml
page.component-1-1.site~rm~dashboard.xml	avm://sitestore/-1;alfresco:site-data;components;page.component-1-1.site~rm~dashboard.xml
page.component-1-1.user~admin~dashboard.xml	avm://sitestore/-1;alfresco:site-data;components;page.component-1-1.user~admin~dashboard.xml
page.component-1-2.user~admin~dashboard.xml	avm://sitestore/-1;alfresco:site-data;components;page.component-1-2.user~admin~dashboard.xml
page.component-1-3.user~admin~dashboard.xml	avm://sitestore/-1;alfresco:site-data;components;page.component-1-3.user~admin~dashboard.xml
page.component-2-1.site~operations~dashboard.xml	avm://sitestore/-1;alfresco:site-data;components;page.component-2-1.site~operations~dashboard.xml
page.component-2-1.site~rm~dashboard.xml	avm://sitestore/-1;alfresco:site-data;components;page.component-2-1.site~rm~dashboard.xml
page.component-2-1.user~admin~dashboard.xml	avm://sitestore/-1;alfresco:site-data;components;page.component-2-1.user~admin~dashboard.xml
page.component-2-2.site~operations~dashboard.xml	avm://sitestore/-1;alfresco:site-data;components;page.component-2-2.site~operations~dashboard.xml
page.component-2-2.site~rm~dashboard.xml	avm://sitestore/-1;alfresco:site-data;components;page.component-2-2.site~rm~dashboard.xml
page.component-2-2.user~admin~dashboard.xml	avm://sitestore/-1;alfresco:site-data;components;page.component-2-2.user~admin~dashboard.xml
page.component-2-3.user~admin~dashboard.xml	avm://sitestore/-1;alfresco:site-data;components;page.component-2-3.user~admin~dashboard.xml
page.component-3-1.site~operations~dashboard.xml	avm://sitestore/-1;alfresco:site-data;components;page.component-3-1.site~operations~dashboard.xml
page.component-3-1.site~rm~dashboard.xml	avm://sitestore/-1;alfresco:site-data;components;page.component-3-1.site~rm~dashboard.xml
page.component-3-1.user~admin~dashboard.xml	avm://sitestore/-1;alfresco:site-data;components;page.component-3-1.user~admin~dashboard.xml
page.component-3-2.site~operations~dashboard.xml	avm://sitestore/-1;alfresco:site-data;components;page.component-3-2.site~operations~dashboard.xml
page.component-3-2.site~rm~dashboard.xml	avm://sitestore/-1;alfresco:site-data;components;page.component-3-2.site~rm~dashboard.xml
page.component-3-2.user~admin~dashboard.xml	avm://sitestore/-1;alfresco:site-data;components;page.component-3-2.user~admin~dashboard.xml
page.component-3-3.site~operations~dashboard.xml	avm://sitestore/-1;alfresco:site-data;components;page.component-3-3.site~operations~dashboard.xml
page.component-3-3.user~admin~dashboard.xml	avm://sitestore/-1;alfresco:site-data;components;page.component-3-3.user~admin~dashboard.xml
page.navigation.site~operations~dashboard.xml	avm://sitestore/-1;alfresco:site-data;components;page.navigation.site~operations~dashboard.xml
page.navigation.site~rm~dashboard.xml	avm://sitestore/-1;alfresco:site-data;components;page.navigation.site~rm~dashboard.xml
page.title.site~operations~dashboard.xml	avm://sitestore/-1;alfresco:site-data;components;page.title.site~operations~dashboard.xml
page.title.site~rm~dashboard.xml	avm://sitestore/-1;alfresco:site-data;components;page.title.site~rm~dashboard.xml
page.title.user~admin~dashboard.xml	avm://sitestore/-1;alfresco:site-data;components;page.title.user~admin~dashboard.xml

If we click through on any of these child nodes, we will see the detailed properties associated with these component nodes. The information shown near the top of the node browser screen for any one of these nodes looks similar to the following table:

Properties

Name	Value
{http://www.alfresco.org/model/content/1.0}name	page.component-1-1.site~operations~dashboard.xml
{http://www.alfresco.org/model/system/1.0}node-dbid	21
{http://www.alfresco.org/model/system/1.0}store-identifier	sitestore
{http://www.alfresco.org/model/content/1.0}content	contentUrl=store://2010/7/29/19/30/56033ae2-0b3c-4290-9422-a3162c9b6bbc.bin|mimetype=text/xml|size=284|encoding=utf-8|locale=en_US_
{http://www.alfresco.org/model/content/1.0}owner	admin
{http://www.alfresco.org/model/system/1.0}node-uuid	UNKNOWN
{http://www.alfresco.org/model/content/1.0}modified	Thu Jul 29 19:30:56 PDT 2010
{http://www.alfresco.org/model/content/1.0}created	Thu Jul 29 19:30:56 PDT 2010
{http://www.alfresco.org/model/system/1.0}store-protocol	avm
{http://www.alfresco.org/model/content/1.0}creator	admin
{http://www.alfresco.org/model/content/1.0}modifier	admin

Here we can see that the value for the property `{http://www.alfresco.org/model/content/1.0}content` is `contentUrl=store://2010/7/29/19/30/56033ae2-0b3c-4290-9422-a3162c9b8bbc.bin|mimetype=text/xml|size=284|encoding=utf-8|locale=en_US_`. This is a bit cryptic, but the first part of the value represents the location of the XML data on disk in the Alfresco repository.

In this example, the following is the file path: `2010/7/29/19/30/56033ae2-0b3c-4290-9422-a3162c9b8bbc.bin`.

If we look at the `Alfresco alf_dir` location on disk, we can locate a file at the path location of `C:\Alfresco\alf_data\contentstore\2010\7\29\19\30\56033ae2-0b3c-4290-9422-a3162c9b8bbc.bin`. The file ends with a binary file extension, but if we open the file in a text editor, we can see that the contents of the file are actually in XML. In this example, we can see the XML fragment for this component:

```
<?xml version="1.0" encoding="UTF-8"?>

<component>
  <guid>page.component-1-1.site~operations~dashboard</guid>
  <scope>page</scope>
  <region-id>component-1-1</region-id>
  <source-id>site/operations/dashboard</source-id>
  <url>/components/dashlets/site-welcome</url>
</component>
```

By using this technique, although it is somewhat tedious, it is possible to find where Share site configuration information for individual components is persisted.

AVM Store Share page nodes

In a similar way, we can also drill down to find persisted Share data for pages. Above, we saw how to find the child node for Share page site-data in the node browser. If we click on that site-data page node, we come to a page where there are two child nodes:

Children				
Child Name	Child Node	Primary	Association Type	Index
site	avm://sitestore/-1;alfresco;site-data;pages;site	true	contains	-1
user	avm://sitestore/-1;alfresco;site-data;pages;user	true	contains	-1

Here we see that page data that is specific to a site and common to all users is stored under a child node named **site**. Page data that is stored as a per-user preference configuration is stored under the **user** node.

If we first investigate the **site** node, we find that it too has child nodes, one for each site defined within Share:

Children				
Child Name	**Child Node**	**Primary**	**Association Type**	**Index**
operations	avm://sitestore/-1;alfresco;site-data;pages;site;operations	true	contains	-1
rm	avm://sitestore/-1;alfresco;site-data;pages;site;rm	true	contains	-1

Clicking on one of the sites, like the **rm** site (the Records Management site shortname), we can see the node within the AVM Store where data for the Records Management site is persisted:

Children				
Child Name	**Child Node**	**Primary**	**Association Type**	**Index**
dashboard.xml	avm://sitestore/-1;alfresco;site-data;pages;site;rm;dashboard.xml	true	contains	-1

If we click through on this node, we can find the XML fragment file in the Alfresco repository where the persisted Records Management dashboard page information is stored.

If we go back to the **user** page node that we saw above and click on that now, we'll find persisted page information grouped by individual users. In this example, the only user defined in the system is user **admin**:

Children				
Child Name	**Child Node**	**Primary**	**Association Type**	**Index**
admin	avm://sitestore/-1;alfresco;site-data;pages;user;admin	true	contains	-1

Clicking on this child node, we can see the user preferences for user admin that are persisted for the user dashboard home page. Finally, clicking through on this node, we would then find the reference to the XML file fragment stored in the Alfresco repository:

Children				
Child Name	**Child Node**	**Primary**	**Association Type**	**Index**
dashboard.xml	avm://sitestore/-1;alfresco;site-data;pages;user;admin;dashboard.xml	true	contains	-1

Modifying existing user dashboards

We saw above that modifying the `presets.xml` configuration file can cause all new user and site dashboards to take on this default information. Any dashboards that had been created prior to the change in the `presets.xml` file would not be affected.

To change dashboard component and page information that existed prior to modifying the `presets.xml` file, it's necessary to manually re-configure the dashboards using the Share user interface. This can be a daunting job if you need to change very many dashboard pages.

Another option to fix outdated dashboards would be to programmatically use the technique of finding the persisted component and page data for each pre-existing dashboard in the AVM store and then add, remove, or overwrite those file fragments with the new dashboard information.

Programmatically accessing persisted dashboard data

The root-scoped object called `sitedata` plays a key role in server-side JavaScript webscripts that access and manipulate Alfresco Share site data. We saw in the previous chapter how the `sitedata` object was used during the creation of the Records Management site. Now, let us see how we could use it to gain access to persisted dashboard component and page data.

Using JavaScript, we can reference a user dashboard page object using the following syntax: `sitedata.getPage("user/admin/dashboard")`. If we also append the `toXML()` method to this object, we can more easily see the contents of the object. It will look something like this:

```
sitedata.getPage("user/admin/dashboard").toXML()

<page>
  <title>User Dashboard</title>
  <title-id>page.userDashboard.title</title-id>
  <description>Users dashboard page</description>
  <description-id>page.userDashboard.description</description-id>
  <authentication>user</authentication>
  <template-instance>dashboard-4-columns</template-instance>
  <page-type-id>generic</page-type-id>
</page>
```

Here we see an XML fragment that describes the dashboard page object. The definition includes the name of the `template-instance`, `title` and `description`. In a similar way, we can query and find the XML content for this `template-instance`:

```
sitedata.findTemplate("user/admin/dashboard").toXML()

<?xml version="1.0" encoding="UTF-8"?>

<template-instance>
  <template-type>org/alfresco/dashboard</template-type>
  <description>Four columns</description>
  <properties>
    <gridClass>yui-g</gridClass>
    <gridColumn1>5</gridColumn1>
    <gridColumn2>5</gridColumn2>
    <gridColumn3>5</gridColumn3>
    <gridColumn4>5</gridColumn4>
  </properties>
</template-instance>
```

Instead of using `sitedata.findTemplate()`, we could have found the `template-instance` XML data using this command: `sitedata.getTemplate("dashboard-4-columns").toXML()`, where we discovered the `template-instance` name `dashboard-4-columns` in the XML result from `getPage()`.

In a similar way, we could query dashboard component information too. For example, consider the following:

```
sitedata.getComponent("page", "component-2-2", "user/admin/
dashboard").toXML()

<?xml version="1.0" encoding="UTF-8"?>

<component>
  <guid>page.component-2-2.user~admin~dashboard</guid>
  <scope>page</scope>
  <region-id>component-2-2</region-id>
  <source-id>user/admin/dashboard</source-id>
  <url>/components/dashlets/my-activities</url>
</component>
```

 A complete description of `sitedata` and other root-scoped objects that are available within the Spring Surf web framework in Share can be found on the Alfresco wiki: `http://wiki.alfresco.com/wiki/Surf_Platform_-_Freemarker_Template_and_JavaScript_API`

In the previous subsection, we mentioned that in some cases it might be desirable to programmatically update large numbers of dashboard configuration settings. The JavaScript code used in Share for manually updating dashboards provides good examples of how to programmatically interact with the `sitedata` root-scoped object to add, modify, and delete dashlets on a dashboard.

Code in the JavaScript file `webapps\share\WEB-INF\classes\alfresco\site-webscripts\org\alfresco\components\dashboard\customize-dashlets.get.js` provides an example of how to find and get references to the dashlets contained on a dashboard page. The JavaScript file `customize-dashboard.post.json.js` in that same directory gives good examples of how to manipulate dashlets. For example, that JavaScript file uses the following code to delete a dashlet:

```
sitedata.unbindComponent("page", regionId, dashboardPage);
```

That same JavaScript file also has an example that demonstrates how to add a new dashlet:

```
sitedata.newComponent("page", newDashlet.regionId, dashboardPage);
```

Creating a new Share theme

With a background understanding of CSS files, creating a new theme within Share is a fairly straightforward task.

The best way to start is to navigate to the `tomcat\webapps\share\themes` directory. There you will see directories, one for each of the standard available themes. Choose one of these directories other than the default one, like **greenTheme**.

Copy this entire folder for the theme and all of the files in it and then rename the folder based on the name of the new theme. We need to make the copy directly in the `webapps\share\themes` directory. Rename the new directory. Here we will just use the name `newTheme`. Copying the default theme folder may work as well, but in early releases of Alfresco theming, there were some problems with using the default folder because the default theme files had some references in them that were valid only for the default theme.

Next copy the file `tomcat\webapps\share\WEB-INF\classes\alfresco\site-data\themes\greenTheme.xml` to `tomcat\shared\alfresco\web-extension\site-data\theme\newTheme.xml`.

The contents of this file should be edited to look something like:

```
<?xml version='1.0' encoding='UTF-8'?>
<theme>
  <title>New Theme</title>
```

```
    <title-id>theme.newTheme</title-id>
  </theme>
```

Finally, restart the Alfresco server's software. That is all you need to do to make a new theme available for configuration in the admin console. After doing that, by making changes to the CSS files and images in the new theme folder, the new look for the theme can be created.

While there is a single theme applied to the whole Share site, that theme can be overridden for a single page by appending the parameter `theme=newTheme` to the URL for the page. For example, the following URL will display the dashboard for the Records Management site using the newly created theme:

`http://localhost:8080/share/page/site/rm/dashboard?theme=newTheme.`

Share site top navigation toolbar

We saw in the previous section how the `presets.xml` file initialized the pages that are assigned to a site. In standard sites, site pages will be links to things like wiki or blog pages. In the Records Management site, there are only two preset page navigation links, and they are both unique to Records Management. Preset Records Management site page links are for the **File Plan** and for **Records Search**.

To see how the Share top navigation toolbar is constructed, it is useful to examine the files in the directory `webapps\share\WEB-INF\classes\site-webscripts\org\alfresco\components\navigation\collaboration-navigation`. The JavaScript file `collaboration-navigation.get.js` builds the list of page links to include in the toolbar. The file `collaboration-navigation.get.html.ftl` contains the FreeMarker markup that specifies the layout of the toolbar. From the markup of the layout, we see that each Share site will always include a link to get to the top-level dashboard for the site at the beginning and another link to access the members of the site as the last item on the toolbar.

Share Site secondary navigation header bar

If we click into any of the pages from the top navigation, a secondary set of menu/ icon links then becomes available. For example, if we are at the dashboard level of the Records Management site and we click on the **File Plan** link, we will go to the **File Plan** page where there is a secondary top navigation toolbar or header bar that includes options like **New Series**, **File**, **Import**, and **Report**:

Like most of the user interface code everywhere else in Share, this secondary toolbar is controlled via a presentation webscript. In the Records Management site, the base name for the webscript is `dod5015-toolbar.*`. For standard Share sites, the corresponding webscript files are named `toolbar.*`, and those files rely heavily on the library files `include\toolbar.lib.js` and `include\toolbar.lib.ftl`. The JavaScript controller and FreeMarker files for these webscripts are located in the directory `webapps\share\WEB-INF\classes\alfresco\site-webscripts\org\ alfresco\components\documentlibrary`.

For Records Management, file `dod5015-toolbar.get.html.ftml` defines the presentation markup for the secondary toolbar. File `dod5015-toolbar.get.js` is the JavaScript controller file and it determines the preferences for the user accessing the page and the available actions that will display in the drop-down action menu that applies to the selected row items.

Summary

In this chapter, we have seen how the Alfresco Records Management site functions within the Alfresco Share application. The Records Management site shares many of the same features as standard Share sites, and we have seen that it can be configured to include some of the same collaboration features used in other Share sites.

We have also seen one big way that the Records Management site differs from standard Share sites, and that is with the document library. Records Management extends the standard site document library to work as a Records Management File Plan. The File Plan is aware of specialized Records Management folder types. A companion Records Search page provides the capability of performing very detailed record searches.

In this chapter, we covered the following topics:

- The basic framework for Alfresco Share sites
- Share dashboards and sites
- Inviting users and managing the members of a Share site
- The Records Management File Plan and Records Search pages

At the end of this chapter, in a 'How does it work?' section, we looked in detail at Share internals for the user and site dashboards. We discussed how dashlets are assigned to dashboards and where their configuration information is persisted in the Alfresco repository.

We now have Alfresco Records Management software up and running and a much better understanding of the Alfresco Share environment in which the Records Management site runs. In the next chapter, we will begin looking at metadata and the Alfresco content model, and specifically examine the content model used by Records Management and how it can be modified or extended.

4
Metadata and the Alfresco Content Model

In *Chapter 3*, we took a high-level tour of Alfresco Share and the Share Records Management site. In this chapter, we will look at the Alfresco Content Model and specifically look at the part of the model that is relevant to Records Management.

In this chapter, we will describe:

- What the Alfresco Content Model is and what elements comprise it
- How to design, create, and deploy a new content model
- How the Alfresco Records Management Content Model is structured

This chapter describes the mechanics for entering and configuring the content model within Alfresco. Each of the basic elements of the content model is discussed—types, aspects, properties, constraints, and associations. We will discuss how you can use these content model building blocks to design and build your own model. We'll then show how a new content model can be installed and made available from the Alfresco Share user interface.

Later in the chapter, we will look in detail at the built-in Alfresco Records Management Content Model. The model reveals much about the inner workings of Records Management within Alfresco and it also provides a very useful example of how a very rich content model can be created.

The Alfresco Content Model

Content and metadata storage is a core capability of an enterprise content management system, and it is an area where Alfresco excels. The content model is the framework that prescribes exactly how content data will be stored and how it later can be searched for retrieval. The model describes the structure, the format, and inter-relationships of content. It also provides the framework for organizing content and assigning meaning to it.

While the Alfresco Content Model is built from a very small set of components, the richness and flexibility of those components enable potentially very complex content models to be created.

The content model is actually segmented into a collection of models. For example, Records Management and Workflow are each implemented as separate models.

Each of the individual **models** contains the description for the specific **types** of content that can be stored in the repository. Each content type contains a fixed set of metadata **properties**. **Constraints** can be applied to properties to limit or to closely define the range of the allowed values for the properties. **Associations** can also be modeled and associated with types to define relationships between content items such as parent-child relationships or content-to-content references. Dynamic properties and associations can be added at runtime by applying **aspects** to the content.

When a new piece of content is added to the Alfresco repository, a structure called a node is created to hold the content. Each node gets added to a tree of nodes in the repository and is associated with at least one other node in the tree that acts as its parent. Every node is assigned a content type from the content model. A node can be associated with only a single content type at any one time, although the type of a node could potentially change. Aspects containing additional properties and associations can also be added to or removed from the node at any time.

Alfresco also supports the ability to set ad hoc properties on a node, ones not defined by properties associated with either the type or with applied aspects. Ad hoc properties can be stored as name-value pairs in a generic property bag associated with a node and are called **residual properties**. While there may be isolated cases where the use of residual properties makes sense, a suggested best practice is to avoid the use of ad hoc properties and to explicitly define all properties that will be needed within the content model.

The model namespace

Creating new content models requires us to assign names to the elements of the models that we define. Our new model must be defined in a way that allows it to globally co-exist with the names used within all other content models that have already been defined.

A common problem that occurs when creating new element names for a content model is to have a name conflict with the name of an element already used by another model definition. Name conflicts can cause the software to not run at all or for data to become accidentally corrupted because of confusion over the naming of the elements.

Suppose, for example, that we decide to add a new property called `container` to a document type that we define in our new custom model. There would be a problem because that name conflicts with the Alfresco repository system content model that already has a property named `container`.

To avoid naming conflicts like this between content models, Alfresco uses **namespaces**. A namespace groups together all the elements of the content model and also provides a way to create names that will guarantee their global uniqueness.

Alfresco namespaces

Namespaces are typically written as URI strings that start with an HTTP address, usually belonging to the author or the author's company, and then followed by a path that describes or organizes the types of elements contained in the namespace. All standard Alfresco namespaces have URIs that start with `http://www.alfresco.org`. The URI typically ends with the version number for the namespace.

The table below shows a list of standard Alfresco Content Model namespaces. The namespace URIs can be quite long and writing code that appends the namespace URI to model element names everywhere can make for some very verbose and clumsy-looking code.

To avoid having to always append the namespace URI to an element name, namespace prefixes are defined that significantly shorten the namespace reference. So, instead of having to refer to an element like {`http://www.alfresco.org/ model/system/1.0`}`container`, we can even simply write `sys:container`. The next table lists the prefixes that are used by convention when referring to Alfresco namespaces. The files defining these models can be found in the `tomcat\webapps\ alfresco\WEB-INF\classes\alfresco\model` directory.

Common Prefix	Namespace	Description
alf	`http://www.alfresco.org`	General Alfresco Namespace
app	`http://www.alfresco.org/model/ application/1.0`	Application Model
bpm	`http://www.alfresco.org/mod el/bpm/1.0`	Business Process Model
cm	`http://www.alfresco.org/model/ content/1.0`	Content Domain Model
d	`http://www.alfresco.org/model/ dictionary/1.0`	Data Dictionary Model
fm	`http://www.alfresco.org/model/ forum/1.0`	Forum Model
st	`http://www.alfresco.org/model/ site/1.0`	Site Model
sys	`http://www.alfresco.org/model/ system/1.0`	Repository System Model
dod	`http://www.alfresco.org/model/ dod5015/1.0`	DoD 5015.2 Records Management Model
rma	`http://www.alfresco.org/model/ recordsmanagement/1.0`	Records Management Model

Important namespaces that you'll see frequently referred to are the Content Domain Model and the Dictionary Model. New content models typically inherit from or reuse definitions of these foundational models. You might also notice the Site Model included in this list. The Site Model supports the management of data related to Alfresco Share sites. At the end of the list, there are also two content models that are used by the Alfresco Records Management implementation that we will talk about towards the end of the chapter.

Types

Types in the Alfresco Content Model provide a way to classify content as it is added to the repository. Every node in the repository is assigned a single type, and the type brings along with it a set of properties, associations, and even aspects that are relevant for that kind of content.

Types must be uniquely named and include the namespace prefix at the beginning of the type name. Available elements that are enclosed by the `<type>` tag for describing the behavior of a type are as follows:

- title—a title for the type. A text string that documents the type.
- description—a description for the type. A text string that documents the type.
- parent—the parent type of this type. Types can inherit from the definition of their parent type. The root type from which all types inherit is called `sys:base`. Subtypes inherit property, association, and constraint definitions from their parent type. Types can be nested to any depth.
- archive—a Boolean flag that indicates when nodes of this type are deleted that they are moved to the archive store as a sort of recycle bin area.
- properties—an element that encloses a list of properties for the type.
- associations—an element that encloses a list of associations for the type.
- mandatory-aspect—an element that encloses a list of aspects for the type.
- includedInSuperTypeQuery—a Boolean that determines if this type is to be searched as part of a query over any of its parent types.
- overrides—an element that encloses a list of properties that override parent properties.

  The following features from parent properties can be overridden:

  - mandatory—a subtype can make a property mandatory, but cannot relax a property declared mandatory by the parent.
  - default—the subtype can override or include a parent default value.
  - constraints—new constraints can be applied to a parent property, but existing constraints inherited from the parent cannot be removed.

Note that when defining both properties and associations for a type, the properties must be listed before the associations. It is also not possible to split the properties within a tag among multiple <properties> tags; only a single <properties> tag can be used within any one type definition. An example of the definition of a content type can be found in the Records Management model for an rma:recordFolder:

```
<type name="rma:recordFolder">

  <title>Record Folder</title>
  <parent>cm:folder</parent>
  <archive>false</archive>

  <properties>
    <property name="rma:isClosed">
      <title>Record Folder Closed</title>
      <description>Indicates whether the folder is
        closed</description>
      <type>d:boolean</type>
      <protected>true</protected>
      <mandatory>true</mandatory>
      <default>false</default>
    </property>
  </properties>

  <mandatory-aspects>
    <aspect>cm:titled</aspect>
    <aspect>rma:recordComponentIdentifier</aspect>
    <aspect>rma:commonRecordDetails</aspect>
    <aspect>rma:filePlanComponent</aspect>
  </mandatory-aspects>

</type>
```

Overrides to properties inherited from the parent type can be defined in the subtype as follows:

```
<type>
  ...
  <overrides>
    <property name="cm:autoVersion">
      <default>false</default>
    </property>
  </overrides>
</type>
```

Properties

Properties are one of the most important components of the definition for types and aspects. All properties in type and aspect definitions are grouped together and enclosed by a single `<properties>` tag. Each property is uniquely named by including a namespace prefix as the initial part of the name. The property name is an attribute of the property called `name`, as in `<property name="rma:location">`.

Available elements that are enclosed by the `<property>` tag for describing the behavior of a property are as follows:

- type—the data type of the property value. This element is required.
- title—a title for the property. A text string that documents the property.
- description—a description of the property. A text string that documents the property.
- mandatory—a Boolean flag indicating whether or not the property is mandatory. Mandatory properties must have a value before an attempt to complete a transaction on a node with that property for it to be successful. The mandatory flag is always enforced by the Alfresco web client. The mandatory flag will also be enforced at the server when the `<mandatory>` tag is further qualified with a *true* value for the `enforced` attribute. When `enforced` is set to *false*, as in `<mandatory enforced="false">`, if the property is not set at the time of the transaction, the transaction will not be blocked, but after the transaction is completed, the node will be marked with the `sys:incomplete` aspect.
- multiple—a Boolean flag that indicates that the property is able to support multiple values. Multiple values are handled as a list.
- index—a Boolean flag that indicates that the property will be indexed and searchable. If this flag is true, there are additional elements enclosed by the tag that configure how the indexing will be performed. By selecting not to index some properties, you can save index space. Very often, it is known in advance that some properties will never need to be searched.

  ○ atomic—a Boolean flag that indicates that the property will be indexed when a transaction on the node with this property completes. The alternative to this is that the property will be indexed as part of a background process that will run after the node transaction is completed. Properties containing binary content are typically indexed in the background.

○ stored—a Boolean value that indicates that the original value of the property before being tokenized should be stored in the index. This should only be done for properties that are expected to be relatively short.

○ tokenized—a value of *true*, *false*, or *both* to indicate that the tokenized value of the property is stored in the index. When the value of the property is processed for indexing, the string will be cleaned, for example, by removing whitespace, and broken into smaller pieces, like individual words. Typically, it is useful to tokenize property values that contain text, but not things like numbers or dates. When the value is *both*, both the original and the tokenized strings are stored.

- constraints—the constraints on the allowed values for the property.
- default—the default value for the property.
- protected—no child of the content type will be able to override this property.

Every property must be typed. This means that each property is associated with a data type that is defined by the `type` element. `type` is the only element of those listed above that is mandatory when defining a property. Alfresco has a wide range of data types available and it's possible to add more if the data type that you need isn't available. However, for most cases, the standard data types offered by Alfresco are most likely sufficient.

Because the core Alfresco software is written in Java, the data types available in a content model parallel very closely the data types available in Java. The following table lists some of the common data types available for use in the Alfresco Content Model. The complete list of Alfresco data types can be found in the file `tomcat\ webapps\alfresco\WEB-INF\classes\alfresco\model\dictionaryModel.xml`.

Data type name	Java equivalent	Description
`d:text`	`java.lang.String`	A text or character string.
`d:mltext`	Alfresco custom type	Multilingual text. Able to store multiple translations of a text string.
`d:content`	Alfresco custom type	Arbitrary content stored as a text or binary stream.
`d:int`	`java.lang.Integer`	32-bit signed two's complement integer.
`d:long`	`java.lang.Long`	64-bit signed two's complement integer.
`d:float`	`java.lang.Float`	Single-precision 32-bit IEEE 754 floating point.
`d:double`	`java.lang.Double`	Double-precision 64-bit IEEE 754 floating point.

Data type name	Java equivalent	Description
d:date	java.util.Date	Date value.
d:datetime	java.util.Date	Date and time value.
d:boolean	java.lang.Boolean	Boolean data, either *true* or *false*.
d:locale	java.util.Locale	Locale to describe a geographical or cultural region.
d:path	Alfresco custom type	A file path.
d:any	java.lang.Object	Any value, regardless of type.

Constraints

Constraints limit the allowed range of values for a property. Within a model XML file, constraints can be defined independently of the definition for any one type or aspect. Constraints defined in this way can then be reused as part of the property definition anywhere within the model.

 Note that there is no limit to the number of constraints that can be applied to a property.

For example, cm:username, which is a property of the type cm:person, refers to the global constraint cm:userNameConstraint. The following XML snippet from contentModel. xml shows how a constraint reference can be made by using the ref attribute:

```
<property name="cm:userName">
  <type>d:text</type>
  <mandatory>true</mandatory>
  <constraints>
    <constraint ref="cm:userNameConstraint" />
  </constraints>
</property>
```

It is also possible to define an **in-line constraint** as part of the definition of the property. In this case, the constraint cannot be applied to any other property outside the one in which it is defined. A simple example of this is the following:

```
<property name="test:constrainedProp">
  <type>d:text</type>
  <constraints>
    <constraint type="LENGTH">
      <parameter name="minLength"><value>0</value></parameter>
      <parameter name="maxLength"><value>100</value></parameter>
    </constraint>
  </constraints>
</property>
```

Types of constraints

Alfresco out of the box supports four types of constraints, which will be discussed in this section.:

REGEX constraint

The REGEX constraint enforces the syntax, spelling, or format for a property value. The constraint expression is written using regular expression syntax. Valid `<parameter>` names for this constraint are as follows:

- expression—the regular expression used to evaluate the incoming string.

- requiresMatch—a Boolean value, set to either *true* or *false*, to specify whether the value must match the regular expression or must not match the expression. The default for this parameter is *true*, that means that the test will fail if the value does not match the regular expression.

An example of a REGEX constraint is `cm:filename`, which is used for matching valid filenames. This constraint is defined as part of the content model. The definition is shown here:

```
<constraint name="cm:filename" type="REGEX">
  <parameter name="expression">
  <value><![CDATA[(.*[\"\*\\\>\<\?\/\:\|]+.*)|(.*[\.]?.*[\.]+$)|(.*[
  ]+$)]]></value>
  </parameter>
  <parameter name="requiresMatch"><value>false</value></parameter>
</constraint>
```

Another simpler example that simply constrains the value of the property to be an all uppercase string is as follows:

```
<constraint name="test:regexExample" type="REGEX">
  <parameter name="expression"><value>[A-Z]*</value></parameter>
  <parameter name="requiresMatch"><value>true</value></parameter>
</constraint>
```

Regular expressions are extremely powerful, but writing one can quickly become quite complex. There are many tutorials available online or books written about how to write them. Resources like `http://regexlib.com/` offer a large library of online regular expressions that can be reused and also provide tools for online interactive debugging of regular expressions.

LENGTH constraint

The LENGTH constraint enforces the lengths of strings to be within a range of values. Valid `<parameter>` names for this constraint are as follows:

- minLength—the minimum allowed length for the string. The value must be non-negative and less than or equal to maxLength.

- maxLength—the maximum allowed length for the string. The value must be greater than or equal to the value of minLength.

Consider the following example of a `LENGTH` constraint where the length of the string for the property value must be between 0 and 100:

```
<constraint name="test:lengthExample" type="LENGTH">
  <parameter name="minLength"><value>0</value></parameter>
  <parameter name="maxLength"><value>100</value></parameter>
</constraint>
```

LIST constraint

The LIST constraint forces the values of a property to be one of the values contained in an enumerated list. Typically, a user will interact with entering the values for a LIST-constrained property by selecting a value from a drop-down list containing all allowed values. Valid `<parameter>` names for this constraint are as follows:

- allowedValues—a list of allowed string values for the property. While the values are strings, it is possible for them to represent non-string values.

- caseSensitive—a Boolean value, set to either *true* or *false*. This flag specifies if the case is case-sensitive. This parameter is optional and the default is *true*.

The Alfresco Content Model implementation for the DoD 5015.2 Records Management specification contains the following example of a `LIST` constraint:

```
<constraint name="dod:imageFormatList" type="LIST">
  <title>Image Formats</title>
  <parameter name="allowedValues">
    <list>
      <value>Binary Image Interchange Format (BIIF)</value>
      <value>GIF 89a</value>
      <value>Graphic Image Format (GIF) 87a</value>
      <value>Joint Photographic Experts Group (JPEG) (all
        versions)</value>
      <value>Portable Network Graphics (PNG) 1.0</value>
      <value>Tagged Image Interchange Format (TIFF) 4.0</value>
      <value>TIFF 5.0</value>
      <value>TIFF 6.0</value>
```

```
      </list>
   </parameter>
   <parameter name="caseSensitive"><value>true</value></parameter>
</constraint>
```

MINMAX constraint

The MINMAX constraint enforces that a numeric value be within a range of numbers. Valid `<parameter>` names for this constraint are as follows:

- minValue—the minimum allowed value for this property. minValue must be less than or equal to the maxValue.

- maxValue—the maximum allowed value for this property. maxValue must be greater than or equal to the minValue.

An example of a constraint on a numeric property that requires the number to be between `0` and `1000` is shown next:

```
<constraint name="test:minMaxExample" type="MINMAX">
   <parameter name="minValue"><value>0</value></parameter>
   <parameter name="maxValue"><value>1000</value></parameter>
</constraint>
```

Custom constraint types can be written too, but doing that is a task that needs to be done using Java. Built-in constraints are defined by the Java package `org.alfresco.repo.dictionary.constraint`. `<property>` values for each constraint correspond to the setter methods of the Java class implementation for the constraint. An example and description on how to do create a custom constraint can be found on the Alfresco wiki: `http://wiki.alfresco.com/wiki/Constraints`.

Associations

Associations are relationships that are created between two types within the content model. Associations are ultimately realized as relationships between nodes in the repository and are controlled by the types assigned to the nodes. Associations must be uniquely named and include the namespace prefix at the beginning of the association name.

Two types of associations are possible—child associations and peer associations. Both types of associations consider one of the types as the source and the other as the target. The source is the type in which the association is defined.

Peer associations

For brevity, within the Alfresco Content Model, a peer association is simply referred to as an `association`. Available elements that are enclosed by the `<association>` tag for describing the behavior of an association are as follows:

- title—the title of the association. A text string to document the association.
- description—a description of the association. A text string to document the association.
- source—an element that groups the parameter elements that define the source of the association:
    - mandatory—a flag that specifies whether having an association is mandatory.
    - many—a flag that specifies whether the source type can be associated with more than one target.
- target—an element that groups the parameter elements that define the target of the association:
    - class—the allowed type for the target element. Selecting a class like `sys:base` would allow the target to be any kind of content, since all types inherit from `sys:base`. This element is required for defining the target.
    - mandatory—a flag that specifies whether having an association is mandatory.
    - many—a flag that specifies whether the source type can be associated with more than one target.

An example of a peer association can be found in `contentModel.xml`. The association here defines a reference from one item to another piece of content:

```
<association name="cm:references">
  <source>
    <role>cm:referencedBy</role>
    <mandatory>false</mandatory>
    <many>true</many>
  </source>
  <target>
    <class>cm:content</class>
    <role>cm:references</role>
    <mandatory>false</mandatory>
    <many>true</many>
  </target>
</association>
```

Child associations

A `child-association` is described by the same set of enclosed elements. Additionally, the following two elements are also supported as part of the `child-association` definition:

- duplicate—is a Boolean flag, either *true* or *false*, that specifies whether or not children of the parent node can have the same name. If it is not allowed, a transaction cannot be committed until this condition is met.

- propagateTimestamps—is a Boolean flag, either *true* or *false*, that specifies when making a change to a child element, that the timestamp of the parent should also be updated.

An example of a child association can be found in the Records Management Content Model. This example shows a holds area that is capable of tracking the holds that have been placed:

```
<child-association name="rma:holds">
  <title>Holds</title>
  <source>
     <mandatory>false</mandatory>
     <many>false</many>
  </source>
  <target>
     <class>rma:hold</class>
     <mandatory>false</mandatory>
     <many>true</many>
  </target>
</child-association>
```

The `mandatory` flag is enforced whenever a node with the association is being committed at the end of a transaction. This holds for both `<association>` and `<child-association>` tags. If the `mandatory` flag is *true,* and if it is enforced, then the commit will fail if the association element does not exist, specified by writing `<mandatory enforced="true">`. If the `mandatory` flag is *true* but not enforced, the commit will succeed, but an aspect called `sys:incomplete` will be applied to the node.

When the two elements, `mandatory` and `many`, are considered together, they define the cardinality of the association. The following table shows how the cardinality can be determined, based on those two elements:

	mandatory = *true*	**mandatory** = *false*
many = *true*	1 or more	0 or more
many = *false*	1	0 or 1

With a child association, if you delete the parent node, the child nodes will be automatically deleted. In a peer association, deleting the source node will break the association, but will not cause any other nodes to be deleted.

Aspects

Aspects are a shorthand method to group together property, association, and constraint definitions. Aspects can be applied to repository nodes, type definitions, or to the definition of other aspects. When an aspect is applied to, for example, a node, the properties and associations defined in the aspect are taken from it and added to those that already exist on the node. Application of aspects to types and to other aspects works in a similar way.

Much of what an aspect does overlaps with the functionality of a type. For example, like types, aspects support inheritance, with the concept of one aspect inheriting from a parent aspect. The one difference between types and aspects is that every node must have one and only one type, while any number of aspects can be applied to a node.

The application of multiple aspects to a node is often compared to multiple inheritance. Aspects can also be thought of as being similar to macros. A macro, once defined, can be reused again by referring to it by its name. In the same sort of way, a common practice in the Alfresco Content Model is to define an aspect and to then apply it to many type and aspect definitions as a mandatory aspect. For example, the aspect cm:titled from the content model is often used in the definition of a type, bringing along with it standard definitions for the properties cm:title and cm:description.

Another advantage of aspects is that they can be dynamically applied at runtime to nodes. For example, when a record is declared within Records Management, only at that time are the properties that are relevant to managing records appended to the node. In this way, only metadata relevant to an object needs to be tracked. Aspects create a clean way to assign metadata to objects and avoid tracking metadata fields that are not relevant to an object.

The definition of an aspect is very similar to that of a type. Aspects must be uniquely named and include the namespace prefix at the beginning of the aspect name. Available elements that are enclosed by the `<aspect>` tag for describing the behavior of an aspect are as follows:

- title—a title for the aspect. A text string that documents the aspect.
- description—a description for the property. A text string that documents the aspect.
- parent—the parent aspect of this aspect. Aspects can inherit from the definition of their parent aspect. Aspects can be nested to any depth in inheritance.
- archive—a Boolean flag that indicates when nodes of this aspect are deleted and are moved to the archive store as a sort of recycle bin area.
- properties—an element that encloses a list of properties for the aspect.
- associations—an element that encloses a list of associations for the aspect.
- mandatory-aspect—an element that encloses a list of aspects for the aspect.
- includedInSuperTypeQuery—a Boolean that determines if this aspect is to be searched as part of a query over any of its parent aspects.
- overrides—an element that encloses a list of properties that override parent properties.

  The following features can be overridden:
  - mandatory—a child aspect can make a property mandatory, but cannot relax a property declared mandatory by the parent.
  - default—the child aspect can override or include a parent default value.
  - constraints—new constraints can be applied to a parent property, but existing constraints inherited from the parent cannot be removed.

A good example of an aspect that is defined in the Alfresco Records Management Content Model is `rma:frozen`. This aspect is applied to records that are subject to a hold:

```
<aspect name="rma:frozen">
  <title>Frozen</title>
  <properties>
    <property name="rma:frozenAt">
      <title>Frozen At Date</title>
      <type>d:date</type>
      <mandatory>true</mandatory>
```

```
      </property>
      <property name="rma:frozenBy">
        <title>Frozen By</title>
        <type>d:text</type>
        <mandatory>true</mandatory>
        <index enabled="true">
          <atomic>true</atomic>
          <stored>false</stored>
          <tokenised>false</tokenised>
        </index>
      </property>
    </properties>
    <mandatory-aspects>
      <aspect>rma:filePlanComponent</aspect>
    </mandatory-aspects>
  </aspect>
```

Creating a new model

We now have a good understanding of the elements that go into defining a content model, and we've seen a few code snippets that show examples of each of the element types, but let's now try to bring all the pieces together by looking at the steps needed to define a new content model from scratch.

Designing the model

Our main goal with the example that we will walk through next is to see what's involved in creating a content model. Therefore, at this point, let's not focus too much on the details of exact properties and metadata. When we look at the File Plan later, we'll want to be more thorough in our analysis. For now, we'll focus on a very high-level outline of the documents within a fictitious company that we will call Typical Company, Inc, and that we will abbreviate as TC.

Before we even start thinking about what sort of XML we need to put together for the TC model description file, it will be a lot easier and quicker overall if we first carefully design what the structure of our content model will look like.

The model that we'll define needs to identify the document types that we will manage. We aren't concerned with the Records Management part of the puzzle just yet. In a later section in this chapter, we'll look in detail at the structure of the Records Management Content Model and see how any document or content type in Alfresco can be placed under Records Management.

A typical company is comprised of a number of departments, and the types of documents in each of those departments are distinctly different. We will classify our documents primarily along department lines. Finance, for example, deals with documents related to general accounting, accounts receivable, accounts payable, payroll, and taxes, to name a few. Whereas, the Legal department has documents related to contracts, litigation, and patents. The metadata associated with each of these different types of documents varies widely.

For the TC model, we will create a base content type called `tc:generalDoc`. `tc:generalDoc` is actually a child type of `cm:content`. By inheriting from `cm:content`, we will automatically have access to the mechanics for storing and managing arbitrary binary content, like Microsoft Office documents, PDF files, images, and text files. We will also make use of a few aspects that are already defined within the standard Alfresco Content Model. `cm:auditable` is one of them. This aspect taps into the auditing capability of Alfresco. With it, we can track detailed information about any changes that happen to the documents, such as who made the change, when the change was made, and exactly what was changed. `cm:titled` is another aspect that `tc:generalDoc` inherits from. It defines the properties in a standard way for the document title and description. The following diagram shows the relationship between types and aspects for the TC model:

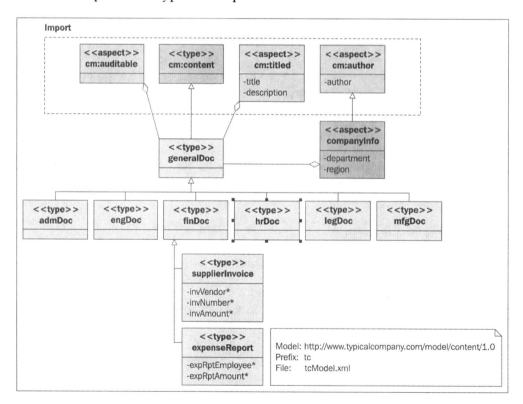

`tc:generalDoc` also inherits from the aspect `tc:companyInfo` properties that maintain the author name, the department, and the global regions in which the company operates. The `tc:companyInfo` aspect is defined in the TC model. `tc:companyInfo` is a child of a pre-existing aspect called `cm:author`, from which it inherits the property for the author name.

Let's divide our base type hierarchy pretty much along department lines. For now, let us consider the documents used within each of the company's six departments (Administration, Engineering, Finance, Human Resources, Legal, and Manufacturing) as the primary document types. These six new document type groups all inherit from `tc:generalDoc`. Metadata that is relevant across the entire group of documents can be inserted into these types.

To avoid making this example too complex, we will limit ourselves to looking at two content types specific to the Finance department—invoices and expense reports. To do that, we will create two types, namely, `tc:supplierInvoice` and `tc:expenseReport`, that both inherit from the type `tc:finDoc`.

Implementing the model file

Each model in Alfresco is defined within a single XML model file. We'll call the file for the model that we've just designed `tcModel.xml`. This custom model file needs to be deployed into the directory `tomcat\shared\classes\alfresco\extension\model` when it is complete. Let's look in detail now at the contents of this model definition file.

The model file header

The file begins with an XML declaration tag. Next, the `<model>` tag defines the name for the model. This tag encloses the entire model definition. Descriptor information for the model includes the `<description>`, `<author>`, and `<version>` tags.

 To avoid potential problems when defining the model name, you should choose a name that is in lowercase and does not contain any spaces or special characters.

```
<?xml version="1.0" encoding="UTF-8"?>
<!-- Definition of new Model -->
<model name="tc:typicalcompany"
  xmlns="http://www.alfresco.org/model/dictionary/1.0">
  <!-- Optional meta-data about the model -->
  <description>Typical Company Model</description>
  <author>Dick Weisinger</author>
  <version>1.0</version>
```

Model import files

The definitions from other models, that this model references, are imported. In our model, we will create properties that reference basic Alfresco content data types defined in the Dictionary model. We also inherit from types and aspects that are defined in the standard Alfresco Content Model. Both of these models are imported here. Any existing model file could be potentially imported in order to reuse previously defined elements.

Each import reference to the external content model includes a long-name `uri` and a short-name `prefix`. The `prefix` is used as a shorthand that is pre-appended to element names from these external models to identify clearly what their origin is:

```
<!-- Imports are required to allow references to definitions
  in other models -->
<imports>
  <!-- Import Alfresco Dictionary Definitions -->
  <import uri="http://www.alfresco.org/model/dictionary/1.0"
    prefix="d"/>
  <!-- Import Alfresco Content Domain Model Definitions -->
  <import uri="http://www.alfresco.org/model/content/1.0"
    prefix="cm"/>
</imports>
```

The model namespace

In a similar way to the syntax used to define the import of external models, we next define the long and short names for this namespace. The `uri` typically identifies the company or individual by whom the namespace is managed. For Typical Company, we will use the `prefix` *tc*.

By convention, the `uri` for the model namespace typically ends with the version number of the model. The `prefix` is shorthand to minimize the possibility of naming clashes with the names of elements in other models. The `prefix` is being bound to this `uri` for use in this file. The `uri` is the true identifier for the namespace. If you were to import this file later into another model definition file, you may decide to use a different `prefix` in that file to refer to this same `uri`, but it is best practice to consistently use the same `prefix` across all files:

```
<namespaces>
  <namespace uri="http://www.typicalcompany.com/model/content/1.0"
    prefix="tc"/>
</namespaces>
```

The model constraints

Next, we get into the actual definition of the various parts of the content model. We start with the definition of the global constraints that will be used within the model.

For the TC model, we will define a single constraint. This constraint will later be associated with the `tc:region` property that we define in the `tc:companyInfo` aspect. This constraint, `tc:regionList`, is a list of global regions that Typical Company breaks down as its sales regions:

```
<constraints>
  <constraint name="tc:regionList" type="LIST">
    <title>List of Company Regions</title>
    <parameter name="allowedValues">
      <list>
        <value>North East</value>
        <value>MidWest</value>
        <value>South</value>
        <value>South West</value>
        <value>West</value>
        <value>Europe</value>
        <value>Asia</value>
        <value>South America</value>
      </list>
    </parameter>
    <parameter name="caseSensitive"><value>true</value></parameter>
  </constraint>
</constraints>
```

The model types

Next, we define the types for the model. The first type declared is `tc:generalDoc`. This type inherits from the standard Content Model type `cm:content`. Because of that, all properties defined by `cm:content` will come along as part of this definition. In addition to that, `tc:generalDoc` also applies a number of `mandatory-aspects`. These aspects are applied immediately whenever a node of this content type is created.

For example, the aspect `cm:auditable` brings with it properties used for auditing purposes like `cm:created`, `cm:creator`, `cm:modified`, `cm:modifier`, and the date and time accessed, `cm:accessed`. The aspect `cm:titled` brings with it the properties `cm:title` and `cm:description`:

```
<types>
  <type name="tc:generalDoc">
    <title>General Document</title>
```

```
      <parent>cm:content</parent>
      <archive>true</archive>
      <mandatory-aspects>
        <aspect>cm:auditable</aspect>
        <aspect>cm:titled</aspect>
        <aspect>tc:companyInfo</aspect>
      </mandatory-aspects>
    </type>
```

Next, we define the types that inherit from `tc:generalDoc`:

```
<type name="tc:admDoc">
  <title>Administrative Document</title>
  <parent>tc:generalDoc</parent>
</type>
<type name="tc:engDoc">
  <title>Engineering Document</title>
  <parent>tc:generalDoc</parent>
</type>
<type name="tc:finDoc">
  <title>Financial Document</title>
  <parent>tc:generalDoc</parent>
</type>
<type name="tc:insDoc">
  <title>Insurance Document</title>
  <parent>tc:generalDoc</parent>
</type>
<type name="tc:legDoc">
  <title>Legal Document</title>
  <parent>tc:generalDoc</parent>
</type>
<type name="tc:mfgDoc">
  <title>Manufacturing Document</title>
  <parent>tc:generalDoc</parent>
</type>
```

Next, we define the two special content types that inherit from the `tc:finDoc` type used for financial documents: `tc:supplierInvoice` and `tc:expenseReport`. Note that all the properties defined for these types are specified as `mandatory`:

```
<type name="tc:supplierInvoice">
  <title>Supplier Invoice</title>
  <parent>tc:finDoc</parent>
  <properties>
    <property name="tc:invVendor">
```

```
          <title>Vendor for Invoice</title>
          <type>d:text</type>
          <mandatory>true</mandatory>
          <index enabled="true">
            <atomic>true</atomic>
            <stored>false</stored>
            <tokenised>false</tokenised>
          </index>
        </property>
        <property name="tc:invNumber">
          <title>Invoice Number</title>
          <type>d:int</type>
          <mandatory>true</mandatory>
        </property>
        <property name="tc:invAmount">
          <title>Invoice Amount</title>
          <type>d:double</type>
          <mandatory>true</mandatory>
        </property>
      </properties>
    </type>

    <type name="tc:expenseReport">
      <title>Expense Report</title>
      <parent>tc:finDoc</parent>
      <properties>
        <property name="tc:expRptEmployee">
          <title>Employee Reporting Expense Report</title>
          <type>d:text</type>
          <mandatory>true</mandatory>
          <index enabled="true">
            <atomic>true</atomic>
            <stored>false</stored>
            <tokenised>false</tokenised>
          </index>
        </property>
        <property name="tc:expRptAmount">
          <title>Amount of Expense Report</title>
          <type>d:double</type>
          <mandatory>true</mandatory>
        </property>
      </properties>
    </type>
  </types>
```

The model aspects

Finally, we define the custom aspects that are used in the TC Content Model. We have a single new aspect, `tc:companyInfo`, which is an aspect that inherits from the parent aspect `cm:author`. This aspect has two properties, namely, `tc:department` and `tc:region`:

```
<aspects>
  <aspect name="tc:companyInfo">
    <title>Department/Region Source information</title>
    <parent>cm:author</parent>
    <properties>
      <property name="tc:department">
        <title>Department</title>
        <type>d:mltext</type>
        <index enabled="true">
          <atomic>true</atomic>
          <stored>false</stored>
          <tokenised>false</tokenised>
        </index>
      </property>
      <property name="tc:region">
        <title>Region</title>
        <type>d:text</type>
        <constraints>
          <constraint ref="tc:regionList" />
        </constraints>
      </property>
    </properties>
  </aspect>
</aspects>
</model>
```

Installing the model

With our content model definition ready, we can now go ahead and install it into Alfresco. There are two options for doing this: **bootstrap deployment** and **dynamic deployment**.

Bootstrap deployment of the model

With bootstrap deployment, the new model is recognized and automatically installed when the Alfresco server starts. Usually, when a model is fully debugged and ready, it will be deployed in this way. The most efficient way to distribute a model to others is by defining the files for bootstrap deployment.

Let's look at how bootstrap deployment works. In the previous section, we created the model file `tcModel.xml` and saved it into the extension area `tomcat\shared\classes\alfresco\extension\model`. However, Alfresco won't automatically recognize the model file without a Spring definition file first referencing it. When the server starts, Spring looks for context configuration files that end in `-context.xml`. For the model file to be picked up, it needs to be referenced from a Spring context file.

We will create a Spring context file called `typicalcompany-model-context.xml` that references the new content and save it to the `tomcat\shared\classes\alfresco\extension` *directory*. In this file, we define a Java bean with a unique `id` called `typicalcompany.dictionaryBootstrap`. The definition specifies the location of our model file `tcModel.xml`. We also reference a properties file to hold any labels associated with the model definition. The properties file is called `typicalcompany-model.properties` *and is stored in the same directory as the* `tcModel.xml` *file.* Note that the model file reference includes the complete filename with the `.xml` extension. However, when referring to the `labels` file, we need to omit the `.properties` extension. If this isn't done, these files won't be properly identified. The context file looks like this:

```
<?xml version='1.0' encoding='UTF-8'?>
<!DOCTYPE beans PUBLIC '-//SPRING//DTD BEAN//EN'
  'http://www.springframework.org/dtd/spring-beans.dtd'>
<beans>
  <!-- Registration of typical company content models -->
  <bean id="typicalcompany.dictionaryBootstrap"
    parent="dictionaryModelBootstrap" depends-
    on="dictionaryBootstrap">
  <property name="models">
    <list>
      <value>alfresco/extension/model/tcModel.xml</value>
    </list>
  </property>
    <property name="labels">
      <list>
        <value>alfresco/extension/model/typicalcompany-
          model</value>
      </list>
    </property>
  </bean>
</beans>
```

There isn't much in the properties file right now. If needed, more can be added to this file later:

```
tc_typicalcompany.description=Typical Company Model
```

Dynamic deployment of the content model

An alternative deployment method to the bootstrap method we just described is dynamic deployment. Dynamic deployment lets you iteratively develop and test the creation of your new content model without having to continually stop and restart the server to test your new changes.

Instead of referencing the model in a configuration file read on server startup, the content model file is deployed directly to the content repository. This is done by first uploading the model file into the repository folder Company Home\ Data Dictionary\Models. Beginning in Share version 3.2R, full access to the Alfresco repository is now available directly from Share, and starting with version 3.3, access to the Alfresco repository in Share is turned on by default.

We can access the Alfresco repository via the **Repository** link along the top of the Share window. Once in the repository, we can then navigate to the Data Dictionary\Models folder. If you have already installed the new content model via the bootstrap approach described in the previous section, and if you would like to try using the dynamic method to install a model using the same type name, first remove any content you had created of that type, remove the model bootstrap files, and then upload the **tcModel.xml** *file to the* **Models** *directory of the repository:*

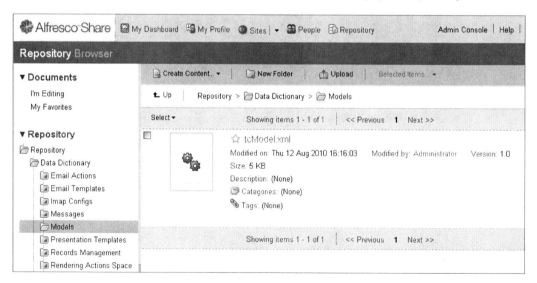

Once the file is uploaded, bring up the dialog to edit the document metadata. In the list of metadata, we can find the **Model Active** checkbox. We can check that box to activate the model:

Once the **Model Active** field is set, the model will become available for use. Each time you subsequently upload a new copy of the model file or edit the XML in the file via the Share inline edit option, the updated model is re-registered and re-activated immediately after being saved. This makes it easy to do interactive development on a model without the need to continually restart the system after every change to the model.

To deactivate a model added via the repository, uncheck the **Model Active** metadata field. To completely delete the model, remove the model file from the repository.

A content model can be removed only if there are no nodes in the repository that are currently associated with the model. Removing property definitions from the model and then saving the model when content is currently stored with those properties will cause errors. It's best to use a development environment during the iterative process of first building a content model.

Exposing a new content model from the Share user interface

Even though the new model is deployed, we're not able to immediately see any signs of it in the Share user interface. By default, the only content type that can be created in Share is of type `cm:content`. New models aren't of much use if we aren't able to access them from the user interface. But we can change that.

Adding Types to the site upload form

When we upload new content to the Document Library area of a site, we are presented with a Flash-based form that allows us to navigate to a local directory and to then select multiple files for upload. By default, there are no options on this form that allow the user to select which content type will be assigned to the files when they are uploaded.

There are two files specific to the Flash-based upload form that need to be overridden to give us the option of selecting from additional content types on upload. The override files need to be placed in the `tomcat\shared\classes\alfresco\web-extension\site-webscripts\org\alfresco\components\upload` directory.

The first one is a JavaScript file that contains a function that defines the array of allowed content types. This is the only function contained in this file. If we decide to expose only invoices and expense report content types from the TC model, the file `flash-upload.get.js` will be modified to look something like the following:

```
function getContentTypes()
{
  // TODO: Data webscript call to return list of available types
  var contentTypes = [
  {
    id: "cm:content",
    value: "type.cm_content"
  },
  {
    id: "tc:supplierInvoice",
    value: "type.tc_invoice"
  },
  {
    id: "tc:expenseReport",
    value: "type.tc_expense"
  }
  ];
```

```
    return contentTypes;
}
model.contentTypes = getContentTypes();
```

Each content type element of the JavaScript array has a `value` that refers to the label of string in a properties file. The value for the `id` is the name of the content type that will be displayed. The second file that needs to be defined is the properties file `flash-upload.get.properties`. First we copy the contents of the original file from `tomcat\webapps\share\WEB-INF\classes\alfresco\site-webscripts\org\alfresco\components\upload` and then we add the following lines to the bottom of the file:

```
type.tc_general=Company General
type.tc_adm=Administration
type.tc_eng=Engineering
type.tc_fin=Finance
type.tc_ins=Insurance
type.tc_leg=Legal
type.tc_mfg=Manufacturing
type.tc_invoice=Invoice
type.tc_expense=Expense Report
```

With these files in place, when we now go to upload new content, we see the changes reflected in the upload form. A drop-down is added that allows the user to select from additional content types:

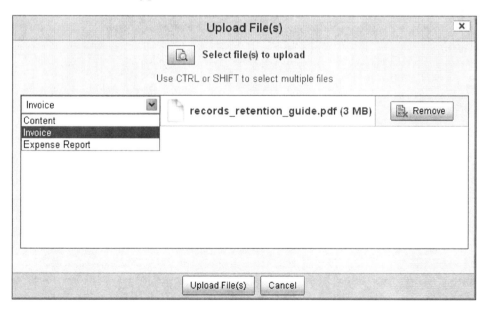

Adding Types to the Change Type action

After uploading new content to the repository, one of the actions available is to be able to change the type of that content. For example, if we uploaded a file and assigned the file to be of type cm:content, we could later change the type to tc:expenseReport.

Again, by default, there are no mappings defined that allow changes between different content types. If you select the **Change Type** action, a dialog is displayed, but no change selections are available.

Options for the **Change Type** action mappings can be made in the share-config-custom.xml file found in the tomcat\shared\classes\alfresco\web-extensions directory.

When we look in this file, we find a section of it with the following code:

```
<types>
  <type name="cm:content">
  </type>
  <type name="cm:folder">
  </type>
</types>
```

This is the section of the code that we want to change. We will add <subtype> elements within the cm:content type block to define the mapping. Since tc:supplierInvoice and tc:expenseReport are content types that inherit from cm:content, it is possible to change nodes that have been assigned cm:content. Changing the type from something like tc:supplierInvoice back to an ancestor type like cm:content, which has fewer properties, isn't allowed:

```
<types>
  <type name="cm:content">
    <subtype name="tc:supplierInvoice" />
    <subtype name="tc:expenseReport" />
  </type>
  <type name="cm:folder">
  </type>
</types>
```

The way this mapping works is that when the **Change Type** action is selected for a document of type cm:content, the subtypes defined here for that type will be displayed from the dialog dropdown. If we then select the **Change Type** action for a document of any type other than cm:content, no change options will be available.

For example, while this isn't the behavior that we want, to demonstrate more clearly how the content change mapping works, consider the following change mapping type definitions:

```
<types>
  <type name="cm:content">
     subtype name="tc:generalDoc" />
  </type>
  <type name="cm:generalDoc">
    <subtype name="tc:supplierInvoice" />
    <subtype name="tc:expenseReport" />
  </type>
  <type name="cm:folder">
  </type>
</types>
```

In this case, we are able to change the content type from cm:content to tc:generalDoc, but no other type directly, while a document of type tc:generalDoc can be changed to either type tc:supplierInvoice or tc:expenseReport.

Going back to the first definition, if we make this change to the configuration file, **Change Type** options will begin to appear in the dialog. That's great, but the text that appears for the items in the drop-down list will show items like **tc_supplierInvoice** and **tc_expenseReport**. We need to create a property file with the mappings that will correctly define the text labels for these items.

To do that, we first create the property file that contains the type labels for our new model. We can create a new file tcmodel.properties and place this file in the tomcat\shared\classes\alfresco\web-extension\messages directory:

```
type.tc_generalDoc=Company General
type.tc_admDoc=Administration Document
type.tc_engDoc=Engineering Document
type.tc_finDoc=Finance Document
type.tc_insDoc=Insurance Document
type.tc_legDoc=Legal Document
type.tc_mfgDoc=Manufacturing Document
type.tc_supplierInvoice=Invoice Document
type.tc_expenseReport=Expense Report Document
```

Then we need to wire this file into Spring so that it can be identified as a properties file. We can do that by creating or extending an existing `custom-slingshot-application-context.xml` file located in the `tomcat\shared\classes\alfresco\web-extension` directory. This new file will reference the `tcmodel.properties` file:

```
<?xml version='1.0' encoding='UTF-8'?>
<!DOCTYPE beans PUBLIC '-//SPRING//DTD BEAN//EN'
  'http://www.springframework.org/dtd/spring-beans.dtd'>
<beans>
  <bean id="webscripts.resources"
    class="org.springframework.extensions.surf.util.
    ResourceBundleBootstrapComponent">
    <property name="resourceBundles">
      <list>
        <value>webscripts.messages.webscripts</value>
        <value>alfresco.messages.common</value>
        <value>alfresco.messages.slingshot</value>
        <value>alfresco.web-extension.messages.tcmodel</value>
      </list>
    </property>
  </bean>
</beans>
```

After we add these files and restart the Alfresco server, we are then able to see the changes. If we upload a file of type `cm:content` and apply the **Change Type** action, we will see the following dialog that allows us to change the content type. When we select a new type from the list, we will immediately see that the metadata properties available for the document are updated to reflect the new properties available in the type:

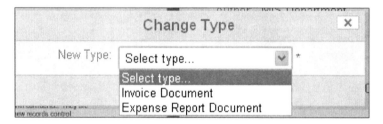

Seeing the new Type applied to a content node

Now that we have created the new content type and are able to assign the type from the interface when new content is created, we can verify that the type information is being correctly saved by using the Node Browser to look at the information in the repository.

You will recall that the Node Browser is a tool available in the Alfresco JSF Explorer client from the Administration area of the client. If you bring up the Explorer client and log in as the user admin and navigate to the Node Browser, you will be able to navigate to a new content item that has the new content type.

One way to get a quick reference to the content item is to note that the node reference is appended at the end of the Share URL when you view the details page for the item.

In the **Node Browser**, we are able to see that the correct type has been applied. We are able to see **Properties** from the new TC model, as well as **Properties** inherited from the System and Standard Content models. We can also see all of the **Aspects** that are currently applied to this node:

Customizing the forms for viewing and editing the new model's metadata

You may have noticed that the forms for editing and viewing metadata for the new document type are showing a lot of properties that most users would not be interested in seeing. What's happening is that we have not yet configured a Share property form to display the metadata for our new types, and by default, all the properties for the type are being dumped into the edit and view property forms.

We can configure and customize the property forms so that they look a bit more appealing, and also remove the properties that don't need to be seen by the end user. Custom forms for Share are added to the `share-config-custom.xml` file. This file is placed in the `tomcat\shared\classes\alfresco\web-extension` directory.

We will add three new `<config>` tag elements to this file. The first specifies that we want to be able to include a CSS file to control the look of the form. We will call that file `typical.css` and it is placed in the `tomcat\webapps\share\custom\form` directory:

```
<!-- Typical company Creation Forms -->
<config>
  <forms>
    <dependencies>
      <css src="/custom/form/typical.css" />
    </dependencies>
  </forms>
</config>
```

Next, we include the configuration for the `tc:supplierInvoice` form. This form will be used to display type properties for all nodes of this type, as determined by the `node-type` evaluation. In a similar way, we also define a `<config>` element for the type `tc:expenseReport` (not shown):

```
<config evaluator="node-type" condition="tc:supplierInvoice">
  <forms>
    <form>
      <edit-form template="/2-column-edit-form.ftl" />
      <field-visibility>
        <hide id="sys:node-uuid" />
        <hide id="sys:store-protocol" />
        <hide id="sys:store-identifier" />
        <hide id="sys:node-dbid" />
        <hide id="cm:created" />
        <hide id="cm:creator" />
        <hide id="cm:modified" />
```

```
            <hide id="cm:modifier" />
            <hide id="cm:accessed" />
            <hide id="cm:contains" />
            <hide id="rma:identifier" />
            <hide id="rma:dbUniquenessId" />
            <show id="cm:name" />
            <show id="cm:title" force="true" />
            <show id="cm:description" force="true" />
            <show id="mimetype"  for-mode="view"  />
            <show id="cm:author" force="true" />
            <show id="tc:department" force="true" />
            <show id="tc:region" force="true" />
            <show id="tc:invVendor" />
            <show id="tc:invNumber"  />
            <show id="tc:invAmount"  />
        </field-visibility>

        <appearance>
          <set id="Invoice Documents"
            appearance="bordered-panel" label="Supplier Invoice" />
          <field id="tc:region">
            <control template="controls/selectone.ftl">
                <control-param name="options">North
                  East,MidWest,South,South West,West,Europe,Asia,South
                  America</control-param>
            </control>
          </field>
          <field id="tc:invVendor" set="Invoice Documents" />
          <field id="tc:invNumber" set="Invoice Documents" />
          <field id="tc:invAmount" set="Invoice Documents" />
        </appearance>
      </form>
    </forms>
  </config>
```

In the form definition, we mark a number of properties as hidden within the <field-visibility> element, and we explicitly mark properties that we want to be visible, like the new tc:invVendor, tc:invNumber, and tc:invAmount properties.

We override the standard template used to display the properties when in edit mode, specifying our own custom template file 2-column-edit-form.ftl. That file is placed into the tomcat\shared\classes\alfresco\web-extension\site-webscripts directory.

In the <appearance> section of the form definition, a bordered panel is defined by the <set> element and the invoice-specific properties are then grouped into the panel by referring to that element. The panel border will be visible on the default view form, but it won't be displayed with the custom edit form template.

The property tc:region is displayed as a dropdown using the control template called selectone. The elements for the dropdown are listed in the definition of the selectone control.

> The form template used here was adopted from the form example available on the Alfresco wiki at http://wiki.alfresco. com/wiki/Forms_Examples

This is the FreeMarker code that is used to define the form display template:

```
<#import "/org/alfresco/components/form/form.lib.ftl" as formLib />

<#if error?exists>
  <div class="error">${error}</div>
<#elseif form?exists>
  <#assign formId=args.htmlid + "-form">
  <#assign formUI><#if
    args.formUI??>${args.formUI}<#else>true</#if></#assign>
  <#if formUI == "true">
    <@formLib.renderFormsRuntime formId=formId />
  </#if>

  <div id="${formId}-container" class="form-container">
    <div class="logoimg"><img class="logoleft"
      src="/share/custom/form/images/typicallogo.png"><span>Finance
        Document</span></div>
    <#if form.showCaption?exists && form.showCaption>
      <div id="${formId}-caption" class="caption freshstart">
        <span class="mandatory-
        indicator">*</span>${msg("form.required.fields")}</div>
    </#if>
    <#if form.mode != "view">
      <form id="${formId}" method="${form.method}" accept-
        charset="utf-8" enctype="${form.enctype}"
        action="${form.submissionUrl}">
    </#if>

    <div id="${formId}-fields" class="form-fields">
      <#list form.structure as item>
        <#if item.kind == "set">
          <@renderSetWithColumns set=item />
        <#else>
```

```
              <@formLib.renderField field=form.fields[item.id] />
          </#if>
        </#list>
      </div>

      <#if form.mode != "view">
        <@formLib.renderFormButtons formId=formId />
        </form>
      </#if>

    </div>
  </#if>

<#macro renderSetWithColumns set>
  <#if set.appearance?exists>
    <#if set.appearance == "fieldset">
      <fieldset><legend>${set.label}</legend>
    <#elseif set.appearance == "panel">
      <div class="form-panel">
        <div class="form-panel-heading">${set.label}</div>
        <div class="form-panel-body">
    </#if>
  </#if>

  <#list set.children as item>
    <#if item.kind == "set">
      <@renderSetWithColumns set=item />
    <#else>
      <#if (item_index % 2) == 0>
      <div class="yui-g"><div class="yui-u first">
      <#else>
      <div class="yui-u">
      </#if>
      <@formLib.renderField field=form.fields[item.id] />
      </div>
      <#if ((item_index % 2) != 0) || !item_has_next></div></#if>
    </#if>
  </#list>

  <#if set.appearance?exists>
    <#if set.appearance == "fieldset">
      </fieldset>
    <#elseif set.appearance == "panel">
        </div>
      </div>
    </#if>
  </#if>
</#macro>
```

Now, on the details page for a document of type `tc:supplierInvoice`, we see a
form that looks as follows:

The edit form that uses the new custom template for the `tc:supplierInvoice` type
now looks like the following:

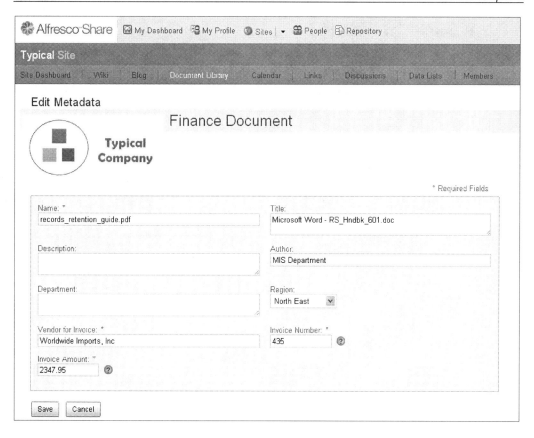

The Records Management Content Model

At this point, we're fairly familiar with the Alfresco Content Model and we can now apply that understanding by looking at the components of the Alfresco Records Management model. The content model descriptor files for the Records Management model can be found in the `tomcat\webapps\alfresco\WEB-INF\classes\alfresco\module\org_alfresco_module_dod5015\model` directory. The content model is broken into two models and two files, namely, `recordsModel.xml` and `dod5015Model.xml`.

The Records Model

Let's look at the first file called `recordsModel.xml`. The relationships defined in that model file can be illustrated in the UML format, as shown in the next diagram:

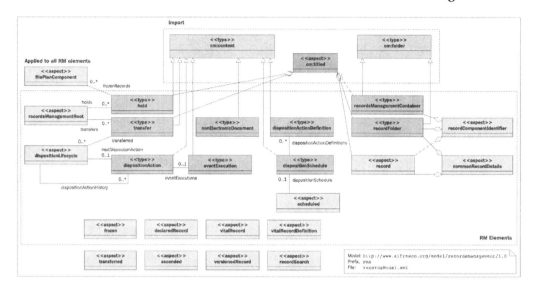

Now, let's look in detail at how the file `recordsModel.xml` is constructed and the definitions that are in it.

The Records Model header

If we look at the top of the `recordsModel.xml` file, we can see the declaration of the Records Model and some header information about the author and version:

```
<?xml version="1.0" encoding="UTF-8"?>

<!-- Definition of Records Management Model -->

<!-- Note: the rma: namespace is defined further on in the document
    -->
<model name="rma:recordsmanagement"
  xmlns="http://www.alfresco.org/model/dictionary/1.0">

  <!-- Meta-data about the model -->
  <description>Records Management Model</description>
  <author>Roy Wetherall</author>
  <version>1.0</version>
```

The main thing to note in this code snippet is the definition of the model name, `rma:recordsmangement`, called out as the `name` attribute in the `<model>` tag.

The Records Model imports

The Records Management Content Model doesn't start from scratch. The elements of this model are built using elements from content models that have already been defined:

```
<!-- Imports are required to allow references to definitions in other
  models -->
<imports>
  <!-- Import Alfresco Dictionary Model Definitions -->
  <import uri="http://www.alfresco.org/model/dictionary/1.0"
    prefix="d"/>
  <!-- Import Alfresco Content Domain Model Definitions -->
  <import uri="http://www.alfresco.org/model/content/1.0"
    prefix="cm"/>
  <!-- Import Alfresco System Model Definitions -->
  <import uri="http://www.alfresco.org/model/system/1.0"
    prefix="sys" />
</imports>
```

This code imports existing foundation content models and defines the model prefixes for creating short references to the elements of the imported models. The Dictionary, Content Domain, and System models are imported, and those models are associated with the prefixes d:, cm:, and sys:, respectively. Most new content models, as best practice, start by importing these three foundation content models, although, in this case, the System model is never directly referenced in the new model definition.

The Records Model namespace

Next, the name of the namespace to associate with the new Records Model is defined. The short-name prefix, rma:, for the namespace is also defined:

```
<!-- Records Management Namespace -->
<namespaces>
  <namespace
    uri="http://www.alfresco.org/model/recordsmanagement/1.0"
    prefix="rma"/>
</namespaces>
```

Some of the things that we don't find here are as interesting as the things that we do find. For example, there is a definition of a Records Management container, something that is essentially a folder with some additional aspects associated with it, but we don't see anything specific for Record Series or Record Categories. Those will be defined later in the dod content model.

The DoD 5015 Records Management Content Model

We've just looked at the elements defined in the rma records content model. The companion content model that Alfresco publishes alongside rma is the DoD 5015.2 Content Model or dod. The dod model builds on the elements defined in rma and while the naming conventions within the rma model are fairly generic, the names used within the dod model follow the terminology of DoD-style Records Management as outlined in the DoD 5015.2 specification. We can see the elements defined by the dod model and the relationships between them in the following UML diagram:

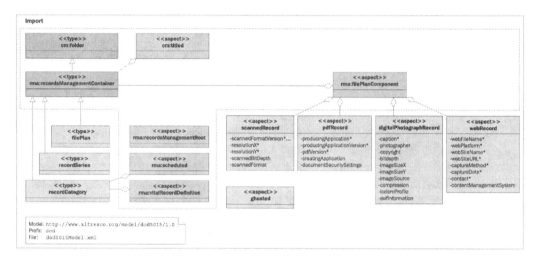

Extending the Alfresco Content Model

We've just toured the Alfresco Records Management Content Model. There's a lot there. Most likely you're impressed with what you've seen, but you are also probably thinking that there are some things in the model that you'd like to change, or you might have some ideas about properties that you think should be added to the model.

Changing part of the standard Alfresco Content Model (like the built-in model for Records Management) can be done, but should not be done lightly, especially if you are making changes to an Alfresco production system where Records Management is already in use.

Unlike other parts of Alfresco, there isn't a mechanism for overriding standard definitions of core content model files with your own files. For example, if you create an override file by modifying one of the files of the standard content model and then place your new file in the `shared\alfresco\extension` area, the new file will not be picked up. To change the definitions found in the standard content model files, you will need to directly make your changes to the core files.

> One best practice with the Alfresco Content Model is that rather than modifying the underlying types, whenever possible, you should create types that extend from the core model.
>
> In the case of Records Management there is some type-dependent behavior wiring that happens in the Records Management application that makes that difficult to do.
>
> If you do need to add new properties, consider creating new aspects that can hold those properties.

Making changes to core files means that you will need to remember that those files must be modified every time there is an upgrade of your Alfresco system, and because of that, you also need to be careful about what changes you make in those files.

To be on the safe side, it is usually best to make only additions and minor changes to standard models, like adding new properties or new associations. Removing properties from the model on a system that has stored content may result in data corruption, and if you remove a property that the application code references, you will probably get errors and, most likely, the application will probably not function correctly. Similar types of problems might occur if you try to change the names of any of the properties.

Having said that though, if you have not yet deployed Records Management, it's a good idea to review the Records Management model to make sure that you find that the model is consistent with how you plan to manage your records. You need to make sure that it is collecting the information that you need. If the model's not right, despite the warnings above, the model probably needs to be changed. Waiting to make changes to the model at some later point after you have already started to store content will likely only lead to future headaches.

But again, changes should not be made without first giving a lot of careful thought to all available options. Don't forget the power available by using aspects too. Aspects can be applied on top of the base model and can help to extend it while avoiding direct changes to it.

Also keep in mind that the Records Management Content Model relates only to the structure of the File Plan and the lifecycle control of records. Metadata associated with your document types are under your complete control and your documents don't become records until they are appropriately filed in the File Plan and declared as records.

At this point, you may see no need for making any changes to the Records Management model. That might change after we go further in our discussion and get more insight into how the Records Management system works. Later on, once we've defined the File Plan and have identified the types of documents that we want to manage, it might be a good idea to circle back and review the Records Management model one more time.

Summary

In this chapter, we covered the following topics:

- The elements of the Alfresco Content Model

- How to create and install a new content model

- How to configure elements of the Share UI to be able to render metadata for a content node

- What the structure of the internal Alfresco Records Management Content Model looks like

At the end of this chapter, we also discussed the general philosophy about when to alter elements of the standard Alfresco Content Model.

There was a lot of information covered in this chapter. But with this information, we are now ready to continue in the design of our Records Management system. In the next chapter, we will look at how to organize our documents and records within the folder hierarchy known as the record File Plan.

5
Creating the File Plan

This chapter explains how the Records Management File Plan is constructed within Alfresco. In the last chapter, we then saw how documents can be modeled as document types within the Alfresco Content Model and can be configured to store almost any kind of file content and metadata. This chapter focuses on the building of a classification and organizational structure called the File Plan. It is within the File Plan where we will store records.

In this chapter, we will describe:

- The benefits of having a well-designed File Plan
- How to design the best structure for the File Plan to meet the needs of your organization
- How to create a File Plan within the Alfresco Share Records Management site

Alfresco Records Management is built based on the specification of the DoD 5015.2 File Plan. We will see how to create record Series, Categories, and Folders that are compliant with that specification.

At the end of this chapter, in a "How does it work?" section, we will discuss from a developer perspective some of the internals of how the **File Plan** page within the Share Records Management site was built. We will see how the **File Plan** page gets bound to the Records Management site, how the Spring-Surf framework is used to lay out the page, and how the YUI client-side user interface library is used to both render the page and to interact with the repository.

The File Plan—a definition

The File Plan, also sometimes known as the "Records Classification Scheme", is the basic structure in Records Management that classifies and groups records together with similar characteristics. International standard ISO 15489 describes the File Plan as an essential component of any Records Management program. Many people consider the File Plan to be the crux of their entire Records Management program. The File Plan classification system is similar to that of the folder or directory structure in a filesystem. It is hierarchical, with the upper-most levels of the hierarchy representing very broad categories and with the lower levels becoming increasingly more specific. The File Plan structure provides a consistent scheme for classifying records that can be applied to any type of record media or format.

Strictly speaking, there is more to the File Plan than just the folder structure and the classification. The File Plan provides a comprehensive outline that also includes instructions for file retention and disposition. Transfer, retention, and disposition are File Plan topics of discussion that we will discuss in the next chapter.

Components of the File Plan

The DoD 5015.2 specification defines three tiers for the File Plan: **Series**, **Category**, and **Folder**. Each of these elements is a container that functions in a way similar to a standard filesystem folder, but that has some special restrictions and characteristics.

It's tempting to refer to all types of containers in the File Plan as simply the "folders" for the File Plan, but doing so can lead to ambiguity since containers at the third-level tier are also called Folders.

Series are stored in the first tier or root-level of the File Plan. These kinds of containers are restricted to hold only Category containers. No Folder containers, records, or standard documents can be filed into a Series.

Categories are stored in the second tier of the File Plan hierarchy under Series. Categories have a restriction similar to that of a Series in that only Folder containers can be filed into them. Similar to Series, no records or documents can be filed into them. A unique capability of Categories is that each one is associated with a disposition schedule and retention rules that are inherited by all the Folders and records that are filed under them.

Folders are stored in the third tier of the File Plan under Categories. No other container, whether it is Series, Category, or Folder, can be stored under a Folder. Only **records** and non-declared **records** can be stored within a Folder.

The DoD 5015.2 specification describes only these three types of containers. The specification is ambiguous about whether a Folder can contain another Folder. The Alfresco implementation does not allow this. Many in the Records Management community agree with this approach and advocate the use of shallow File Plan hierarchies. Using three levels of containers is fairly standard. Allowing more nested levels to exist under a Category than just Folders could complicate the management of lifecycle rules:

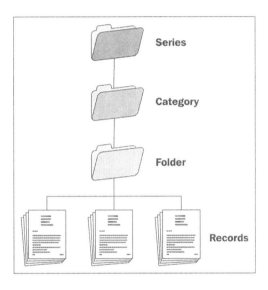

 The File Plan is a Records Management term that originated with the management of paper and physical records. 'File' refers to paper documents and 'Plan' refers to the strategy for classifying records. Traditionally, with the management of paper records, documents or files are stored as records in physical folders, that in turn are stored in drawers, and the drawers in turn are part of a larger filing cabinet. In this way, the three tiers of containers used for storing paper records based on a File Plan are: filing cabinet, drawer, and folder.

Benefits of the File Plan

Working on creating a File Plan that is a good match for the types of records that you will be managing is well worth your time. The benefits of creating a File Plan include:

- Allows staff members to consistently recall File Plan classifications when filing and retrieving records

- Enables compliance with statutory and regulatory requirements

- Provides an audit trail for activities that have occurred in the organization

- Allows records to be disposed of when they are no longer needed

Looking at the Alfresco example File Plan

It is useful to look at the structure of the sample File Plan included with the Alfresco Records Management module. This plan is a standard example and actually corresponds to an example that comes along with the DoD 5015.2 specification.

We can install the sample File Plan by going to the Records Management console on the administrator's Share top-level dashboard page. Once there, we can see the option for installing the sample Records Management data. Let's click on that link to start the install process. The install adds the sample File Plan to all other records or containers that you may have already created yourself within the File Plan:

Records Management
Configuration and Setup for Records Management site.
Records Management Site
Load Test Data
Management Console

Clicking on the **Load Test Data** label runs an import of an ACP file into the Alfresco repository. The ACP file with the sample File Plan is located here: `tomcat\webapps\alfresco\WEB-INF\classes\alfresco\module\org_alfresco_module_dod5015\bootstrap\DODExampleFilePlan.acp`.

After installing the test data set, we can navigate over to the Records Management site and into the **File Plan** page. We can see that the test plan consists of four Series, each containing a number of categories:

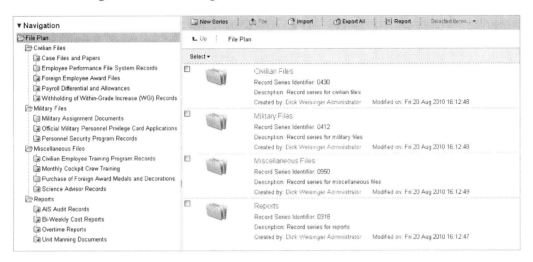

At this point, it is useful to gain some familiarity with how the File Plan works within Alfresco by navigating through the File Plan structure via both the navigation tree in the left panel and the main display area on the right.

When we are through looking at this sample File Plan and we no longer need it, it is easy to remove it by navigating back to the top of the Plan, selecting all four of the Series, and then choosing **Delete** from the **Selected Items...** menu.

Another sample File Plan is available as a data file that accompanies this book. Unlike the example that ships with Alfresco that is based on the DoD-5015.2, the structure of this example has much greater detail than the one from the DoD, and it resembles more closely the File Plan of a typical organization.

There are two files that make up the sample File Plan that can be downloaded from Packt Publishing. The file FilePlan.xlsx is an Excel spreadsheet and describes the File Plan. The file SampleFilePlan. acp is a file in the ACP format that can be imported directly into Alfresco using the **Import** button on the **File Plan** page of the Records Management site.

A second ACP file, also named SampleFilePlan.acp, is available as a downloadable file for *Chapter 6*. That version of the File Plan also includes disposition schedules, as discussed in *Chapter 6*.

Best practice for creating the File Plan

File Plan designs are usually created using one of two types of approaches, namely, either the plan is architected to parallel the company's organizational chart or else the structure calls out the functions and activities of the organization.

 Organizations may already have File Plans being used for managing non-electronic records. If so, that's good, but before deciding to adopt the same plan, it should be reviewed to see if it adequately represents all the record types that we plan to organize electronically.

File Plans based on organizational hierarchy

Designing the File Plan to parallel your company's organizational hierarchy has the advantage of clearly identifying records with a business unit. This approach makes it easy for individuals within the organization to know where to go within the File Plan to file their records. While making the filing process easy is especially important in organizations where record filing is decentralized, modeling the File Plan on the organizational structure does have some problems and *is generally not recommended*.

For example, organizations tend to change frequently, and those changes will then need to be updated in the File Plan. It may be necessary to have to even re-file or move records into the folders of the new organization. If corresponding updates aren't made to the plan after the organizational change, then the structure of the File Plan will be out of date. This can become particularly exasperating to anyone not familiar with the history of the organization. Ideally, the basic File Plan structure should change very infrequently. That's the first problem with this approach.

Another problem with this approach is that it typically results in having records cluster together that have different retention and disposition rules. It then becomes difficult to apply record lifecycle instructions to many records at one time. Over the long term, this approach can become very tedious.

 One common mistake made when designing a File Plan is to create one Folder for each employee. The employee then uses this folder to file their e-mail and other electronic records. This type of filing structure, while seemingly convenient, defeats the purpose of even having File Plan. It makes the process of finding records difficult, and the task of assigning lifecycle instructions to records almost impossible.

File Plans based on business processes and activities

An alternative approach for modeling the File Plan is to structure the plan based on the processes, activities, and transactions that occur in the business. Designing the File Plan in this way has a number of advantages, chief of which is the fact that doing so will usually make it possible for similar types of records to cluster together.

Similar types of records will usually also share the same lifecycle instructions. For example, records of the same type typically will also have similar rules for access and security, rules for prioritizing storage, and rules for retention and disposition. While there may be some exceptions, grouping similar records in this way simplifies the overall records program administration.

Another technique for creating File Plans that can lead to trouble is to name elements of the File Plan after the lengths of time for retention periods. For example, naming folders "Two Year Retention", "Five Year Retention", and "Fifteen Year Retention" will cause problems. With this kind of structure, anyone outside of the Records Management office will have a hard time knowing where to file records or where to start looking for specific kinds of records. It can also complicate the task of freezing records as part of a legal hold.

Best practice for File Plan design

We've just seen that one advantage of using a File Plan laid out to mirror the organization chart for the business is that it makes it easier on infrequent users of the records system to immediately know where they should go to file their records. This is especially useful when filing responsibilities are decentralized to many users across various business groups. The administration of the records program becomes easier when records are grouped together by business activity and function.

A best practice frequently used when designing the File Plan is to blend the two approaches.

For example, at the root level of the File Plan, Series can be created that correspond to high-level business functions within the organization. While not always the case, the File Plan root-level Series can usually be mapped to points that lie near the top of the organizational structure. Series in an organization typically have names like Administration, Human Resources, Legal, and Finance.

At the second tier of the File Plan, the Category level names are usually best selected by choosing the names of processes that are part of the business function that the Series represents. For example, under the Series called Finance, there might be Categories that include things such as Audits, Billings, Expense Reports, and Supplier Invoices.

At the third tier of the File Plan, Folders are created that typically specify an entity and/or time period that corresponds to the records that are to be filed. Folders under the Category of Supplier Invoices, for example, could be named based on the Supplier Name, like "ADD Solutions", "Zimmer Electronics", and so forth. Folders under the Category of Expense Reports could be created based on the names of employees, like "Jones, Harold".

Choosing the right naming convention for Folders may have a lot to do with how we expect the records to cluster. Consider the Billings Category in the Finance Series. Folders under Billings can be named after the entities that are billed, such as a name of a company. But if there are many entities that will be billed, and the billings to those entities are infrequent or one-time, then it may make sense to group them by billing period rather than by entity names. In that case, Folders would be named by date, such as "2011-03".

To summarize, a best practice approach for building a File Plan structure is to create three tiers as follows:

- Business Function (Series)
- Process Name (Category)
- Transaction (Folder)

This approach for creating the structure of the File Plan is often readily understood by infrequent Records Management users as to where they should look when they need to file or retrieve records. This structure also tends to group records with similar lifecycle instructions together.

Other types of rules, such as those around security and storage media, also need to be applied to records. The groupings of records defined using this File Plan structure typically work well for that too, but if the requirements get too granular, it may be necessary to break up folders into multiple additional folders.

Creating the File Plan

Once the design for the File Plan is done, we are then ready to start implementing the plan within Alfresco.

Adding containers to the File Plan

Designing a good File Plan is really the hard part. Building out the structure within the Alfresco File Plan area is straightforward, but may take a bit of time if our plan has many folders. Let's walk through the steps on how to do that now.

Creating a Series

From the root level of the **File Plan**, we are able to create new **Series**. After navigating to the root, we will see the option for adding a **New Series** across the toolbar at the top left. Note that there are no other options available here for creating other types of containers like Categories or Folders, nor is there an option to **File** any records here. This is to be expected because the rules of the DoD 5015.2 File Plan structure do not allow anything other than a **Series** to be created at the root of the File Plan:

Note that while the File Plan in the Share Records Management site is quite good at restricting users from creating container types or records where they are not allowed, it is possible to bypass this guidance. For example, Share site folders and files, including those of the Records Management site can be browsed from the Repository option of Share or by using the Alfresco JSF Explorer client. Adding, deleting, or changing anything in the File Plan by using these tools bypasses the Records Management interface and has the possibility of corrupting the data that is stored in the File Plan.

After clicking on the **New Series** button, we see a pop-up form that collects information about the **Name** and **Description** of the Series that we will create. Note that an asterisk marks fields that are mandatory. In this case, only the **Name** field is mandatory:

After filling out the fields on this form, click on **Submit**, and the new Series container will then appear at the root level of the File Plan. We can then navigate into the new Series by clicking on it.

Creating a Category

From within the Marketing Series we just created, we are now ready to create a new **Category**. Again, in the File Plan toolbar at the top of the page, we can see that we now have the possibility of creating a **New Category**. We can also see in the breadcrumb area on the second line of the toolbar, our current position within the **File Plan**:

In a similar way to the Series creation, we can create the new **Category** by clicking on the **New Category** button. We then see the following pop-up form:

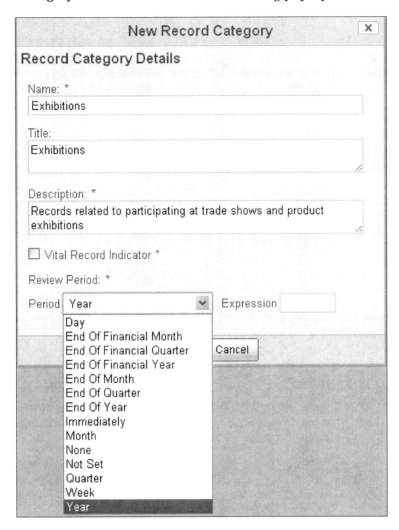

The **Category** creation form is similar to the form used for the creation of a Series. The **Name**, **Title**, and **Description** are collected. In this case, both the **Name** and the **Description** are mandatory. At the bottom of the form are fields for specifying if this Category will be used to hold **vital records** and whether or not there is to be a **Review Period** for the records stored under this Category.

Vital records are records that contain information that can help an organization reconstruct and continue operations after the event of a disaster. Typically about 3-5 percent of records in an organization are categorized as vital.

All vital records must be periodically reviewed to make sure that they are current and still relevant. If the vital indicator is selected on the creation form, then it will also be necessary to choose the **Review Period** that we would like to set for records under this Category. It is also possible to set up a review period for records that are not vital. In that case, entering a review period is optional.

There are two widgets on this form used to specify the frequency for the review. The **Review Period** drop-down lets us select a unit for determining the period. The period together with the field labeled **Expression** lets us specify a number of period units. The default value for the number of periods is 1. For example, selecting "End of Year" and 2, would mean that the Review period for records under this Category would be at the end of every two years after the document was first declared a record.

The disposition schedule is assigned to a Category. The disposition schedule normally must be defined for the Category prior to creating any Folders or records underneath it. The next chapter will discuss in more detail the steps necessary for setting up the disposition schedule and associating the schedule with the Category.

Creating a Folder

Next, after navigating into the newly created Category, we can see, on the toolbar, that we now have an option to create a new **Folder**. Click on the **New Folder** link in the upper-left of the toolbar:

On the pop-up form, information to describe the name of the new Folder is specified. The **Name** of the Folder is the only mandatory field that needs to be completed on this form:

After submitting the form, the new Folder is created and is then shown within the Category.

File Plan container metadata

Like any content within Alfresco, the File Plan containers, that is, the Series, Categories, and Folders are associated with metadata. We saw when looking at the Records Management Content Model that the content types for these containers correspond to `dod:recordSeries`, `dod:recordCategory`, and `rma:recordFolder`. All of these content types inherit from the base content type of `cm:folder` and they also contain metadata specific to their function within the File Plan.

Recall that we discussed metadata and document and record properties in the context of the Content Model in the last chapter. Metadata is structured data that describes other data. The metadata for a record tracks information about its content, context, and lifecycle. Metadata is used to help locate and manage records, and also to better understand the content of records. Metadata can include information like the record name, description, author, access permissions, and information about when the record should be destroyed or transferred.

The configuration of the Content Model controls which metadata is stored with each of the containers and which pieces of data are mandatory. As described in the chapter on the Content Model, adding new metadata fields can be done easily, but removing any existing fields should be avoided. Removing fields can cause existing data to possibly become corrupted or for the software to fail because it expected those fields that were deleted, to exist.

From the File Plan, the metadata for any container can be navigated to by selecting the **View Details** actions for that container:

From the details page for the container, the **Metadata** corresponding to it is displayed. From this screen, the metadata can't be edited. However, users with sufficient permission to edit container metadata can do so from the **Edit Metadata** pop-up dialog:

Copy and move of File Plan containers

We need to remember that File Plan containers are similar to normal folders within Share, but are subject to a few additional rules. For example, we've mentioned that there are restrictions about where containers within the File Plan can be copied or moved.

For example, there is no option to move a Series. A Series is already positioned at the root level of the plan and is restricted from being placed under a Category or Folder. A Series can be copied, but only as a Series with a different name under the File Plan root.

Similarly, a Category can only be moved or copied to a position under a Series, and a Folder can only be moved or copied to a position under a Category. Records can only be moved or copied to positions within Folders:

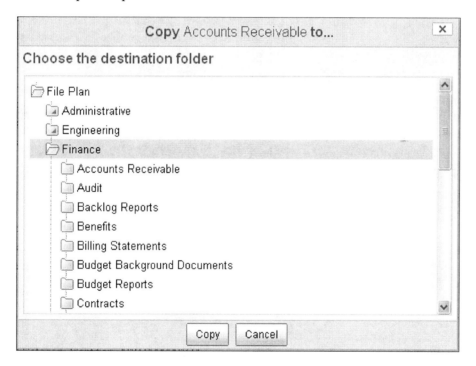

How does it work?

We have now seen how to set up and build the File Plan in Alfresco by nesting the Series, Category, and Folder containers. The File Plan page in the Records Management Share site is interesting to study in terms of understanding how it is constructed. It provides an excellent example for how pages can be built using the Spring-Surf web development framework.

How the File Plan page is set by the preset

As a first step, let's see how the **File Plan** page gets associated with the Records Management site. The **File Plan** page is automatically configured as part of the Records Management site when it is installed. But the **File Plan** page is a special one that is not available to be added to the configuration of standard Share sites.

We saw earlier how the Share Records Management site dashboard was configured with settings in the presets.xml file found in the tomcat\webapps\share\WEB-INF\classes\alfresco\site-data\presets directory. The presets file also defines the default configuration pages for the Records Management site.

The presets.xml configuration file defines a <preset> tag called rm-site-dashboard that contains a single <pages> tag, that in turn defines a <page> called "site/${siteid}/dashboard". Later on, we will see how the configuration data defined here can be looked up to reference the page ID "site/rm/dashboard":

```
<page id="site/${siteid}/dashboard">
  <title>Records Management Site Dashboard</title>
  <title-id>page.rmSiteDashboard.title</title-id>
  <description>Records Management site's dashboard page</description>
  <description-id>page.rmSiteDashboard.description</description-id>
  <template-instance>dashboard-3-columns</template-instance>
  <authentication>user</authentication>
  <properties>
    <sitePages>[{"pageId":"documentlibrary"}, {"pageId":"rmsearch"}]
    </sitePages>
      <pageMetadata>
        {"documentlibrary":{"titleId":"page.rmDocumentLibrary.title",
          "descriptionId":"page.rmDocumentLibrary.description",
          "type":"dod5015"}}
      </pageMetadata>
  </properties>
</page>
```

The `<sitePages>` tag defines the two pages that are associated by default with the Records Management site: `documentlibrary` and `rmsearch`. The `rmsearch` page is unique to the Records Management site and corresponds to the **Records Search** page. The `documentlibrary` page is commonly used by other Share sites, but when used on the Records Management site, it is called the **File Plan** page. It behaves quite a bit differently than the standard **Document Library** page.

The File Plan extends from the standard Share **Document Library** pages, but the behavior is quite different because standard behavior of the `documentlibrary` page is overridden with new values that are defined in the `<pageMetadata>` tag for the `title`, `description`, and `type` properties.

The `titleId` and `descriptionId` text strings referred to in the `<pageMetadata>` tag are defined in the file `dod5015.properties` found in the `tomcat\webapps\share\WEB-INF\classes\alfresco\messages` directory:

```
page.rmDocumentLibrary.title=File Plan
page.rmDocumentLibrary.description=Records Management File Plan with Tree view
```

We see here that the normal label on the navigation bar of the **Document Library** is overridden with the string **File Plan** and that the description string is similarly overridden.

The File Plan, as extended from the Document Library

Let's look in more detail at how the `documentlibrary` page behaves within the Records Management site. To trace back the behavior of the Document Library, we'll start by looking at the `documentlibrary` page definition file `documentlibrary.xml` that is located in the `tomcat\webapps\share\WEB-INF\classes\alfresco\site-data\pages` directory:

```xml
<?xml version='1.0' encoding='UTF-8'?>
<page>
  <title>Document Library</title>
  <title-id>page.documentLibrary.title</title-id>
  <description>Document library with Tree view</description>
  <description-id>page.documentLibrary.description</description-id>
  template-instance>documentlibrary</template-instance>
  <authentication>user</authentication>
</page>
```

The `<template-instance>` for the page is similarly named `documentlibrary`. We can then look up the `template-instance` file `documentlibrary.xml` in the `tomcat\webapps\share\WEB-INF\classes\alfresco\site-data\template-instances` directory:

```
<?xml version='1.0' encoding='UTF-8'?>
<template-instance>
  <template-type>org/alfresco/documentlibrary</template-type>
  <properties>
    <pageFamily>documentlibrary</pageFamily>
    <container>documentLibrary</container>
  </properties>
</template-instance>
```

Here we finally find out that the template is defined in the `tomcat\webapps\share\WEB-INF\classes\alfresco\templates\org\alfresco` directory. When we look in that directory, there are two files of interest there named `documentlibrary.ftl` and `documentlibrary.js`.

The Document Library JavaScript controller file

The JavaScript controller file `documentlibrary.js` calculates two properties that are assigned to the **model**. One is called the `doclibType`, which is used to distinguish the type of page to render, the standard **Document Library**, or the **File Plan**. The other is the `rootNode`, that is, a string containing the root path in the Alfresco repository.

The following three functions are at the top of the file `documentlibrary.js` and we will have a look at them shortly:

```
function toRepoType(appType){}
function fromRepoType(repoType){}
function getLocationType(){}
```

The main code of the controller file is at the bottom of the file:

```
var objLocation = getLocationType(),
  doclibType = fromRepoType(objLocation.containerType),
    scopeType = objLocation.siteId !== null ? "" : "repo-";
model.doclibType = doclibType == "" ? scopeType : doclibType + "-";
var rootNode = "alfresco://company/home",
  repoConfig = config.scoped["RepositoryLibrary"]["root-node"];
if (repoConfig !== null)
```

```
{
    rootNode = repoConfig.value;
}
model.rootNode = rootNode;
```

There isn't that much code here, but let's walk through it to understand what is happening in the controller. The controller, as we recall, sets the parameters in the model that will later be available for use by the FreeMarker template when constructing the page presentation.

Getting the Location Type

First, the variable objLocation is set by calling the getLocationType() function defined near the top of the documentlibrary.js file. The results of this function distinguish whether we are dealing with the **File Plan** or with the standard **Document Library** page. Let's step into that function now:

```
function getLocationType()
{
    // Need to know what type of node the container is
    var siteId = page.url.templateArgs.site,
        containerId = template.properties.container,
        containerType = "cm:folder",
        appType = "";
    if (siteId !== null)
    {
        var p = sitedata.getPage("site/" + siteId + "/dashboard");
        if (p != null)
        {
            pageMetadata = eval('(' + p.properties.pageMetadata + ')');
            pageMetadata = pageMetadata != null ? pageMetadata : {};
            doclibMeta = pageMetadata[page.id] || {};
            if (doclibMeta.titleId != null)
            {
                // Save the overridden page title into the request context
                context.setValue("page-titleId", doclibMeta.titleId);
            }
            appType = doclibMeta.type;
        }
        var connector = remote.connect("alfresco");
        result = connector.get("/slingshot/doclib/container/" +
            siteId + "/" + containerId + "?type=" + toRepoType(appType));
        if (result.status == 200)
        {
```

```
      var data = eval('(' + result + ')');
      containerType = data.container.type;
    }
  }

  return (
  {
    siteId: siteId,
    containerType: containerType
  });
}
```

The function `getLocationType()` first retrieves the page object definition for the Records Management dashboard in the variable `p` by looking up the page associated with `"site/rm/dashboard"`. It looks this information up from the `sitedata` root-scoped object that contains the page data from the `presets.xml` file definition that we saw earlier. The `presets.xml` configuration file information is then stored into the page object.

From the page object, we can extract the parameters specific to the page that we are currently on, that is, the `documentLibrary` page. The name of the current page is stored in `page.id`. `docLibMeta` contains the override information that was specified in the `presets.xml` file `<pageMetadata>`. From it, we can retrieve, set, and override the value for the `title` and also set the variable `appType` to `dod5015`.

Getting the File Plan root node via a service call

At the end of `getLocationType()`, a remote service call is made to the Alfresco repository to determine the container type and the top root-level node reference for the document library. All top level folders in the File Plan will be children of this node. In this case, the service URL looks like:

```
http://localhost:8080/alfresco/service/slingshot/doclib/container/rm/
documentLibrary?type=dod:filePlan
```

The request returns information in the form of the following code:

```
{
  "container":
  {
    "nodeRef": "workspace://SpacesStore/98c5a184-9901-4b7c-9e16-
      91522f2ccb2a",
    "type": "dod:filePlan"
  }
}
```

We can validate the information returned by the service by looking up the reference of the node returned in the JSF Explorer client Node Browser tool. By doing that, we can see that the node returned is indeed of type `dod:filePlan`. Finally, the function `getLocationType()` returns this value as the `type` and the `siteId` "rm":

Setting doclibType in the model data

Now let's return to the controller code at the bottom of the file `documentlibrary.js`. We see that the `doclibType` prefix will be set to `dod5015-`. This prefix is later used to distinguish between the **File Plan** and **Document Library** pages when rendering the page in the FreeMarker template. Normally, the prefix is `repo-` that corresponds to the standard **Document Library** page:

```
var objLocation = getLocationType(),
   doclibType = fromRepoType(objLocation.containerType),
   scopeType = objLocation.siteId !== null ? "" : "repo-";

model.doclibType = doclibType == "" ? scopeType : doclibType + "-";
```

Setting the root node in the model data

Next, the value for the root node is set in the model. The value for the root node is initialized either in the standard `tomcat\webapps\share\WEB-INF\classes\alfresco\share-config.xml` file or in the `tomcat\shared\classes\alfresco\web-extension\share-config-custom.xml` extension override file. The root node is initialized with code similar to the following:

```
<config evaluator="string-compare" condition="RepositoryLibrary">
...
   <!-- Root nodeRef for top-level folder. -->
   <root-node>alfresco://company/home</root-node>
...
</config>
```

The JavaScript controller code looks like the following snippet of code. The configuration for the `root-node` in the `RepositoryLibrary` is returned via the scoped `config` variable. The value defaults to `alfresco://company/home`. This is the path in the Alfresco repository under which content will be stored:

```
// Repository Library root node
var rootNode = "alfresco://company/home",
  repoConfig = config.scoped["RepositoryLibrary"]["root-node"];
if (repoConfig !== null)
{
  rootNode = repoConfig.value;
}

model.rootNode = rootNode;
```

Reading XML configuration data

We have just seen how we can access Share configuration file information that is defined in JavaScript XML files from server-side JavaScript. The XML configuration information stored in any of the following files is available for access from both the JavaScript controller and FreeMarker template files:

- `tomcat\shared\classes\alfresco\web-extension\share-config-custom.xml`

- `tomcat\webapps\share\WEB-INF\classes\alfresco\share-config.xml`

- `tomcat\shared\classes\alfresco\web-extension\webscript-framework-config-custom.xml`

`<config>` tags in these files are called "**scoped configs**" if the element contains an evaluator attribute (something like `<config evaluator="string-compare" condition="DocumentLibrary">`). In the case where there is no `evaluator`, the tag is referred to as a "**global config**".

For example, the following section of the `share-config-custom.xml` file shows the configuration for a global config:

```
<config replace="true">
  <flags>
   <client-debug>true</client-debug>
   <client-debug-autologging>false</client-debug-autologging>
  </flags>
</config>
```

The global config value for the flag `client-debug` can then be accessed in JavaScript in the following way:

```
config.global.flags.getChildren("client-debug").get(0).value
```

 Global and scoped config information is also accessible from FreeMarker templates using a similar syntax. There is a more detailed explanation on the Alfresco wiki: `http://wiki.alfresco.com/wiki/Web_Scripts`

The information from scoped configs can be accessed in a similar way. Consider the following code from the `share-config-custom.xml` file:

```
<config evaluator="string-compare" condition="DocumentLibrary"
  replace="true">
  <aspects>
    <!-- Aspects that a user can see -->
    <visible>
      <aspect name="cm:generalclassifiable" />
      <aspect name="cm:complianceable" />
      <aspect name="cm:dublincore" />
      <aspect name="cm:effectivity" />
      <aspect name="cm:summarizable" />
      <aspect name="cm:versionable" />
      <aspect name="cm:templatable" />
      <aspect name="cm:emailed" />
      <aspect name="emailserver:aliasable" />
      <aspect name="cm:taggable" />
      <aspect name="app:inlineeditable" />
    </visible>
  </aspects>
  <types>
    <type name="cm:content"></type>
    <type name="cm:folder"></type>
  </types>
</config>
```

The following JavaScript code will count and return the number of `<aspect>` tags as 11:

```
config.scoped["DocumentLibrary"]["aspects"].childrenMap["visible"].
  get(0).childrenMap["aspect"].size()
```

Values for the names of the aspects can be found as shown next. This example returns the string value for the `name` attribute of the first `aspect` in the list as `cm:generalclassifiable`:

```
config.scoped["DocumentLibrary"]["aspects"].childrenMap["visible"].
  get(0).childrenMap["aspect"].get(0).attributes["name"].toString()
```

Inner-element data can be returned by using `value`, as shown in the next example that uses the `SitePages` list defined in the `share-config.xml` file:

```xml
<config evaluator="string-compare" condition="SitePages">
  <pages>
    <page id="calendar">calendar</page>
    <page id="wiki-page">wiki-page?title=Main_Page</page>
    <page id="documentlibrary">documentlibrary</page>
    <page id="discussions-topiclist">discussions-topiclist</page>
    <page id="blog-postlist">blog-postlist</page>
    <page id="links">links</page>
    <page id="data-lists">data-lists</page>
  </pages>
</config>
```

The following JavaScript will return the inner-element value of `calendar` for the first `<page>` tag:

```
config.scoped["SitePages"]["pages"].childrenMap["page"].get(0).value
```

The value of `calendar` for the `id` attribute of the first `<page>` tag is returned with the following code:

```
config.scoped["SitePages"]["pages"].childrenMap["page"].get(0).
  attributes["id"].toString()
```

 An alternative and perhaps less complex way to process and traverse the XML structure of the global and scoped config information is to use **E4X**, which is a JavaScript XML API. More information can be found about E4X at `https://developer.mozilla.org/En/E4X/Processing_XML_with_E4X`.

The Document Library FreeMarker presentation

We continue now to see how the **File Plan** page of the Records Management site in Share is rendered. We have seen above that the JavaScript controller file `documentlibrary.js` populates values of the `model`. The values in the `model` are then passed to the FreeMarker template file `documentlibrary.ftl` that controls the layout and ultimate display of the **File Plan** page.

FreeMarker page layout for the File Plan

Code from the FreeMarker layout file `documentlibrary.ftl` is shown below. This file defines a basic skeleton description of the overall structure and layout of the page. The design is such that components are plugged into the page layout with the real work for rendering of the page being deferred to each of the individual components that are referenced on it.

What is important to note here is the `<@region>` tags in the code. Each of these tags maps to a template instance file that in turn corresponds to a Surf component that will ultimately be displayed in that position on the page:

```
<@templateBody>
  <div id="alf-hd">
    <@region id="header" scope="global" protected=true />
    <@region id="title" scope="template" protected=true />
    <@region id="navigation" scope="template" protected=true />
  </div>
  <div id="bd">
    <@region id=doclibType + "actions-common" scope="template"
      protected=true />
    <div class="yui-t1">
      <div id="yui-main">
        <div class="yui-b" id="divDocLibraryDocs">
          <@region id=doclibType + "toolbar" scope="template"
            protected=true />
          <@region id=doclibType + "documentlist" scope="template"
            protected=true />
        </div>
      </div>
      <div class="yui-b" id="divDocLibraryFilters">
        <@region id=doclibType + "filter" scope="template"
          protected=true />
        <@region id=doclibType + "tree" scope="template"
          protected=true />
```

```
        <@region id=doclibType + "tags" scope="template"
          protected=true />
        <@region id=doclibType + "fileplan" scope="template"
          protected=true />
        <@region id=doclibType + "savedsearch" scope="template"
          protected=true />
      </div>
    </div>
    <@region id=doclibType + "html-upload" scope="template"
      protected=true />
    <@region id=doclibType + "flash-upload" scope="template"
      protected=true />
    <@region id=doclibType + "file-upload" scope="template"
      protected=true />
  </div>
</@>

<@templateFooter>
  <div id="alf-ft">
    <@region id="footer" scope="global" protected=true />
  </div>
</@>
```

Alfresco page components

From the region id and the scope for the `<@region>` tag of an Alfresco page template, the name for the corresponding component descriptor filename can be constructed.

The naming convention for a component descriptor filename is:
`<scope>.<regionid>.<page>.xml`.
`<scope>` corresponds to `global`, `template`, or `page`. When the `<scope>` is global, the `<page>` component of the file name is dropped.

Component descriptor files can be found in the `tomcat\webapps\share\WEB-INF\classes\alfresco\site-data\components` directory.

The XML of each component descriptor file contains a `<url>` tag that uniquely identifies the webscript files needed to render the component. There's a sure-fire way to find the exact location of the webscript files that we describe below, but most of the components that we will be looking at can be found under the directory `tomcat\webapps\share\WEB-INF\classes\alfresco\site-webscripts\org\alfresco\components`. The relative path under this directory often matches the path of the `<url>` in the component descriptor. An exact match is made when the `<url>` value for the component descriptor matches the `<url>` value in the webscript file.

For example, consider the component descriptor file `global.header.xml`. We see that the `<url>` in this file is defined to be `/components/header`. The contents of that file are as follows:

```
<?xml version='1.0' encoding='UTF-8'?>
<component>
  <scope>global</scope>
  <region-id>header</region-id>
  <source-id>global</source-id>
  <url>/components/header</url>
</component>
```

The URL also gives us a good clue as to where to find the corresponding webscript files for the component. If we look in the directory `tomcat\webapps\share\WEB-INF\classes\alfresco\site-webscripts\org\alfresco\components\header`, we can find the file `header.get.desc.xml`. That file contains the matching webscript `<url>` tag value of `/components/header` that we are looking for:

```
<webscript>
  <shortname>Global Header Component</shortname>
  <description>Header component used across the whole
    application</description>
  <url>/components/header</url>
</webscript>
```

In that same webscripts directory, we find the following other files needed for rendering the header component:

Webscript component file	Description
`header.get.desc.xml`	The descriptor file for the component.
`header.get.head.ftl`	Markup to support the rendering of the component that will be included in the page `<head>` tag, such as the import of a JavaScript file or the link to a CSS page.
`header.get.html.ftl`	The actual FreeMarker markup for the component.
`header.get.js`	The JavaScript controller file to calculate information to be displayed in the FreeMarker template.
`header.get.properties`	The properties file with the definition of text for labels.

The surest way to identify the location of a component webscript is to use the webscripts browser page in Share. The URL for that page is `http://localhost:8080/share/service/index`. To access this page, we will need to have Share administrator privileges. From this page, we can click on the **Browse by Web Script URI** link, and from there, navigate to find where the webscript files are actually stored:

 Web Scripts Home

Spring WebScripts - v1.0.0 (Milestone 3 357) schema 1,000

273 Web Scripts

Online documentation.

Index
Browse 'admin-console' Web Scripts
Browse 'dashlet' Web Scripts
Browse 'rm-console' Web Scripts
Browse 'site-dashlet' Web Scripts
Browse 'user-dashlet' Web Scripts

Browse all Web Scripts
Browse by Web Script URI
Browse by Web Script Package
Browse by Web Script Lifecycle

Maintenance
Alfresco Javascript Debugger
Web Script Installer

[Refresh Web Scripts]

Components on the File Plan page

Now that we know how to locate the components and rendering webscripts for a page, we can map the components identified by the `<@region>` tag on the page template to the components that will then be rendered at those page positions.

The file `documentlibrary.ftl` is written to support both the standard Share site **Document Library** and the Records Management site **File Plan** pages. We've seen above that the JavaScript controller has calculated and populated a value for the `doclibType` variable in the model.

The string value for `doclibType` will be "repo-" when `documentlibrary.ftl` is used to render the **Document Library** page, but it will have the string value of "dod5015-" when the **File Plan** page is being rendered. The `doclibType` string is used to build the name for many of the `<@region>` tag ids with logic like the following:

```
id=doclibType + "toolbar"
```

In the **File Plan** case, for example, this would resolve to the ID of "dod5015-toolbar". In the Document Library case, this simply resolves to "toolbar". In this way, it is possible to specify which component to use, based on the page rendering type.

The next table shows the mapping from the `<@region>` tags for the **File Plan** page, to their component descriptor files, and then to the `url` that identifies the components:

Region id and scope	Component descriptor file	URL
id="header" scope="global"	global.header.xml	/components/header
id="title" scope="template"	template.title. documentlibrary.xml	/components/title/ collaboration-title
id="navigation" scope="template"	template.navigation. documentlibrary.xml	/components/navigation/ collaboration- navigation
id="dod5015- actions-common" scope="template"	template.dod5015- actions-common. documentlibrary.xml	/components/ documentlibrary/ dod5015/actions-common
id="dod5015- toolbar" scope="template"	template. dod5015-toolbar. documentlibrary.xml	/components/ documentlibrary/ dod5015/toolbar
id="dod5015- documentlist" scope="template"	template.dod5015- documentlist. documentlibrary.xml	/components/ documentlibrary/ dod5015/documentlist
id="dod5015- filter" scope="template"	N/A Does not exist.	N/A Does not exist.
id="dod5015-tree" scope="template"	template.dod5015-tree. documentlibrary.xml	/components/ documentlibrary/ dod5015/tree
id="dod5015-tags" scope="template"	N/A Does not exist.	N/A Does not exist.
id="dod5015- fileplan" scope="template"	template. dod5015-fileplan. documentlibrary.xml	/components/ documentlibrary/ dod5015/fileplan

Region id and scope	Component descriptor file	URL

`id="dod5015-`
`savedsearch"`
`scope="template"`
	`template.dod5015-`
	`savedsearch.`
	`documentlibrary.xml`
		`/components/`
		`documentlibrary/`
		`dod5015/savedsearch`

`id="dod5015-`
`html-upload"`
`scope="template"`
	`template.dod5015-`
	`html-upload.`
	`documentlibrary.xml`
		`/components/upload/`
		`dod5015/html-upload`

`id="dod5015-`
`flash-upload"`
`scope="template"`
	`template.dod5015-`
	`flash-upload.`
	`documentlibrary.xml`
		`/components/upload/`
		`dod5015/flash-upload`

`id="dod5015-`
`file-upload"`
`scope="template"`
	`template.dod5015-`
	`file-upload.`
	`documentlibrary.xml`
		`/components/upload/`
		`dod5015/file-upload`

`id="footer"` `scope="global"`	`global.footer.xml`	`/components/footer`

The next figure shows visually where the components for the regions will display on the File Plan page. Some of the regions that are defined are for pop-up dialogs, such as the dialog for uploading a file to the repository:

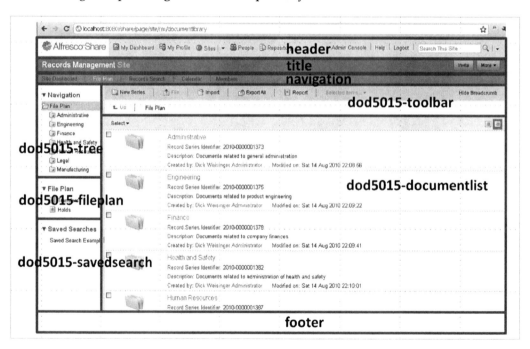

The File Plan Document List

Of the components and regions on the File Plan page, of particular interest is the one called dod5015-documentlist. This component fills the largest panel of the screen and is the one that typically receives the main attention from the user of the page.

As we just saw, the webscript that renders this component consists of files with names of the form dod5015-documentlist.get.*. Let's take a look at some of these files to see how the Document List works.

The Document List controller file

The JavaScript controller file for the Document List webscript is dod5015-documentlist.get.js. The purpose of the controller file is to populate the model for the presentation. The controller file for the Document List is fairly straightforward. It calculates and returns the array of user preferences and an array of available actions.

User preferences

The JavaScript code in the controller file dod5015-documentlist.get.js first tries to calculate user preferences. The part of the code that does that is as follows:

```
const PREFERENCES_ROOT = "org.alfresco.share.documentList";

var result = remote.call("/api/people/" +
  stringUtils.urlEncode(user.name) + "/preferences?pf=" +
  PREFERENCES_ROOT);
if (result.status == 200 && result != "{}")
{
  var prefs = eval('(' + result + ')');
  try
  {
    // Populate the preferences object literal for easy look-up
      later
    preferences = eval('(prefs.' + PREFERENCES_ROOT + ')');
    if (typeof preferences != "object")
    {
      preferences = {};
    }
  }
  catch (e)
  {
  }
}
```

A remote call is made here to the Alfresco repository API, specifically for retrieving information about people. The API call will hit the Alfresco Preferences Service. When logged in as user admin, the service address called resolves to the following:

```
remote.call ("/api/people/admin/preferences?pf=org.alfresco.share.
documentList");
```

This will call the following URL:

```
http://localhost:8080/alfresco/service/api/people/admin/
preferences?pf=org.alfresco.share.documentList
```

The result of making this call is a response that looks like this:

```
{"org":{"alfresco":{"share":{"documentList":{"showFolders":true}}}}}
```

The only preference being stored in the result of this example for user admin is the flag showFolders with the value of true.

 More information about the **REST Alfresco API** services can be found on the Alfresco wiki at http://wiki.alfresco.com/wiki/3.0_REST_API#Preferences_Service.

The call to the **Preference Service** via the API retrieves information that has been cached about the user in the Alfresco repository. Preference information is stored in the cm:preferenceValues attribute associated with the cm:preferences aspect that is applied to a node of type cm:person.

Using the Node Browser administration tool, we can find exactly where in the repository the preference information is stored. In this case, it is stored as an attribute for a node in the repository store called workspace://SpacesStore with a path of /sys:system/sys:people/cm:admin.

The value assigned to cm:preferenceValues refers to content stored on disk that contains the preference information:

{http://www.alfresco.org/model/content/1.0}preferenceValues	contentUrl=store://2010/8/11/15/25/fce3c447-43f4-4998-aeb5-58c6502af4ae.bin|mimetype=text/plain|size=52|encoding=utf-8|locale=en_US_

Just out of curiosity, we can find and then look and see the text contents of that file:

```
{"org.alfresco.share.documentList.showFolders":true}
```

Actions

The other calculation made in the JavaScript controller file dod5015-documentlist.
get.js is to find the available actions for the Document List:

```
var prefActionSet, order, actionSet, actionSetId, actionId,
  defaultOrder;
var myConfig = new XML(config.script),
    prefActions = preferences.actions || {};

for each (var xmlActionSet in myConfig..actionSet)
{
  actionSet = [];
  actionSetId = xmlActionSet.@id.toString();
  prefActionSet = prefActions[actionSetId] || {};
  defaultOrder = 100;

  for each (var xmlAction in xmlActionSet..action)
  {
    defaultOrder++;
    actionId = xmlAction.@id.toString();

    actionSet.push(
    {
      order: prefActionSet[actionId] || defaultOrder,
      id: actionId,
      type: xmlAction.@type.toString(),
      permission: xmlAction.@permission.toString(),
      href: xmlAction.@href.toString(),
      label: xmlAction.@label.toString()
    });
  }
  actionSets[actionSetId] = actionSet.sort(sortByOrder);
}
```

One interesting thing that is happening in this script is the use of the `config` variable. We saw earlier in this chapter how we can use `config` to access scoped information stored in XML configuration files. In this script, the reference `config.script` retrieves the XML stored in the companion webscript file `dod5015-documentlist.get.config.xml`:

The XML data in that file is formatted as follows:

```
<documentList>
  <actionSets>
    <actionSet id="empty"></actionSet>

    <actionSet id="recordSeries">
      <action type="simple-link" id="onActionViewDetails"
        href="{recordSeriesDetailsUrl}" label="actions.view-details"
        />
      <action type="simple-link" id="onActionEditDetails"
        permission="UpdateProperties" href="{editMetadataUrl}"
        label="actions.edit-details" />
        . . .
    </actionSet>

    <actionSet id="recordCategory">
      <action type="simple-link" id="onActionViewDetails"
        href="{recordCategoryDetailsUrl}" label="actions.view-
        details" />
      <action type="simple-link" id="onActionEditDetails"
        permission="UpdateProperties" href="{editMetadataUrl}"
        label="actions.edit-details" />
        . . .
    </actionSet>
      . . .

  </actionSets>
</documentList>
```

After loading the XML, an array of `actionSets` are constructed that manage the list of available actions for each type of repository object. Depending on the type of object selected in the data grid, subject to the permissions that the user has, this is the list of actions that will become available. The action list for a Series container in the File Plan looks something like the following. Here, the actions are **View Details**, **Edit Metadata**, **Manage Permissions**, and so forth:

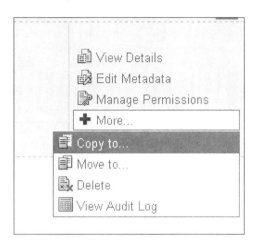

The Document List Data Table

The Document List displays all the items that are in the container corresponding to the current position in the File Plan. We've seen how the server-side Surf framework is used to define the layout of the File Plan page. The actual display of the items in the Document List is handled on the client using JavaScript and AJAX.

Defining and rendering the Data Table

The webscript file, `dod5015-documentlist.get.head.ftl`, identifies files that will be imported into the `<head>` section of the File Plan page. Two JavaScript files, `documentlist.js` and `dod5015-documentlist.js`, are specified for import with this file:

```
<#include "../component.head.inc">
<!-- DoD 5015.2 Document List -->
<@link rel="stylesheet" type="text/css"
  href="${page.url.context}/components/documentlibrary/
  documentlist.css" />
<@link rel="stylesheet" type="text/css"
  href="${page.url.context}/components/documentlibrary/dod5015-
  documentlist.css" />
<@script type="text/javascript"
  src="${page.url.context}/components/documentlibrary/
```

```
    documentlist.js"></@script>
<@script type="text/javascript"
    src="${page.url.context}/components/documentlibrary/dod5015-
    documentlist.js"></@script>
```

The first of these files, documentlibrary.js, is a Share file used in the display of the **Document Library** page for standard Share sites. It defines the Alfresco. DocumentList class. The second file, dod5015-documentlist.js, overrides some of the methods of the first file which is the superclass. The method overrides features that are specific for Records Management functionality. The class defined in this second file is Alfresco.RecordsDocumentList. The RecordsDocumentList class is the one that is instantiated for use on the **File Plan** page.

Share uses the YUI library, which provides the framework for the client-side user interface. These two JavaScript files make extensive use of YUI event handling and the **YUI Data Table** widget. In total, these two files are several thousand lines of code long, and because of their length, we will only be able to touch on a few highlights from each of them.

The DocumentList *superclass* defines a method called onReady that is implemented as the function DL_onReady(). This method is fairly long and isn't shown here. Among other things, it initializes the widgets needed for the document list and sets up a number of event handlers. Among the various things that are initialized in that function is a call to the method _setupDataTable() to initialize the YUI Data Table to display the items in the repository:

```
_setupDataTable: function DL__setupDataTable()
{
  var me = this;

  // DataTable column defintions
  var columnDefinitions =
  [
    { key: "nodeRef", label: "Select", sortable: false, formatter:
      this.fnRenderCellSelected(), width: 16 },
    { key: "status", label: "Status", sortable: false, formatter:
      this.fnRenderCellStatus(), width: 16 },
    { key: "thumbnail", label: "Preview", sortable: false, formatter:
      this.fnRenderCellThumbnail(), width: 100 },
    { key: "fileName", label: "Description", sortable: false,
      formatter: this.fnRenderCellDescription() },
    { key: "actions", label: "Actions", sortable: false, formatter:
      this.fnRenderCellActions(), width: 200 }
  ];

  // DataTable definition
```

```
this.widgets.dataTable = new YAHOO.widget.DataTable(this.id + "-
    documents", columnDefinitions, this.widgets.dataSource,
{
    renderLoopSize: this.options.usePagination ? 16 : 32,
    initialLoad: false,
    dynamicData: true,
    MSG_EMPTY: this.msg("message.loading")
});
```

The `columnDefinitions` variable in the *method* `_setupDataTable()` defines the cells for each row of the data table. This method sets the width and formatting method for rendering the cell of each row in the table:

Cell label	Format function
Select	`fnRenderCellSelected()`
Status	`fnRenderCellStatus()`
Preview	`fnRenderCellThumbnail()`
Description	`fnRenderCellDescription()`
Actions	`fnRenderCellActions()`

The `columnDefinitions` is then used as an input parameter to create a new YUI Data Table for rendering on the page. The other important parameter used in creating the Data Table is the **Data Source**. The data source is based on an Alfresco repository service called `doclist`, which returns the row values for display on this page.

The `dod5015-documentlist.js` file defines the data source, as seen in the following code:

```
_setupDataSource: function DL__setupDataSource()
{
    var me = this;

    // DataSource definition
    this.widgets.dataSource = new
        YAHOO.util.DataSource(Alfresco.constants.PROXY_URI +
```

```
      "slingshot/doclib/dod5015/doclist/");
   this.widgets.dataSource.responseType =
     YAHOO.util.DataSource.TYPE_JSON;
   this.widgets.dataSource.responseSchema =
   {
     resultsList: "items",
     fields:
     [
       "index", "nodeRef", "type", "isFolder", "mimetype", "fileName",
         "displayName", "status", "title", "description", "author",
       "createdOn", "createdBy", "createdByUser", "modifiedOn",
       "modifiedBy", "modifiedByUser", "size", "version",
       "contentUrl", "actionSet", "tags",
       "location", "permissions", "dod5015"
     ],
     metaFields:
     {
       paginationRecordOffset: "startIndex",
         totalRecords: "totalRecords"
     }
   };
   ...
```

This method specifies a data source that will be connected to a repository web service. It specifies the fields or properties that should be returned for each row in the result. The base URL for the web service is defined as: `Alfresco.constants.` `PROXY_URI + "slingshot/doclib/dod5015/doclist/"`, which will typically resolve to look something like: `http://localhost:8080/alfresco/service/slingshot/` `doclib/dod5015/doclist`.

The method called `_buildDocListParams` near the bottom of `documentlist.js` builds a parameter string that is appended to the base data source URL to further qualify what type of results are needed to be returned. For example, the data source might call something similar to the following URL to find all the Category containers under a Series container named "Health and Safety":

```
http://localhost:8080/alfresco/service/slingshot/doclib/dod5015/
doclist/all/site/rm/documentLibrary/Health%20and%20Safety?filter=p
ath&noCache=1282251487169
```

The result of this URL is a JSON data packet that contains a list of all of the Category containers and the properties associated with each one of them. The data associated with each result row is then made available to each of the cell formatting functions that we saw above and are used for rendering the types of cells in the Data Table.

Retrieving Content Object with an Alfresco Repository webscript

We've just seen how the File Plan page is filled with a list of repository object data. The repository service that is being called to populate the Data Table of the Document List is an Alfresco repository webscript. The files defining this repository webscript can be found here: `tomcat\webapps\alfresco\WEB-INF\classes\ alfresco\templates\webscripts\org\alfresco\slingshot\documentlibrary\ dod5015-doclist*`.

The webscript descriptor file, `dod5015-doclist.get.desc.xml`, identifies the URL formats that the `doclist` webscript responds to. In this file, we see that there are multiple URL formats that this script will respond to. The format that we matched with the URL of the last example is: `slingshot/doclib/dod5015/doclist/{type}/ site/{site}/{container}/{path}`.

The URL that we used contained `slingshot/doclib/dod5015/doclist/all/site/ rm/documentLibrary/Health%20and%20Safety`.

```
<webscript>
  <shortname>doclist</shortname>
  <description>Document List Component - dod5015 doclist data
    webscript</description>
  <url>/slingshot/doclib/dod5015/doclist/{type}/site/{site}/
{container}
  /{path}</url>
  <url>/slingshot/doclib/dod5015/doclist/{type}/site/{site}/
{container}
</url>
  <url>/slingshot/doclib/dod5015/doclist/{type}/node/{store_type}/
    {store_id}/{id}/{path}</url>
  <url>/slingshot/doclib/dod5015/doclist/{type}/node/{store_type}/
    {store_id}/{id}</url>
  <format default="json">argument</format>
  <authentication>user</authentication>
  <transaction allow="readwrite"
    buffersize="0">required</transaction>
</webscript>
```

Summary

In this chapter, we covered the following topics:

- What a File Plan is and the File Plan structure recommended by the DoD 5015.2 specification
- What is the best practice approach for specifying a File Plan
- How to create the Series, Category, and Folder containers of the File Plan

At the end of this chapter, we included a detailed discussion about how the File Plan in the Records Management site was implemented as an extension of the standard Alfresco Share Document Library. We saw how the **File Plan** page is configured to be available in the Records Management site via the `presets.xml` file. We also saw some of the internals for how the **File Plan** page was built using Spring-Surf webscripts and the YUI client-side library for building rich application interfaces.

One part of the File Plan skipped over in the discussion in this chapter was the creation of the Disposition schedule that is associated with File Plan categories. The Disposition schedule defines lifecycle instructions for the records within a Category. This is an important part of the File Plan and one that deserves a detailed explanation. That is why we have dedicated the whole of the next chapter to an explanation of the File Plan disposition schedule.

Creating Disposition Schedules

6

In the last chapter, we designed the overall structure of the File Plan. An important part of the File Plan is the disposition schedule, which includes information about how long records will be retained. In this chapter, we will look in detail at the meaning of the disposition schedule and we will see how to configure it within Alfresco. Specifically, we will describe:

- The disposition schedule as the descriptor for the final stage of a record's lifecycle
- Example disposition schedules
- The process for creating a disposition within Alfresco
- How to import and export the File Plan

At the end of this chapter, in a "How does it work?" section, we look in detail at developer internals of the Share web pages used to configure the disposition schedule for a record Category within the Records Management site. We will see how it is built from the YUI library using the Spring-Surf web framework. We will also see how Share communicates with the Alfresco repository using data web scripts.

What is the disposition schedule?

In the previous chapter, we discussed how to design the File Plan and we looked at the steps needed to build the structure for the File Plan within Alfresco. One part of creating the File Plan that we haven't discussed yet in great detail is the assignment of the disposition schedule to the elements of the File Plan. The disposition schedule will be the main topic of this chapter.

Disposition instructions

The **Disposition Schedule** forms the instructions and steps that describe what happens at the end of the life of a record. In short, the disposition describes the steps needed to remove or dispose of a record from the Records Management system. The possible steps for the disposition include **retention**, **transfer**, and ultimately **destruction**.

Regulations or company policy often requires that a record be retained for a certain period of time. At some point, the record may need to be moved or transferred to another location for permanent or long-term archival. When the record no longer needs to be retained or is no longer needed, it may be destroyed.

The record lifecycle

Disposition focuses only on the tail end of the life of a record. The early steps in the lifecycle of a record aren't considered at all in the instructions of the disposition. For example, the disposition doesn't include the time when the record was first created, when it was still just a document outside of the Records Management system.

At some point in time, when a document is recognized as having business significance, the document will be brought into the Records Management system and filed into a Folder of the File Plan.

After being moved into the File Plan, the document first becomes an **undeclared record**, and usually, shortly after filing, is then **declared** as a record. But, prior to declaration, it is necessary to complete all mandatory metadata fields on the document.

Records declared and located in the File Plan are automatically associated with a disposition schedule. The disposition is inherited from the record Category in which the record is located.

Once the document is in the File Plan and is declared as a record, it is available as a reference. While the content of the record is not changeable, the metadata of a record can be changed, and any change to the metadata will be tracked in the audit log for the record. The only option for replacing the content of a record is to first obsolete it and to then file a new record.

The next diagram shows the full lifecycle of a document. The record lifecycle that we discussed in *Chapter 1* refers only to the disposition schedule applied once the document is declared as a record. Prior to becoming a record, as a document, frequent changes and versioning are common, and once declared as a record, during the record retention period, it is no longer changed, but used as a reference:

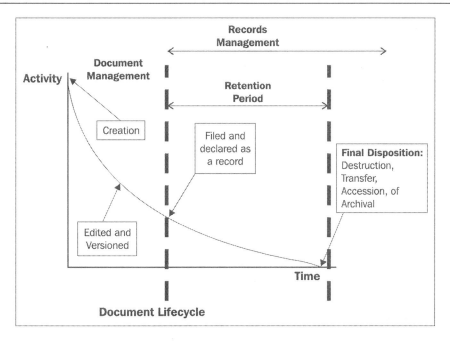

Document Lifecycle

Cutoff

Cutoff is a term that simply refers to the point in time when the disposition instructions of a record go into effect. In Alfresco, cutoff typically occurs as the first step in the disposition schedule. The process of cutoff is the event that starts the clock on the record's retention period.

Cutoff can occur at either the Folder level or at the record level. The disposition schedule can be correspondingly configured to support either type of behavior. When cutoff occurs at the Folder level, all records that have been filed in that Folder will also be cut off. But when cutoff occurs at the record level, the containing Folder itself will not get cut off, just the records that are within it.

File Plans are often set up such that during a fixed time period, like a month, a quarter, or a year, records are filed into the Folder corresponding to that period. At the end of the filing period, the Folder and the records that have been filed in it will all be cut off. After the cutoff of the Folder, a new Folder is then typically opened corresponding to the next filing period.

Retention

The retention period is the length of time before the final disposition that a record is required to be kept. As we just saw, within the disposition, the retention period is kicked off the moment a record is cut off.

Destruction

Destruction is one of the most frequent end-of-life actions taken on records. In the case of destruction, electronic records must be erased by the records management program so that the data is totally overwritten and it is not possible for it to be reconstructed.

Paper records are typically destroyed by shredding, pulping, or burning. Often the destruction of paper records is outsourced to companies that specialize in record destruction.

In the DoD 5015.2 standard, the Department of Defense stipulates that records designated to be destroyed must be destroyed in a "manner such that the records cannot be physically reconstructed". In a specification separate from DoD-5015.2, the methods for the destruction of classified materials are described. DoD-5220.22-M, the National Industrial Security Program Operating Manual, specifies that:

"Classified material may be destroyed by burning, shredding, pulping, melting, mutilation, chemical decomposition, or pulverizing (for example, hammer mills, choppers, and hybridized disintegration equipment)."

Transfer

Transfer refers to the physical moving of records from one location to another. Typically, it also implies to the transferring of control or custody of the management of the records. Particularly in the world of paper records, usually in order to reclaim local storage space, transfer is an inevitable step for records that are to be permanently archived and preserved, but which are no longer needed for performing daily operations.

For electronic records, where the storage space required to archive the records may be minimal, the transfer of records for archival and preservation may mean moving them from one storage system to another while still keeping them under the management of the same agency or authority. Typically though, archival is performed by a different agency or organization from the one that originally created the record, one that specializes in the long-term storage of records.

Examples of record transfer scenarios include the following:

- Transfer from the originating organization to a long-term archival
- Transfer from the creating organization to a successor organization
- Transfer from the archive back to the originating organization
- Transfer between archives
- Transfer between two systems in an organization
- Transfer of records between business units or business partners that both require access to the same records, but when both parties do not have access to the same records system

Of these scenarios, the first, the transfer of records from the originating organization to an archive, is perhaps the most common.

Any transfer of record data between two organizations or two systems requires that both parties in the transfer agree on the transfer format prior to the transfer being made. Often, the relationship between the two parties requires that, over time, many data transfers will need to be made. In that case, as a matter of efficiency, it is useful to define a specification for the standard transfer format for the data being transferred. A specification promotes reuse and can speed the flow of data between the two parties.

Depending on the organizations involved in the transfer, the transfer process may involve a number of steps. For example, often it is necessary to get signoff, or even multiple signoffs, before the record can be transferred. The transfer format may also require that metadata be reformatted or that file data be converted to a different electronic file formats.

Once electronic records have been successfully transferred from the records system and the receipt of the new system is received and confirmed, the records can then be destroyed in the original system.

Accession

Accession is a special kind of transfer that refers to the legal and physical transfer of records to another body. It is usually used specifically relative to federal agencies that transfer their permanent records to the National Archives (NARA) or that transfer their temporary records to the Federal Records Center (FRC).

Inheritance of the disposition

The disposition schedule is created and associated with Category containers. In Alfresco, the disposition is configured from the details page for the Category.

Disposition instructions defined on the Category will be inherited at either the Folder or record level. When the disposition is created, we specify which type of inheritance we want, at either the Folder or the record level. A disposition instruction applied at the Folder level will affect the Folder and all of the records in the Folder. A disposition instruction applied at the record level will be applied to each record individually:

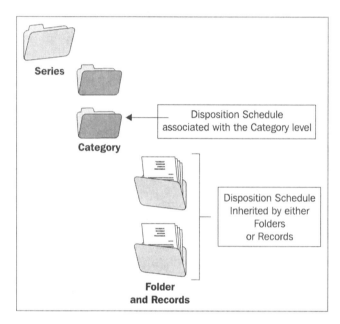

Disposition example—application at the Folder level

Let's now consider an example of a disposition schedule. The example that we will use is fairly simple, having only two steps, but not all that uncommon to a disposition that would be used in practice. In this example, the first step of the disposition is a trigger to cutoff the Folder at the end of the quarter. All during the quarter, e-mails, paper records, and electronic records are filed and declared within the Folder. Then, at the end of the quarter, the Folder is cutoff.

The process of cutting off the Folder causes all records in the Folder to also be cut off. Cutoff signals the start of a retention period that is applied to the Folder and to all of the records in it. In this example, the retention period lasts for a quarter of a year. At the end of the second quarter, the retention period is complete and the Folder is then available for destruction:

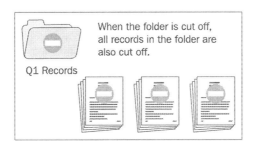

After the destruction of the Folder, a stub of the Folder, and a stub for each of the records in the Folder still remain. The Folder and record stubs maintain a complete set of metadata and an audit log for all the actions that have occurred on the Folder and records:

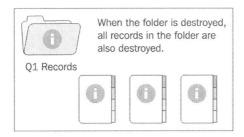

Record destruction removes only the content part of the record, that is, the file data. The metadata for the record is not removed. Alfresco stores file content on disk. After the content is destroyed, the associated file stored in the repository can no longer be found, even when searching on the local drive.

In the diagram below, we see the disposition as applied to a single Folder of a Category. In this example, there are additional Folders not shown that parallel the one we look at. These other Folders would activate one in each subsequent quarter.

For example, a parallel Folder called "**Q2** records" would have active filings all through the second quarter, be cutoff at the start of the third quarter, and then be subject to destruction at the start of the third quarter. When the disposition is applied at the Folder level in this way, we see that there is a kind of rolling Folder structure, with a new Folder being opened each time one of the Folders is cutoff.

The diagrams shown here use notation similar to that used within Alfresco. The red circle with a white bar represents a Folder or record that has been cut off. The blue circle with the white lower case "i" represents a Folder or record that has been destroyed and remains as a stub within the plan. The "i" indicates that the stub remains for information only.

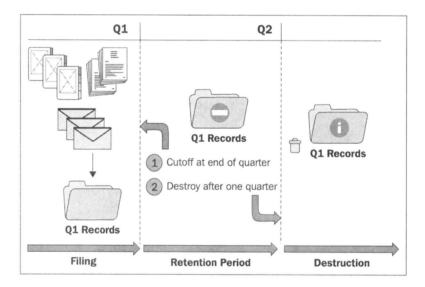

Disposition example—application at the record level

Now consider an example where the disposition schedule is applied at the record level. In this case, we look at how purchase orders are handled in the Finance department. The File Plan is structured so that there is a record Series called "Finance", under which there is a record Category that is called "Purchase Orders".

Within the Category, Folders organized by the names of the companies to whom the purchase orders are sent. In this example, we see the Folder corresponding to the company "STM Technology".

Similar to the previous example, a record related to a purchase order sent to STM Technology is filed into the Folder. The new record is cut off at the end of the quarter, but unlike the previous example, the containing Folder is not affected by the cutoff:

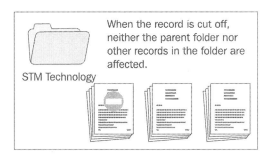

Cutoff of the record starts the clock moving on the retention period. After five years, the document is then destroyed, which results in the content of the record being removed. The record is available as a stub, still containing a complete set of metadata and audit history:

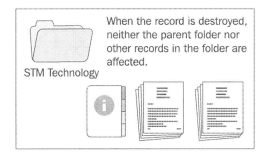

Unlike the previous example where all records within the Folder were at the same point in the disposition schedule, records in the Folder for this example may be at different stages of the disposition. There may be some records that are not yet cutoff, some which are at different points of fulfilling the retention schedule, and some where only the stub of the destroyed record remains:

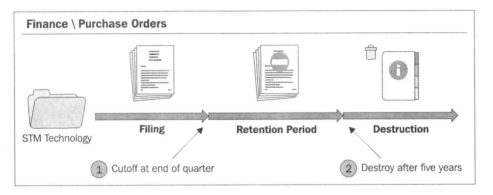

Creating the disposition schedule

Let's now look in greater detail at the steps needed to create a disposition schedule. The disposition schedule is best created and associated with the Category immediately when the Category is created. We'll see below that the addition or editing of a disposition schedule will have some restrictions once Folders and records begin to be placed into the Category.

The review

While strictly not part of the disposition, a review period can be scheduled for records that are filed under a Category. During the creation of the File Plan structure, we saw how reviews could be specified as part of the Category definition.

Once the Category is created, the information that specifies the review period is saved as metadata and can be changed at a later date:

The review period for a record is recurring. That is, after one review is completed, the next review will be scheduled based on the specified frequency of reviews. Reviews are typically associated with vital records. In fact, reviews are mandatory when dealing with vital records. But even for record Categories that will not hold vital records, a review period can be specified.

Based on the review period entered for the Category and the date when the record was filed, the value of a metadata field called the **Next Review Date** is calculated. The value for the review date can be seen on the details page of the record to be reviewed:

Once a record is reviewed, the next review period for the record is automatically rescheduled. Rescheduling can be done by using the **Edit Review Date** option:

The disposition schedule

Once the new Category has been created, the disposition schedule for it should be specified next. That can be done by going to the **View details** screen for the record Category.

On the details page for the Category, the center section of the screen has an area where the disposition information can be entered. The entry of the information is split into two parts, namely, **General** and **Disposition Steps**:

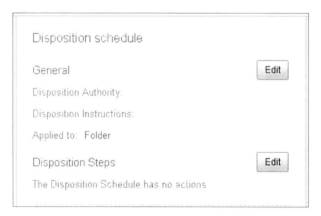

The disposition schedule is attached to a Category and applies to the folders and records under that Category. We will see in *Chapter 8* that electronic and the stub placeholders for non-electronic records are both filed in similar ways, and the steps of the disposition are applied identically to both types of records.

General information for the disposition

In the **General** section, information is edited by clicking on the first of the two **Edit** buttons.

On the screen that is displayed next, text labels can be entered that describe the **Disposition Authority** and **Disposition Instructions**. The **Disposition Authority** corresponds to the name of the Authority document or policy with which these instructions comply. The **Disposition Instructions** is a text label that summarizes the steps that make up the disposition schedule. The label entered here for the **Disposition Instructions** gets displayed as part of the metadata for each record under this Category to indicate the nature of the disposition.

The **Applied to** drop-down specifies if the disposition is to be applied at the Folder or at the record level. As discussed earlier, and as we will see below, this flag plays an important role in the functioning of the disposition:

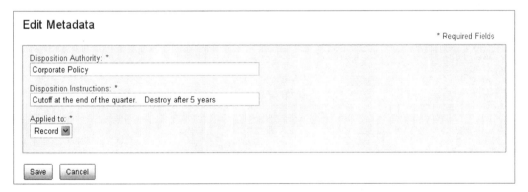

When the disposition is attached at the Folder level, then the date for the next step of the disposition to be run is shown as the **Disposition As Of Date** field attached at the Folder level and the records within the Folder do not track this date. In the other case, when the disposition is attached at the record level, then the **Disposition As Of Date** field is part of the metadata for each record under the Category, and the Folders under the Category do not track this field:

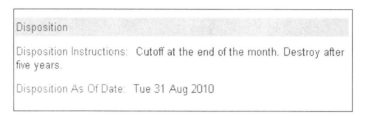

The disposition steps

After clicking on the second of the two **Edit** buttons, the one marked **Disposition Steps**, we see the following screen displayed. Within this screen, the steps for the disposition can be configured:

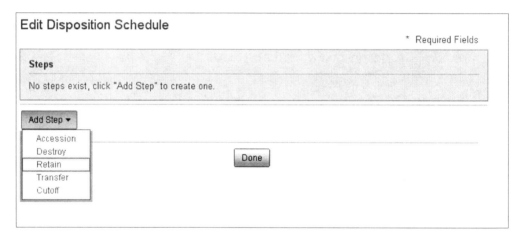

Disposition steps are added sequentially in the order in which they are to be executed for the disposition. There are only five types of steps that can be added, and there are rules about the order in which these step types can be added.

The allowable disposition step types are as follows:

Type of disposition Step	Description
Cutoff	The point in time from which a retention period begins.
Retain	A period of time during which the record is held before being destroyed.
Transfer	The transfer of records from one location to another.
Destroy	The deletion of content from the record that prevents the reconstruction of it.
Accession	Accession means to acquire property. In this context, it is the process of transferring both records and their metadata to NARA, the National Archives. This is a step that is reserved for government agencies.

The rules for adding disposition steps are as follows:

- The first step must be of type **Cutoff** or **Retain**
- No two steps in the disposition schedule can be of the same type
- No steps can be added once the **Destroy** step has been used

In most cases, the disposition schedule is very simple and consists of just two or three steps. The rules are such that it is possible to create nonsensical schedules, such as a disposition with the three steps of **Retain-Accession-Cutoff**, but in practice, the rules for structuring the steps work quite well.

Examples of disposition schedules are shown in the next diagram. Here we see, for example, **Cutoff** followed by **Destroy** and **Cutoff** followed by **Transfer**:

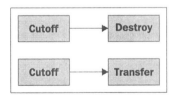

Next, we will look at the details of how to configure the disposition steps. Built into each step is the notion of a waiting period. The action for the step cannot occur until it is triggered by some event or some amount of time that has elapsed. While one possible step in the disposition schedule is a step type explicitly called **Retain**, the waiting period of the trigger actually often serves the purpose of modeling retention so that an explicit **Retain** step is not needed.

Note that if the disposition schedule is applied at the Folder level and the Folder contains no records or some undeclared records, the Folder will not be cut off. It will only be cut off when it contains at least one declared record and no undeclared records.

Configuring a simple disposition schedule

Let's look at a simple yet often recurring disposition schedule. In this case, similar to the example we discussed earlier, consider the schedule for cutoff of a Folder at the end of each month, followed by a one-month retention, and then destruction. We will model the cutoff, retention period, and destruction with just two steps.

First, we select **Cutoff** as the first step type to add. Next, we configure the cutoff to occur at the end of the month after being filed. This means that Folders under this record Category and all records filed during the month are cutoff at the end of the month. Note that it is mandatory to enter a description on this screen to explain what happens during this step of the disposition. When we have finished adding information for this step, we click on **Save**:

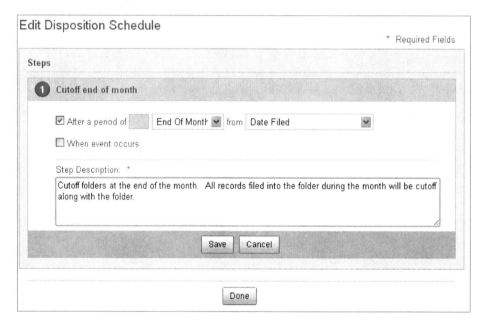

Then, we add the **Destroy** step. In configuring this step, we need to specify how long the records are retained prior to destruction. Our example calls for a retention period of one month. We can enter that period information, a description for the step, and then finally click on **Save**.

With that, we have completed the specification for the steps of a simple disposition schedule. We can now click on the **Done** button. After that, there is nothing else we need to do in setting up the disposition for this Category:

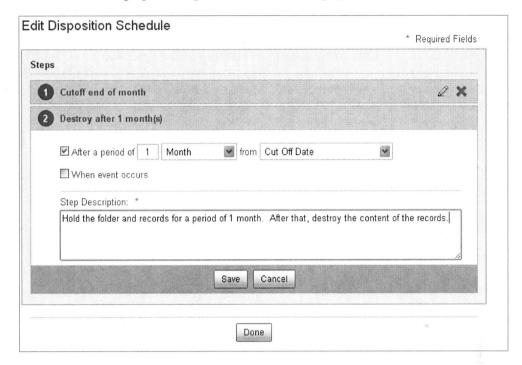

Time-based triggers

In both of the steps for the disposition that we just created, we used time-based triggers to specify when an action would occur. Cutoff occurred at the end of the month, and destruction occurred after a one month retention.

A **time period** is specified by entering a value for the time period unit and the period value. To activate the time period fields on the form, it is first necessary to click on the checkbox next to the label **After a period of**.

The available unit types of **Immediately, Day, Week, Month, Quarter**, and **Year** are straightforward to understand. A **Week** offsets a date by seven days and a **Quarter** offsets the date by three months. The period value is a multiplier that specifies how many units are to be offset, such as by **2 Quarters** or **4 Weeks**.

Also easy to understand are the period unit values of **End of Month, End of Quarter**, and **End of Year**. It is also possible to specify a period value with these "**End of**" type units. For example, **2 End of Month** means the last day of the next month.

Other available unit types include **Financial End of Month, Financial End of Quarter**, and **Financial End of Year**. The calendar for the fiscal year is something that, as we might expect, is configurable. It is set up in a configuration file located in the Alfresco repository source area. By default, these values are specified relative to a fiscal year beginning September 1st. The file to configure the definition for the organization's fiscal year is `tomcat\webapps\alfresco\WEB-INF\classes\alfresco\period-type-context.xml`.

There is also a unit type called **XML Duration**. Using this type of format, we can create an arbitrary date offset. **XML Duration** is based on a standard notation for representing date offsets or durations defined by the standard ISO 8601.

 More information about ISO 8601 time and time durations can be found here at `http://www.w3.org/TR/xmlschema-2/#adding-durations-to-dateTimes`

An ISO 8601 duration is represented as a string in the format `PnYnMnDTnHnmnS`. "`P`" is always used at the beginning of the string to mark the string as containing an ISO 8601 time duration. "`Y`" refers to years; "`M`" refers to months; "`D`" refers to days, "`T`" is used to separate the date from the time; "`H`" refers to hours; "`m`" refers to minutes; and "`S`" refers to seconds. For example, the string "P1M2D" would mean an offset of one month and two days.

 As of Alfresco version 3.3.1, there is a bug in creating disposition steps that does not allow us to enter the XML Duration value.

The period offset is relative to one of the following four events listed in the dialog drop-down:

- The date filed
- The publication date
- The cutoff date
- The disposition action date

The date filed and the publication date are properties that are defined in the aspect called `rma:record`. Note that the date filed is set the first time that the document is placed into the records File Plan. The date filed is stored in the property `rma:dateFiled`. Note that this is not the same as the date that the record was declared. When a document is declared a record, the aspect `rma:declaredRecord` is applied to the document and the property `rma:declaredAt` within that aspect tracks the date of declaration.

The publication date is the property `rma:publicationDate`. It is a mandatory property that must be completed before a document can be declared as a record.

The cutoff date is the property `rma:cutOffDate`. It is attached to the record at the time of cutoff when the aspect `rma:cutOff` is applied.

The disposition action date refers to the date on which the previous step action was completed.

Event-based triggers

In addition to time-based triggers, it is also possible to specify event-based triggers. To activate the controls on the dialog to specify an event-based trigger, we must first click on the checkbox next to the label **When event occurs**.

After doing that, the form will dynamically reconfigure itself to expose a button with a drop-down menu. From the list of menu items displayed when clicking on this button, we can select the name of the event that we would like to be able to trigger off of. The values in the drop-down list are strings that will later be used to label a button associated with a record or folder. A user will later click on that button to trigger the action for this step of the disposition.

After selecting the event from the drop-down menu, it will be added to the list of events that can trigger the action:

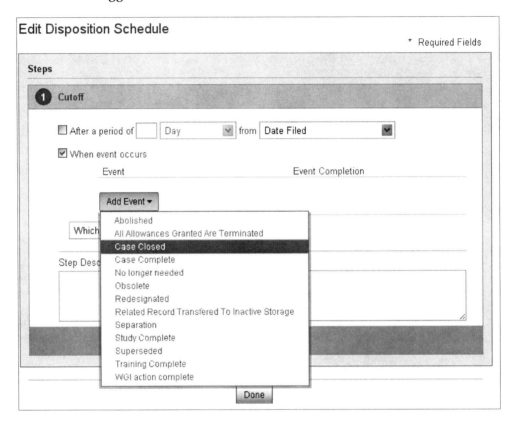

Trigger precedence

It is possible to combine a time-based trigger with one or multiple event-based triggers. It is also possible to specify multiple event-based triggers. When more than one trigger is configured, it is necessary to also select a flag to indicate the precedence of the triggers.

The two options for handling precedence are either that the action will not occur until all trigger conditions have been met, or that the action will occur when one of the trigger conditions is met. The two options that we use can be specified in a drop-down that appears immediately below the event-trigger button.

Making changes to the disposition schedule

After the disposition has been configured, it is possible to go back and make edits to the definition. But there are some restrictions or limitations about what can be edited.

There is generally no problem trying to edit the schedule immediately after creating it before any Folders or records are added to the category. Right after creating the schedule, each step of the disposition can be both edited and deleted.

Deleting steps of the disposition schedule

The red **X** next to an item in the list of disposition steps is for deletion. Clicking on it will delete that step from the disposition schedule.

We need to be careful about what steps we delete because it's possible to get the list of steps in a state that normally would not be allowed during creation. For example, if we have a two-step schedule that consists of cutoff and destruction, we are not prevented from deleting the cutoff step. But after doing that, the destruction step remains by itself. This is a configuration that we normally would not have been able to build.

We'll also find that the red **X** for deletion will not be available as soon as Folders or records are placed under the Category. The behavior is slightly different depending on whether we are applying the disposition to the Folder or the record level.

If the disposition is applied at the Folder level, as soon as a Folder is created within the Category, the red **X** for deletion is no longer available on the disposition schedule. Similarly, when the disposition is applied at the record level, the disposition steps can no longer be deleted after a record is placed under the Category. When the Folders and records under the Category are removed, then the red **X** for deletion will again be available:

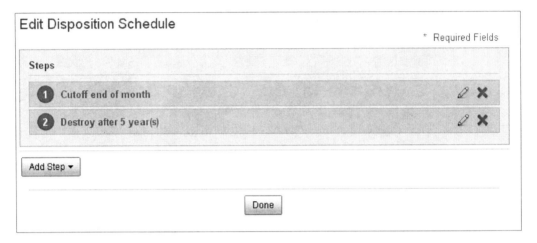

Editing steps of the disposition schedule

It is possible to do some limited editing of the steps of the disposition schedule. While the type of step, such as cutoff, retain, or destroy, can't be changed, the parameters for the step can be. Time-based trigger periods can be edited and event triggers can be added or removed.

Edits made to the parameters of the disposition steps will flow down to the Folders and records under the Category. For example, if a record was to be held for three years prior to destruction, and the retention period is later changed to five years, the already existing records under the Category will update to take on the new disposition schedule.

Importing and exporting File Plan data

It is often convenient to be able to both import and export data to and from the File Plan. In this section, we will show how this can be done.

Importing a File Plan

We've described how it is possible to totally build out all of the Series, Categories, and Folders needed to specify the File Plan for the organization. When creating the File Plan for the very first time, there often is no other option but to do it manually. But in certain cases, it is useful to be able to import an existing File Plan definition or parts of one. This is particularly handy when cloning a File Plan on one Alfresco system and moving it to another. This feature also could be used as the final step of an automated process for importing parts of the File Plan. For example, an automated tool might be used to build an import file containing Folders corresponding to a company's many employees.

In order to have a working example, in addition to the sample File Plan provided by Alfresco, this book comes with another sample File Plan. This plan is perhaps more typical of many companies than the sample DoD plan used within Alfresco. The File Plan was modeled on a manufacturing company. It is not intended to be complete, nor should any part of it be adopted for actual use without first carefully reviewing it to see that it meets your needs.

An Excel spreadsheet, `FilePlan.xlsx`, which comes with this book, gives a complete description of the sample File Plan. The companion file `SampleFilePlan.acp` is an importable version of the plan. The **ACP** (Alfresco Content Package) file contains the complete structure for the record Series, record Categories, Folders, and disposition schedules. The version of this ACP file used for the last chapter contained only Series and Categories.

To import this file, from the toolbar on the **File Plan** page in the Records Management site, click on the link called **Import.** The following dialog is displayed, after which you can navigate to the location of the ACP file and then upload it:

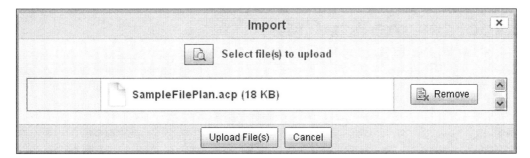

After uploading the ACP import file, the screen will refresh, and you can see the contents of the sample File Plan. The structure of the plan will look something like the following screenshot:

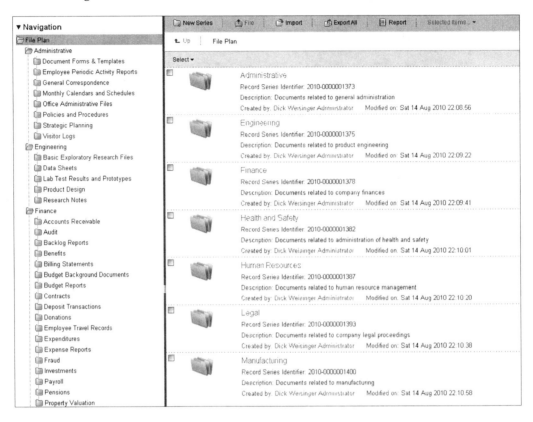

Exporting the File Plan

Just as easily as we have imported a File Plan, the current state of the File Plan can also be exported to an ACP or ZIP file at any time. This feature comes in handy while designing the structure of the plan. It allows us to backup or take snapshots of the current state of the File Plan.

Making backups of the entire File Plan is easy. Simply click on the **Export All** button of the **File Plan** page toolbar. You'll be given the option to save the export file as either a ZIP file or as an ACP file. ZIP files are useful when exporting data to non-Alfresco systems. You should select the ACP file option when you later intend to import the file to this or another Alfresco instance.

The data exported will include the complete structure of the File Plan, including Series, Categories, and Folders. Any records that are stored in the File Plan will also be included in the export file. Because of that, if there is a lot of content in the system, the export file can grow to be quite large.

> Note that, on import, Alfresco systems may be sensitive to the version of Alfresco that was used to create the ACP file. One example is with thumbnails. Thumbnails for content items started being stored as renditions beginning with version 3.3. Because of that, ACP files created prior to version 3.3 with thumbnails included as part of the exported content may not directly import into a 3.3+ system.

How does it work?

Now that we've seen how specification of the disposition schedule works from a user perspective, let's examine some of the internals that occur when the Category and disposition schedule are configured.

The Category details page

First, let's look at the details page for a record Category. To do that, we'll do a bit of investigation to find out where the definition for this Spring-Surf page is defined. If we navigate to a category and select the **View details** option, we can see that the URL in the location field of the browser is something like `http://localhost:8080/share/page/site/rm/record-category-details?nodeRef=workspace://SpacesStore/96b977ad-b4f7-472b-a10c-ccb0c06151c6`.

We can trace backwards from this URL to find the pages that render and control the Categories detail page. The clue here in this URL is the string `record-category-details`. Starting with the page descriptor file `tomcat\webapps\share\WEB-INF\classes\site-data\pages\record-category-details.xml`, we can see that the `<template-instance>` for the page is defined to be that same name, `record-category-details`:

```
<?xml version='1.0' encoding='UTF-8'?>
<page>
  <title>Record Category Details</title>
  <title-id>page.recordCategoryDetails.title</title-id>
  <description>Record Category Details page for Records
    Management</description>
  <description-id>
    page.recordCategoryDetails.description</description-id>
```

```
    <template-instance>record-category-details</template-instance>
    <authentication>user</authentication>
  </page>
```

Next, tracing into the `template-instance` descriptor file `tomcat\webapps\share\WEB-INF\classes\site-data\template-instances\record-category-details.xml`, we will find the location for the template defined in the `<template-type>` tag:

```
  <?xml version='1.0' encoding='UTF-8'?>
  <template-instance>
    <template-type>org/alfresco/record-category-details</template-type>
    <properties>
      <pageFamily>documentlibrary</pageFamily>
      <container>documentLibrary</container>
    </properties>
  </template-instance>
```

This gives us the path to where the template is defined. By looking there, we can find the FreeMarker layout template for the Category details page. That file is `tomcat\webapps\share\WEB-INF\classes\alfresco\templates\org\alfresco\record-category-details.ftl`:

```
  <#include "include/alfresco-template.ftl" />
  <#assign doclibType="dod5015-">
  <@templateHeader>
    <@link rel="stylesheet" type="text/css"
      href="${url.context}/templates/folder-details/folder-details.css"
      />
    <@script type="text/javascript"
      src="${url.context}/modules/documentlibrary/doclib-
      actions.js"></@script>
    <@script type="text/javascript"
      src="${page.url.context}/templates/folder-details/folder-
      details.js"></@script>
    <@script type="text/javascript"
      src="${page.url.context}/templates/folder-
      details/${doclibType}folder-details.js"></@script>
  </@>
  <@templateBody>
    <div id="alf-hd">
      <@region id="header" scope="global" protected=true />
      <@region id="title" scope="template" protected=true />
      <@region id="navigation" scope="template" protected=true />
    </div>
    <div id="bd">
```

```
  <@region id=doclibType + "actions-common" scope="template"
    protected=true />
  <@region id=doclibType + "path" scope="template" protected=true
    />

  <div class="yui-gb">
    <div class="yui-u first">
      <div class="folder-details-comments">
        <@region id=doclibType + "folder-metadata-header"
          scope="template" protected=true />
        <@region id=doclibType + "folder-metadata" scope="template"
          protected=true />
      </div>
    </div>
    <div class="yui-u">
      <@region id=doclibType + "disposition" scope="template"
        protected=true />
    </div>
    <div class="yui-u">
      <@region id=doclibType + "folder-actions" scope="template"
        protected=true />
      <@region id=doclibType + "folder-links" scope="template"
        protected=true />
    </div>
  </div>

</div>

<script type="text/javascript">//<![CDATA[
new Alfresco.RecordsFolderDetails().setOptions(
{
  nodeRef: new Alfresco.util.NodeRef("${url.args.nodeRef}"),
  siteId: "${page.url.templateArgs.site!""}"
});
//]]></script>
</@>

<@templateFooter>
  <div id="alf-ft">
    <@region id="footer" scope="global" protected=true />
  </div>
</@>
```

By looking at this template layout file, we can pull off the regions where components are to be plugged into it. We need to match the `region id` with the `scope` for each `<@region>` tag. The component descriptor files for this page are found in the directory `tomcat\webapps\share\WEB-INF\classes\alfresco\site-data\components`:

RegionId and scope	Component descriptor file	URL
`id="header"` `scope="global"`	`global.header.xml`	`/components/header`
`id="title"` `scope="template"`	`template.title.` `documentlibrary.xml`	`/components/title/` `collaboration-title`
`id="navigation"` `scope="template"`	`template.navigation.` `documentlibrary.xml`	`/components/navigation/` `collaboration-navigation`
`id="dod5015-` `actions-common"` `scope="template"`	`template.dod5015-` `actions-common.` `record-category-` `details.xml`	`/components/` `documentlibrary/dod5015/` `actions-common`
`id="dod5015-` `path"` `scope="template"`	`template.dod5015-` `path.record-category-` `details.xml`	`/components/folder-` `details/dod5015/path`
`id="dod5015-` `folder-metadata-` `header"` `scope="template"`	`template.dod5015-` `folder-metadata-` `header.record-` `category-details.xml`	`/components/folder-` `details/folder-metadata-` `header`
`id="dod5015-` `folder-metadata"` `scope="template"`	`template.dod5015-` `folder-metadata.` `record-category-` `details.xml`	`/components/form`
`id="dod5015-` `disposition"` `scope="template"`	`template.dod5015-` `disposition.record-` `category-details.xml`	`/components/fileplan/` `disposition`
`id="dod5015-` `folder-actions"` `scope="template"`	`template.dod5015-` `folder-actions.` `record-category-` `details.xml`	`/components/folder-` `details/dod5015/folder-` `actions`
`id="dod5015-` `folder-links"` `scope="template"`	`template.dod5015-` `folder-links.record-` `category-details.xml`	`/components/folder-` `details/folder-links`
`id="footer"` `scope="global"`	`global.footer.xml`	`/components/footer`

The `<@region>` tags reference the pluggable components that will be displayed on this page. By looking at the markup used by each of the components combined with the markup of the base FreeMarker template, we can map the location for each of these regions to their location on a screenshot for the web page:

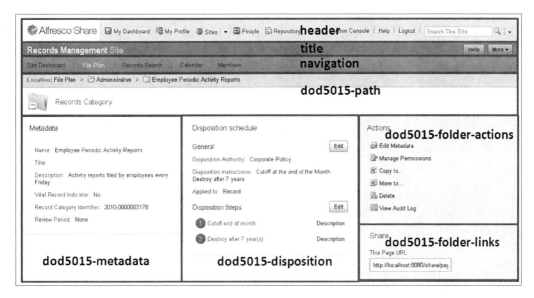

The edit disposition instructions page

When we discussed the Alfresco content types earlier, we saw that there is a content type that is called `rma:dispositionschedule` that holds a set of lifecycle instructions for the Category container.

Let's review the relationship of the Category container to the disposition schedule by looking again at the UML diagram for the Records Management content model. In the model, these two entities are called the **dod:recordCategory** and the **rma:dispositionSchedule**:

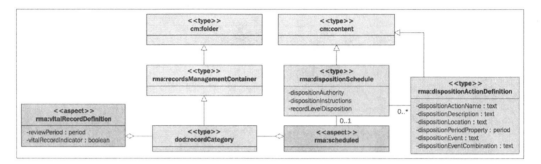

Because every **dod:recordCategory** has **rma:scheduled** as a mandatory aspect, each **dod:recordCategory** also has a single **rma:dispositionSchedule** attached to it as a child association, and the disposition schedule in turn can be attached with multiple **rma:dispositionActionDefinition** child associations.

We can investigate the relationship between the record Category and disposition schedule by seeing how it is applied in practice. Let's see how this works by making use of the Node Browser again in the Alfresco JSF Explorer client. If we navigate in the Node Browser to a Category node, we can see that it indeed has a child relationship to an `rma:dispositionSchedule`. We do this by first navigating to the Alfresco store called `workspace://SpacesStore` and, within that store, navigate to the node with this path: `app:company_home/st:sites/cm:rm/cm:documentlibrary/cm:Finance/cm:Benefits`.

 The File Plan being used in this description corresponds to the sample File Plan included with this book.

In the Node Browser, we can see a list of the child nodes that are attached to the Category node. The first node in that list is called the `dispositionSchedule` and the **Association Type** for it is also called the `dispositionSchedule`. All the other child associations correspond to nodes of type `rma:recordFolder`. They are Folder nodes and have the **Association Type** of `contains`. From the perspective of the standard Share UI of the File Plan, the `contains` nodes are the ones that will be picked up for display as Folders within the Category:

Children

Child Name	Child Node	Primary	Association Type	Index
dispositionSchedule	workspace://SpacesStore/3aa26e6f-cad8-4163-9eec-e40e8723acc5	true	dispositionSchedule	0
_Benefit_Name [Naming Convention]	workspace://SpacesStore/cbfcc52c-275c-49ce-bc80-05bbd77c1d26	true	contains	1
Health Care Insurance	workspace://SpacesStore/ad63bd9e-a5b4-4af5-91f3-9c6ec769be46	true	contains	2
Dental Insurance	workspace://SpacesStore/b34763aa-0710-40eb-81b1-a3d88480ecd1	true	contains	3
Disability Insurance	workspace://SpacesStore/8495c16b-bc5f-4fe5-b2c1-962b8356bad8	true	contains	4
Life Insurance	workspace://SpacesStore/513d1d9f-31d5-4289-aefa-3929ac3994d3	true	contains	5
Domestic Partner Benefits	workspace://SpacesStore/99823c04-e742-43cb-8d6b-8460c5a1aeee	true	contains	6
Paid Time Off	workspace://SpacesStore/16c53b2a-4928-4761-acda-3a25a8d3a43a	true	contains	7

Going back to the **Category Details** page, let's now click on the top **Edit** button marked **General** within the **Disposition Schedule** area of the Category details page:

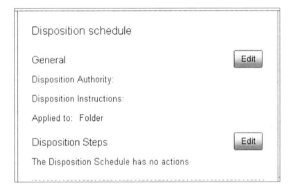

After doing that, an **Edit Metadata** screen is shown. The screen itself isn't too interesting, and actually, you will probably find it familiar. This screen is the same one that is used by the Share document library and File Plan when editing standard content metadata.

The type of content here though is really no different, even though the node whose metadata is being edited is of type `rma:dispositionSchedule` and not of `cm:content` type that we are more familiar with. The form that is used to edit the metadata will vary based on the type associated with the node. Note that the unique reference to the node is passed in to the `edit-metadata` page as the final parameter of the URL:

There are three properties that are editable for the disposition schedule. Of these, the **Disposition Authority** and **Disposition Instructions** are both labels and the **Applied to** field is a Boolean.

Immediately, when a Category is created, the child association to a node of type `rma:dispositionSchedule` exists. If we were to look at that disposition node in the Node Browser right after being created, we would see that nothing is set yet. There are no child associations and the labels for the Authority and the Instructions have not yet been initialized. After saving the **Edit Metadata** page, the properties on the disposition will be updated.

The create disposition steps page

When the second **Edit** button of the disposition schedule area of the **Category details** page is pressed, a new page called `disposition-edit` is called. A screen like the following is displayed, showing the steps of the disposition schedule:

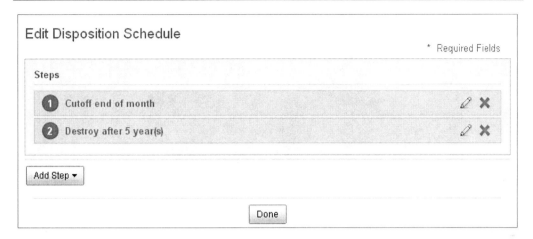

Again, by looking at the URL, we can investigate where this page is defined. The Spring-Surf page descriptor for this screen is the file `tomcat\webapps\share\WEB-INF\classes\alfresco\site-data\pages\disposition-edit.xml`.

```
<?xml version='1.0' encoding='UTF-8'?>
<page>
  <id>disposition-edit</id>
  <title>Edit Disposition Schedule</title>
  <title-id>page.dispositionEdit.title</title-id>
  <description>Page for editing the disposition
    schedule</description>
  <description-id>page.dispositionEdit.description</description-id>
  <template-instance>disposition-edit</template-instance>
  <authentication>user</authentication>
</page>
```

This page descriptor defines the `<template-instance>` tag with the value of `disposition-edit`. The `template-instance` definition can be found in the file `tomcat\webapps\share\WEB-INF\classes\alfresco\site-data\template-instances\disposition-edit.xml`.

```
<?xml version='1.0' encoding='UTF-8'?>
<template-instance>
  <template-type>org/alfresco/disposition-edit</template-type>
  <properties>
    <pageFamily>documentlibrary</pageFamily>
  </properties>
</template-instance>
```

From this file, we in turn find the definition for the template location. It is in the path `tomcat\webapps\share\WEB-INF\classes\alfresco\templates\org\alfresco\disposition-edit.ftl`. This FreeMarker layout file doesn't have much happening in it. The top three `<@region>`s are the standard `header`, `title`, and `navigation` regions, and the bottom one is the standard `footer`:

```
<#include "include/alfresco-template.ftl" />
<#import "import/alfresco-layout.ftl" as layout />
<@templateHeader>
  <@link rel="stylesheet" type="text/css"
    href="${url.context}/templates/disposition-edit/disposition-
    edit.css" />
</@>

<@templateBody>
<div id="alf-hd">
  <@region id="header" scope="global" protected=true />
  <@region id="title" scope="template" protected=true />
  <@region id="navigation" scope="template" protected=true />
  <h1 class="sub-title"><#if
    page.titleId??>${msg(page.titleId)!page.title}<#else>$
    {page.title}</#if></h1>
</div>
<div id="bd">
  <@region id="disposition-edit" scope="template" protected=true />
</div>
</@>

<@templateFooter>
  <div id="alf-ft">
    <@region id="footer" scope="global" protected=true />
  </div>
</@>
```

Components of the disposition edit webscript

The real `<@region>` of interest here is the one called `disposition-edit`. We can look up the definition of this component in the file `tomcat\webapps\share\WEB-INF\classes\site-date\components\template.disposition-edit.disposition-edit.xml`. There we will find the identifying URL of the component as `/components/fileplan/disposition-edit`. This then finally leads us to the webscript descriptor file `tomcat\webapps\share\WEB-INF\classes\alfresco\site-webscripts\org\alfresco\components\fileplan\disposition-edit.get.desc`.

The working parts of the webscript itself consist of the files `disposition-edit.get.head.ftl`, `disposition-edit.get.html.ftl`, and `disposition-edit.get.js`, all of which are in the same directory.

The JavaScript controller file `disposition-edit.get.js` calls into the Alfresco repository and retrieves the list of values used in the drop-downs of the page:

```
// Call the repo to create the site
var scriptRemoteConnector = remote.connect("alfresco");
var repoResponse = scriptRemoteConnector.get("/api/rma/admin/
listofvalues");
```

The URL for this service call resolves to something like `http://localhost:8080/alfresco/service/api/rma/admin/listofvalues`. The response to this URL is a JSON object that contains the available list of disposition actions, events, period types, period properties, and audit event. These values are collected, added to the model, and made available for display in the FreeMarker presentation template.

The file `disposition-edit.get.html.ftl` specifies the rendering of the layout for the `disposition-edit` component. In the file `disposition-edit.get.head.ftl`, the client-side JavaScript file `tomcat\share\components\fileplan\disposition-edit.js` is imported into the final page. This file is where some of the more interesting page interactions are handled.

Disposition edit client-side JavaScript

The file `disposition-edit.js` is used on the client. It describes a YUI object called `Alfresco.DispositionEdit` that handles the dynamics and interactions with the user on the page. When the page initializes, this object is created and runs through the onReady() method. The last step of that method is to call the `_loadActions()` method that loads and displays the disposition schedule steps.

The method makes the following AJAX call into the repository to retrieve the disposition schedule and the instructions for the steps of the schedule:

```
Alfresco.util.Ajax.jsonGet(
{
  url: Alfresco.constants.PROXY_URI_RELATIVE + "api/node/" +
    this.options.nodeRef.replace(":/", "") + "/dispositionschedule",
  successCallback:
  {
  ...
```

The URL of the AJAX service call, when substituted with the node reference for the Category node, will resolve to something that looks like `http://localhost:8080/alfresco/service/api/node/workspace/SpacesStore/0ff56759-b216-4c95-a4ed-dc5119e72b69/dispositionschedule`.

The JSON response to this request returns all the data for the disposition schedule and the associated actions. These are then processed and loaded for display on the screen for specifying the disposition steps:

```
{
  "data":
  {
    "url":
      "\/alfresco\/service\/api\/node\/workspace\/SpacesStore\
      /0ff56759-b216-4c95-a4ed-dc5119e72b69\/dispositionschedule",
    "nodeRef": "workspace:\/\/SpacesStore\/3aa26e6f-cad8-4163-9eec-
      e40e8723acc5",
    "authority": "Corporate Policy",
    "instructions": "Cutoff at end of month. Destroy after 5 years",
    "recordLevelDisposition": true,
    "canStepsBeRemoved": true,
    "actionsUrl":
      "\/alfresco\/service\/api\/node\/workspace\/SpacesStore\
      /0ff56759-b216-4c95-a4ed-dc5119e72b69\/dispositionschedule\
      /dispositionactiondefinitions",
    "actions":
    [
  {
    "id": "c87359e6-bdda-45ad-aa9b-cdea5411a470",
    "url":
      "\/alfresco\/service\/api\/node\/workspace\/SpacesStore\
      /0ff56759-b216-4c95-a4ed-dc5119e72b69\/dispositionschedule\
      /dispositionactiondefinitions\/c87359e6-bdda-45ad-aa9b-
      cdea5411a470",
    "index": 0,
    "name": "cutoff",
    "label": "Cutoff",
    "description": "Cutoff at end of month.",
    "period": "monthend|",
    "periodProperty": "rma:dateFiled",
        "location": "",
    "eligibleOnFirstCompleteEvent": true
  }
      ,
  {
```

```
    "id": "5fd679c4-0e4c-455e-a745-b1f0927d2edd",
    "url":
      "\/alfresco\/service\/api\/node\/workspace\/SpacesStore\
      /0ff56759-b216-4c95-a4ed-dc5119e72b69\/dispositionschedule\
      /dispositionactiondefinitions\/5fd679c4-0e4c-455e-a745-
      b1f0927d2edd",
    "index": 1,
    "name": "destroy",
    "label": "Destroy",
    "description": "Destroy after 5 years",
    "period": "year|5",
    "periodProperty": "rma:cutOffDate",
        "location": "",

    "eligibleOnFirstCompleteEvent": true
  }

  ]
  }
}
```

In the JSON response, we see that the `dispositionSchedule` node has two child node associations, one for each of the steps in the disposition. We can also see that in the Node Browser:

Children

Child Name	Child Node	Primary	Association Type	Index
cutoff	workspace://SpacesStore/c87359e6-bdda-45ad-aa9b-cdea5411a470	true	dispositionActionDefinitions	0
destroy	workspace://SpacesStore/5fd679c4-0e4c-455e-a745-b1f0927d2edd	true	dispositionActionDefinitions	1

Summary

One of the most important things to configure within the File Plan is the retention schedule—the specification for how long a type of record needs to be retained before being disposed of. In the DoD 5015.2 specification, retention schedules are a key component of the disposition schedule. In this chapter, we learned how to configure the disposition schedules. We covered the following topics:

- How to configure the disposition schedule
- The types of steps that can be created in a disposition schedule

- The difference between applying the disposition at the Folder and record levels
- How to configure both time and event-based triggers

At the end of the chapter, in a 'How does it work' section, we looked, in detail, at how the Alfresco site Edit disposition web page is constructed. In particular, we covered:

- How the page was built as a Spring-Surf web page
- Some examples of YUI web client components and the use of the YUI framework to handle client-side event processing
- The relationship between the disposition schedule and its record Category in the content model
- How AJAX calls from the client can retrieve content from the Alfresco repository to populate data into the client web page

In both this chapter and the last, we covered the setup and configuration of the Records Management File Plan. With the File Plan now in place, we are ready to actually begin filing content into the plan and we will discuss some of the many ways that filing can be done within Alfresco in the next chapter.

7
Filing Records

In the last chapter, we saw how to set up the File Plan for a Records Management system. In this chapter, we now turn to look at the many ways in which records can be filed into the plan.

In this chapter, we will describe:

- How to file both electronic and non-electronic records from within Share
- How to mount the File Plan as a drive that can be filed to directly from the desktop
- How to file from within an e-mail client
- How to bulk file large numbers of documents

At the end of this chapter, in a "How does it work?" section, we will look at Share internals to examine two different aspects of records filing: electronic file uploads and non-electronic record registrations.

The file upload process is streamlined by making use of the Flash upload control in the YUI library. We'll look at how this control works and see how it enables multi-file uploads from the browser to be as quick and easy as uploading a file from a thick client application.

The non-electronic record registration provides a good example of how Alfresco forms can be displayed as part of a dynamic pop-up dialog.

Filing—more than one way

Filing is the process of classifying records and then correctly placing records into the File Plan. While the Records Management site within Alfresco Share makes web client filing straightforward and easy, Alfresco provides numerous other ways for records to be filed into the records system.

The many different interfaces that Alfresco offers to interact with the repository can shrink the learning curve and accelerate acceptance of the system. For example, many users are enthusiastic to learn that they can continue to interact with the Alfresco repository just like it were a shared file server. Many users also spend much of their time using e-mail, and for those users, Alfresco features are built into their favorite e-mail clients, like IMAP folders and SMPT inbound e-mail, both of which can significantly streamline a user's access to the repository.

Alfresco provides tools for getting many records into the system quickly. Bulk import methods, like the client Flash upload dialog in the web client, integration with scanners, and command-line upload scripts, allow large numbers of records to be captured and filed very quickly.

In this chapter, we will look in detail at some of the many different ways to file into the Records Management system.

While there may be more than one way to file a record, all the different filing methods access the records repository in a consistent way based on the user's access rights. Different ways of filing allow different styles of working to be accommodated, making the system easier and more convenient to access. But this flexibility does not imply any inconsistency in terms of policies.

Consistency is a best practice for Records Management programs and it provides credibility to the program. Consistency means that the same policies and procedures are applied repeatedly without exception under a variety of conditions. No matter what the location, no matter what type of media, no matter which business group, records across all parts of the organization are treated in a similar manner.

In *Chapter 1*, we discussed a number of drivers that motivate organizations to adopt Records Management systems. Different motivators can mean that different groups within the organization may have different objectives or goals for what they would like to achieve with Records Management.

For example, Finance and Accounting business units may be particularly focused on financial records required to comply with regulations, while the Legal business unit may have a greater focus on the maintenance of corporate legal records. These different business units also often have different workflows and different ways of doing business.

Despite these differences in objectives, the organization is best served when all records are treated in the same way. Only by doing this can the organization demonstrate the legal credibility of their records program. The flexibility in the many ways that records can be filed in the Alfresco system means that it is easier for all business units to contribute to and interact with the records system while still being consistent with organization-wide record standards.

Filing an electronic record from Share

Now that the File Plan is set up, it is easy to start filing records directly by using the Records Management site within Share.

Recall that records can be filed into only the record Folders of the File Plan. It is not possible to put records into either Series or Categories. To prevent us from doing so, the **File** icon on the toolbar is visible but grayed out, and not selectable when positioned within either Series or Category containers.

From the **File Plan** page of the Records Management site, we can navigate into a Folder of the File Plan. When we are within a Folder container, the **File** icon of the toolbar then becomes available for selection:

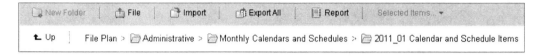

Clicking on the **File** button will display a dialog that prompts us to enter the type of record that we would like to file, either **Electronic** or **Non-electronic**. In this first example, we would like to file an **Electronic** record, so we select that option:

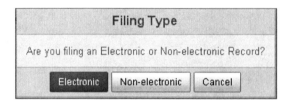

At the top of the dialog for uploading files, there is an option to specify the **Record Type** for the files that will be uploaded. The drop-down menu shows five different types of records:

- Default
- Scanned Record
- PDF Record
- Digital Photograph Record
- Web Record

The file being uploaded is created by default as type cm:content. Recall that we saw in *Chapter 4* in the discussion of the Content Model that cm:content is the base document type in Alfresco from which all other documents types with content inherit from. Selecting a **Record Type** from the drop-down applies an aspect and the associated properties of that aspect to the record.

We saw near the end of *Chapter 4* that the record type aspects listed here are part of the dod content model. These aspects define the record types and their property sets that are recommended for use by the DoD 5015.2 specification. In Appendix B (which is available for download from the Packt Publishing website), the properties associated with these record type aspects are listed in greater detail.

These record types are defined in the Content Model file `tomcat\` `webapps\alfresco\WEB-INF\classes\alfresco\module\` `org_alfresco_module_dod5015\model\dod5015Model.xml`. In that file, in a similar way, new record types could be defined to extend the list here and existing record type definitions can be modified.

If we don't apply a record type aspect and leave the **Record Type** value as **Default**, no additional aspect properties will be applied to the record.

 Each of the four non-default record-type aspects has at least one property that is mandatory. Recall that before a document can be declared a record, all mandatory metadata needs to be defined.

The following diagram shows the four record-type aspects and the metadata properties associated with each one:

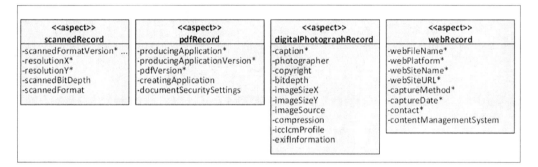

 Note that a record type aspect is something that can also be applied later, after the file has been uploaded, while it is still in the state of an undeclared document.

Next, the files that we wish to upload are selected and finally the **Upload Files** button is clicked on. After that, files are uploaded using Flash. The dialog is dynamic and provides feedback on the status of the upload, indicating the state of upload for each file and a counter that shows how many of the files have completed. After the upload is done, the label **Upload Files** on the dialog button will change to **OK**:

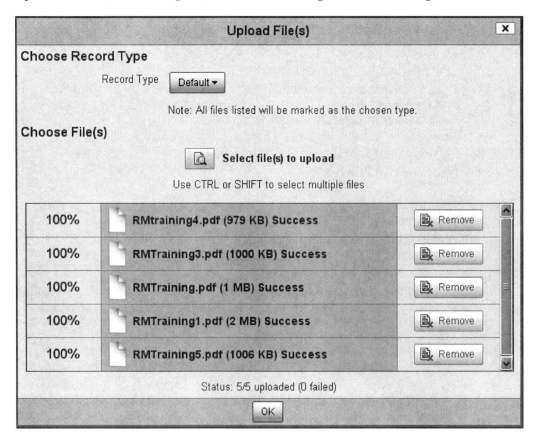

After clicking on **OK**, the contents for the Folder will be refreshed and we see that the files have been uploaded. Note that the documents at this point are still denoted as Undeclared Records.

Undeclared Records are documents that have been placed into the File Plan, but that have not yet entered into the steps of the disposition schedule. The record lifecycle does not begin until the record is actually declared as a record. The process of filing the document into the File Plan adds properties to it that are needed for processing it as a record, like the unique record ID and the date the record was filed. The additional properties are from the record aspect that is applied to the document when it is filed.

Note that the system will not allow you to file two records with the same name into a Folder. Within a Folder, the record names must be unique.

Filing a non-electronic record from Share

We just saw that when filing into a Folder, a dialog first prompts to see whether an electronic or non-electronic record is to be filed. In the last section, we then saw how an electronic record is filed. In this section, we will look at the case of a non-electronic record.

When we select **Non-electronic** record filing, we are presented with a form to collect metadata associated with the record we are about to file. By filing a non-electronic document, we create a stub entry that references a physical document within the Records Management site that contains no file content. The non-electronic record typically refers to a paper record, but the record could be stored on any type of media, including, for example, older, but popular, archival media types like microfilm, aperture cards, and microfiche:

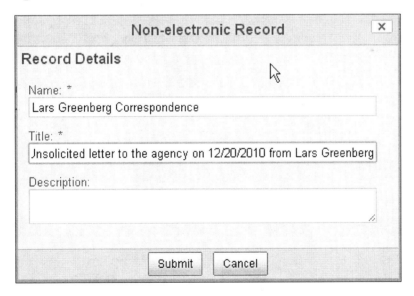

After completing the metadata for the **Non-electronic** record, we click on the **Submit** button. After doing that, a new **Undeclared Record** entry is added to the Folder. The thumbnails for all non-electronic records are represented with the same icon:

After filing the record, additional information about it can be entered by editing the metadata to include information such as the location of the physical record, the media type it is stored on, and the format.

Filing from another Share site

Since we are using the Records Management site within Share, it is likely that we are also using standard Share sites to manage other types of documents, content, and collaboration data in our organization.

We've seen earlier that Share sites are especially good at providing a central point for organizing the content associated with a project, such as a project's documents, files, schedules, and discussions.

Standard Share sites, for example, can be used to manage the process for creating new documents, making use of document management capabilities like versioning and workflow. At some point, documents from within a Share site could then be moved and filed into the Records Management system.

Filing a document from a standard Share site into the Records Management site is easy to do. From within a Share site **Document Library**, a document is selected and marked to be moved:

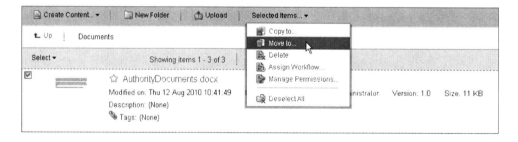

Within the pop-up dialog that displays, it is then possible to navigate into the **File Plan** of the Records Management site and then file the document as a record:

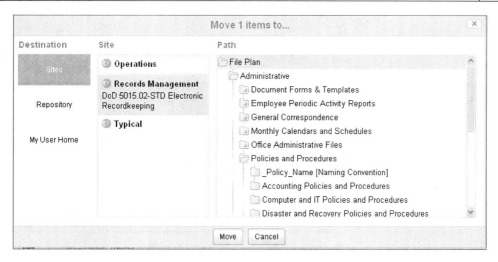

Filing a record from a CIFS mounted drive

CIFS is one of the most popular ways to access the Alfresco repository from a desktop without having to use a specialized software application. We can use CIFS to file records within the Records Management site or documents into a standard Share site, **Document Libraries**.

What is CIFS?

CIFS stands for **Common Internet File System**. It is a protocol that was originally created by Microsoft to allow a Windows 95/98/NT client machine to access files stored on another Windows machine. It allows remote access to files on another computer.

Alfresco's CIFS technology is based on a Java implementation of the protocol created by Microsoft called JLAN. But JLAN is richer than just CIFS. It also supports NFS and FTP protocols as well as authentication like Kerberos, NTLM, and Active Directory. Alfresco acquired JLAN in 2005 and later converted it into an Open Source technology using a GPLv2 license.

> The JLAN technology is embedded in Alfresco and it is also available as a standalone product. It was originally developed by Gary Spencer. A high-level technical specification for the JLAN technology can be found at http://www.alfresco.com/products/aifs/.

Filing with CIFS

With JLAN, Alfresco is able to emulate the CIFS protocol. The Alfresco repository can respond to CIFS protocol requests, making it appear and act just like an external file server. That means that applications that can interact with CIFS servers, such as Windows Explorer, are able to connect to the Alfresco CIFS interface. Users can navigate through the folders and documents of Alfresco just like the folders and files of a file server. Filing into Alfresco becomes as simple as dragging a document from the desktop into the CIFS-mounted drive.

Only Alfresco Share users are able to map to and connect to the Alfresco CIFS drive. During each operating system session, the user will need to authenticate with Share in order to access the mapped drive. The user gains access to the CIFS drive with the same user credentials as with the Share web client and has the same access permissions to elements of the File Plan as in the web client:

Configuring CIFS

If we've installed an Alfresco "full setup" version for the Windows platform, CIFS may already be active on our server. If so, that's great. Let's look at what may need to be changed in the configuration of the CIFS drive.

Remember that CIFS emulates the access of a file server on a remote machine. Because of that, access to the Alfresco CIFS interface is referenced with a unique host name. By default, when Alfresco starts, CIFS is assigned a host name constructed by taking the host name of the Alfresco server and appending the letter "A" to it. For example, since my computer name is DW_FTK_CA, the Alfresco CIFS server that runs on it, by default, is called **DW_FTK_CAA**.

The format for accessing an Alfresco repository path is \\machinename\Alfresco\ path; for example, the path to the Records Management File Path on my machine would be written as \\DW_FTK_CAA\Alfresco\Sites\rm\documentLibrary.

To make sure that we have the correct Alfresco CIFS path, we can look it up in the Alfresco JSF Explorer client by navigating to the folder within the repository that we would like to map as the root for our CIFS drive. By moving the mouse over the icon to the right of the folder name directly under the path breadcrumb, the correct CIFS path for reaching the directory is displayed:

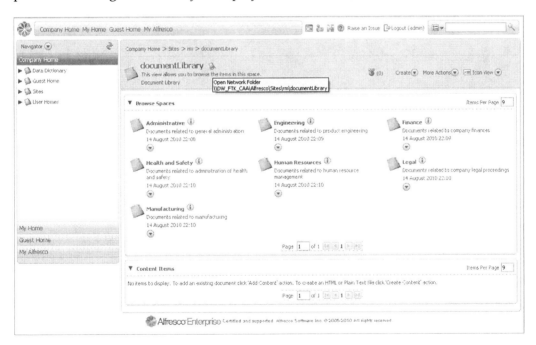

Once we know the CIFS path for the repository folder, we can then map it as an accessible remote folder. For example, on a Windows operating system, the CIFS drive can be mapped using Windows Explorer. Within the **Map Network Drive** dialog available from the **Tools** menu in Windows Explorer, the CIFS path can be entered and assigned to a drive letter, as shown in the screenshot below:

Troubleshooting CIFS

CIFS is a great option for making it easy to access the repository and users typically love it, but getting it set up can sometimes cause problems. If CIFS didn't work for us right out of the box, there are some things we can do to try to troubleshoot it.

If, for example, we don't see CIFS paths showing up on the page of a folder in the repository within the JSF Alfresco Explorer client, it means that the CIFS server is probably not running. Other reasons it may not work include issues with DLLs on Windows, improper port settings, and authentication setting conflicts.

Checking to see whether the CIFS server is running

To investigate whether the CIFS server is actually running, we first need to know the name of our machine. Make sure that we have the correct name for our machine. In Windows, we can find the machine name by using the `net` command from a DOS command line:

```
C:\>net config workstation

Computer name                          \\DW_FTK_CA

Full Computer name                     DW_FTK_CA

User name                              Dick
```

Using `nbtstat`, we can then check whether the CIFS drive is available. We should see two entries for the CIFS drive when we do the following:

 Make sure that we've started the Alfresco server before running this command.

```
C:\>nbtstat -n

Local Area Connection 1:
Node IpAddress: [172.16.1.135] Scope Id: []

                 NetBIOS Local Name Table

       Name              Type         Status
    ---------------------------------------------

       DW_FTK_CA      <00>  UNIQUE    Registered

       DW_FTK_CA      <20>  UNIQUE    Registered

       DW_FTK_CAA     <20>  UNIQUE    Registered

       DW_FTK_CAA     <00>  UNIQUE    Registered
```

Here we see `DW_FTK_CAA`, which is the CIFS server, included in the list. If we don't see the CIFS server in this list, it has definitely not started up, and we'll need to troubleshoot what might have gone wrong.

Missing NetBIOS DLL

On a Windows machine, JLAN needs to find `win32netbios.dll` on the system path. A copy of this file is in the `<Alfresco>\bin` directory. If we don't already have a copy of this DLL in the `C:\Windows\System32` folder, we should copy it over to that location.

Problems with ports

Another common problem is that the ports that CIFS needs to use may already be used by something else. The standard ports that CIFS tries to use are TCP 139/445 and UDP 137/138. When Alfresco is running and CIFS is working correctly, running `netstat` on Windows helps us check to see if those ports are being used. To do this, we shut down the Alfresco server and look for activity on these ports. If we come across a conflict, we need to reconfigure CIFS to run on different ports:

```
C:\>netstat -an |find /i "listening" |find "139"
   TCP    172.16.1.135:139        0.0.0.0:0              LISTENING

C:\>netstat -an |find /i "listening" |find "445"
   TCP    0.0.0.0:445             0.0.0.0:0              LISTENING

C:\>netstat -an |find /i "UDP" |find "137"
   UDP    172.16.1.135:137        *:*

C:\>netstat -an |find /i "UDP" |find "138"
   UDP    172.16.1.135:138        *:*
```

Configuring a different set of ports can be done by overriding the standard ports in the `tomcat\shared\classes\alfresco-global.properties` file. For example, the following entries could be added to that properties file to define non-privileged ports to be used with CIFS, after first verifying that there is no existing conflict with these new port assignments too:

```
cifs.tcpipSMB.port=1445
cifs.netBIOSSMB.namePort=1137
cifs.netBIOSSMB.datagramPort=1138
cifs.netBIOSSMB.sessionPort=1139
```

CIFS server name is too long

The maximum length of a machine name in Windows is 10 characters. If our server machine name is 10 characters long, a CIFS machine name constructed by appending the letter "A" to it will fail because the CIFS machine name would be too long for Windows. In that case, we should override the default CIFS name with our own. We can define a new CIFS machine name shorter than 10 characters in the `alfresco-global.properties` file by adding the following line to it:

```
cifs.serverName=ShortName
```

Conflicts with authentication settings

Note also that CIFS isn't compatible with certain Alfresco authentication systems that do not support CIFS, such as LDAP or Active Directory. If we have changed our authentication scheme to use either of those systems, then that is a problem. In those cases, CIFS will be automatically disabled. In order to get both CIFS and LDAP to work together, or to use some other authentication system, we have to set up what is called an authentication chain.

> Complete information for configuring CIFS, NFS, and FTP is available on the Alfresco wiki at `http://wiki.alfresco.com/wiki/File_Server_Subsystem#SMB.2FCIFS_Server_Configuration`. Some tips about getting CIFS running on Windows can be found here at `http://wiki.alfresco.com/wiki/CIFS_Windows`

Filing from an e-mail client with IMAP

Following in the same theme of being able to access Alfresco without needing to start up the Share application, Alfresco's **IMAP** integration, available since version 3.2, allows users to access the Alfresco repository via their e-mail client.

What is IMAP?

IMAP or **Internet Message Access Protocol** is a standard Internet protocol that allows an e-mail client to access e-mail on a remote mail server. IMAP is a feature available on most popular modern e-mail clients, such as Outlook, Outlook Express, Apple Mail, and Thunderbird.

IMAP allows the e-mail client to be able to interact with the Alfresco repository. Folders within Alfresco can be exposed as IMAP folders and grouped within the e-mail client folder list, for example, appearing under the list of folders with entries such as the user's inbox or sent folders.

Filing with an IMAP e-mail client

Filing into Alfresco via the Alfresco IMAP folder is easy. It is just a matter of locating the folder to which we want to file within the Alfresco folder hierarchy and then dragging the e-mail into that folder.

Similarly, we can also file by right-clicking on an item in the inbox and then selecting the option of **Move to Folder**. Doing that will display a list of all available folders in Outlook, including the Alfresco IMAP folder, and from that list, the correct Alfresco folder can be selected in which to file:

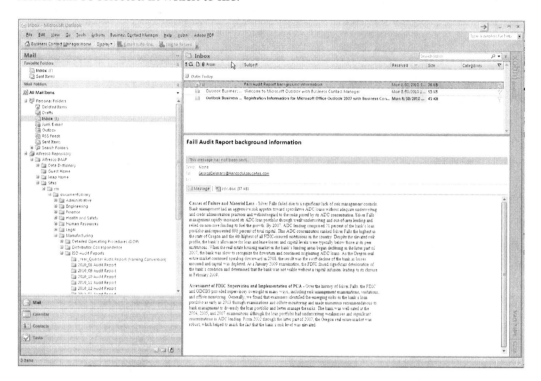

Configuring IMAP

For users to access Alfresco using IMAP, there are configurations that need to be made on both the server and the client.

Configuring IMAP to run on the server

The Alfresco IMAP server can be turned on by configuring the `tomcat\shared\classes\alfresco-global.properties` file. It isn't available by default. Adding the following lines to the global properties file will enable it:

```
imap.server.enabled=true\
imap.server.port=143
imap.server.host=formtek.com
```

Here `imap.server.host` is the name of our network server. The value used for the host name should be the IP address or the DNS address for the outward-facing network. After adding these lines to the `alfresco-global.properties` file, recycle the Alfresco server. During startup, in the Alfresco log file, we will notice an entry that should confirm that the IMAP server successfully started:

```
11:09:44,203  INFO  [repo.imap.AlfrescoImapServer] IMAP service
started on host:port formtek.com:143.
```

Next, log in to Share as the user admin and, from the **My Sites** dashlet on the home page, notice that there are two stars to the left of the **Records Management** site name. Click on the one on the right with the tiny e-mail image. Doing this will make the **Records Management** site visible to privileged users as IMAP folders from their e-mail clients:

The Alfresco IMAP server is now ready to communicate with e-mail clients. The default repository mount location for the IMAP server is the `Company Home` directory of Alfresco.

There are variations to this default configuration that can be made. The mount point can be configured to be at a different folder in the repository, and it is also possible to define more than a single mount point.

For example, adding these three lines to the previous configuration will restrict the mount point to being at the top of the File Plan:

```
imap.config.server.mountPoints.default.rootPath=/${spaces.company_
home.childname}/st:sites/cm:rm/cm:documentLibrary
imap.config.server.mountPoints.value.AlfrescoIMAP.
mountPointName=Records
imap.config.server.mountPoints.value.AlfrescoIMAP.modeName=MIXED
```

A description of all the available configuration settings for the IMAP server can be found on the Alfresco wiki at `http://wiki.alfresco.com/wiki/The_IMAP_Subsystem`.

Configuring IMAP on e-mail clients

Getting the IMAP server to run is relatively painless, but getting it to work on individual e-mail clients is a bit more work, with the method for configuring each client being slightly different. Let's look here to see what is necessary to configure Outlook 2007 to recognize Alfresco as a mount point.

IMAP configuration for Outlook 2007

Outlook is probably one of the most common e-mail clients. Let's look to see how an Outlook 2007 client can be set up to connect to the Alfresco repository.

From the Outlook client, select the **Tools | Account Settings** menu item. After doing that, the **Account Settings** dialog should display. Stay on the left-most tab labeled **E-mail**. Below that tab, click on the **New** option. If an **Auto Account Setup** screen appears, select the option to **Manually configure server settings** near the bottom of that dialog.

At that point, our screen should look something like the following screenshot:

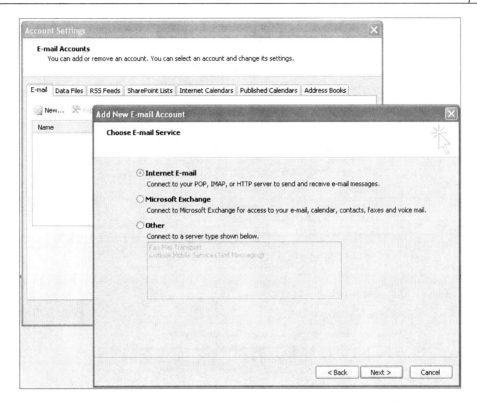

On the **Choose E-mail Service** dialog, select the top option for specifying an **Internet E-Mail** account:

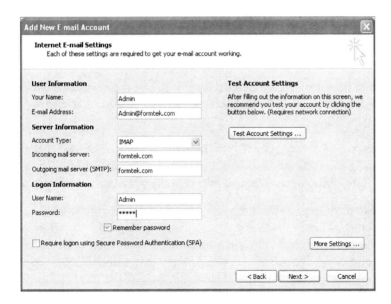

Then on the **Add E-mail Account** screen, define the information for connecting to the Alfresco IMAP server.

Click on **More Settings**, and we can then enter the name that will be displayed for the IMAP folder in Outlook. After entering the name, click on **OK** and go back to the parent dialog:

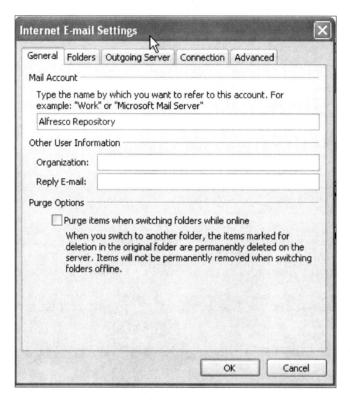

We can now test the connection. After doing that, the configuration is finished. We can click on **Next** and then on **Finish** to create the new e-mail account.

Immediately after doing that, the IMAP mapping becomes active and we see the mounted Alfresco repository show up in the left-hand panel of the Outlook window. Let's try dragging something into one of the File Plan folders, and after doing that, we can verify in Share that we have indeed successfully filed an e-mail from Outlook.

It's also possible to drag an e-mail from the File Plan back into the inbox or another folder in Outlook. When browsing through the File Plan folders, all e-mails filed into the repository display within Outlook as normal e-mail documents, showing the body and attachments. The Alfresco IMAP folder functions like any other Outlook folder.

Outlook is also able to browse records that are not e-mails but which are filed in the File Plan. When we browse to a record that is not an e-mail, we see the metadata for the record displayed as the body of the e-mail. The body of the e-mail also contains links to the record content. For example, clicking on the **Content URL** link will launch the file content for the record.

 It is possible to configure the template that is used to display the metadata in the e-mail body. By changing the template, the layout format can be customized. The template can be found stored in the repository in the directory `/Company Home/Data Dictionary/Imap Configs/Templates`.

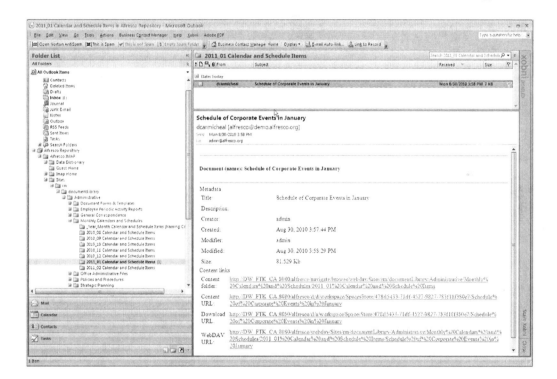

 Additional information about configuring Outlook and other IMAP e-mail clients that can connect to the Alfresco repository can be found on the Alfresco wiki: `http://wiki.alfresco.com/wiki/IMAP`

Filing to Alfresco via FTP

One more way to file records into the Alfresco repository is by connecting to the Alfresco repository using FTP. Again, access to the repository is very easy to do, this time using any standard FTP client. In the figure below, we see access to the Alfresco File Plan using the FTP client **Filezilla**.

In a similar way to CIFS and IMAP, Alfresco can run as an FTP server. By default, the Alfresco server uses port 21, and no additional configuration should be needed. Although with FTP, as with both CIFS and IMAP, problems can occur in setting up the server when the port that Alfresco attempts to run on is already being used by another process:

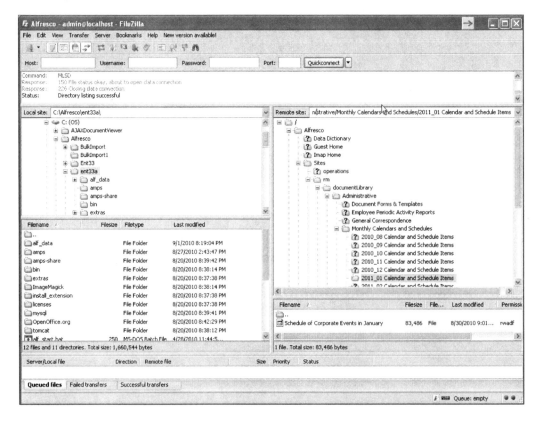

Bulk import

Let's now discuss one way to import a large number of records into the File Plan at one go. One existing tool that will let us do this is called the Alfresco Bulk Filesystem Import tool. The Import tool imports into Alfresco, from a specified directory that is local to the Alfresco server, the folder structure underneath that directory and all the files that are contained within it.

The Alfresco Bulk Filesystem Import tool can be downloaded from Google Code at `http://code.google.com/p/alfresco-bulk-filesystem-import/`. The import tool was written by Peter Monks, an employee of Alfresco.

An unsupported add-on

The Import tool was intended to support the import of folders and files into the standard Alfresco repository. The tool works fairly well in being able to import files quickly and has achieved some amount of popularity in the Alfresco community. However, one caveat is that the Import tool isn't part of the standard Alfresco product and, as such, isn't officially supported. If we have a lot of files to import though, it is definitely something worth checking out.

Bulk import and Records Management considerations

The other thing to note is that it is likely that the Import tool was not built with any thought about Records Management in mind, and because of that, and because of the special characteristics of the records File Plan, there are some considerations that we need to keep in mind when applying the Import tool to Records Management content.

Bulk import can't import disposition information

One problem to note in particular is with record Categories. The tool does not provide a way to be able to associate a disposition schedule with the Category.

If the intent is to have the disposition schedule apply at the record level, the Import tool won't help because once records are filed under a Folder of the Category, it is no longer possible to go back and create a disposition schedule as one that applies at the record level. If Categories, Folders, and records are imported with a single batch run, this then causes a problem.

On the other hand, if the disposition is to be applied at the Folder level, importing Categories should work, but dispositions will need to be added to each Category after the tool is run.

For Records Management purposes, it is probably best to limit the use of the Import tool to the bulk import of Folders and records into the File Plan. The File Plan Series and Category structure should already be in place when the tool is run.

Installing bulk import

Installing the Import tool is easy and quick to do. First, the Alfresco server should be shut down. Then, download and copy the AMP file for the Import tool and place it in the `amps` directory under the `alfresco` root. Finally, from within the `alfresco` root directory, run the `apply_amps.bat` batch file.

Simple interface to access bulk import

After installing the tool, there is a very simple web page that we can bring up to try it. If we go to the URL `http://localhost:8080/alfresco/service/bulk/import/filesystem`, we will see a page similar to the following:

Next, we need to prepare some files for import. As an example, let's place files into a local server directory called `BulkImport`.

 Note that the Import tool will fail to work correctly when run from a client machine that specifies a path that is not available for the server to reach.

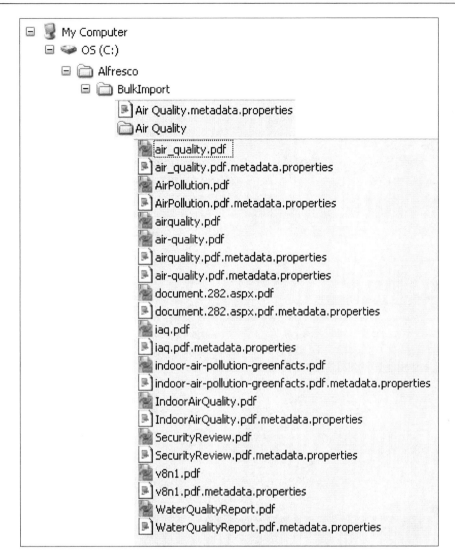

Bulk import shadow files

Associated with each folder and file to be imported into the directory is a corresponding "shadow" properties file that contains the metadata for that item. The naming convention for the "shadow" files is to simply append `.metadata.properties` to the file or folder name.

In this example, there is a single folder and 11 content items, and each item is associated with a "shadow" file. For the folder, the properties file `Air.Quality.metadata.properties` has the following contents:

```
type=rma:recordFolder
cm\:name=Air Quality
cm\:title=Air Quality
rma\:identifier=2010-0000000001f
```

The properties file specifies that the content model type for the imported folder be `rma:recordFolder`, which is a Records Management Folder. We specify the name and title of the Folder. We also specify a unique record identifier for it, something that is generally automatically assigned when the Folder is created via the web application. The identifier needs to be just that, a unique string.

Similarly, one property file to hold associated metadata is defined for each of the files. An example of one of the property files is shown as follows:

```
type=cm:content
aspects=rma:declaredRecord,cm:author
cm\:name=Study on Air Quality in Jakarta, Indonesia
cm\:title=Study on Air Quality in Jakarta, Indonesia
cm\:author=Bulk Import
rma\:originator=Dick Weisinger
rma\:originatingOrganization=Formtek, Inc.
rma\:publicationDate=2010-11-21T10:15:00.000Z
rma\:dateFiled=2010-11-21T10:15:00.000Z
rma\:declaredAt=2010-11-21T10:15:00.000Z
rma\:declaredBy=Dick Weisinger
rma\:identifier=2010-0000000001b
```

Auto-declaration of records

In this file, we declare the content model type to be `cm:content`. We also attach two aspects to the imported content, namely, `cm:author` and `rma:declaredRecord`. By adding the `rma:declaredRecord` aspect, we are able to simulate the **autodeclaration** of this record at the time of import.

We need to be careful here. Before a record can be declared, it is first necessary that all mandatory metadata be completed. `rma:originator`, `rma:originatingOrganization`, and `rma:publicationDate` are all mandatory fields, and because of that, we make sure that we include values for them here.

Similar to the case of the imported Folder, we also specify a unique value for the `rma:identifier` here.

Metadata and dates

Note that the properties that are datetime values, such as `rma:dateFiled`, need to be specified as values formatted using the ISO 8601 time format. The validation of the time format is very strict and the string needs to be complete in specifying the date and time down to the millisecond with time zone suffix, as shown in the code example above.

 ISO 8601 is discussed again in more detail in *Chapter 10*, relative to creating search queries.

Running the tool

Once the content and properties files are in place, running the Import tool is straightforward. The path to the local files and folders to be imported is specified, and the target folder within Alfresco is specified. The import process is quick, and the tool updates its progress every few seconds. After the import is complete, a results screen like the following one displays the status and summary of the import job.

In this example, we see that the folder and all 11 content items have been successfully imported. All of the content items that have all mandatory metadata completed are marked as having been filed, are declared as records, and have been linked to the Category disposition schedule:

Bulk Filesystem Import Tool Status

Alfresco Enterprise v3.3.0 (64)

General Statistics	
Current status:	Idle
Start Date:	2010-08-27 10:05:20.187PM
End Date:	2010-08-27 10:05:23.390PM
Duration:	0d 0h 0m 3s 203ms
Successful:	Yes
Source (read) Statistics	
Files read:	11
Files skipped:	0
Folders read:	2
Folders skipped:	0
Target (write) Statistics	
Content items created:	11
Content items updated:	0
Content items skipped:	0
Spaces created:	0
Spaces skipped:	1

Initiate another import

Filing by scanning

While paper is being increasingly replaced by the use of electronic files and forms, many organizations must still deal with large amounts of new paper records on a day-to-day basis. Many organizations must also deal with large volumes of historical paper documents and records. Paper is still very much a reality today for organizations, but there are compelling reasons to convert paper documents and records into electronic ones.

Being able to bring paper documents into the records system can both improve work efficiencies and save a tremendous amount of physical space. The costs for scanning have also been dropping. Both scanner hardware and imaging software over the last decade have become cheap, fast, and reliable. Because of those benefits, many organizations use scanning on a regular basis to digitize their paper documents and records.

Scanning can either be centralized or distributed. The type of approach that is best for an organization is often a function of the nature of the operation.

For example, some organizations receive large amounts of mail and find that they save money by using an economy-of-scale approach. These organizations have centralized their scanning within their mailrooms to capture documents electronically as soon they are received and opened.

In other industries, particularly professional services and health care, rather than being centralized, scanners are becoming increasingly distributed, typically across multiple branch offices. Each office can then scan documents and records immediately on receipt, enabling quicker processing and updating of the central repository.

Identify which records to scan

While digitizing records can bring about efficiencies and cost savings, that doesn't necessarily mean that all documents and records are good candidates for scanning. Rather than to try to scan everything and to then later cull low-value items from the repository after they have been entered, it is far more cost-efficient to identify and simply exclude low-value documents from scanning.

Metadata and classification

Once digitized, a scanned record isn't that much different than any other type of electronic record filed in the system. But capturing document metadata and then correctly filing the record is typically harder when the record originated as a scanned image. Ideally, we'd like to be able to automate as much of the scan process as possible.

We've already seen, for example, that the header information from electronic record types such as PDF and Microsoft Office bring with them a significant amount of existing metadata. When these Office documents are filed into Alfresco, the information from their file headers is immediately extracted and mapped to metadata properties in Alfresco. But this technique usually doesn't work as well with scanned images because the header of scanned images usually provides much less information than what is found in the header of office documents.

To help with the input of metadata, **OCR (Optical Character Recognition)** software is often used immediately after scanning a document to capture the text contained in the image. Metadata can then be derived from the scanned image by matching the OCR text with the regions on the page where the text for metadata fields are known to be located. Text retrieved from OCR can also be used to assist with the auto-classification and correct filing of the record.

Another technique often used when scanning images is to include scan separator pages or barcodes on the pages that the scanner reads. This allows the software to identify pages that are scanned as belonging to a certain record type or as having certain properties.

OCR and auto-classification technology has gotten to be very good, and for many applications, it is at a point where it is good enough for the task at hand. Unfortunately, for some applications, the error rate of text and barcode recognition may be too high and considered as not sufficiently reliable. In those cases, intervention in the scan process may be needed, making it necessary to either validate the extracted metadata or to manually have to enter data.

Filing scanned images

Alfresco isn't in the scanning business and has left scan integration as a piece for its technology partners to build. To fill the gap, a number of Alfresco partners have developed their own solutions to capture and move scanned images and the associated metadata into the Alfresco repository.

One company that offers complete scan integration with Alfresco is Kofax Image Products. Kofax sells computer hardware, software, and services and has a long history of creating scan software and hardware. Kofax has offered a "release script" as a third party extension to Alfresco since 2006. The script integrates with Kofax software to offer a direct path from scanning and OCR to release into the Alfresco repository.

> Information about the Kofax scan solution can be found on the Alfresco wiki: `http://wiki.alfresco.com/wiki/Kofax_Release_Script`. The Kofax solution is by far the best known of the available scan integrations with Alfresco, but other scan solutions can also be found on the Alfresco Forge, a resource for storing software and features for Alfresco that have been contributed by the community: `http://forge.alfresco.com/search/?type_of_search=soft&words=scan`

Alfresco offers multiple APIs which make the process of integrating with third-party software fairly easy. A tight integration between Alfresco and scanning software can be achieved using the API methods available in the Alfresco Java API and the Alfresco REST API. Low-volume scan capture can also be achieved using some of the other techniques that we've already discussed in this chapter, such as Share multi-filing, CIFS, FTP, or Bulk Import.

Other ways to file

We've seen now that Alfresco is extremely flexible and is able to "ingest" content from a variety of sources using standard protocols that are available out of the box. We have not discussed all the possibilities. Inbound e-mail processing, WebDAV, and third-party browser plugins, for example, are some of the other popular ways that are also useful for bringing content into the Alfresco repository.

> Inbound e-mail processing is a particularly interesting technique that allows users to send e-mails directly to the repository to be automatically filed. Using this technique, for example, important e-mails can be automatically filed by cc-ing the e-mail to the repository. More information can be found about using Inbound SMTP e-mail processing on the Alfresco wiki: `http://wiki.alfresco.com/wiki/Inbound_Email_Server_Configuration`.

Besides the many out-of-the-box approaches for capturing content, Alfresco also offers APIs for Java, PHP, CMIS, REST, SOAP, and JSR-170 that can be used by developers for integrating Alfresco with other software applications.

How does it work?

We will now look at how some of the internals work for filing records within Share. First, we will look at the Flash-based **Upload File** dialog for filing electronic files. Then we will also look at the internals of the dialog form used for registering non-electronic records.

Internals of electronic file upload

One of the interesting features of Alfresco Share that we discussed earlier in this chapter is the ability to quickly multi-select many files for upload at one time. Share has one of the best browser-based multi-file upload implementations available.

Traditional HTML web pages are very awkward when it comes to the handling of the uploading of files. HTML file uploads are possible because of a feature of the HTML `<form>` tag. File uploads in HTML require that the form be declared with `multipart` encoding and include input fields of type "file".

There are numerous restrictions for security reasons about how client-side JavaScript can interact with the input field and the HTML form. By using AJAX and dynamic HTML, it may be possible to work around some of those restrictions, but in terms of development, it is convoluted and equivalent to standing on your head.

Share bypasses the limitations of HTML file uploads and instead uses, by default, an Adobe Flash component to assist with file upload. The result is an upload process that is fast and elegant.

Let's investigate to see how Flash-based uploads work within Share.

File uploads for the Records Management site is initiated from the **File Plan** page. In the "How does it work?" section in the chapter discussing the File Plan, we have already looked at some of the internals of how that page works.

We saw earlier that the file document library.ftl defines the overall layout for the **File Plan** page. Within that file, there are three <@region> tags that relate to file uploads. We've seen in previous chapters that <@region> tags are used to define reusable components on a Spring-Surf web page. Normally, the file upload components are hidden and displayed only when the dialogs need to be visible. The regions are:

Region name	Description
dod5015-file-upload	Dialog that prompts the user to either file an electronic or non-electronic document.
dod5015-html-upload	Dialog to upload a single file using a standard HTML multi-part form submit.
dod5015-flash-upload	Dialog to select and upload multiple files at one time using a Flash component.

The files corresponding to the component definitions for these regions can be found in the directory tomcat\webapps\share\WEB-INF\classes\alfresco\site-webscripts\org\alfresco\components\upload.

The launch of the upload form is initiated by clicking on the toolbar **File Plan** button called **Upload**. The JavaScript controller for the Toolbar component on the File Plan is found in the file dod5015-toolbar.get.js. This file is in the tomcat\webapps\share\components\documentlibrary directory. The event handler for mouse clicks on the **Upload** button is also handled in this file.

The onFileUpload method pops up a standard Alfresco pop-up window with three buttons prompting the user to select from non-electronic file upload, electronic file upload, or cancel:

```
onFileUpload: function DLTB_onFileUpload(e, p_obj)
{
  var me = this;

  Alfresco.util.PopupManager.displayPrompt(
  {
    title: this.msg("message.file.type.title"),
    text: this.msg("message.file.type"),
    buttons: [
    {
      text: this.msg("button.electronic"),
      handler: function DLTB_onFileUpload_electronic()
      {
        this.destroy();
        me.onElectronicRecord.call(me);
      },
      isDefault: true
```

```
      },
      {
        text: this.msg("button.non-electronic"),
        handler: function DLTB_onFileUpload_nonElectronic()
        {
          this.destroy();
          me.onNonElectronicDocument.call(me);
        }
      },
      {
        text: this.msg("button.cancel"),
        handler: function DLTB_onFileUpload_cancel()
        {
          this.destroy();
        }
      }]
    });
  }
```

In this code, we see the method defined to handle the display of the electronic upload window:

```
onElectronicRecord: function DLTB_onElectronicRecord()
{
  if (this.fileUpload === null)
  {
    this.fileUpload = Alfresco.getRecordsFileUploadInstance();
  }
  // Show uploader for multiple files
  this.fileUpload.show(
  {
    siteId: this.options.siteId,
    containerId: this.options.containerId,
    uploadDirectory: this.currentPath,
    filter: [],
    mode: this.fileUpload.MODE_MULTI_UPLOAD,
    thumbnails: "doclib",
    onFileUploadComplete:
    {
      fn: this.onFileUploadComplete,
      scope: this
    }
  });
}
```

Here we see the toolbar code calling into the code for the upload components. The call to `Alfresco.getRecordsFileUploadInstance()` creates `Alfresco.RecordsFileUpload`, as defined in the `dod5015-fileupload.js` file. That component checks to see whether the user has Flash installed or not, and depending on that, decides which pop up to display next.

If Flash is installed, the component `Alfresco.RecordsFlashUpload` is used, which enables multi-file uploads, otherwise the `Alfresco.RecordsHtmlUpload` component is used to upload files on a one-by-one basis.

When Flash is not available, the dialog that is displayed is as follows. We can see that with this pop up, the user is limited to selecting only a single file at a time for upload:

In the case where the user has Flash installed, then the upload process is based on Flash and is handled by the two JavaScript files: `flash-upload.js` and `dod5015-flash-upload.js`, which extends from the former file. These are client-side JavaScript files and are located in the `tomcat\webapps\share\components\upload` directory.

The **File Plan** page upload dialog borrows via inheritance much of the same functionality that is used for file upload by the standard Share site Document Library. One main difference with the File Plan version of the upload dialog and the standard version is the additional button at the top of the dialog with a drop-down menu for selecting a record type.

The values that show up in the **Record Type** drop-down menu are populated from a hardcoded JavaScript array that is defined in the file `dod5015-flash-upload.get.js`.

The record type selector button, the upload button, and the cancel buttons are all buttons built using YUI. The main panel where files to be uploaded are listed is also a YUI control, the data table. We discussed previously how the YUI data table is used in the `documentlist` component of the File Plan page and lists the records stored at the current path in the File Plan.

But the magic of the dialog is due to the Flash upload control. The Flash component is front and center in the dialog. It is displayed as the icon for the button to launch the file selector dialog, and it behaves differently as compared to standard HTML components. If we right-click the mouse on the file select button, we'll see some Flash-specific menu options that aren't available with any of the other buttons on the screen:

 File upload of multiple files in Share is made possible with the YUI 2 Uploader component `http://developer.yahoo.com/yui/uploader/`.

The YUI library includes an SWF file that handles the actual Flash upload. On startup of the Flash upload component, an instance of the YUI uploader object is constructed. The following code is from the `onReady` method from the file `flash-upload.js`:

```
// Create and save a reference to the uploader so we can call it later

this.uploader = new YAHOO.widget.Uploader(this.id + "-flashuploader-
    div",
    Alfresco.constants.URL_CONTEXT + "themes/" +
    Alfresco.constants.THEME + "/images/upload-button-sprite.png",
      true);
this.uploader.subscribe("fileSelect", this.onFileSelect, this, true);
this.uploader.subscribe("uploadComplete",this.onUploadComplete, this,
    true);
this.uploader.subscribe("uploadProgress",this.onUploadProgress, this,
    true);
```

```
this.uploader.subscribe("uploadStart",this.onUploadStart, this,
    true);
this.uploader.subscribe("uploadCancel",this.onUploadCancel, this,
    true);
this.uploader.subscribe("uploadCompleteData",this.
    onUploadCompleteData, this, true);
this.uploader.subscribe("uploadError",this.onUploadError, this,
    true);
this.uploader.subscribe("contentReady", this.onContentReady, this,
    true);
```

The first argument passed in to the YUI uploader constructor is the HTML element where the upload button will be located on the pop up, as specified in the FreeMarker template file dod5015-flash-upload.get.html.ftl. We also note here that the upload icon for the button is customizable by the Share theme.

Once the uploader control is created, subscriptions to uploader events are created next, each with a reference to the handler method corresponding to the event.

Clicking on the Flash select file button launches the selection dialog from Flash. After files have been selected, the onFileSelect handler method is called to process the results. This handler populates the data table of the upload dialog with the names of the files selected. The YUI data table was created and initialized in the onReady() method by making a call to _createEmptyDataTable():

```
// Definition of the data table column
var myColumnDefs = [
  { key: "id", className:"col-left", resizable: false, formatter:
    formatLeftCell },
  { key: "name", className:"col-center", resizable: false, formatter:
    formatCenterCell },
  { key: "created", className:"col-right", resizable: false,
    formatter: formatRightCell }
];

// The data tables underlying data source.
var myDataSource = new YAHOO.util.DataSource([]);
myDataSource.responseType = YAHOO.util.DataSource.TYPE_JSARRAY;
myDataSource.responseSchema =
{
  fields: ["id", "name", "created", "modified", "type", "size",
    "progress"]
};

YAHOO.widget.DataTable._bStylesheetFallback = !!YAHOO.env.ua.ie;
var dataTableDiv = Dom.get(this.id + "-filelist-table");
this.dataTable = new YAHOO.widget.DataTable(dataTableDiv,
  myColumnDefs, myDataSource,
```

```
{
  scrollable: true,
  height: "100px",
  width: "620px",
  renderLoopSize: 0,
  MSG_EMPTY: this.msg("label.noFiles")
 });
this.dataTable.subscribe("postRenderEvent", this.onPostRenderEvent,
  this, true);
this.dataTable.subscribe("rowDeleteEvent", this.onRowDeleteEvent,
  this, true);
```

Here we see that the `DataSource` is set up to populate the data table from a JavaScript array that holds the result list of selected files that are returned by the YUI Uploader component. The fields in the data of the response are specified. The `onFileSelect` method then adds rows with the file information to the table.

When we are ready to upload the selected files, the user clicks on the **Upload Files** button, and the click handler `onUploadButtonClick()` calls the _ `uploadFromQueue()` method to start the upload, looping over and starting the upload process for each of the files. The files are actually uploaded when the YUI Flash Uploader posts the file information back to the repository using a URL similar to `http://localhost:8080/share/proxy/alfresco/api/upload;jsessionid=44 06234BCC8F787ADCB202EA369792D8`.

Internals of non-electronic record filing

From a developer's perspective, the implementation of the dialog for filing a non-electronic record is interesting because it demonstrates how to include an Alfresco form in a pop-up dialog.

We saw above how JavaScript code for the **Upload** button on the File Plan page is invoked when the **Upload** button is pushed. Similarly, the `onNonElectronicDocument` method in the `dod5015-toolbar.js` file controls the dialog for uploading non-electronic files.

At the start of this method, labels for the title and header are prepared. The variable `destination` is also set. The value for `destination` is the node reference for the Folder where the non-electronic record is to be placed after it is created:

```
onNonElectronicDocument: function DLTB_onNonElectronicDocument()
{
  var destination =
    this.modules.docList.doclistMetadata.parent.nodeRef,
    label = "label.new-rma_nonElectronicDocument",
```

```
  msgTitle = this.msg(label + ".title"),
  msgHeader = this.msg(label + ".header");
// Intercept before dialog show
var doBeforeDialogShow = function DLTB_onNonElectronicDocument_
doBeforeDialogShow(p_form, p_dialog)
{
  Dom.get(p_dialog.id + "-dialogTitle").innerHTML = msgTitle;
  Dom.get(p_dialog.id + "-dialogHeader").innerHTML = msgHeader;
};
```

After that, the method becomes more interesting. We create the URL that will make the Form service render the creation form for a record of type `rma:nonElectronicDocument`:

```
var templateUrl =
  YAHOO.lang.substitute(Alfresco.constants.URL_SERVICECONTEXT +
  "components/form?itemKind={itemKind}&itemId={itemId}&destination
  ={destination}&mode={mode}&submitType={submitType}
  &showCancelButton=true",
{
  itemKind: "type",
  itemId: "rma:nonElectronicDocument",
  destination: destination,
  mode: "create",
  submitType: "json"
});
```

Using the YUI string substitution utility function, the variable `templateUrl` is created. If we convert this into a URL and call it directly from the browser, we can get an idea about how the form in the pop up will look. Using the following URL, where we have appended the `htmlid http://localhost:8080/share/service/components/form?itemKind=type&itemId=rma:nonElectronicDocument&destination=workspace://SpacesStore/0da4440e-9cea-4af4-b951-18c03342ad6b&mode=create&submitType=json&showCancelButton=true&htmlid=rm`, we see something like the following screenshot:

```
title

header

Name:* [          ]
Title:* [          ]

                [                              ]
Description: [                              ]
[ Submit ]  [ Cancel ]
```

This is the raw, unformatted content of the form. The next step then is to create the Alfresco dialog that will actually display as a pop up containing the form. In the createRecord method, the size of the dialog is set as well as methods for handling success or failure of the item creation:

```
// Using Forms Service, so always create new instance
var createRecord = new Alfresco.module.SimpleDialog(this.id + "-
  createRecord");

createRecord.setOptions(
{
  width: "33em",
  templateUrl: templateUrl,
  actionUrl: null,
  destroyOnHide: true,
  doBeforeDialogShow:
  {
    fn: doBeforeDialogShow,
    scope: this
  },
  onSuccess:
  {
    fn: function DLTB_onNonElectronicDocument_success(response)
    {
      var fileName = response.config.dataObj["prop_cm_name"];
      YAHOO.Bubbling.fire("metadataRefresh",
      {
          highlightFile: fileName
      });
      Alfresco.util.PopupManager.displayMessage(
      {
        text: this.msg("message.new-record.success", fileName)
      });
```

```
      },
      scope: this
    },
    onFailure:
    {
      fn: function DLTB_onNonElectronicDocument_failure(response)
      {
        Alfresco.util.PopupManager.displayMessage(
        {
          text: this.msg("message.new-record.failure")
        });
      },
      scope: this
    }
  }).show();
}
```

When the form is finally rendered within the dialog, it looks like the following screenshot:

Very similar logic is used to pop up a form for the Folder creation dialog. See the method onNewContainer(), also defined in the file dod5015-toolbar.js.

Summary

In this chapter, we covered the following topics:

- Filing electronic and non-electronic records from Share
- Filing records with CIFS and FTP protocols with the help of JLAN
- How to go about scanning and bulk loading of documents

In the last part of this chapter, we've looked in detail at how the file upload process works when filing directly into the File Plan in Share. We also saw how an Alfresco form is popped up within a standard dialog for collecting metadata needed to file a non-electronic record.

In the last chapter, we saw how to design and build the File Plan in the Records Management site. This chapter showed us many different ways to file records within it. In the next chapter, we will look at how to manage and work with records in the system.

8
Managing Records

So far, we have covered how to design and implement a Records Management File Plan. We've also looked at the many different ways in which records can be filed into the plan. Now, in this chapter, we will discuss how to manage records once they have been filed.

Once a record is filed into the File Plan and declared as a record, it is subject to the instructions of the record Category's disposition schedule under which it is filed. The possible steps and states that make up a disposition schedule and that define the lifecycle for a record are described in detail in *Chapter 9*.

This chapter looks at record features that are common to and available for all or most lifecycle states that a record can be in. The first part of this chapter covers the details for how to access, view, and interact with record content and metadata from the user interface. The latter part of the chapter then describes code internals for how some of these capabilities have been implemented within Alfresco.

In particular, we will discuss the following in this chapter:

- The actions that are available to perform on records
- How to trigger a manual event for a record
- How to track the audit history for a record
- How to create reference links between records

Records Details

Much of the description in this chapter focuses on record features that are found on the Records Details page. An abbreviated set of metadata and available actions for the record is shown on the row for the record in the File Plan. The Details page for a record is a composite screen that contains a complete listing of all information for a record, including the links to all possible actions and operations that can be performed on a record. We can get to the Details page for a record by clicking on the link to it from the **File Plan** page:

The Record Details page provides a summary of all available information known about a record and has links to all possible actions that can be taken on it. This is the central screen from which a record can be managed.

The Details screen is divided into three main columns. The first column on the screen provides a preview of the content for the record. The middle column lists the record **Metadata**, and the right-most column shows a list of **Actions** that can be taken on the record. There are other areas lower down on the page with additional functionality that include a way for the user to manually trigger events in the steps of the disposition, to get URL links to file content for the record, and to create relationship links to other records in the File Plan:

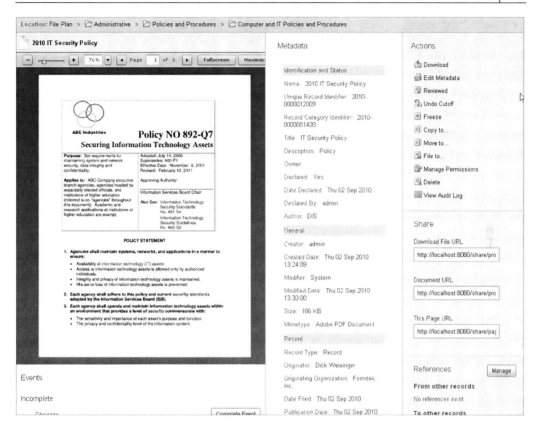

Alfresco Flash previewer

The web preview component in the left column of the Record Details page defines a region in which the content of the record can be visually previewed. It is a bit of an exaggeration to call the preview component a **Universal Viewer**, but it does come close to that. The viewer is capable of viewing a number of different common file formats and it can be extended to support the viewing of additional file formats.

Natively, the viewer is capable of viewing both Flash SWF files and image formats like JPEG, PNG, or GIF. Microsoft Office, OpenOffice, and PDF files are also configured out-of-the-box to be previewed with the viewer by first converting the files to PDF and then to Flash.

The use of an embedded viewer in Share means that client machines don't have to have a viewing application installed to be able to view the file contents of a record. For example, a client machine running an older version of Microsoft Word may not have the capability to open a record saved in the newer Word DOCX format, but within Share, using the viewer, that client would be able to preview and read the contents of the DOCX file.

The top of the viewer has a header area that displays the icon of a record alongside the name of the record being viewed. Below that, there is a toolbar with controls for the viewing of the file:

At the left of the toolbar, there are controls to change the zoom level. Small increments for zoom in and zoom out are controlled by clicking on the "+" and "-" buttons. The zoom setting can also be controlled by the slider or by specifying a zoom percentage or display factor like **Fit Width** from the drop-down menu.

For multi-page documents, there are controls to go to the next or previous pages and to jump to a specific page. The **Fullscreen** button enlarges the view and displays it using the entire screen. **Maximize** enlarges the view to display it within the browser window.

Image panning and positioning within the viewer can be done by using the scrollbar or by left-clicking and dragging the image with the mouse. A print option is available from an item on the right-mouse click menu.

Record Metadata

The centre column of the Record Details displays the metadata for the record. There are a lot of metadata properties that are stored with each record. To make it easier to locate specific properties, there is a grouping of the metadata, and each group has a label.

The first metadata group is **Identification and Status**. It contains the **Name, Title,** and **Description** of the record. It shows the **Unique Record Identifier** for the record, and the unique identifier for the record Category to which the record belongs. Additional **Metadata** items track whether the record has been **Declared**, when it was **Declared**, and who **Declared** it:

```
Metadata


Identification and Status

Name:  2010 IT Security Policy

Unique Record Identifier:  2010-0000012009

Record Category Identifier:  2010-
0000001420

Title:  IT Security Policy

Description:  Policy

Owner:

Declared:  Yes

Date Declared:  Thu 02 Sep 2010

Declared By:  admin

Author:  DIS
```

The **General** group for metadata tracks the **Mimetype** and the **Size** of the file content, as well as who **Created** or last made any modifications to the record. Additional metadata for the record is listed under groups like **Record**, **Security**, **Vital Record Information**, and **Disposition**.

 The **Record** group contains the metadata fields **Location**, **Media Type**, and **Format**, all of which are especially useful for managing non-electronic records.

Record actions

In the right-most column of the Record Details page, there is a list of **Actions** that are available to perform on the record. The list displayed is dynamic and changes based on the state of the record. For example, options like **Declare as Record** or **Undo Cutoff** are only displayed when the record is in a state where that action is possible:

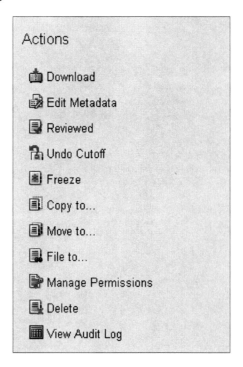

Download action

The **Download** action does just that. Clicking on this action will cause the file content for the record to be downloaded to the user's desktop.

Edit Metadata

This action displays the **Edit** form matching the content type for the record. For example, if the record has a content type of cm:content, the **Edit** form associated with the type cm:content will be displayed to allow the editing of the metadata.

Items identified with asterisks are required fields. Certain fields contain data that is not meant to change and are grayed out and non-selectable:

Copy record

Clicking on the **Copy to** action will pop up a repository directory browser that allows a copy of the record to be filed to any Folder within the File Plan. The name of the new record will start with the words "Copy of" and end with the name of the record being copied.

Only a single copy of a record can be placed in a Folder without first changing the name of the first copy. It isn't possible to have two records in the same Folder with the same name.

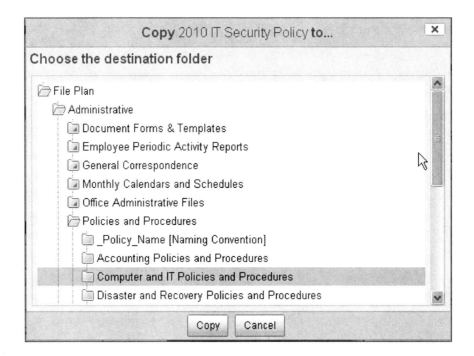

Move record

Clicking on the **Move to** action pops up a dialog to browse to a new Folder for where the record will be moved. The record is removed from the original location and moved to the new location.

File record

Clicking on the **File to** action pops up a dialog to identify a new Folder for where the record will be filed. A reference to the record is placed in the new Folder. After this operation, the record will basically be in two locations. Deleting the record from either of the locations causes the record to be removed from both of the locations.

After filing the record, a clip status icon is displayed on the upper-left next to the checkbox for selection. The status indicates that one record is filed in multiple Folders of the File Plan:

Delete record

Clicking on the **Delete** action permanently removes the item from the File Plan. Note that this action differs from **Destroy** that removes only the file content from a record as part of the final step of a disposition schedule. We will discuss **Destroy** more in the next chapter.

Audit log

At any point in the lifecycle of a record, an audit log is available that shows a detailed history of all activities for the record. The record audit log can help to answer questions that may come up such as which users have been involved with the record and when specific lifecycle events for the record have occurred. The audit log also provides information that can confirm whether activities in the records system are both effective and compliant with record policies.

The **View Audit Log** action creates and pops up a dialog containing a detailed historical report for the record. The report includes very detailed and granular information about every change that has ever been made to the record.

Each entry in the audit log includes a timestamp for when the change was made, the user that made the change, and the type of change or event that occurred. If the event involved the change of any metadata, the original values and the changed values for the metadata are noted in the report.

By clicking on the **File as Record** button on the dialog, the audit report for the record itself can be captured as a record that can then be filed within the File Plan. The report is saved in HTML file format. Clicking on the **Export** button at the top of the dialog enables the audit report to be downloaded in HTML format:

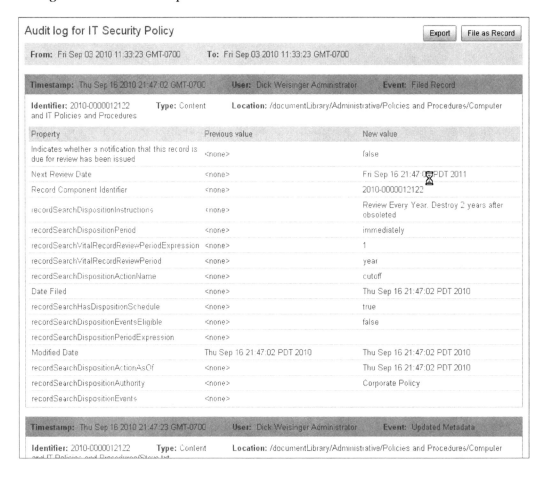

The Audit log, discussed here, provides very granular information about any changes that have occurred to a specific record. Alfresco also provides a tool included with the Records Management Console, also called Audit, which can create a very detailed report showing all activities and actions that have occurred throughout the records system. The Audit tool is described later in *Chapter 10*.

Links

Below the **Actions** component is a panel containing the **Share** component. This is a standard component that is also used in the Share Document Library. The component lists three URL links in fields that can be easily copied from and pasted to. The URLs allow record content and metadata to be easily shared with others.

The first link in the component is the **Download File URL**. Referencing this link causes the content for the record to be downloaded as a file. The second link is the **Document URL**. It is similar to the first link, but if the browser is capable of viewing the file format type, the content will be displayed in the browser; otherwise it is downloaded as a file. The third link is the **This Page URL**. This is the URL to the record details page.

Trying to access any of these three URLs will require the user to first authenticate himself/herself before access to any content will be allowed.

Events

Below the Flash preview panel on the Details page for the record is an area that displays any **Events** that are currently available to be manually triggered for this record. Remember that each step of a disposition schedule is actionable after either the expiration of a time deadline or by the manual triggering of an event.

Events are triggered manually by a user needing to click on a button to indicate that an event has occurred. The location of the event trigger buttons differs depending on how the disposition in the record Category was applied. If the disposition was applied at the Folder level, the manual event trigger buttons will be available on the Details page for the Folder. If the disposition was applied at the record level, the event trigger buttons are available on the Record Details page. The buttons that we see on this page are the ones available from the disposition being applied at the record level.

The event buttons that apply to a particular state will be grouped together based on whether or not the event has been marked as completed. After clicking on completion, the event is moved to the **Completed** group. If there are multiple possible events, it takes only a single one of them to complete in order to make the action available. Some actions, like cutoff, will be executed by the system. Other actions, like destruction, require a user to intervene, but will become available from the Share user interface:

 We'll see in *Chapter 12* how custom events can be created with a tool that is part of the Records Management Console.

References

Often it is useful to create references or relationships between records. A reference is a link that relates one record to another. Clicking on the link will retrieve and view the related record.

In the lower right of the Details page, there is a component for tracking references from this record and to other records in the File Plan. It is especially useful for tracking, for instance, reference links to superseded or obsolete versions of the current record.

To attach references, click on the **Manage** button on the **References** component:

Then, from the next screen, select **New Reference**:

A screen containing a standard Alfresco form will then be displayed. From this screen, it is possible to name the reference, pick another record to reference, and to mark the type of reference.

Available reference types include:

- SupersededBy / Supersedes
- ObsoletedBy / Obsoletes
- Supporting Documentation / Supported Documentation
- VersionedBy / Versions
- Rendition
- Cross-Reference

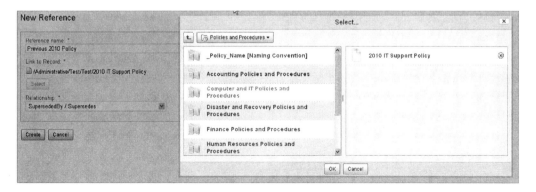

After creating the reference, you will then see the new reference show up in the list:

How does it work?

We've now looked at the functionality of the details page for records and the Series, Category, and Folder containers. In this "How does it work?" section, we'll investigate in greater detail how some of the internals for the record Details page work.

The Details page

To investigate the Details page, let's first start with the URL for the page. The format for the URL is something like this:

```
http://localhost:8080/share/page/site/rm/document-
details?nodeRef=workspace://SpacesStore/3d3a5066-59bf-45cd-b025-
4e5484c9b9af
```

We can see that the `pageid` used within this URL is `document-details`. We can then look up the page description file and find that it is the file `tomcat\webapps\share\WEB-INF\classes\alfresco\site-data\pages\document-details.xml`.

The page descriptor file references the `<template-instance>` as `document-details`. If we look that up, we find the file `tomcat\webapps\share\WEB-INF\classes\alfresco\site-data\template-instances\document-details.xml`.

From the template instance descriptor file, we find that the template path is `org/alfresco/document-details`. From that, we locate the FreeMarker and JavaScript template files for the page. The files are `document-details.ftl` and `document-details.js` in the directory `tomcat\webapps\share\WEB-INF\classes\alfresco\templates\org\alfresco`.

The JavaScript controller for the Details page

The JavaScript controller file `document-details.js` for the Details page is quite short. It relies heavily on the code from the file `documentlibrary.js` that it imports. Recall that we have already reviewed the file `documentlibrary.js` when we discussed the **Document Library**.

The file `documentlibrary.js` has code that recognizes that we are running in the Records Management site. That code sets the variable `doclibType` to the string `"dod5015"` and adds it to the `model`. The file `document-details.js` also stores the variable `jsType` in the `model` with the value of `"Alfresco.RecordsDocumentDetails"`:

```
<import
  resource="classpath:/alfresco/templates/org/alfresco/
  documentlibrary.js">
function toJSType(doclibType)
{
  var type = "Alfresco.DocumentDetails";
  switch (String(doclibType))
  {
    case "dod5015":
      type = "Alfresco.RecordsDocumentDetails";
      break;
  }
  return type;
}
model.jsType = toJSType(doclibType);
```

The FreeMarker template for the Details page

Now let's look at the FreeMarker template file. The layout for the Details page is somewhat similar to the **Document Library** and Category Details pages that we've looked at previously. The `document-details.ftl` page is also used by the standard document Details page by sites other than the Records Management site. When we examine the `document-details.ftl`, we can see at the beginning of the file that there are client-side JavaScript files imported.

Included files for the Details page

The files imported include:

- `components/blog/postview.css`
- `templates/document-details/document-details.css`
- `components/blog/blogdiscussions-common.js`

- components/blog/blog-common.js
- modules/documentlibrary/doclib-actions.js
- templates/document-details/document-details.js
- templates/document-details/${doclibType}document-details.js

There are a number of files related to blog entries referenced, but these files are outside the context of the record Details page. The four main `include` files of interest are:

- templates\document-details\document-details.js
- templates\document-details\dod5015-document-details.js
- templates\document-details\document-details.css
- modules\documentlibrary\doclib-actions.js

Initialize the RecordsDocumentDetails object

Skipping to the bottom of the file `document-details.ftl`, we see the following code that will be executed when the page is loaded on the client:

```
<script type="text/javascript">//<![CDATA[
  new ${jsType}().setOptions(
  {
    nodeRef: new Alfresco.util.NodeRef("${url.args.nodeRef}"),
    siteId: "${page.url.templateArgs.site!""}",
    rootNode: new Alfresco.util.NodeRef("${rootNode}")
  });
//]]></script>
```

We have just seen when we discussed the JavaScript controller that the variable `jsType` evaluates to `Alfresco.RecordsDocumentDetails`. An object of this type is instantiated on page load. The `Alfresco.RecordsDocumentDetails` object is defined in the file `dod5015-document-details.js`, which we just saw included on this page.

This new object is created with elements initialized for `nodeRef`, `siteId`, and `rootNode` members. The `nodeRef` is passed in from the URL.

FreeMarker components on the Details page

In the main body of the web page, as defined by FreeMarker, we can see a number of components defined by the use of the `<@region>` tags:

```
<@templateBody>
  <div id="alf-hd">
    <@region id="header" scope="global" protected=true />
    <@region id=doclibType + "title" scope="template" protected=true
      />
    <@region id=doclibType + "navigation" scope="template"
      protected=true />
  </div>
  <div id="bd">
    <@region id=doclibType + "actions-common" scope="template"
      protected=true />
    <@region id=doclibType + "actions" scope="template"
      protected=true />
    <@region id=doclibType + "path" scope="template" protected=true
      />
    <div class="yui-g">
      <div class="yui-g first">
        <#if (config.scoped['DocumentDetails']['document-
          details'].getChildValue('display-web-preview') == "true")>
        <@region id=doclibType + "web-preview" scope="template"
          protected=true />
        </#if>
        <#if doclibType?starts_with("dod5015")>
        <@region id=doclibType + "events" scope="template"
          protected=true />
        <#else>
        <div class="document-details-comments">
          <@region id=doclibType + "comments" scope="template"
            protected=true />
          <@region id=doclibType + "createcomment" scope="template"
            protected=true />
        </div>
        </#if>
      </div>
      <div class="yui-g">
        <div class="yui-u first">
          <@region id=doclibType + "document-metadata-header"
            scope="template" protected=true />
          <@region id=doclibType + "document-metadata"
            scope="template" protected=true />
```

```
            <@region id=doclibType + "document-info" scope="template"
              protected=true />
            <@region id=doclibType + "document-versions"
              scope="template" protected=true />
          </div>
          <div class="yui-u">
            <@region id=doclibType + "document-actions"
              scope="template" protected=true />
            <@region id=doclibType + "document-links" scope="template"
              protected=true />
            <#if doclibType?starts_with("dod5015")>
              <@region id=doclibType + "document-references"
                scope="template" protected=true />
            </#if>
          </div>
        </div>
      </div>

      <@region id="html-upload" scope="template" protected=true />
      <@region id="flash-upload" scope="template" protected=true />
      <@region id="file-upload" scope="template" protected=true />
    </div>
    ...
  </@>
```

Based on the Region ID and Scope, we can trace through descriptor files to find the following summary of region tags, excluding the regions for the upload dialogs that are not available from the context of the records Details page. Note that the regions corresponding to document comments are not available on the records Details page:

Region	Scope	URL
Header	global	/components/header
dod5015-title	template	/components/title/collaboration-title
dod5015-navigation	template	/components/navigation/collaboration-navigation
dod5015-actions-common	template	/components/documentlibrary/dod5015/actions-common
dod5015-actions	template	N/A
dod5015-path	template	/components/document-details/dod5015/path
dod5015-web-preview	template	/components/preview/web-preview
dod5015-events	template	/components/fileplan/events

Region	Scope	URL
dod5015-document-metadata-header	template	/components/document-details/document-metadata-header
dod5015-document-metadata	template	/components/form
dod5015-document-info	template	/components/document-details/document-info
dod5015-document-actions	template	/components/document-details/dod5015/document-actions
dod5015-document-links	template	/components/document-details/document-links
dod5015-document-references	template	/components/document-details/dod5015/document-references
Footer	global	/components/footer

The region `dod5015-actions-common` is used to pull in some additional `include` files for use on the page. The file `tomcat\webapps\share\WEB-INF\classes\alfresco\site-webscripts\org\alfresco\components\documentlibrary\dod5015-actions-common.get.header.xml` has the following contents:

```
<#include "../component.head.inc">
<!-- DoD 5015.2 Actions -->
<@script type="text/javascript"
  src="${page.url.context}/components/documentlibrary/actions.js">
  </@script>
<@script type="text/javascript"
  src="${page.url.context}/components/documentlibrary/dod5015-
  actions.js"></@script>
<!-- Simple Dialog -->
<@script type="text/javascript"
  src="${page.url.context}/modules/simple-dialog.js"></@script>
<!-- DoD 5015.2 Copy-To, Move-To, File-To -->
<@link rel="stylesheet" type="text/css"
  href="${page.url.context}/modules/documentlibrary/site-folder.css"
  />
<@script type="text/javascript"
  src="${page.url.context}/modules/documentlibrary/site-
  folder.js"></@script>
<@script type="text/javascript"
  src="${page.url.context}/modules/documentlibrary/dod5015-copy-move-
  file-to.js"></@script>
<!-- DoD 5015.2 File Transfer Report -->
<@script type="text/javascript"
  src="${page.url.context}/modules/documentlibrary/dod5015-file-
  transfer-report.js"></@script>
```

We can then see where on the final rendered page the component for each region will be placed, as shown in the following screenshot:

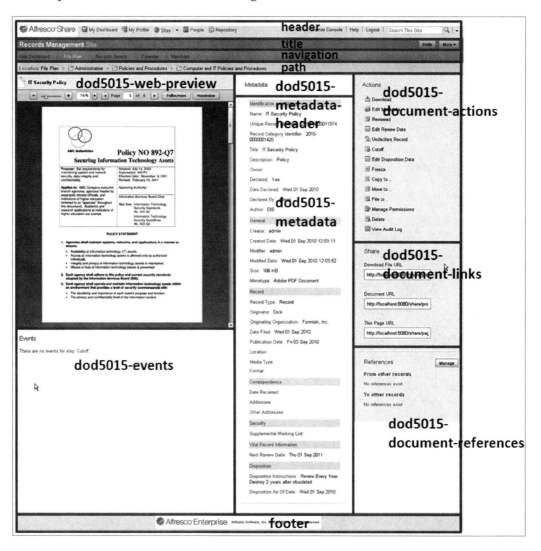

Let's now look in more detail at some of the page components. We don't have space to go through all of them, but let's pick a few that have some interesting characteristics.

The web preview component

The files that define the **web preview** component can be found in the directory
`tomcat\webapps\share\WEB-INF\classes\alfresco\siter-webscritps\org\`
`alfresco\components\preview`.

Web preview include files

The file `web-preview.get.head.ftl` defines the additional files to be included to
support the display of the page on the client:

```
<#include "../component.head.inc">
<@link rel="stylesheet" type="text/css"
  href="${page.url.context}/components/preview/web-preview.css" />
<@script type="text/javascript"
  src="${page.url.context}/components/preview/web-
  preview.js"></@script>
<@script type="text/javascript"
  src="${page.url.context}/js/flash/extMouseWheel.js"></@script>
```

The web preview controller JavaScript

The file `web-preview.js` is run when both the page and the web preview
component are initialized. The code in this file checks to make sure that a valid
node reference was passed in:

```
// Check mandatory parameters
var nodeRef = args.nodeRef;
if (nodeRef == null || nodeRef.length == 0)
{
  status.code = 400;
  status.message = "Parameter 'nodeRef' is missing.";
  status.redirect = true;
}
```

Next, it attempts to find the metadata associated with this record from the node
reference:

```
var json = remote.call("/api/metadata?nodeRef=" + nodeRef);
if (json != null && json.toString().trim().length() != 0)
{
  var node = {},
    n = eval('(' + json + ')');
```

This will make a remote call into the Alfresco repository to retrieve metadata for the
current node. The URL for the service request will be of the form:

`http://localhost:8080/alfresco/service/api/`

```
metadata?nodeRef=workspace://SpacesStore/3d3a5066-59bf-45cd-b025-
4e5484c9b9af.
```

Next, the code tries to extract the `cm:content` property from all object metadata for the record:

```
mcns = "{http://www.alfresco.org/model/content/1.0}",
content = n.properties[mcns + "content"];
```

The value for the content variable contains a string of concatenated properties for the stored file. For example, the information will look as follows:

```
contentUrl=store://2010/9/1/12/3/08ac3a0d-0ccf-44f8-a65d-
1ef4666076d5.bin|
mimetype=application/pdf|
size=108932|
encoding=utf-8|
locale=en_US_
```

Embedded in this string, the `contentUrl` refers to the directory where the Alfresco content store is located. Also encoded in the string are values for the `mimetype`, `size`, `encoding`, and `locale`.

The JavaScript code then continues to check to see if an image or Flash preview of the document is available for viewing:

```
// Call repo for available previews
json = remote.call("/api/node/" + nodeRef.replace(":/", "") +
  "/content/thumbnaildefinitions");
var previews =  eval('(' + json + ')');
```

A call to the Alfresco repository is made here to see what types of renditions are available for this record. It does this by using the following web service URL:

```
http://localhost:8080/alfresco/service/api/node/workspace/
SpacesStore/3d3a5066-59bf-45cd-b025-4e5484c9b9af/content/
thumbnaildefinitions
```

In this example, the response to the web service JSON looks like the following:

```
[    "doclib",
     "webpreview",
     "avatar",
     "medium",
     "imgpreview"
]
```

We see that a `web preview` rendition for this document is already available. This isn't the first time that this document has been viewed on the Details page. The first time that someone accesses the Details page for the record, the Flash `web preview` file is created.

The rest of the `web-preview.js` controller file constructs a node object to be returned as part of the model.

The web preview FreeMarker template

The file `web-preview.get.html.ftl` contains the markup that describes the display of the web preview component. The top of this file contains JavaScript run on the client when the web preview component is loaded that creates an `Alfresco. WebPreview` object:

```
<#if (node?exists)>
<script type="text/javascript">//<![CDATA[
new Alfresco.WebPreview("${args.htmlid}").setOptions(
{
  nodeRef: "${node.nodeRef}",
  name: "${node.name?js_string}",
  icon: "${node.icon}",
  mimeType: "${node.mimeType}",
  previews: [<#list node.previews as p>"${p}"<#if (p_has_next)>,
    </#if></#list>],
  size: "${node.size}"
}).setMessages(
  ${messages}
    );
//]]></script>
</#if>
```

The remainder of the file is the FreeMarker markup for the layout of the component:

```
<div class="web-preview shadow">
  <div class="hd">
    <div class="title">
      <h4>
        <img id="${args.htmlid}-title-img"
          src="${url.context}/components/images/generic-file-32.png"
          alt="File" />
        <span id="${args.htmlid}-title-span"></span>
      </h4>
    </div>
  </div>
  <div class="bd">
```

```
      <div id="${args.htmlid}-shadow-swf-div" class="preview-swf">
        <div id="${args.htmlid}-swfPlayerMessage-
          div">${msg("label.preparingPreviewer")}</div>
      </div>
    </div>
</div>
```

Client-side JavaScript

On the client, the JavaScript file that provides the dynamics for the web preview component is the file `components\preview\web-preview.js`. This JavaScript file contains the definition of the object `Alfresco.WebPreview`.

The JavaScript will check to see if the content is already an image or Flash SWF format that can be viewed as-is or whether a Flash rendition is needed to be viewed. The previewer is capable of viewing both images, Flash or FLEX, so documents with content of this file format type need not have their content converted to Flash in order to preview them.

Alfresco converts office documents, in either Microsoft Office or OpenOffice formats, to PDF using the OpenOffice SDK. Those intermediate PDF files are then converted to Flash SWF objects using the PDF2SWF utility that is part of SWFTools. In the same way, if there is a file format that needs to be previewable, it can be added if there is a tool that exists to convert the file into either PDF or SWF formats.

A service call is then made back to the Alfresco repository to retrieve the Flash preview content. If the preview doesn't already exist, it will be generated. An example of what that service call looks like is the following:

```
http://localhost:8080/share/proxy/alfresco/api/node/workspace/
SpacesStore/3d3a5066-59bf-45cd-b025-4e5484c9b9af/content/thumbnails/
webpreview?c=force&noCacheToken=12833886
```

The actual web preview is enabled by a Flash SWF file that is embedded in the page.

The ActionScript source code for the Alfresco SWF previewer component is not available in the WAR file of a standard Alfresco installation. It can be found in the Alfresco Subversion source code repository under `root\projects\slingshot\ source\as\webpreviewer`.

Alfresco community source code can be downloaded from this Subversion URL: `http://svn.alfresco.com/repos/ alfresco-open-mirror/alfresco/HEAD/`.

The software that detects and checks for a valid version of the Flash player in the browser and embeds the Alfresco Flash previewer object on the web page is called SWFObject.

 Alfresco uses SWFObject 1.5 that is part of YUI 2.0. SWFObject is written by Geoff Stearns and released under the MIT license. The SWFObject JavaScript Flash Player is hosted on the code.google.com website at http://code.google.com/p/swfobject/.

The code in the file web-preview.js that embeds the previewer looks like this:

```
var so = new YAHOO.deconcept.SWFObject(Alfresco.constants.URL_CONTEXT
    + "components/preview/WebPreviewer.swf", swfId, "100%", "100%",
    "9.0.45");
so.addVariable("fileName", this.options.name);
so.addVariable("paging", previewCtx.paging);
so.addVariable("url", previewCtx.url);
so.addVariable("jsCallback", "Alfresco.util.ComponentManager.get('" +
    this.id + "').onWebPreviewerEvent");
so.addVariable("jsLogger", "Alfresco.util.ComponentManager.get('" +
    this.id + "').onWebPreviewerLogging");
so.addVariable("i18n_actualSize", this.msg("preview.actualSize"));
so.addVariable("i18n_fitPage", this.msg("preview.fitPage"));
so.addVariable("i18n_fitWidth", this.msg("preview.fitWidth"));
so.addVariable("i18n_fitHeight", this.msg("preview.fitHeight"));
so.addVariable("i18n_fullscreen", this.msg("preview.fullscreen"));
so.addVariable("i18n_fullwindow", this.msg("preview.fullwindow"));
so.addVariable("i18n_fullwindow_escape",
    this.msg("preview.fullwindowEscape"));
so.addVariable("i18n_page", this.msg("preview.page"));
so.addVariable("i18n_pageOf", this.msg("preview.pageOf"));
so.addVariable("show_fullscreen_button", true);
so.addVariable("show_fullwindow_button", true);
so.addParam("allowScriptAccess", "sameDomain");
so.addParam("allowFullScreen", "true");
so.addParam("wmode", "transparent");
```

The code embeds the Flash control into the web page and passes into it the filename, that is, the record name in the repository. It also sets a flag to indicate whether the file is multi-page and requires paging. The url is a path to the Flash or image rendition of the record to view. Text labels are set as well as some parameters to specify how the component will be viewed, such as with or without the **Full Window** mode.

The metadata component

The dod5015-metadata component is interesting in that it simply displays the standard metadata form for the record. From the file tomcat\webapps\share\WEB-INF\classes\alfresco\site-data\components\template.dod5015-document-metadata.document-details.xml, we see that the standard form component is parameterized with properties that define the itemId, formId, and mode:

```
<?xml version='1.0' encoding='UTF-8'?>
<component>
  <scope>template</scope>
  <region-id>dod5015-document-info</region-id>
  <source-id>document-details</source-id>
  <url>/components/form</url>
  <properties>
    <itemKind>node</itemKind>
    <itemId>{nodeRef}</itemId>
    <formId>rm</formId>
    <mode>view</mode>
  </properties>
</component>
```

The form identified with the tag <form id="rm"> and of the document type cm:content is defined in the file tomcat\webapps\share\WEB-INF\classes\alfresco\dod-5015-form-config.xml.

The events component

The dod5015-events component is defined by the files tomcat\webapps\share\WEB-INF\classes\alfresco\site-webscripts\org\alfresco\components\fileplan\events.get.*. The file events.get.head.ftl includes the client-side JavaScript file components\fileplan\events.js.

The file events.get.html.ftl defines the FreeMarker layout for the component. The layout is divided into three <div> components, one to show the events that have completed, one to list events that have not yet completed, and another for a pop-up dialog that is normally hidden but pops up to collect information from the user when the event is manually completed.

There is no JavaScript controller file for this component. Most of the work for this component is done by the client-side JavaScript file events.js.

We can see in the code in the events.js file that a data webscript is called to find the next available events for this record:

```
url: Alfresco.constants.PROXY_URI_RELATIVE + "api/node/" +
  this.options.nodeRef.uri + "/nextdispositionaction"
```

This will resolve to a URL of the form:

```
http://localhost:8080/share/proxy/alfresco/api/node/
workspace/SpacesStore/0ee56658-9518-4b2e-a679-8c2fd8aa0b59/
nextdispositionaction
```

In this example, the JSON webscript response looks like the following:

```
{
  "data":
  {
    "url":
      "\/alfresco\/s\/api\/node\/workspace\/SpacesStore\/0ee56658-
      9518-4b2e-a679-8c2fd8aa0b59\/nextdispositionaction",
    "name": "destroy",
    "label": "Destroy",
    "eventsEligible": false,
    "asOf": "2020-10-01T12:23:19.828-07:00",
    "events":
    [
      {
        "name": "obsolete",
        "label": "Obsolete",
        "complete": false,
        "automatic": true
      },
      {
        "name": "no_longer_needed",
        "label": "No longer needed",
        "complete": false,
        "automatic": false
      },
      {
        "name": "superseded",
        "label": "Superseded",
        "complete": false,
        "automatic": true
      }
    ]
  }
}
```

The JavaScript code then iterates through these events to render the **Events** component:

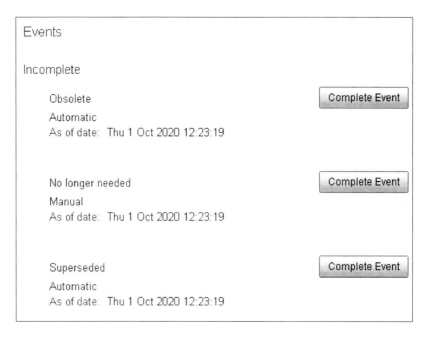

The references component

This component provides more good examples on how to build Alfresco pages using Spring-Surf. Multiple new pages are used to implement this functionality. Clicking on the **Manage** button of this component will bring up a new page with `pageid` `rmreferences`. Then, clicking on the **New References** button of that page brings up yet another page with `pageid new-rmreference`.

In a similar way to that described above and in earlier chapters, it is possible to trace through the chain of files from the `pageid`'s to the components, JavaScript controller code, and FreeMarker templates for these pages to see how they have been constructed.

Summary

In this chapter, we covered the following concepts:

- How to perform common operations on records like file, copy, move, and delete
- How to see the audit history for a record
- How to add links from one record to other records that have been superseded or obsoleted
- How to manually trigger an event on a record

Then, at the end of this chapter, in a "How does it work?" section, we analyzed the record Details page, breaking it into its constituent page components, and looked in detail at how some of the components work. One unique capability of Alfresco that we spent some time discussing is the built-in Flash viewer. We also saw that the metadata component on the Details page is nothing other than an embedded standard Alfresco form.

This chapter has focused on how to manage records of the File Plan once they have been filed. In the next chapter, we will follow a record all the way through its lifecycle.

Following the Lifecycle of a Record

9

We've looked in detail at how to create the disposition schedule that defines the lifecycle instructions for a record. This chapter will show how those instructions are carried out and managed during an actual record lifecycle.

In this chapter, we will discuss:

- How an undeclared record is first filed and then declared
- What the steps are in transferring a record to another location
- How accession is a special type of transfer and how it differs from a standard transfer
- The difference between destruction and deletion of records
- How to freeze documents requested for legal purposes

In the last part of the chapter, we will again go into some developer specifics on how the Alfresco Records Management system is built in a section called "How does it work?". The information is useful to developers (or those who are just curious) for understanding how the Share Records Management system can potentially be modified or extended to meet the requirements of your organization.

We discuss in detail how to configure some background processes that are responsible for sending out notification e-mails and also for automatically triggering time-based events that are defined in File Plan disposition schedules.

We will look at how File Plan Holds and Transfers are implemented, and we also will see how transfer reports are automatically generated and filed.

Undeclared records

When a document is first filed into the File Plan, it is placed into a Folder of the plan and is assigned a unique record identifier and marked as an **undeclared record**.

When filing a document into the File Plan, it is also assigned a number of aspects that are specific to managing records, such as the `rma:record` aspect. These aspects bring along with them many records-specific properties.

However, since undeclared records, by definition, have not yet been declared, the disposition schedule of the Category that the record is filed under doesn't yet affect it. You might think that it's possible to upload a new version of file content for an undeclared record, much like you can for a standard document, but that isn't allowed.

Undeclared records can also potentially be blockers. In the case of a disposition schedule that is applied at the Folder level, if an undeclared record exists in a Folder with that disposition, the Folder's disposition steps will be blocked. For example, even though a folder may be due for cutoff, it can't occur until only declared records are filed in the Folder.

Specifying mandatory metadata

Prior to being declared as a record, it is first required that all mandatory metadata for an undeclared record be completed. This is a requirement of the DoD 5015.2 specification, and the reasoning behind doing it is understandable. It wouldn't be a good idea to allow records to be declared when some critical pieces of information about them are still missing.

 The DoD 5015.2 specification can be found on-line at `http://www. js.pentagon.mil/whs/directives/corres/pdf/501502std. pdf`. We will also discuss it in more detail in Appendix A (which is available for download from the Packt Publishing website) of this book.

However, unfortunately, the need to specify mandatory metadata can complicate the filing process. Because of the need to first specify metadata, there are, in effect, three steps needed to file and declare a record: first file the document in a File Plan Folder, complete the mandatory metadata, and then declare it as a record.

If there are many records that need to be filed, it is sometimes desirable to be able to automate the process of filing records. In *Chapter 7*, we have already looked at the Bulk Import method that enables files to be uploaded, metadata to be automatically attached, and for the document to be declared as a record, all in a single step.

A good solution for automating the filing process would be to be able to add an Alfresco rule to the File Plan Folder. The rule could run a script when an item enters the folder that could auto-populate mandatory fields and then declare the item as a record. However, we have our hands tied here a bit because, as of Alfresco 3.3, rules for Records Management containers have been disabled. The workflow chapter has been deleted.

We've already seen when we looked at the content model that, by default, there are a number of mandatory properties in the `rma:record` aspect.

At least three of the mandatory properties for the record are not automatically populated at the time of filing. These mandatory properties include the `rma:originator`, `rma:publicationDate`, and the `rma:originatingOrganization`. These fields are specified by the DoD-5015 specification as mandatory.

However, if your organization does not need to comply with DoD-5015 to the letter and has no particular need for these metadata fields, one possibility is to simply override the `rma` content model and mark these fields as non-mandatory. This can simplify the process of filing followed immediately by declaration of the record.

Declaring the record

Once the item has been filed and all mandatory metadata has been specified for it, it is possible to declare it as a record. Not until the mandatory metadata has been completed does the **Declare** action become an option:

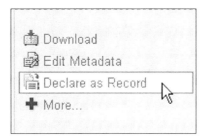

To declare the record, we select the **Declare as Record** action on the item. Immediately after declaring the item, the **Undeclared Record** indicator on the record is removed, and a new action appears in the list: **Undeclare Record**.

Record review

We saw that a property of record Categories is the specification of a review period for each record that is filed under the Category. All vital records require a review. Other types of records can optionally be specified for review.

When the Category is created, a review date, relative to the filing of the record, is specified, such as at the end of the month, quarter, or year.

Once a record comes up for review, an action for marking the record as **Reviewed** becomes available. Clicking on the **Reviewed** action marks the review as having occurred in the audit log of the record:

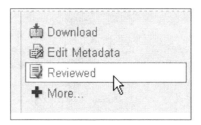

It is also possible to change or update the date of review for a record. After the review of the record, if it is desired to schedule another periodic review, the review date can be updated to reflect the date of the next review:

Closing a Folder

Prior to Folder cutoff, a Folder can be marked as closed. It is not possible to file records to a closed Folder. Filing to the Folder is only possible again if the Folder is re-opened. When a Folder is cutoff, it is automatically closed.

Cutoff

Cutoff is the start date from which the retention period for a record begins. When cutoff is initiated from a time-based criterion, records and folders designated for cutoff are automatically marked as cutoff with no user intervention.

When cutoff is initiated by a manual event, the **Cutoff** action for the item immediately becomes available. The user can then either manually cut off the item by clicking on the **Cutoff** action or wait until the background cron job later identifies the item as due for cutoff and then automatically applies cutoff. As we'll see later in this chapter, the background cron job runs, by default, every 15 minutes:

Once the item is cutoff, an action to manually undo the cutoff becomes available. When a folder is cutoff, it is also closed to any new filings. Items that are cutoff are marked with a small status icon that shows a filled red circle enclosing a white horizontal bar.

Transfer

Transfer is the process of moving records from the system to another location. It is a process that, once kicked off, actually includes a number of substeps.

Consider a records Category with the following disposition schedule. After cutoff, records in this Category are to be retained for two years, then transferred to a long-term storage facility, and then, ultimately destroyed:

Let's see what happens in the File Plan after the record is cut off and the retention period expires. At the end of the retention period, the following action labelled **Transfer** becomes available for the record:

When we click on the **Transfer** link, we initiate the steps for the transfer to start. After doing that, if PDF files were part of the transfer bundle, the first thing that is presented to the user is a pop-up dialog that asks to check that the PDF files in the transfer bundle include an embeddable font:

If fonts are not embedded within the PDF file, then when viewed, Adobe Acrobat or Reader will try to make a best guess on which available alternative font can substituted for the font that was originally used when the file was created. If the same font isn't available, the look and layout of the document might be significantly different from what was intended.

 By using Adobe Acrobat, it is possible to see if the fonts used in the file are embedded or not. In Acrobat, bring up the **Document Properties** dialog by selecting the **File | Statistics...** menu item. Then in the **Fonts** tab, verify that all fonts listed are marked as embedded.

Once the transfer process begins, the record or folder selected for transfer is marked with a green arrow transfer icon. The transfer is still "in process" at this point. There are more steps before it is completed. In our example, we see in the File Plan that the record is marked with both cutoff and the transfer icons:

IT Security Procedures (Corporate-wide IT Procedures)

Unique Record Identifier: 2010-0000012857

Date Filed: Sat 4 Sep 2010 21:26:47   Publication Date: Thu 16 Sep 2010

Originator: Dick Weisinger   Originating Organization: Formtek, Inc

On the File Plan page, along the left-hand panel in a section labelled **File Plan**, there is an entry for **Transfers**. If we click on this link, we will get a list of all **Transfer** bundles that are in progress:

Transfer 0000012857 (Los Angeles Long Term Storage)

Created on: Sat 4 Sep 2010 21:30:06   By: Dick Weisinger Administrator

If we click on the transfer link, which in this example is **Transfer0000012857**, we will be taken to another screen that shows the records that are to be included in the transfer.

To the right of this entry, there are some available actions for the transfer bundle:

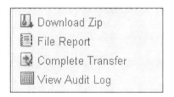

Clicking on the first of these links, **Download Zip**, we get a ZIP file that could be sent to the location where the records are being transferred to. In this example, the location is an offsite archival system.

The bundled ZIP file that we create contains each of the files corresponding to the file content of the records being transferred and an additional file that is in XML and contains all the metadata for the transfer records in the bundle.

After the records have been sent, we can create a report that documents the contents of the transfer, where they were sent, and who did it. This document itself can be retained and filed as a record. To create and file this report, we click on the **File Report** link. The format and sample contents of the transfer report are as follows. We'll look later in this chapter at the internals for how the **Transfer Report** is generated:

Transfer Report

Transfer Date: Sat Sep 04 21:30:06 PDT 2010

Transfer Location: Los Angeles Long Term Storage

Performed By: admin

Disposition Authority: Corporate Policy

Transferred Items

IT Security Procedures (Unique Record Identifier: 2010-0000012857) declared by admin on Sat Sep 04 21:27:08 PDT 2010

The report is then filed and shows up as an **Undeclared Record** in the File Plan:

⚠ Undeclared Record

report_91804 12403736159422 html

Unique Record Identifier: 2010-0000012876

Modified on: Sat 4 Sep 2010 22:06:51   Modified by: Dick Weisinger Administrator   Size: 1 KB

Description: (None)

Transfer to the remote location may take some time, even if the data exchange is primarily done electronically. Once the receiving authority is able to successfully process the transfer bundle, on our side, we will mark that the transfer has been completed. We do that by clicking on the **Complete Transfer** link action on the transfer bundle.

Once the transfer is complete, the transfer bundle is then removed from the **Transfers** area. The transfer status icon on the transferred records and folders in the File Plan changes to indicate that the transfer is complete:

In some organizations, transfer operations are chained, with one transfer successively following another one. Ultimately though, the record is destroyed.

In this example, the next step scheduled after the transfer is an immediate destruction of the document. The **Destroy** action now becomes available.

Accession

Accession is a very special type of transfer operation. It typically only applies to federal agencies that have an obligation for transferring their records to the **National Archive and Records Administration**, or **NARA**, for permanent storage.

The mechanics of accession are similar to those of the standard transfer process. The difference between transfer and accession is that, with accession, the organization that had been managing the records transfers not only just the records, but also all responsibility and authority for them to another organization, typically NARA. Under a normal transfer, the organization performing the transfer would continue to maintain complete authority over them, although they may no longer reside in the original records system after the transfer.

 More information about NARA can be found at their website: http://www.archives.gov/.

In a way similar to how we configured transfers, we can set up a **Disposition Schedule** that uses accession. Consider the case of a disposition with immediate cutoff after filing, followed by five years retention, accession to NARA, and then destruction:

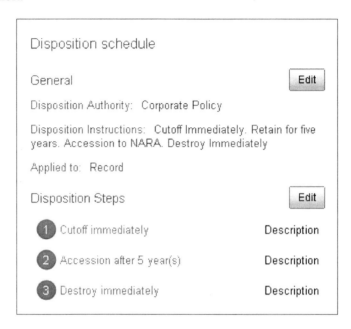

In this example, when a record is filed, it will be immediately cut off. After a five year retention period, the record then becomes available for accession. At that point, the **Accession** action item becomes available for the record:

After clicking on the **Accession** action, in the same way as for a transfer, the item is moved to the **Transfers** area under the **File Plan** header in the left navigation panel:

As with standard transfers, the same actions are available for accessions. The Accession bundle can be downloaded and transferred as a ZIP file. A report on the accession transfer can be filed and then the transfer can be completed.

After the action **Complete Transfer** is taken, the transfer item is then removed from the **Transfers** list. At that point, the original record still exists in the File Plan, but it is marked as having been transferred. In the example disposition schedule shown above, after a transfer is competed, the record is then available for destruction:

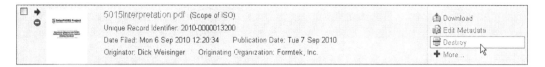

Destruction

As we've seen earlier, **Destruction** is the last stage of a record lifecycle. After a record has been retained and is no longer needed or has been transferred from the repository to a new location, the document is available for destruction.

In the previous section on Accession, we looked at the example of a record that had destruction as the final step of its disposition, immediately after the record was transferred for accession.

If we select the **Destroy** action for a record that is available for destruction, we are presented with the following dialog:

After confirming that we would like to destroy the record, there is a second **Confirmation** screen:

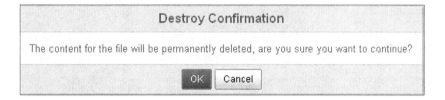

After confirming a second time, the file contents of the record are deleted. With the file content for the record missing, just a stub entry for the record remains in the system. The stub still contains the complete metadata for the record and also all the audit history information that has been logged for the record. In the document list, the entry for the item shows a small status icon of a trash can and the thumbnail for the item is changed to a picture of an icon with an information mark, which indicates the record has been destroyed and the metadata is available for information only:

> Don't confuse **Destroy** and **Delete** actions. **Delete** permanently removes the record, including all metadata and audit information from the system. **Destroy** removes the file content from the record while maintaining a complete audit trail and metadata for the record, and marks the item with an icon as having been destroyed.

Audit log

The **Audit log** contains the complete history of every action that was performed on a record. A **Timestamp**, **Event** name, and **User** is recorded for each action. Both the **Previous** and **New** values for every property that changed when an action occurred are noted in the log:

Audit log for 5015Interpretation.pdf			Export	File as Record

From: Mon Sep 06 2010 13 26 51 GMT-0700   To: Mon Sep 06 2010 13:26:51 GMT-0700

Timestamp: Mon Sep 06 2010 12 20 34 GMT-0700   User: Dick Weisinger Administrator   Event: Filed Record

Identifier: 2010-0000013200   Type: Content
Location: /documentLibrary/Administrative/Test2/qqqq/5015Interpretation.pdf

Property	Previous value	New value
Record Component Identifier	<none>	2010-0000013200
recordSearchDispositionInstructions	<none>	Cutoff Immediately. Retain for five years. Accession to NARA. Destroy Immediately
recordSearchDispositionPeriod	<none>	immediately
recordSearchVitalRecordReviewPeriodExpression	<none>	0
recordSearchDispositionActionName	<none>	cutoff
recordSearchVitalRecordReviewPeriod	<none>	none
Date Filed	<none>	Mon Sep 06 12 20 34 PDT 2010
recordSearchHasDispositionSchedule	<none>	true
recordSearchDispositionEventsEligible	<none>	false

From the **Audit log** pop-up, two buttons near the upper right allow the log to be either exported or filed as a record. For both cases, an HTML version of the audit log is used.

Hold or freeze

Freezing a document or Folder means to temporarily suspend any lifecycle instructions that would normally apply. In particular, the action of record destruction is not permitted when a record is frozen.

If a Folder that has been frozen is due for cutoff, for example, the Folder delays the cutoff action until the freeze has been removed. Similarly, if an item exceeds its retention period while it is frozen, it will not advance to the next step of the disposition until the freeze has been removed.

Once a record has been frozen, it stays in its current location in the File Plan and is marked as being frozen. A frozen record cannot be modified. If a Folder is frozen, the records within the Folder inherit the freeze, and no records can be moved from that Folder, even if the records were added to the Folder after the freeze occurred.

Responding to a hold request

The terms **freeze** and **hold** have the same meaning. Very often, the reason for putting a freeze on records or Folders is due to a legal request, sometimes referred to as a **legal hold**. Lawyers, for example, may request to see all records that contain specific keywords within the body of the record content or within the metadata.

Freezing records

To perform the freeze, we first find the documents or folders that we want to include in the freeze. For example, we might decide to freeze all records related to our IT policies. In the example here, we select the Folder related to IT policies and we select the action **Freeze** from the drop-down menu:

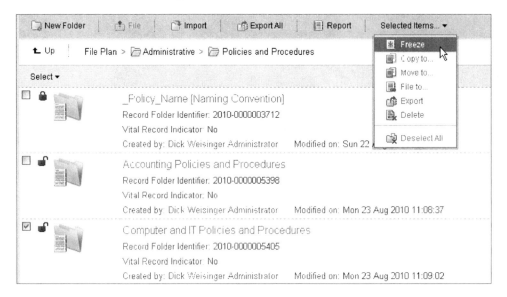

Before the freeze is applied, it is necessary to enter some descriptive information as to why the records are being frozen. After entering the text, we click on the **Freeze Record(s)** button:

The Folder that we selected is then frozen and is marked as such in the document list of the File Plan:

Locating records on hold

We will also notice now that a new package has been added to the **Holds** area that includes the Folder that we just put on hold. The **Holds** area can be reached under the label **File Plan** on the lower left of the File Plan page:

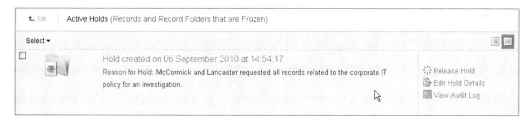

The entry in the **Holds** area shows the new package, marked with the date and time that the hold was made. The description of the reason for the hold is also displayed on this page. In the actions area on the right-hand side of the row entry, we see that we can **Release** the current hold, **Edit** the text that describes the reason for the hold, and also look at the **Audit Log**.

If we click through on this entry, we can get a list of the contents that are bundled into this package, that is the Folder which we froze. Clicking through into the Folder shows that the Folder record contents are also frozen. Items that are frozen are indicated as such with a blue snowflake icon, shown in the status area on the row of the item:

Items included as part of the hold package can be removed from it by selecting the **Unfreeze** action. In this way, it is possible to exclude items from a freeze. Note that it isn't possible to add new items to a hold package from the user interface once the hold has been placed.

Creating an export package of requested records and metadata

Once the items have been frozen, it is then possible to bundle the records and the metadata for those items to create an export package. The package is suitable for transport to the requesting party.

To **Export** the package, we first locate the package in the **Holds** area and then click through it to see the contents of the package. We select all the items contained in the package, and then choose **Export** from the drop-down menu:

Then, on the next screen, we select the option to **Export** the package as a **ZIP** file:

 If the package is intended to be sent to another Alfresco system, then selecting **ACP** as the desired format can ease the task of importing the data into the other system.

After a brief pause, the ZIP file is downloaded to our local computer. After opening the ZIP file, in this example, we see four policy records that were in the IT Policy Folder and a fifth file that contains the metadata for the Folder and records:

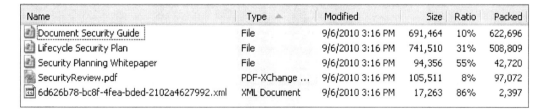

Name	Type ▲	Modified	Size	Ratio	Packed
Document Security Guide	File	9/6/2010 3:16 PM	691,464	10%	622,696
Lifecycle Security Plan	File	9/6/2010 3:16 PM	741,510	31%	508,809
Security Planning Whitepaper	File	9/6/2010 3:16 PM	94,356	55%	42,720
SecurityReview.pdf	PDF-XChange ...	9/6/2010 3:16 PM	105,511	8%	97,072
6d626b78-bc8f-4fea-bded-2102a4627992.xml	XML Document	9/6/2010 3:16 PM	17,263	86%	2,397

The metadata contains the information to match the files packaged in the bundle with the original content files for the records in the package. All known information for the records is included in the dump, including values for the properties inherited from both content types and aspects.

Releasing the hold

Once there is no longer a need to keep the Folders and records of a hold frozen, the hold can be removed. To do this, the **Release Hold** action can be selected for the package within the Hold area:

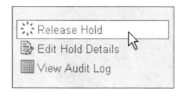

Once the hold is released, the hold package is removed from the hold area. All freeze icons are removed from any of the items that were in that package.

The File Plan report

Another option available on the **File Plan** page is the creation of a File Plan report. The option is available from the toolbar. Clicking on the **Report** button launches the File Plan report starting from the current location in the File Plan path:

The report is launched as a pop-up into a separate browser window along with a **Print** dialog already opened. After printing or canceling out of the print dialog, we can look at the report pop-up and see that it contains a diagram of the File Plan structure, complete with node names, descriptions, and disposition instructions.

There is no save button on the report pop-up, but the report can be saved in HTML from the browser by right-clicking and then selecting **Save As**. A problem with the report is that it may be too verbose for very large File Plans. As noted earlier, a partial plan can be printed by first positioning yourself somewhere in the File Plan other than the root when creating the report:

User: Dick Weisinger Administrator
Date and Time: 06 Sep 2010 15:42:58 GMT-0700 (PDT)

Administrative

Path: /
Record Series Identifier: 2010-0000001373
Description: Documents related to general administration

Document Forms & Templates

Path: /Administrative/
Record Category Identifier: 2010-0000001441
Disposition Authority: Corporate Policy

Disposition Schedule:
1. Cutoff Immediately
2. Retain until obsoleted or superseded
3. Destroy 2 years after obsoleted or superseded.

Corporate Report Templates

Path: /Administrative/Document Forms & Templates/
Record Folder Identifier: 2010-0000003915

Corporate Style Guide Documents

Path: /Administrative/Document Forms & Templates/

How does it work?

We've looked at the types of steps that can be performed on a record during its lifecycle. In this "How does it work?" section, let's look slightly more deeply at some of those steps.

The unique record ID

When a record container, such as the Series, Category, or Folder is created, or when a record is filed, a unique record identifier for the record is created. Many companies are already using an internal convention for creating unique record IDs.

The record ID naming convention within Alfresco is YYYY-SeqNumber, that is, the year followed by a unique sequence counter. An example of this is the record ID 2010-0000003909.

Ideally, it would be nice if the unique record IDs were easily configurable, but the code for generating the record ID is hardcoded in a Java file. That file is `root\modules\dod-5015\source\java\org\alfresco\module\org_alfresco_module_dod5015\action\impl\FileAction.java`:

```
// Calculate the filed date and record identifier
Calendar fileCalendar = Calendar.getInstance();
String year = Integer.toString(fileCalendar.get(Calendar.YEAR));
QName nodeDbid =
  QName.createQName(NamespaceService.SYSTEM_MODEL_1_0_URI, "node-
  dbid");
String recordId = year + "-" +
  padString(recordProperties.get(nodeDbid).toString(), 10);
recordProperties.put(RecordsManagementModel.PROP_DATE_FILED,
  fileCalendar.getTime());
recordProperties.put(RecordsManagementModel.PROP_IDENTIFIER,
  recordId);
```

Background jobs

There are two background jobs that support the correct functioning of Alfresco Records Management. One is a notification function that alerts users when vital records become due for review. The second job checks to see if any cutoff or retention periods have expired and automatically updates those records based on the steps in the disposition schedule.

Both types of background jobs are scheduled and run by Quartz, that is the scheduler component that is built into Alfresco. These two jobs are configured within the file `tomcat\webapps\alfresco\WEB-INF\classes\module\org_alfresco_modfule_dod5015\rm-job-context.xml`.

More information can be found about Quartz on their home page at `http://www.quartz-scheduler.org/`.

More information can be found about scheduling cron jobs in Alfresco on the wiki pages at `http://wiki.alfresco.com/wiki/Scheduled_Actions`.

Review notifications

Review notifications are sent to specified users of the Records Management site when vital records come up for review.

Configuring the notification e-mail bean

The file `rm-job-context.xml` specifies the configurations for scheduled job beans. Consider the following section of code in that file:

```
<!-- Notify Of Records Due For Review Job
Sends out emails of records due for review
-->
<bean id="scheduledNotifyOfRecordsDueForReviewJobDetail"
  class="org.springframework.scheduling.quartz.JobDetailBean">
  <property name="jobClass">
    <value>org.alfresco.module.org_alfresco_module_dod5015.job.
NotifyOfRe
  cordsDueForReviewJob</value>
  </property>
  <property name="jobDataAsMap">
    <map>
      <entry key="recordsManagementService">
        <ref bean="recordsManagementService"/>
      </entry>
      <entry key="recordsManagementNotificationService">
        <ref bean="recordsManagementNotificationService"/>
      </entry>
      <entry key="nodeService">
        <ref bean="nodeService" />
      </entry>
      <entry key="searchService">
        <ref bean="searchService" />
      </entry>
      <entry key="transactionService">
        <ref bean="transactionService" />
      </entry>
      <!--  Subject for email -->
      <entry key="subject">
        <value>${rm.notification.subject}</value>
      </entry>
      <!--  Role to notify -->
      <entry key="role">
       <value>${rm.notification.role}</value>
      </entry>
    </map>
  </property>
</bean>
```

The `jobClass` property sets the bean to use the Java class `org.alfresco.module.` `org_alfresco_module_dod5015.job.NotifyOfRecordsDueForReviewJob`. This class does the work of checking for vital records that are up for review and then sends out the e-mail.

An important part of this code snippet is the last two entries of the property `map` named `jobDataAsMap`. The first of these, called the subject, defines the string to be used for the subject of the e-mail that is sent out. The second, called the role, is the name of the role to whom the notification e-mails will be sent.

By checking in the file `tomcat\webapps\alfresco\WEB-INF\classes\alfresco\` `module\org_alfresco_module_dod5015\alfresco-global.properties`, we can see the configurations for the labels of both of these entries:

```
# Notification configuration
rm.notification.role=RecordsManager
rm.notification.subject=Alfresco Records Management Notification
```

We see that, by default, only users with the role of `RecordsManager` are configured to receive the e-mails.

Configuring the e-mail notification cron schedule

In the same `rm-job-context.xml` file, the cron schedule for the Review notification e-mail is configured.

That block of XML in the file looks like the following:

```
<bean id="scheduledNotifyOfRecordsDueForReviewJobTrigger"
  class="org.alfresco.util.CronTriggerBean">
  <property name="jobDetail">
    <ref bean="scheduledNotifyOfRecordsDueForReviewJobDetail" />
  </property>
  <property name="scheduler">
    <ref bean="schedulerFactory" />
  </property>
  <property name="cronExpression">
    <value>0 0/15 * * * ?</value>
  </property>
</bean>
```

This section sets up the cron expression that is used to determine how frequently to check for and send out vital review e-mail messages. Cron jobs are system background jobs that can be scheduled to occur on a regular basis. The cron expression that specifies the schedule for the job can be interpreted by looking at the meaning for each field of the expression. We see that, by default, the job is set up to run every 15 minutes:

Position	Field name	Value	Meaning
1	Seconds	0	At zero seconds into the minute
2	Minutes	0/15	Every 15 minutes starting on the hour
3	Hours	*	Every hour
4	Day of Month	*	Every day
5	Month	*	Every month
6	Day of Week	?	No specific day of the week

 For a more in-depth description of how cron jobs can be configured within Alfresco, see the Alfresco wiki: `http://wiki.alfresco.com/wiki/Scheduled_Actions`.

Configuring the contents of the notification e-mail

The FreeMarker template for the contents of the text body of the e-mail notification is stored in the Alfresco repository. The file with the template can be found under / `Company Home/Dictionary/Records Management/Records Management Email Templates`. The name of the template document is `Notify Records Due For Review Email.ftl`.

The content for the e-mail layout template is shown next:

```
The following vital records are due for review:

<#list records as record>
  - ${record.properties["rma:identifier"]!}
    ${record.properties["cm:name"]!}<#if record_has_next>,
  </#if>
</#list>
```

It is pretty minimal, but contains all the information needed for the notification. Customization of the layout is easy to do by just modifying this file and saving the new files to the repository. The subject for the e-mail can also be modified as we just saw in the Records Management module `alfresco-global.properties` file (it is different from the standard Alfresco configuration file with the same name).

An example of what the file looks like when it is actually sent is shown next:

Configuring outbound e-mails

In order for Alfresco to be able to send e-mail notification messages, the server must be enabled to send outbound e-mails. An outbound e-mail server can be configured by adding and completing the following lines in the standard `alfresco-global.properties` file:

```
mail.host=<the name of your SMTP host>
mail.port=<the port that your SMTP service runs on (the default is
    25)>
mail.username=<the username of the account e-mail will be sent from>
mail.password=<the password>
```

 To find out more about how to configure outbound e-mails from Alfresco, consult the Alfresco wiki: `http://wiki.alfresco.com/wiki/E-mail_Configuration`.

Manually checking for records requiring review

You may be interested, for troubleshooting purposes or just out of curiosity, to know how to check which vital records are candidates for sending review e-mail notifications.

We saw above in the configuration of the bean that the Java class that controls e-mail notifications is called `NotifyOfRecordsDueForReviewJob`. When we look in that Java source file (that is possible because Alfresco is open source software), we can see what happens when the scheduled job is run.

If you have a need to add other notification e-mails within the Records Management system, the code provided by the Java class `NotifyOfRecordsDueForReviewJob` provides a great starting-point template for new development.

The flow of the code is basically just two steps. First, check to see if any records meet the criteria that they are up for review, but no e-mail notifications have yet been sent, and second, send out the e-mails to the users in the Role configured to receive them.

The check to see if any records exist is done by making a query with Lucene. The Lucene query is as follows:

```
+ASPECT:"rma:vitalRecord"
  +(@rma\:reviewAsOf:[MIN TO NOW] )
  +( @rma\:notificationIssued:false OR
  ISNULL:"rma:notificationIssued"
  )
```

The three parts to the query look only for records that are vital records, which have a review date that has been exceeded, and for which e-mail notifications have already been sent.

Using the Node Browser in the Alfresco JSF Explorer client, we can then check to see which records meet this criteria. To do that, we browse into the `workspace://SpaceStore` area and select the search type from the drop-down to be **Lucene**. After doing that, we enter the above query to see if there are any records that meet the criteria:

 The Java class `NotifyOfRecordsDueForReviewJob` can be found in the Alfresco source repository at `http://svn.alfresco.com/repos/alfresco-open-mirror/ alfresco/HEAD/root/modules/dod-5015/source/java/org/alfresco/module/org_alfresco_module_dod5015/job/`.

Tracking the scheduler

Another thing you may wish to do for troubleshooting purposes, or just plain curiosity, is to watch the real time logger of the application server for messages from the scheduler that are being logged.

That is easy to do; we just add the following lines to the bottom of the `tomcat\webapps\alfresco\WEB-INF\classes\log4j.properties` file and restart the server:

```
log4j.logger.org.alfresco.module.org_alfresco_module_dod5015.
  job=debug
log4j.logger.org.alfresco.module.org_alfresco_module_dod5015.
  notification=debug
log4j.logger.org.alfresco.module.org_alfresco_module_dod5015.
  jscript=debug
```

After doing this, we will see quite a few log messages related to the background jobs. Remember, based on the default setting that we saw above, that the job will be run every 15 minutes as the scheduler runs the review notification job:

We will see messages like this:

```
13:45:00,343 DEBUG
  [org_alfresco_module_dod5015.job.NotifyOfRecordsDueForReview
  Job] Job NotifyOfRecordsDueForReviewJob starting.
  13:45:00,390 User:System DEBUG
  [org_alfresco_module_dod5015.notification.Records
  ManagementNotificationServiceImpl] Sending notification email to
  dweisinger@formtek.com
  13:45:00,859 DEBUG
  [org_alfresco_module_dod5015.job.NotifyOfRecordsDueForReview
  Job] Job NotifyOfRecordsDueForReviewJob finished
```

Lifecycle tracking

The second type of background job that is set up to run by default within the Records Management module is a lifecycle tracker job. This job, like the Review notification job, is also primarily configured within the context file `rm-job-context.xml`.

Configuring the disposition lifecycle bean

A block section of XML in the context file defines the bean for the scheduled lifecycle job. The code that configures it is as follows:

```
<!-- Disposition Lifecycle Job -->
<bean id="scheduledDispositionLifecyceleJobDetail"
  class="org.springframework.scheduling.quartz.JobDetailBean">
```

```
<property name="jobClass">
  <value>org.alfresco.module.org_alfresco_module_dod5015.job.
    DispositionLifecycleJob</value>
</property>
<property name="jobDataAsMap">
  <map>
    <entry key="nodeService">
      <ref bean="nodeService" />
    </entry>
    <entry key="searchService">
      <ref bean="searchService" />
    </entry>
    <entry key="recordsManagementActionService">
      <ref bean="recordsManagementActionService" />
    </entry>
    <entry key="transactionService">
      <ref bean="transactionService" />
    </entry>
  </map>
</property>
</bean>
```

There are a number of standard services that are configured here. The main thing of interest to us in this discussion though is the value set for the `jobClass` property. This refers to a Java class `org.alfresco.module.org_alfresco_module_dod5015.job.DispositionLifecycleJob` where we can find additional information about the inner workings of this scheduled job.

Configuring the lifecycle cron schedule

We see also in the file `rm-job-context.xml` that the lifecycle cron job is, just as in the case we saw above for review e-mail notifications, scheduled to be sent out every 15 minutes:

```
<bean id="scheduledDispositionLifecyceleJobTrigger"
  class="org.alfresco.util.CronTriggerBean">
  <property name="jobDetail">
    <ref bean="scheduledDispositionLifecyceleJobDetail" />
  </property>
  <property name="scheduler">
    <ref bean="schedulerFactory" />
  </property>
  <property name="cronExpression">
    <value>0 0/15 * * * ?</value>
  </property>
</bean>
```

As an aside, it might be good to reconfigure the two background jobs to not occur at the same time. In fact, depending on the usage of your system, it may be possible to reduce the frequency of checks to only once or a few times per day.

Manually checking for lifecycle records

In a similar way to how we checked for records that are up for review, we can also manually check to see which records should be getting identified by the lifecycle tracker job.

By examining the Java source code, we can find that the query that the job makes to identify records that need updating uses the following Lucene search criteria:

```
+TYPE:"rma:dispositionAction"
+(@rma\:dispositionAction:("cutoff" OR "retain"))
+ISNULL:"rma:dispositionActionCompletedAt"
+( @rma\:dispositionEventsEligible:true OR @rma\:dispositionAsOf:[MIN
  TO NOW] )
```

We see here that records themselves are not specifically being searched for here. Objects of the type disposition action, or `rma:dispositionAction`, are being tracked.

Logging information for the lifecycle scheduler

The log4j settings that we defined above for the review e-mail notification also apply to the lifecycle scheduler. Using those settings, you will see log messages being printed for both types of cron jobs.

The File Plan component

In the File Plan chapter, we saw that the component called `dod5015-fileplan` on the **File Plan** page contains links that, when clicked on, will show all the items that are in-progress for **Holds** and **Transfers**:

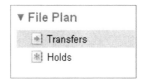

The files that control the `dod5015-fileplan` component are found in `tomcat\webapps\share\WEB-INF\classes\alfresco\components\documentlibrary\dod5015-fileplan.*`.

On examination of the component files, we find that they are surprisingly simple. For example, there is a controller JavaScript file, `dod5015-fileplan.get.js`, but it is empty. TheFreeMarker template for the component is in the file `dod5015-fileplan.get.html.ftl` and it is very short:

```
<#assign filterIds = "">
<div class="filter fileplan-filter">
  <h2>${msg("header.fileplan")}</h2>
  <ul class="filterLink">
    <li><span class="transfers"><a rel=""
      href="#">${msg("label.transfers")}</a></span></li>
    <li><span class="holds"><a rel=""
      href="#">${msg("label.holds")}</a></span></li>
  </ul>
</div>
<script type="text/javascript">//<![CDATA[
  new Alfresco.component.BaseFilter("Alfresco.DocListFilePlan",
    "${args.htmlid}").setFilterIds(["transfers", "holds"]);
//]]></script>
```

The FreeMarker file defines a very simple layout. The labels for the elements of the component are defined in the file `dod5015-fileplan.get.properties`:

```
## Title
header.fileplan=File Plan

## Filters
label.transfers=Transfers
label.holds=Holds
```

We see that most of the dynamics for the component are orchestrated by client-side JavaScript. At the bottom of the FreeMarker template above, we see that on the client, a JavaScript object called `Alfresco.component.BaseFilter` is instantiated.

The `BaseFilter` object is defined in the file `tomcat\webapps\share\js\alfresco.js`. The method called `setFilterIds()` is called from the above script in the FreeMarker file:

```
setFilterIds: function BaseFilter_setFilterIds(p_aFilterIds)
{
  // Register the filter
  Alfresco.util.FilterManager.register(this.name, p_aFilterIds);
}
```

In this method, the filter IDs are then registered and associated with the Transfer and File Links.

Linking to the transfer and hold pages

When either the **Transfers** or **Holds** links are clicked on, the page is re-rendered. Appended to the page URL is the `filter` parameter that specifies the type of filter to apply when re-rendering the page.

For example, the URL for the `transfers` page has the `filter` parameter appended to the end: `http://localhost:8080/share/page/site/rm/documentlibrary#fil ter=transfers`.

The value of the `filter` parameter then controls the rendering of the page.

Rendering transfer and hold Items

In *Chapter 5*, when we discussed the rendering of the **File Plan** page, we saw how the JavaScript files **dod5015-documentlist.js** *and* **documentlist.js** control the display of items in the center document list component. The same JavaScript files are used here in the rendering of the transfer and hold items:

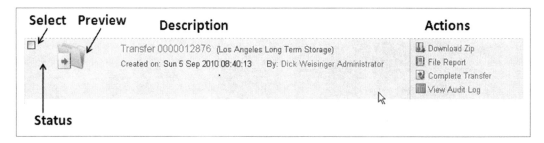

As we saw before, the document list is based on a YUI Data Table control. Each row of the table has five cells that are labeled **Select**, **Status**, **Preview**, **Description**, and **Actions**, and each column of the table has a function that controls the rendering of the column's cells.

Within the column rendering functions for the Data Table are conditionals that control the type of page markup that is used when rendering a row of the table. The markup used will differ depending on whether the row type is for a `folder` or for a `record-series`, for example. In the two cases that we are considering now, the row `type` referred to in the `dod5015-documentlist.js` file is either `transfer-container` or `hold-container`.

Finding transfer items

We just saw that the value for the parameter `filter` controls how the **File Plan** page is rendered. The `filter` value also controls the content on the page. The value for `filter` is passed in as an argument to the data webscript that finds the rows of data that are then displayed on the page.

We saw earlier when we discussed the File Plan how the JavaScript method _`buildDocListParams` in the file `documentlist.js` builds the data webscript URL to determine which items to display on the **File Plan** page.

In the case of transfers, in a similar way, a URL is constructed that looks like the following:

```
http://localhost:8080/alfresco/service/slingshot/doclib/dod5015/
doclist/all/site/rm/documentLibrary?filter=transfers&noCac
he=1283705102828
```

This URL looks like the one we saw earlier. But note that here we are applying the `transfers` filter to the results. We can trace this service call into the Alfresco repository by looking at the data webscript `tomcat\webapps\alfresco\WEB-INF\classes\alfresco\templates\webscripts\org\alfresco\slingshot\documentlibrary\dod5015-doclist.get.*`.

In the file `dod5015-doclist.get.js` in the function `getDocList()`, the Lucene query string for the filter type is determined. The query string is looked up within the method `Filters.getFilterParams()` in the file `dod5015-filters.lib.js`. We will come back to this file when we look at Records Management search in more detail in the next chapter. For now, from this file, we can find that the filter query that is used to find all transfers looks like the following:

```
+PATH:"/app:company_home/st:sites/cm:rm/cm:documentLibrary//*"
+TYPE:"{http://www.alfresco.org/model/recordsmanagement/1.0}transfer"
```

As a step to satisfy our curiosity again, we can paste this Lucene search criteria into the Node Browser within the `workspace://SpacesStore` store. After doing that, we'll see a screen that looks like the following:

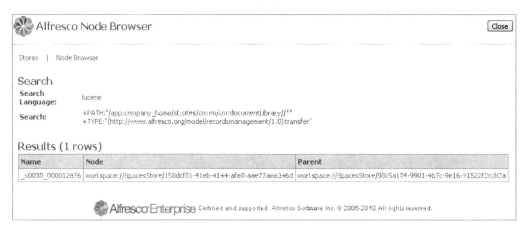

Finding hold items

In the same way, we can trace what happens when the user clicks on the **Holds** link in the File Plan left panel. In the file `documentlist.js`, a call is made to the Alfresco repository with a URL that applies the filter named `holds`:

```
http://localhost:8080/alfresco/service/slingshot/doclib/
dod5015/doclist/all/site/rm/documentLibrary?filter=holds&noCac
he=1283705102828
```

Then in the file `dod5015-doclist.get.js`, a call is made into the method `Filters.getFilterParams()` in the file `dod5015-filters.lib.js`. That method then looks up the Lucene query that is used to find all holds, the results of which populate the rows of the YUI Data Table in the document list component. The Lucene query to find the rows looks like this:

```
+PATH:"/app:company_home/st:sites/cm:rm/cm:documentLibrary//*"
+TYPE:"{http://www.alfresco.org/model/recordsmanagement/1.0}hold"
```

Transfer report

We saw above how a report can be generated that documents the transfer of records. The generation of the report is triggered by selecting the **File Report** action for an item appearing in the transfer list:

The **actions** that are available from the document list component of the **File Plan** page are defined in the file `tomcat\webapps\share\WEB-INF\classes\alfresco\components\documentlibrary\dod5015-documentlist.get.config.xml`.

In that file, we can find the actions that are available for each type of row that is displayed in the YUI Data Table of the document list. In particular, we can find the `actionSet` associated with the transfer items:

```
<actionSet id="transferContainer">
  <action type="simple-link" id="onActionDownloadZip"
    permission="AuthorizeAllTransfers" href="{transfersZipUrl}"
    label="actions.download-zip" />
  <action type="action-link" id="onActionFileTransferReport"
    permission="AuthorizeAllTransfers" label="actions.file-report" />
  <action type="action-link" id="onActionTransferComplete"
    permission="AuthorizeAllTransfers" label="actions.transfer-
    complete" />
  <action type="action-link" id="onActionViewAuditLog"
    permission="AccessAudit" label="actions.view-audit-log" />
</actionSet>
```

Here we see that the action for creating and filing a transfer report has the `id` `onActionFileTransferReport`. These action `id`s can be mapped to JavaScript methods that will be called when the action item is selected.

The client-side JavaScript methods for standard document list actions are defined in the two files, namely, `actions.js` and `documents.js` in the `tomcat\webapps\share\components\documentlibrary\` directory. For example, in this file, there are `onActionXXX` methods such as `onActionCopyTo` and `onActionMoveTo`.

For the Records Management module, additional actions are defined in the `dod5015-actions.js` file. In that file, we find the definition for `onActionFileTransferReport`:

```
onActionFileTransferReport: function RDLA_onActionFileTransferReport(
assets)
```

```
{
  if (!this.modules.fileTransferReport)
  {
    this.modules.fileTransferReport = new
      Alfresco.module.RecordsFileTransferReport(this.id + "-
      fileTransferReport");
  }
  this.modules.fileTransferReport.setOptions(
  {
    siteId: this.options.siteId,
    containerId: this.options.containerId,
    path: this.currentPath,
    fileplanNodeRef: this.doclistMetadata.filePlan,
    transfer: assets
  }).showDialog();
}
```

That method will pop up the dialog to select the location where the generated report will be filed:

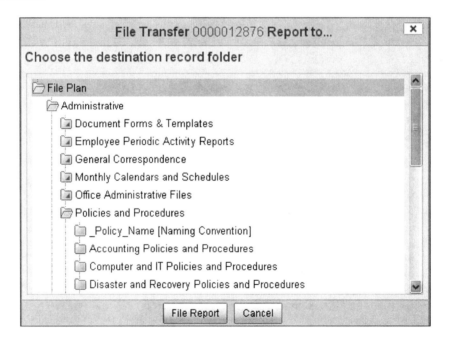

The JavaScript object `Alfresco.module.RecordsFileTransferReport` is defined in the file `tomcat\webapps\share\modules\docuemntlibrary\dod5015-file-transfer-report.js`.

After the user selects the location for where to file the transfer report by clicking on the **File Report** button, the onOK function for the dialog is called to process the request. This function then kicks off the process of creating and filing the report:

```
onOK: function RMCMFT_onOK()
{
  // create the webscript url
  var transferNodeRefParts =
    this.options.transfer.nodeRef.split("/"),
      transferId = transferNodeRefParts[transferNodeRefParts.length -
        1],
    url = Alfresco.constants.PROXY_URI + "api/node/" +
      this.options.fileplanNodeRef.replace(":/", "") + "/transfers/"
      + transferId + "/report";
  // Post file transfer report request to server
  Alfresco.util.Ajax.jsonPost(
  {
    url: url,
    dataObj:
    {
      destination: this.selectedNode.data.nodeRef
    },
  ...
```

The function builds a URL that points to an Alfresco repository web service and then POSTs a request to it. The format for the URL used looks like the following:

```
http://localhost:8080/share/proxy/alfresco/api/node/workspace/
SpacesStore/98c5a184-9901-4b7c-9e16-91522f2ccb2a/transfers/158dcf81-
41eb-4144-afe8-aae77aee346d/report
```

On the repository server side, the format of the request URL corresponds to the webscript tomcat\webapps\alfresco\WEB-INF\classes\alfresco\templates\ webscripts\org\alfresco\rma\transferreport.post.desc.xml. In that file, the matching URL signature is defined as follows. This matches the URL that was just created:

```
<url>/api/node/{store_type}/{store_id}/{id}/transfers/{transfer_id}
  /report</url>
```

This webscript can be processed by mapping to a Java service implementation in the Alfresco source code in the file root\modules\dod-5015\source\java\module\ org_alfresco_module_dod5015\script\TransferReportPost.java.

In that file, we can find the code that generates the transfer report. The Java code there writes an HTML file with the report information and then files that report in the requested location.

Unfortunately, the format for the report is hardcoded in Java so that any change to customize the report will require a change to the Java code.

 This example also shows how Share handles Document Library and File Plan actions in general. More information about Share Document Library actions can be found on the Alfresco wiki at `http://wiki.alfresco.com/wiki/Custom_Document_Library_Action`.

Summary

We covered the following concepts in this chapter:

- How lifecycle steps like record declaration, cutoff, retention, transfer, and destruction work
- How to create an export package to respond to a legal request
- How transfer and hold packages are accessed directly from File Plan links
- How to create a File Plan Report
- What various status icons, including cutoff, transfer, and destruction mean

In the "How does it work?" section, we dug into the internals of some items that included the following:

- How and where the unique record ID is created when a record is filed
- How Review Notifications are configured and what the process is for sending them
- How the Lifecycle cron job is configured and how it automatically updates records and Folders based on their disposition schedules
- How transfer packages are tracked within Records Management
- How hold packages are tracked within Records Management
- How transfer reports are generated and sent

In this chapter, we discussed in detail the different steps that make up record lifecycles. In the next chapter, we will look at the search capabilities of Alfresco Share and at a special Records Search feature that was specifically built around the special requirements for locating records.

10
Searching Records and Running Audits

In this chapter, we will see one of the biggest benefits of using an Electronic Records Management (ERM) system, namely, Search. When using a traditional paper-based records management system, finding records with any criteria other than the filing structure enforced by the File Plan is very difficult and time consuming.

Search is an excellent complement to the capabilities provided by the File Plan. Search improves the accuracy of locating important records and it is a necessary tool for being able to respond to legal and e-Discovery requests in a timely way.

In this chapter, we will now describe:

- How to perform basic and complex searches using the **Records Search** page
- How to create and use saved searches
- How to audit the actions and events that have occurred in the records system

Search and Records Management

We've spent much of this book discussing the File Plan. The File Plan is central to many of the concepts of Records Management. It is a well-understood organizational tool for categorizing and filing records, and it assists in locating records and in managing record lifecycles.

But over the last decade, with the wider introduction of Electronic Records Management (ERM) systems, search has become an important complementary tool to the File Plan. With search, the ability to locate records efficiently has improved dramatically. E-Discovery, by its very definition, would not exist today without search.

Authorization and search

In this chapter, we focus on how the **Records Search** page can be used to query items within the Records Management site. Similar to the way that Alfresco authorization limits which parts of the File Plan tree structure a user can see and navigate, the results from any search query made by the user are filtered such that only the items in the system that the user has read permission access to will be included in the results.

Records Search page

In order to comply with the extensive search requirements found in the DoD 5015.2 specification, the Records Management site includes a special page dedicated to search over the File Plan and the records that are in it. The **Records Search** page can be accessed by clicking on the link in the navigation area under the **Records Management Site** title:

Single-field search form

Document and record search forms can traditionally become very complex. Attempting to cram the labels and entry fields for tens of properties on a single screen is a challenge, both for developers to layout and for users to understand.

In the design of the **Records Search** page, Alfresco tried to opt towards simplicity. Typical user searches include very few properties as part of their search criteria, but in order to comply with the DoD 5015.2 specification, it is necessary to be able to search over all possible properties of the records system, so that simplifying the form by excluding some of the properties from the display was not an option.

> *The DoD 5015.2 specification mandates that the records system "Allow searches using any combination of the record category, record, and/or folder metadata elements, including organization-defined and system-generated metadata".*

The solution that Alfresco came up with was to create a **Records Search** form that tries to model the simplicity of the single-field search form popularized by Google. Alfresco also modeled the query syntax used for the records search form on Google's syntax by allowing additional search criteria qualifiers to be added to the search string.

With Google search, for example, searches can be restricted to be across only the pages of a given website by including the following query fragment with the search string: `site:website.com`.

The resulting design of the **Records Search** page is a single-field form that is familiar to casual users and that provides power users the ability to formulate very complex searches. The downside of the form is that some users may struggle a bit if they don't fall into the category of power users and if they need to do more than just the very basic searches.

To assist the non-power user in using the search form, Alfresco has created a couple of options. They have added a drop-down menu to help guide the user in adding qualifying search criteria. They have also added **Saved Searches** that can be used to capture frequently occurring searches and to then turn those searches into "canned" ones that can be easily called up and later reused.

The Search form

Let's look in greater detail now at the user interface of the **Records Search** page:

The main panel on the **Records Search** page is tabbed. The **Criteria** tab shows the main query field and the **Results** tab displays the search results after a search has been run.

A search is initiated by clicking on the **Search** button. After the search is complete, the open tab switches from **Criteria** to **Results** and displays the hits found from the search. If we switch back to the **Criteria** tab, the search criteria just entered is still retained. All search criteria can be re-initialized by clicking on the **New Search** button in the upper-right of the screen.

Basic search

A simple search can be run by simply typing a word into the text search field. For example, if we type the word **Security** and click on the **Search** button, we will get search hits from records that have the word **Security** within the content of the record:

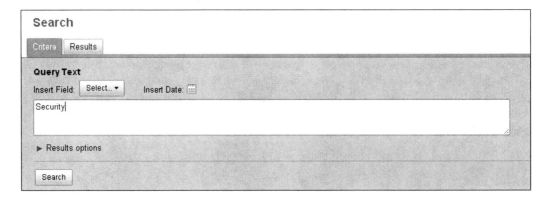

The search results are then displayed in the **Results** tab, as shown in the next screenshot. If we then click again on the **Criteria** tab, we will see our original search criteria:

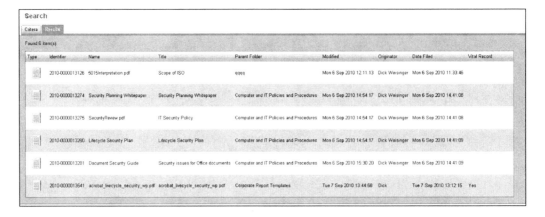

Property search

The search criteria can be extended to include search over metadata properties as part of the criteria. For example, we could search for just the records with the value of Scope of ISO as their cm:title property by entering:

```
cm:title:"Scope of ISO"
```

The syntax for searching over properties is `<property-name>:<value>`. However, remembering the names of all the available searchable properties is a bit of a challenge. To help with that, Alfresco included a drop-down menu on the tab labeled **Insert Field**. Any property that is searchable can be included in the query. Many, if not most, of the searchable fields are available from this list.

Clicking on the drop-down menu shows a cascading list of the possible metadata properties that can be searched over:

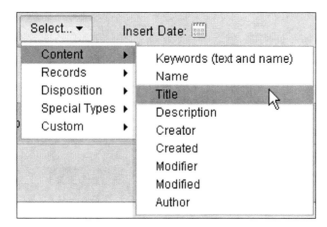

For example, if we select **Content | Title** from the menu, in the search field, the value `title:` will be auto-filled, based on the current position of the cursor in the search field.

In this way, we can select the correct property name from the menu and then fill in the search value for the property. Note that, in this case, the property name auto-filled was `title:` and does not include the namespace prefix `cm:` as we used above in our example.

The use of namespace prefixes with the property names that can be selected from the drop-down menu is inconsistent. Many of the properties do not need a prefix, but some do. When entering a property name and in doubt of whether to include the prefix or not, it is usually best to include it.

Date search

Search can be a bit unforgiving when it comes to entering dates as criteria for search. The format must be in the form "YYYY-MM-DD". Entering anything other than that format will not work. To help ensure that the correct date format is used, the **Criteria** tab includes an **Insert Date** button.

Clicking on that button will pop up a calendar from which a date can be selected and auto-filled into the search field. Note that the value for the date must be enclosed in double quotes:

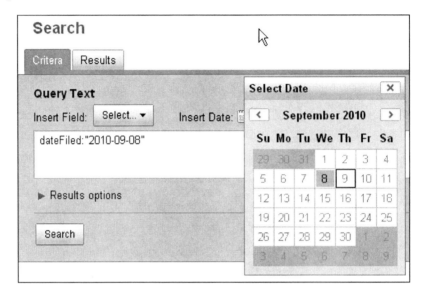

Search filters

In addition to how we've seen that property search criteria can be used to qualify a search, a search can be further qualified by using filters that are labeled as **Components** on the **Criteria** tab.

To see these, we need to expand the **Criteria** tab by clicking on the arrow next to the **Results options** label. Most of what gets exposed in the expanded **Criteria** tab is related to formatting and display of the result set, and we'll get to that next. However, for now, we will discuss the selections in the **Components** list located along the right-hand side. The options in that list can be used to further filter the results of the query:

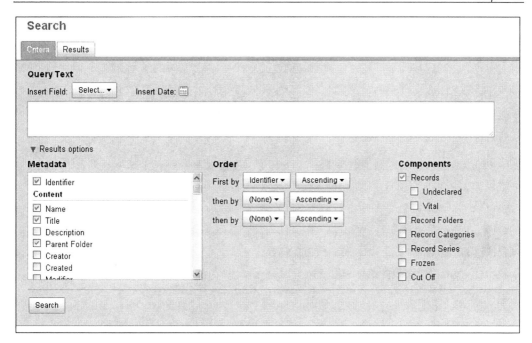

Unlike properties which are appended to the search string in the main search field and that are visible to the user, selection of items from the **Components** list causes criteria to be added to the search string just prior to search, and this additional criterion is not displayed to the user.

For example, selecting the **Record Folders** checkbox from under **Components** would result in the query string being appended with the additional criterion:

```
TYPE:"rma:recordFolder
```

Similarly, selecting either **Record Categories** or **Record Series** would append the following criteria:

```
TYPE:"dod:recordCategory"
TYPE:"dod:recordSeries"
```

By default, when the **Records Search** page is opened, the **Records** checkbox is checked. This causes the following criterion to be appended:

```
ASPECT:"rma:record"
```

For either the checkboxes of **Undeclared** or **Vital** to be selected, it is necessary that **Records** also be checked. If **Records** is checked and **Undeclared** is not checked, then the following criterion is added:

```
ASPECT:"rma:declaredRecord"
```

When **Vital** is checked, then the following is applied to the query string:

```
ASPECT:"rma:vitalRecord"
```

Selecting **Frozen** and **Cut Off** values apply the following, respectively:

```
ASPECT:"rma:frozen"
ASPECT:"rma:cutOff"
```

Restricted File Plan search

Searches made from the **Records Search** page are constrained to show results only from within the File Plan. In order to ensure that the search results are constrained, the following additional criterion that limits the PATH of the search is appended to the search string in the background, prior to actually running the query:

```
PATH:"/app:company_home/st:sites/cm:rm/cm:documentLibrary//*"
```

While this value for the search path restricts us to records and documents only within the File Plan, we could, potentially, further restrict the search within the File Plan by adding an even more restrictive PATH criterion to the search query string.

For example, if we wanted to limit our search to find only records that are under a record Series named `Finance`, we could include the following criterion. Note that the name of the Series includes the prefix `cm:`

```
PATH:"/app:company_home/st:sites/cm:rm/cm:documentLibrary/
cm:Finance//*"
```

Note that the path consists of QNames separated by /, and the QNames in the path must be properly escaped if they contain special characters. Later in this chapter, we will discuss how to properly escape QNames.

Search result columns

The left-most section of the expanded area of the **Criteria** tab labeled **Metadata** shows a list of properties that can be included as columns in the search result list that is returned from the query.

By checking the name of a property in this list, we are specifying that it should be included as a column in the search results. The items in this list correspond to the same items that were in the drop-down property names.

There isn't a limit to how many properties can be selected, but since each property selected corresponds to a column in the results table displayed in the **Results** tab, selecting too many will cause the right-most edge of the table to push to the left, making it necessary for the user to scroll to the right to see all of the data.

Result list search order

The search order of the return search result list can be sorted by primary, secondary, and tertiary columns. The sort order can be specified in the section of the **Criteria** tab under **Results options** labeled as **Order**:

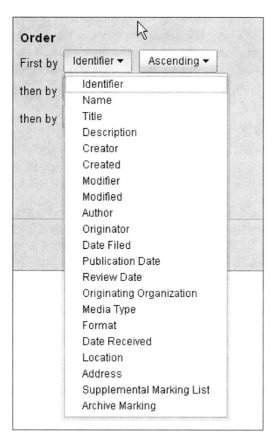

By default, the results are sorted only by a primary column. The default search property is called **Identifier** and it corresponds to the unique record identifier for the item. The default search order is **Ascending**.

The value of the sort property used in the search can be selected from the drop-down list. The sort property need not be a property that is displayed in the search results.

The sort order direction for the results can be selected as either **Ascending** or **Descending**.

Selecting a value for the primary sort criterion is required and is enforced by the user interface. Secondary and tertiary sort criteria are optional.

Clearing the search criteria

The search criteria can be cleared on the form by clicking on the **New Search** button on the upper right. After doing that, the main criteria field is cleared and the sections labeled **Order** and **Components** are set back to their default states. Note that the selections in the **Metadata** multi-select list that control which columns will be displayed do not get reset. To reset everything, we need to refresh the page.

The Results tab

The **Results** tab is a convenient screen for immediately seeing the results of the search. Since the result data is drawn via AJAX to this second tab on the window, the entire screen will not refresh, making the user experience a little bit nicer.

The left-most column of the data table for the search results list is called **Type** and it is displayed as an icon that identifies the type of object that the row represents, like a record or a Folder. A URL link to the object details page for a given row in the results is also available and can be seen by moving the mouse either across the icon or across the text for the unique record identifier that is listed by default in the second column.

The result rows can be sorted by clicking on the label for the column that we wish to sort by. Clicking again on the column label will toggle the sort order back and forth between ascending and descending:

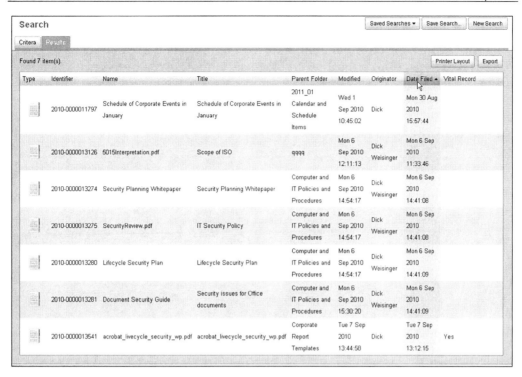

Clicking on the **Printer Layout** button causes the page to redraw, removing the title and navigation information from the top of the page, making room for more data to be displayed in the data table.

Clicking on the **Export** button will dump and download all of the search result information into an ACP file. The file will include the file content as well as all metadata. Recall that an ACP file contains complete information about the directory structure, content data, and metadata about records in the repository. ACP files are in a format that allows the data to be easily imported into an Alfresco system.

Syntax errors

As of Alfresco 3.3, the error handling from syntax errors in the search string on the Records Search page are somewhat cryptic. For example, if the property name is incorrectly spelled or if the value for the property is not well formatted or escaped, an error will be thrown. Typically, the text of the error message doesn't give any indication as to the reason for the error other than a **Wrapped Exception** occurred and that the script **Failed to execute**:

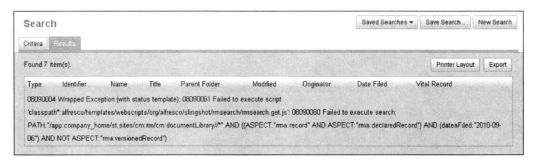

Have no fear though. Simply click on the **Criteria** tab again and re-edit your query. When having problems, referring back to the summary of the query language syntax in the next section can help.

FTS-Alfresco query language

The **Records Search** page provides a user interface for collecting the user search criteria for objects within the File Plan. The query is formulated using the **FTS-Alfresco query language**, where FTS stands for Full Text Search.

At the heart of the FTS-Alfresco queries is the **Lucene** search engine, but it provides richer constructs than what are available by just using Lucene.

Searching for a term

To search for a single word or term that is located somewhere within the file content of a record, the search can consist of just that word, much like a standard search engine. When the search is run, any property that is of type `d:content`, like `cm:content`, will be considered in the search. Consider the following example:

```
digital
```

This is equivalent to using the qualifier `TEXT` as a prefix to the search string:

```
TEXT:digital
```

Searching for a phrase

Phrases can be searched by using double quotes to enclose multiple words or terms. For example:

```
"electronic digital signature"
```

Quotes can be embedded within double quotes by escaping each of the quotes, such as in the following:

```
"\"electronic digital signature\""
```

Wildcard search

Wildcard search patterns are supported. The asterisk operator (*) matches zero or more characters, and the question mark (?) matches a single character. Wildcard characters can also be embedded within the double quotes of a phrase. For example, consider the following examples:

```
ele*ic
elect??nic
"ele*ic digital"
"electronic ?igital"
```

Conjunctive search

AND can be used to combine a term or phrase when both of the two search fragments are to be included in the results. The use of the operator AND is not case sensitive. and could also be used. For example, the following would have the same result::

```
electronic "digital signature"
electronic AND "digital signature"
TEXT:electronic AND TEXT:"digital signature"
```

Disjunctive search

OR can be used to combine a term or phrase when it is sufficient that either of the search fragments are to be included in the results. The default is that search fragments are ORed together:

```
electronic OR "digital signature"
```

Negation

Terms and phrases can be negated using any one of NOT, !, or -. Consider these examples, all of which are equivalent:

```
NOT electronic AND "digital signature"
!electronic AND "digital signature"
-electronic AND "digital signature"
```

 Note that standalone negations are not supported. Negation can only be used when at least one other element is included as part of the query.

Properties

Not only file content, but the values of metadata properties can also be searched. The syntax for searching properties is as follows:

```
<property-name>:<search-value>
```

Note that there can't be any whitespace before or after the colon separator.

The property-name is the property name that is used by either the content type or aspect. The name of the property needs to be qualified by including the full namespace or else use the namespace prefix.

For example, the following two searches are equivalent; the first one uses the prefix and the second one uses the full namespace:

```
cm:content:digital
{http://www.alfresco.org/model/content/1.0}content:digital
```

Other examples of searches over property values include the following:

```
cm:creator:admin
rma:originator:Dick*
sys:node\-dbid:13620
```

Note that hyphens within the property names need to be escaped, like the example here with the property sys:node-dbid.

Special fields

In addition to properties, there are some special fields that can be included in the search. The special fields are formatted in the same way as properties. Most of the special fields are abbreviations for commonly used properties. Some of the special fields are shown in the next table:

Special field name	Example	Comment
TEXT	`TEXT:digital`	Searches over all `d:content` type properties for a node. `cm:content` is the principle property of type `d:content`.
ALL	`ALL:digital` `ALL:"digital signature"`	Searches over all properties with text or content.
KEYWORDS	`KEYWORDS:digital`	Searches over name, title, description, and content.
ID	`ID:"workspace:// SpacesStore/098757a5-5497- 4fc4-922f-537cd0cc80b0"`	Searches for the record with this NodeRef. Same as `sys:store\- identifier:SpacesStore AND sys:node\- uuid:"098757a5-5497-4fc4- 922f-537cd0cc80b0"`.
PARENT	`PARENT:"workspace:// SpacesStore/ada82211-b408- 4db9-a484-8fcf2966ad51"`	Searches for records that are children of this NodeRef.
QNAME	`QNAME:"cm:Security_x0020_ Policy"` `QNAME:"cm:May_0x0020_ Invoices"`	Search for the **Qualified name** (QName) for the node. The namespace prefix, followed by a colon and the object name. See below for ISO-9075 encoding QNames.
ISNULL	`ISNULL:"cm:description"`	Searches for nodes where this property is NULL. The property is referred to by QName within double quotes. Unset properties are treated as NULL.
ISNOTNULL	`ISNOTNULL:"cm:description"`	Searches for nodes where this property is not NULL. The property is referred by QName within double quotes.

Special field name	Example	Comment
ISUNSET	`ISUNSET:"cm:description"`	Searches for nodes where this property is not set. The property is referred to by QName within double quotes.
TYPE	`TYPE:"rma:recordfolder"`	Searches for nodes of this content type. The type value is referred to by QName within double quotes.
CLASS	`CLASS:"cm:content"`	Searches for nodes of this class. The class value is referred to by QName within double quotes.
ASPECT	`ASPECT:"cm:author"` `ASPECT:rma\:cutoff` `ASPECT:rma_x003a_cutOff`	Searches for nodes with this aspect applied. The aspect value is referred to by QName within double quotes.

When referring to the QName as the value for one of the special fields, it is usually easiest to simply enclose the QName within double quotes. As we saw in the last example for ASPECT, it is also possible to not use double quotes, but to either escape the colon or to use the **ISO-9075** encoding.

It is also possible to use the fully qualified namespace as part of the special field search criteria. For example, instead of `ASPECT:"cm:author"`, we could use `ASPECT:"{http://www.alfresco.org/model/content/1.0}author"`.

Escaping QNames

Note that QNames are ISO-9075 encoded. The formula to do ISO-9075 encoding is as follows:

`"_x"` + <4-digit hex code> + `"_"`

Some commonly occurring characters that frequently appear as part of a QName and need to be encoded are the following:

Space	_x0020_
!	_x0021_
"	_x0022_
#	_x0023_
$	_x0024_
%	_x0025_

&	_x0026_
'	_x0027_
(	_x0028_
)	_x0029_
*	_x002a_
+	_x002b_
,	_x002c_
-	_x002d_
.	_x002e_
/	_x002f_
:	_x003a_
;	_x003b_
=	_x003d_

Escaping characters not in a QName

Other than QNames, characters within property names and their values can be escaped by using the backslash character \:

```
sys:node\-dbid:13620
```

Grouping

Parentheses can be used to group elements of the query. For example, consider the following:

```
(ASPECT:"rma:record" AND ASPECT:"rma:declaredRecord") AND
(QNAME:"cm:Security_x0020_Policy" OR QNAME:"cm:Continuity_x0020_
Policy") AND (NOT ASPECT:"rma:versionedRecord")
```

Items in the innermost parentheses will be evaluated first.

Boolean

Booleans are tested for in the search as either `true` or `false`, as in the following line:

```
rma:recordSearchHasDispositionSchedule:true
```

Dates

Date searching is supported for properties that are of type d:datetime, but the date must be in ISO 8601 format. That is, it must be of the form "yyyy-MM-ddTHH:mm:ss.sssZ".

Values of **TODAY** and **NOW** can also be used as values within search criteria. Both refer to today's date.

The use of **ISO 8601** dates in the **Records Search** screen is less rigid than in other areas of Alfresco. The date value used in the query need not be in full ISO 8601 format with both time and date components. For example, consider the following date searches:

```
rma:reviewAsOf:"2011-09-07"
rma:reviewAsOf:"2011-09-07T00:00:00.000Z"
rma:reviewAsOf:TODAY
```

ISO 8601 is a standard for representing date and time formats and time durations. We discussed ISO 8601 in more detail in *Chapter 7* relative to specifying time elements for time-based triggers. In *Chapter 8*, we also saw how it was used for formatting time and date information for stored metadata. You can find more information about this standard here at http://www.iso.org/iso/date_and_time_format and here at http://www.iso.org/iso/iso_catalogue/catalogue_tc/catalogue_detail.htm?csnumber=40874.

Ranges

It is also possible to search over property ranges for a number of data types that include d:text, d:datetime, d:int, and d:long. **MIN** and **MAX** can be used when searching numeric or date ranges:

Range type	Example	Comment
Inclusive [#1 To #2]	`sys:node\-dbid:[13620 TO 13625]`	Uses square brackets. This example searches all values between 13620 and 13625 inclusive.

Google-like Inclusive
#1..#2
	`sys:node\-dbid:13620..13625`
	
	`sys:node\-dbid:"13620".."13625"`
		Separates the min and max values with two periods. This example is equivalent to the previous one.

Range type	Example	Comment
Exclusive <#1 TO #2>	`sys:node\-dbid:<13620 TO 13625>`	Uses angle brackets. This example searches all values between 13620 and 13625 inclusive.
Left-Inclusive [#1 TO #2>	`sys:node\-dbid:[13620 TO 13625>`	Inclusive of the left value, exclusive of the right one. This search does not include 13625.
Right-Inclusive <#1 TO #2]	`sys:node\-dbid:<13620 TO 13625]`	Exclusive of the left value, inclusive of the right one. This search does not include 13620.
Unbounded Lower Range [MIN TO #1]	`sys:node\-dbid:[MIN TO 13620]`	Search over everything less than 13620 inclusive.
Unbounded Upper Range [#1 TO MAX]	`sys:node\-dbid:[13620 TO MAX]`	Search over everything greater than 13620 inclusive.

The above methods for applying ranges work for dates too. For example, consider a date search with an unbounded lower range and upper value of TODAY that is either inclusive or exclusive:

```
rma:dateFiled:[MIN TO TODAY]
rma:dateFiled:[MIN TO TODAY>
rma:dateFiled:[MIN TO "2011-02-10"]
```

Dates should be enclosed in double quotes within the brackets.

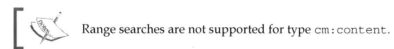 Range searches are not supported for type `cm:content`.

Proximity searches

Google-style proximity word searches are allowed. Consider the text value for the field `rma:recordSearchDispositionInstructions`: "Review every year. Destroy 2 years after obsoleted."

The following search would find a match on this field:

```
rma:recordSearchDispositionInstructions:("Review" * "year")
```

Mandatory elements

Prefixing an element of the query with + indicates that that term, phrase, or group is mandatory.

Optional elements

Prefixing an element of the query with | indicates that that term, phrase, or group is optional. The score of the item increases if it does match. Note that there must be a match with at least one element of the query for an item to be included in the result set.

Operator precedence

The following hierarchy of operator precedence exists:

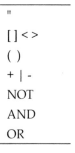

```
"
[ ] < >
( )
+ | -
NOT
AND
OR
```

 A much more detailed description of FTS-Alfresco queries can be found on the Alfresco wiki at http://wiki.alfresco.com/wiki/Full_Text_Search_Query_Syntax.

Example searches

Here are a few example search strings:

Find all records that are available for destruction.	`dispositionActionName:destroy and dispositionActionAsOf:[MIN TO NOW]`
Find all records due for cutoff before January 1, 2011.	`dispositionActionName:cutoff and dispositionActionAsOf:[MIN TO "2011-01-01"]`
Find all records that are due for transfer.	`dispositionActionName:transfer and dispositionActionAsOf:[MIN TO NOW]`

Saved searches

Search queries can get complex and it is tedious to have to re-enter the search criteria each time the search needs to be run. Saved searches are a solution to this problem.

Saved searches capture the complete state of all the settings for the widgets within the **Criteria** tab, including the query text, the filter components, the metadata corresponding to the search results columns, and the sort order. Once captured, the saved search can be recalled and re-run with just a few clicks of the mouse.

Creating a saved search

To save the current state of the **Criteria** tab as a saved search, from the **Criteria** tab, click on the **Save Search** button:

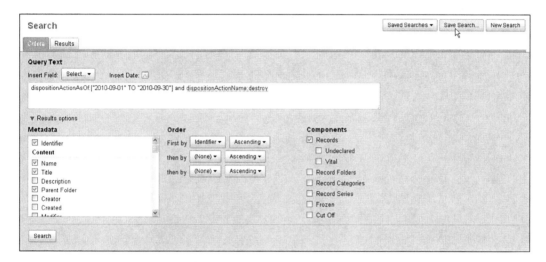

A dialog will pop up where the **Name** and **Description** for the saved search can be entered:

After clicking on the **Save** button, the saved search then becomes available for later reuse. It is added to a list of available searches that show up on the **Saved Search** button drop-down menu. It also becomes available from the **File Plan** page in the left navigation area of that page.

When the **Saved Search** is recalled from the **Records Search** page drop-down menu, the search is not run immediately. Instead, the state of the **Criteria** tab widgets get reset to the state they were in when the save search criteria was captured. The search criteria can then be either edited or simply re-run by clicking on the **Search** button.

When the saved search is accessed by clicking on the name of the search in the **File Plan** page navigation, the saved search is run and the results are presented in the File Page:

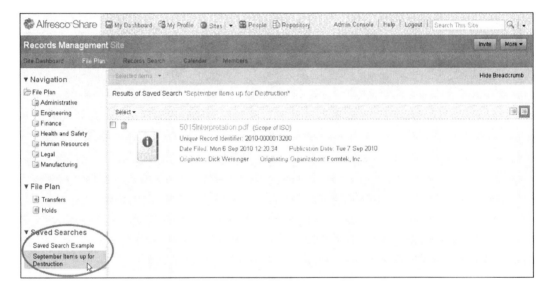

Editing a saved search

A saved search can be edited by first going to the **Records Search** page and then recalling the saved search criteria into the **Criteria** tab. After making changes to the query, the state of the **Criteria** tab can then be re-saved by selecting **Save Search** and then entering the same name for the search as the name of the original query.

After saving the query, we can verify that it was successfully saved by first clicking on **New Search** to clear out the existing search criteria and then selecting the name of the saved query that we just saved from the drop-down menu. We should see the edited version of the saved query search criteria.

Deleting a saved search

In the current design, there is no way from within the Records Management site to delete a saved search. That's not good because often a saved search has only a limited life, after which it will no longer be used.

Fortunately, the workaround for this missing feature is not difficult. To delete a saved search, we navigate to the top level of the File Plan from the Share **Repository** link.

Click on the **Repository** link at the top of the Share page and then navigate to the **Repository | Sites | rm** directory. From this directory, we can navigate into a directory called `Saved Search`.

The entries in that directory correspond to the names for each of the existing Records Management saved searches. From this directory, a saved search entry can be selected and then deleted.

After deleting the saved search entry, we can navigate back to the Records Management File Plan and verify that the saved search has been removed from the list of those available:

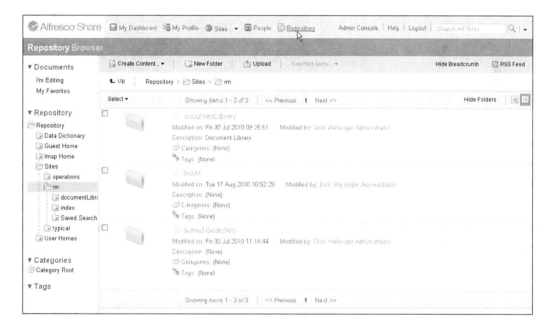

Note that any user who is a member of the Records Management site is able to access the Record Search page. While users will be prevented from seeing any items for which they have no authorization to see, any user is able to create a saved search. Once a saved search is created, it is seen and is available for use by all members of the Records Management site.

Records Management audits

To ensure compliance, a Records Management program will undergo periodic audits. Sometimes the audits will be internal and other times they will be external.

For internal audits, a best practice is either to perform frequent limited-scope audits or to conduct periodic full audits that examine all aspects of the system. The more routine and commonplace the practice of conducting internal audits become for your organization, the easier it will be when it becomes necessary to go through an external audit.

Purpose of the records audit

The reasons for conducting an audit include the following:

- To ensure that the agreed upon practices and policies are being adhered to, and to provide proof of that fact
- To ensure that the program is complying with the requirements of regulatory and oversight bodies
- To ensure that records are legally defensible
- To improve the Records Management process

Regular internal audits are also good tests to ensure that your organization is prepared for any sort of external audit. External audits, requested, for example, by regulatory agencies, may need to be conducted sometimes with as little as a one week prior notice.

Planning for the audit

The actual approach selected for the audit should be designed for your organization to ensure that it is appropriate and effective. Planning for the audit is critical to ensure that it is successful.

It should be determined early on who has the overall responsibility for carrying out the audit and what will be the roles and responsibilities for those who participate in the audit.

It should also be made clear exactly what is the scope and methodology that will be used for conducting the audits. If there are to be different types of audits, they should also be identified.

It is also important to appropriately schedule the time needed for any resources that will participate in the audit to ensure that disruption to normal work will be minimized.

Ideally, the process for the audit should be formally drawn up and agreed to, well before the audit is undertaken. Getting everything on paper early helps ensure the success of the audit. It also helps make the process repeatable.

When the process is written, it also allows for easy annotation and changes so that future audits can be improved on the next go-around when the steps of the written process are followed. Seeing the whole plan on paper also makes it possible to identify any gaps in the process or potential duplication of effort.

Things to look for in the audit

Compliance with internal policies and regulatory bodies often require that the disposition schedules that have been implemented are consistent with the requirements. This entails carefully reviewing all disposition schedules in the system.

If your organization is subject to review from regulatory bodies, it is important to understand which groups could potentially request an external audit. Review authority documents to understand what aspects of your records system or process could potentially be reviewed for compliance.

While it is important to review all aspects of the records system, it often makes sense to define a scope to the audit with a special focus on areas where non-compliance with policies is most risky or that could be most damaging to the organization.

Prior to the audit, it is also useful to review the results of any previous audits and to note problems that have been uncovered in the past. These also are areas that should receive focus during the next audit review.

Much of what an audit tries to do is to compare actual results versus expected results.

Any review of the records system needs to consider the following:

- Are the current retention periods used in the disposition appropriate?
- Are the record activities over the period since the last review consistent with the expected filings and system usage?
- Are activities being completed within the required dates?
- Is there any reason to revise the instructions for any of the dispositions, to clarify or to make them more consistent with stated policies?
- Does the structure of the File Plan continue to be relevant? Do some Series or Categories need to be added or made obsolete?
- Is there any reason to believe that not all records are being filed? If so, which record Categories seem to be lacking? Which groups in the organization are most out of compliance?
- Is there any reason to believe that some users have permissions to access parts of the system that they should not have access to?

Generally, the audit is not interested in the actual content of the records themselves, but in some cases, content is also checked, especially if the records audit includes inspection of financial information. A variety of universal standards may need to be complied with, for example, such as **GAAP** (generally accepted accounting procedures). In that case, the way in which financial data is recorded in the records themselves may also be included as part of the review audit.

 It is good practice prior to an audit to review all authority documents with which the organization needs to comply with to see if there have been any updates or revisions to the stated requirements.

Deliverables from the records audit

At the end of the audit, a report is created that estimates compliance percentage, record activities, and any suggestions for changes or improvements.

Once the report is completed, it should be made available and signed-off by members of the Records Management steering committee and key stakeholders. Audit sign-off can be done informally, but it is best if there is a formal process that includes a sign-off sheet where each person who has reviewed the report signs the sheet to indicate their review.

The audit report should be treated as a record. It should be filed and maintained in the records system.

Audits make sure that processes are running as intended. Regular audits promote good business practices. An audit typically highlights areas of the business where improvements to processes can be made.

If any shortcomings are identified in the audit, they should be prioritized by their severity and urgency, and should be addressed accordingly. Another benefit of the audit is that very often, totally outside of the records management process, the report uncovers aspects of business processes that could also be improved.

If appropriate, it is often useful to communicate findings from the audit across the whole organization when there is information in the results that the organization can use to improve and learn.

The Audit tool

An audit will require that all aspects of the records system be examined. Much of the audit goes into a review of the details of the File Plan structure. However, an audit will typically try to address many questions around system usage too.

To support questions about usage, Alfresco provides an Audit tool that is available from the Alfresco Records Management console.

Accessing the Audit tool

To get to the **Audit** tool, start with the Records Management dashlet, available from the Share home page, and click on **Management Console**:

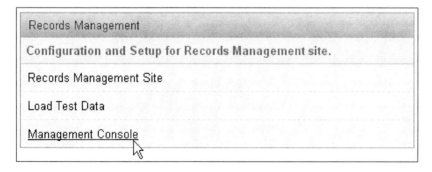

With the current version of Share, any user is able to add the Records Management dashlet to their homepage dashboard. Adding the dashlet would allow any user to be able to access the **Management Console** page. While this may not be the best design, users without appropriate access rights won't be able to get much farther than that. Each tool on the console page requires permission rights in order to access it. Without the appropriate permission, the user will be presented with a screen that says **Access Denied**.

We'll see in the next chapter how permissions or capabilities are assigned on a role basis. A user must belong to a role with the `Access Audit` capability assigned to it in order to get to the Audit tool. Only the Records Management Administrator and Records Management Records Manager roles have this capability.

Using the Audit tool

On the console, **Audit** is the first tool that is listed. We'll discuss the **Audit** tool in detail now, and then in *Chapter 12*, we will discuss some of the other features that are available on the Records Management console.

Running an Audit report

By default, all actions of any significance within the Records Management system are recorded to the Audit log. Once recorded, log entries cannot be edited or changed in any way.

When we click on the **Apply** button on the upper-right of this screen, we see a complete log of all activities. The report that is created displays a **Timestamp** for each entry, the **User** who performed the action, the **Role** of the user, and the actual **Event** or action that took place:

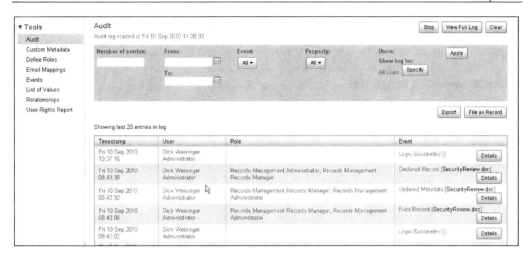

Sometimes there is additional information associated with the event that can't easily be fitted into the standard log report format. To see the complete set of information captured for a particular event, click on the **Details** button on the far right of each row.

For example, when we click on the **Details** button of the third row, as shown in the previous screenshot, we can get very complete information for what properties were changed as part of an update metadata action:

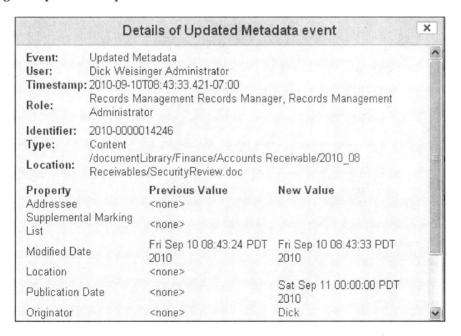

Filtering the report by event

There is a drop-down called **Event** from which we can specify filters that will limit the types of events displayed in the audit log list. The default is for all events to be included in the list displayed.

From the **Event** drop-down list, we can see the types of actions that are being recorded into the log. That list includes the following action types:

UI event label	Internal key name for event
Accession	accession
Closed Record Folder	closeRecordFolder
Completed Accession	accessionComplete
Completed Event	completeEvent
Completed Transfer	transferComplete
Created Object	Create RM Object
Cut Off	cutoff
Declared Record	declareRecord
Delete Object	Delete RM Object
Destroyed Item	destroy
Filed Record	file
Froze Item	freeze
Login Failed	Login.Failure
Login Succeeded	Login.Success
Opened Record Folder	openRecordFolder
Relinquished Hold	relinquishHold
Reversed Completed Event	undoEvent
Reversed Cut Off	unCutoff
Reviewed	reviewed
Set Record As A Digital Photographic Record	applyDigitalPhotographRecord
Set Record As A Scanned Record	applyScannedRecord
Set Record As A Web Record	applyWebRecord
Set Record As PDF A Record	applyPdfRecord
Setup Recorder Folder	setupRecordFolder
Transferred Item	transfer
Undeclared Record	undeclareRecord

UI event label	Internal key name for event
Updated Disposition Action Definition	broadcastDispositionActionDefinitionUpdate
Updated Disposition As Of Date	editDispositionActionAsOfDate
Updated Hold Reason	editHoldReason
Updated Metadata	Update RM Object
Updated Review As Of Date	editReviewAsOfDate
Updated Vital Record Definition	broadcastVitalRecordDefinition

> The auditable events that are displayed in the drop-down are specified in the Java source file: `HEAD/root/modules/dod-5015/source/java/ org/alfresco/module/org_alfresco_module_dod5015/audit/ RecordsManagementAuditServiceImpl.java`. In that file, the auditable event items are defined in a hash map. The key for each item in the hash map is the name of the event used internally in the software. This is shown in the second column. The first column is the value for the hash entry and it corresponds to the text label for the event name, as displayed in the UI.

Filtering the report by property

There are some event types that, as part of the event, make a modification or change to metadata properties. It is possible to set filters that will show the items in the audit log result list that involved specific metadata properties.

To filter by property, there is a drop-down under the label **Property** that shows all Records Management properties organized in a way that is identical to how we saw them presented on the **Records Search** page:

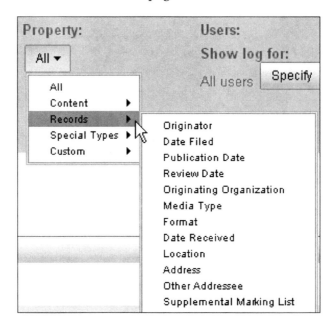

Filtering the report by user

In a similar way, it is also possible to filter the entries displayed in the audit log by the user that was involved in each of the events.

By clicking on the **Specify** button under the **Users** label, it is possible to add filters that will limit the results to include only entries that involved the specified users:

Filtering the report by date

The audit log report can also be filtered based on the timestamps of the entries. It is possible to specify a beginning date and an ending date for the date filter. Either one or both of the **From** and **To** fields can be entered to specify the range criteria for the filter. After applying the date filter, only log entries with timestamps within those dates will be included in the results:

Audit log viewing options

By default, the maximum number of rows that are included in the result is 20. This number can be changed by entering a different value in the **Number of entries** field on the upper left.

The rows of the log can be sorted by clicking on the column header label of the row that we wish to sort by. Each click on the row header will cause the results list to be sorted, based on the row values for that column.

Viewing the full log

If the button **View Full Log** on the upper right is clicked, in a new browser window, a complete log of all entries that match the filtering criteria will be displayed. The entries are sorted in an ascending chronological order:

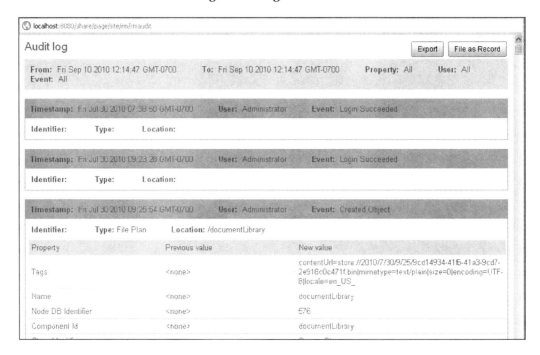

Filing the Audit log report

After an Audit log report has been run, it is possible to store the log results to the File Plan. In both the **View Full Log** pop-up browser window and within the Audit tool main screen, there are buttons labeled **File As Record**.

The same action is taken from both of these buttons. The complete report with all entries and all descriptive data and properties are included in a report that is first created and then filed. Even if the Audit tool limited the number of rows displayed in the browser, the report that is filed will be inclusive of all rows that match the filter criteria.

After the record has been filed, a popup will be displayed that will indicate success:

The report is filed as a self-contained HTML file. Note, depending on the filtering criteria, this file can be quite large.

Export the Audit log report

Both the Audit tool and the full log pop-up screens have buttons to **Export** the Audit log report. The file exported is the same HTML report that we just discussed for the **File As Record** button.

Stopping, starting, and clearing the Audit log

By default, audit logging for Records Management is turned on immediately by default after installing the Records Management site.

It is recommended that you do not turn off logging. While logging to the Audit log can take up some storage space, it isn't really enough to warrant concern. The value of logging far outweighs any storage costs involved in maintaining the logs. If the volume of storing log information becomes a problem, consider the use of the audit clear capability that we will discuss later in this section.

If you still decide that you don't need to be logging or, for some reason, do not want to perform system logging, the audit logging for Records Management events can be turned off.

On the upper left of the Audit tool, there is a **Stop** button that can turn it off:

Stopping logging though does not clear out any log entries that have already occurred, and audit reports can still be run against the information that has already been collected.

The **Stop** button toggles into a **Start** button once the button is pressed again. Turning logging back on is just a matter of clicking on the button again.

There is also a **Clear** button on the Audit tool screen. Used properly, this feature can be very useful, especially for systems with lots of activity. However, clearing the audit log should be done only after careful thought.

Clicking on **Clear** will clear all log data that is currently in the system. It can be used in a scenario where audit log reports are periodically run; those reports are filed into the File Plan, and then, immediately after filing the reports, the audit log is cleared. In this way, the data stored internally to support the audit log is the only data that has been collected since the last report period.

Making a report in this way will allow us to keep a record of all system activity, but the data will not be kept active, and the clearing out of that data potentially can provide a small bump in the performance of the system.

How does it work?

In this "How does it work?" section, we look in detail at how repository webscripts are used to assist the Share-based Records Management web pages retrieve data to support search and audits.

The Records Search page

As we've done previously, it is a matter of tracing back from the `pageid` to determine how a Share page works. Let's do this one more time, this time by using the URL of the **Records Search** page.

From the `tomcat\webapps\share\WEB-INF\classes\alfresco\site-data\presets\presets.xml` file, we can see the site page definitions for the Records Management site:

```
<sitePages>[{"pageId":"documentlibrary"}, {"pageId":"rmsearch"}]</
sitePages>
```

When clicking on the Records Search link, we can also see that the URL for the page is `http://localhost:8080/share/page/site/rm/rmsearch`. From this, we know that the `pageid` for Records Search is `rmsearch`.

If we navigate to `tomcat\webapps\share\WEB-INF\classes\alfresco\site-data`, and then look in the `pages` directory, we find the page description file for `pageid` `rmsearch`. From this file, we notice that the value for `<template-instance>` is `rmsearch`.

By navigating to `site-data\template-instances`, we can then find the descriptor file `rmsearch.xml` that identifies the `<template-type>` value as `org/alfresco/rmsearch`.

Then, looking under the `tomcat\webapps\share\WEB-INF\classes\alfresco\templates\org\alfresco` directory, we can find the FreeMarker template file `rmsearch.ftl` that describes the layout for the **Records Search** page. It's a small file and includes standard `<@region>` tags that place the `header`, `title`, `navigation`, and `footer` areas.

The body element is where the unique component for this page is defined. There is just this one component:

```
<div id="bd">
  <div class="yui-t1">
    <div id="yui-main">
      <@region id="search" scope="template" protected=true />
    </div>
  </div>
</div>
```

Here we see the `<@region>` called `search` defined with `template` scope. Next, we can look up the URL, which is the unique identifier for this region. The file `tomcat\webapps\share\WEB-INF\classes\alfresco\site-data\components\template.search.rmsearch.xml` defines the URL as `/components/rmsearch/rmsearch`.

We can look up that URL using the service URI tool at `http://localhost:8080/share/page/index/uri/`. There we can see that the descriptor for this user interface webscript is `alfresco/site-webscripts/org/alfresco/components/rmsearch/rmsearch.get.desc.xml`.

From the location of the descriptor filename for the search component, we can identify the other relevant webscript files in that same directory as `rmsearch.get.head.ftl`, `rmsearch.get.html.ftl`, `rmsearch.get.js`, and `rm.search.get.properties`.

The controller for the component `rmsearch.get.js` adds custom metadata properties to the model. The file `rmsearch.get.html.ftl` is where the main FreeMarker layout for the page is located.

DataSource and data webscript

Searches from the Records Search page are sent back to a data webscript in the repository. Within the client-side JavaScript file `tomcat\webapps\share\components\rmresults-common\rmresults-common.js`, the framework to call the webscript is set up.

The DataSource includes the base URI for communicating with the webscript. The `onReady()` method of the JavaScript `Alfresco.RecordsResults` that is defined in the JavaScript file initializes the `DataSource`:

```
// DataSource definition
var uriSearchResults = Alfresco.constants.PROXY_URI +
  "slingshot/rmsearch/" + this.options.siteId + "?";
this.widgets.dataSource = new
  YAHOO.util.DataSource(uriSearchResults);
this.widgets.dataSource.responseType =
  YAHOO.util.DataSource.TYPE_JSON;
this.widgets.dataSource.connXhrMode = "queueRequests";
```

Depending on your configuration, the URI will resolve to something like `http://localhost:8080/share/proxy/alfresco/slingshot/rmsearch/rm?`.

The signature for the service is `/alfresco/service/slingshot/rmsearch/{site}?query={query?}&sortby={sortby?}`.

The webscript descriptor file for the service is located in the Alfresco repository WAR in the `tomcat\webapps\alfresco\WEB-INF\classes\alfresco\templates\webscripts\org\alfresco\slingshot\rmsearch` directory. The results are formatted with the `rmsearch.get.json.ftl` file. The controller for the webscript is the file `rmsearch.get.js`.

In this file, we see that the search query is formatted and uses the FTS-Alfresco query language.

Further, the `getSearchResults()` function in this file locks down the query so that the search is constrained to be only within the File Plan:

```
// suffix the rm doclib fileplan site PATH query
var alfQuery = 'PATH:"' + SITES_SPACE_QNAME_PATH + 'cm:' +
  search.ISO9075Encode(siteId) + '/cm:documentLibrary//*"';

// build up final query components
if (query != null && query.length != 0)
{
  alfQuery += ' AND (' + query + ')';
}
```

The default maximum number of search results rows to display is the property `maxResults`, which is set as 500 in the file `rmresults-common.js`.

Saved searches

We saw above that saved searches for the Records Management site are stored in the **Repository | Sites | rm** area of the repository.

We can see that saved searches are saved in the JSON format. For example, the content of a saved search file looks something like the following:

```
{
  "sort": "rma:identifier/asc",
  "query": "(ASPECT:\"rma:record\" AND ASPECT:\"rma:declaredRecord\")
    AND (document) AND NOT ASPECT:\"rma:versionedRecord\"",
  "description": "",
  "name": "document",
  "params": "terms=document&records=true&undeclared=false&vital=false
&folders=
  false&categories=false&series=false&frozen=false&cutoff=false"
}
```

When the **Records Search** page is initialized, it retrieves the list of available saved searches to include in the drop-down menu attached to the `Saved Searches` button.

The client-side JavaScript file `tomcat\webapps\share\components\rmsearch\rmsearch.js` retrieves the saved searches in the initialization method `onReady()`:

```
// retrieve the public saved searches
// TODO: user specific searches?
Alfresco.util.Ajax.request(
{
  url: Alfresco.constants.PROXY_URI +
    "slingshot/rmsavedsearches/site/" + this.options.siteId,
  successCallback:
  {
    fn: this.onSavedSearchesLoaded,
    scope: this
  },
  failureMessage: me._msg("message.errorloadsearches")
});
```

The URL evaluates to something like `http://localhost:8080/share/proxy/alfresco/slingshot/rmsavedsearches/site/rm`.

We also note the comments in the code here that there are no user-specific saved searches. Saved searches are available for all Records Management users to access.

Custom properties

Custom properties can be assigned to records, Folders, Categories, and Series. When the rmsearch page is first invoked, the page collects any custom properties to include as searchable parameters.

The controller file for the rmsearch page, tomcat\webapps\share\WEB-INF\ classes\alfresco\site-webscritps\org\alfresco\components\rmsearch\ rmsearch.get.js, connects to the Alfresco repository and calls the backend data webscript to retrieve any custom properties.

Four service calls are made, one for each of the four different Records Management object types. Examples of the URLs that are called include:

```
http://localhost:8080/alfresco/service/api/rma/admin/custompropertyde
finitions?element=record,
```

```
http://localhost:8080/alfresco/service/api/rma/admin/custompropertyde
finitions?element=recordFolder, and
```

```
http://localhost:8080/alfresco/service/api/rma/admin/custompropertyde
finitions?element=recordCategory
```

We will look again at custom Records Management properties in *Chapter 12*, but for now, let's see what happens after a custom property called Archive_Marking for a record Series is defined. In this case, the data webscript to search custom properties attached to a Series returns a JSON response that looks like the following:

```
{
  "data":
  {
    "customProperties":
    {
      "rmc:Archive_Marking":
      {
        "dataType": "d:text",
        "label": "Archive Marking",
        "description": "",
        "mandatory": false,
        "multiValued": false,
        "defaultValue": "",
```

```
        "protected": false,
        "propId": "Archive_Marking",
        "constraintRefs":
        [
        ]
      }
    }
  }
}
```

It's interesting to note that the content model prefix comes back as `rmc` that stands for the Records Management Custom model (namespace `http://www.alfresco.org/model/rmcustom/1.0`).

The Records Management Custom Model is stored as an object in the Alfresco Repository in the path `\Company Home\Data Dictionary\Records Management\recordsCustomModel.xml`.

The custom metadata property **Archive Marking** shows up at the bottom of the Metadata pick list:

The Audit tool

Let's also look a bit at some of the internals of the Audit log. We've already seen quite a bit about how Share Spring-Surf-based pages are constructed. Rather than looking at the page construction in this section, in this case, let's trace the audit data a bit to see how it is being retrieved.

If we look at the Records Management Console page, we can find that the client-side JavaScript code that manages the dynamics of the Audit tool is in the file `tomcat\webapps\share\components\console\rm-audit.js`.

The onReady() method in that file sets up the URI of a webscript service call for determining the contents of the audit log:

```
onReady: function RM_Audit_onReady()
{
  this.initEvents();
  //initialize data uri
  //an audit log for node and not in console (all nodes)
  if (this.options.nodeRef)
  {
    var nodeRef = this.options.nodeRef.split('/');
    this.dataUri = YAHOO.lang.substitute(Alfresco.constants.PROXY_URI
      + "api/node/{store_type}/{store_id}/{id}/rmauditlog", {
      store_type: nodeRef[0], store_id: nodeRef[1], id: nodeRef[2]
      });
  }
  else {
    this.dataUri =
      Alfresco.constants.PROXY_URI+'api/rma/admin/rmauditlog';
  }
  this.initWidgets();
}
```

We find that the URL is something of the form http://localhost:8080/share/proxy/alfresco/api/rma/admin/rmauditlog.

If we dump the contents of the JSON response from using just this URL request to a browser with no additional parameters, we will see that it returns a complete, unfiltered list of all audit log entries.

This URL also takes a number of parameters that can be used to filter the results:

Parameter name	Description
size	The maximum number of entries to return.
user	Filter results to include only entries from this user.
event	Filter results to include only entries that match this event.
from	Filter results to include only log entries after this date. (yyyy-MM-dd format).
to	Filter results to include only log entries before this date. (yyyy-MM-dd format).

For example, a request to the webscript to see the last 10 events that were performed by the user admin to update the metadata property `cm:title` during the month of September, 2010 would look like the following:

```
http://localhost:8080/share/proxy/alfresco/api/rma/admin/rmauditlog
?user=admin&event=Update%20RM%20Object&size=10&property=cm:title&fr
om=2010-09-01&to=2010-09-30.
```

Summary

In this chapter, we discussed the **Records Search** page and the Audit tool of the Records Management console. We also discussed the importance of setting up a policy for having regular records program audits and how the Audit tool in the Records Management console can be used to assist in performing audits.

In particular, we covered the following topics in this chapter:

- How to specify search criteria in the **Criteria** tab of the Records Search page
- How to construct complex FTS-Alfresco searches
- How to apply search filters and ordering rules
- How to escape search criteria that use special characters with QNames, property names, and values
- How to save and reuse queries in both the Records Search and File Plan pages
- How to run and file audit reports

At the end of the chapter, in a "How does it work?" section, we examined, in detail, some developer internals related to the following items:

- How internally the Share page in Records Management calls a repository webscript to carry out records search
- How saved searches are stored and retrieved
- How the repository webscript supports the retrieval of audit information

In the next chapter, we will discuss how to configure security and permissions for the Alfresco Records Management system.

11
Configuring Security and Permissions

Keeping records secure is one of the highest priority goals of any Records Management system. By definition, the Records Management system is designed to store documents that are vital to the operations of the organization. In this chapter, we will examine how security and access controls can be applied so that users are able to access only the functionality and content that is appropriate for their role.

In particular, we will describe in this chapter:

- How to create users and groups within Alfresco Share
- How to view the permissions of existing Records Management roles
- How to modify and create new Records Management roles
- How to set access rights for areas in the File Plan

Creating users

Before a user is able to gain access to the records File Plan, they must have access to the Share Records Management site, and before getting access to the site, they must first become a user of the Share application. Let's look briefly at how Share users are created and how users are then able to subscribe to sites within Share.

Adding a new Share user

The tool that allows us to create a new Share user is available from the **Tools** area within the **Admin Console**. To get to this page, as a user admin, we click on the **Admin Console** link that can be found at the top of every Share page. After that, we can then move into the **Users** tool that is available from the left-hand panel navigation area:

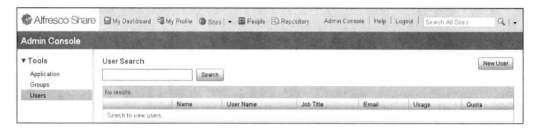

There is a **Search** field at the top of the page that lets us check to see if a user that we plan to add is already in the system. Users can be searched for by full or partial matches to either their first name or their last name.

There are some limitations to **User Search**. A search by user name or e-mail address will fail, and there is a limit of displaying only 100 users at one time. It also isn't possible to get a complete list of all users from this screen. One unwieldy solution to find all users in the system is to use the search criteria "A | B | C | D | E | F | G | H | I | J | K | L | M | N | O | P | Q | R | S | T | U | V | W | X | Y | Z".

To add a new user, we click on the **New User** button. After doing that, we are presented with the screen for adding a new user.

At a minimum, we need to enter the following information for each new user that we create:

- **First Name**
- **Last Name**
- **Email** address
- **User Name**
- **Password**

Optionally, two other pieces of information can be entered when a new user is created:

- **Groups** that the user will belong to

- Maximum disk space **Quota** that the user may consume (leaving bank implies no restriction)

After entering the user information, we click on **Create User** to add the user to the system. If there are many users to be added at one time, the **Create and Create Another** button can save some time by keeping the Add User page open and clearing the fields after a user is entered so that a new user can be immediately entered after one is created:

There is a lot more user information that can be tracked and managed than what was collected on the user creation form. This additional information can be entered and viewed on the **Profile** page for the user.

If we search for the new user that we just created, we can then click on the username in the user list row. We then see the **Profile** page for the user. While administrators are able to update the profile page for a user, users can also update their own profiles:

New user access to Share

After a user has been created in the system, they will then be able to log in to Share. Newly created users will not yet be members of any sites within Share. To join a Share site, the user will either need to subscribe to or be invited to the site.

When the new user logs in to Share, they will immediately be sent to their homepage dashboard. The dashboard page can be customized by each user and the layout that they select will be remembered as a preference and available each time they visit their homepage.

User admin

Most of our discussion in this book about operations within the Records Management site so far has been from the perspective of the user admin. It is vital that the admin account remains secure. Admin either has the privilege to perform any operation in the system or is in the position to be able to acquire any privileges that are not already assigned.

The user admin basically holds all the keys to the system and is thus an important user account that needs to be secured. The default password for the user admin is admin. This is a well known and insecure password that should be changed, especially in a production system, at the very first opportunity.

Groups and Records Management

Groups provide a way to aggregate users and other groups into a single logical entity that can be used when performing operations like assigning permissions. In Alfresco, there is a default user group called EVERYONE. Every user in the system is at least a member of the EVERYONE group and most users also belong to other groups.

To examine groups within Share, we return to the **Admin Console** and this time we bring up the **Groups** tool:

The layout of the **Groups** tool is very similar to that of the **Users** tool. As with **Users**, there is a group **Search** field at the top of the page. In a similar way, a search here also requires that the search criteria entered be at least one character long. Because of this limitation, finding a comprehensive list of all groups using the **Search** field isn't easy.

Browsing groups

Unlike the **Users** tool, the **Groups** tool has another option for browsing over all entries. There is a button to the right of the page called **Browse**. The **Browse** button makes the process of finding and managing groups much easier to use. When we click on the **Browse** button, we get a list of all the available groups, and within the **Groups** browse tool, we are also able to inspect, add, and edit groups:

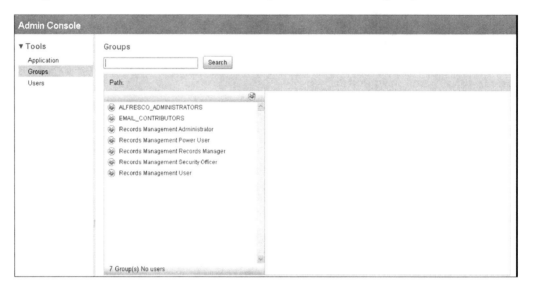

All groups except the EVERYONE group that all users belong to are shown here. The bottom five groups are of particular interest to us because they are specific to Records Management.

 The Records Management groups will only be visible within the **Groups** tool after the Records Management site has been created and has been accessed at least once.

The Records Management groups are:

- **Records Management Administrator**
- **Records Management Power User**
- **Records Management Records Manager**
- **Records Management Security Officer**
- **Records Management User**

These groups are directly associated with the roles and permissions that relate to the specific duties of the different types of users within the Records Management program.

Alfresco groups are used in two different ways with Records Management. Groups aggregate many users into a single entity that, when operated on, applies the operation to all users contained in the group. For example, inviting a group to become a member of a Share site causes all users in that group to be invited.

The five Records Management groups that we discussed above are special in that they are directly associated with the roles and permissions available within Records Management. These groups are managed by the **Define Roles** tool within the Records Management console. When a new role is created, a new group corresponding to that role is also created. Similarly, when the role is deleted, the group corresponding to that role is also deleted.

Adding a new group

To the right, above the list of available groups, there is a small circular icon. If we move our mouse over it, we see that this button lets us create new groups.

 To create a new Records Management role and the associated group for managing users within that role, use the **Define Roles** tool in the Records Management console.

Groups created from this screen can be used for performing operations like inviting by group to join a Share site. We can also assign a group created from this screen to one of the groups associated with a Records Management role.

Deleting a group

From the left-most list of the Group **Browse** feature, it is possible to delete any of the standard Share groups. Delete is also available from the list returned after a search by group name:

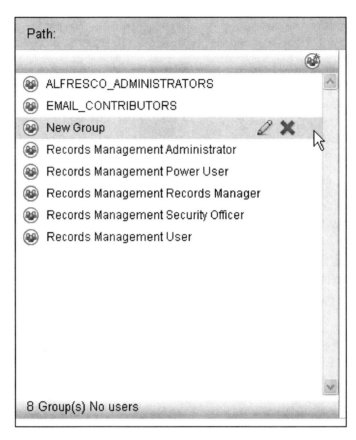

Groups created by the **Define Roles** tool should not be deleted using this screen. These types of groups are automatically deleted when their associated role is deleted.

Editing groups

Clicking on the pencil icon next to the group name lets you edit the display name for the group:

 Once a group is created, it isn't possible to change the group **Identifier** name.

Adding members to a group

We can add members to a group by first selecting the group that we would like to add to, and then clicking on the "Add user" icon in the list to the right of the group list. It is also possible to add not only users to the group, but other groups also:

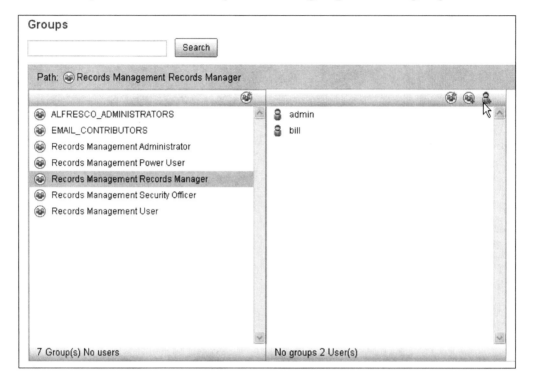

Adding users to groups associated with a Records Management role automatically assigns the permissions associated with that role to the user.

Member access to the Records Management site

Access to the Records Management site is only available to those users who have subscribed to it. The Records Management site is, by default, a public site within Share and available only by subscription to Share users.

Subscribing to the Records Management site

It is possible for a user to subscribe to the Records Management site by going to the **Site Finder** page and searching for the site called **rm** and then clicking on the **Join** button once it has been located:

At this point, the user has access to the dashboard of the Records Management site, but before being able to access any records in the File Plan, the user also needs to be a member of one of the Records Management role groups.

If we want to prevent users from being able to self-subscribe to the site, we can change the visibility of the site from **Public** to **Private**. To do that, we log in as the user who is the site manager of the Records Management site, that is, the user who originally installed it.

We then access the dashboard of the Records Management site. From the **More** menu next to **Customize Dashboard**, select **Edit Site Details**:

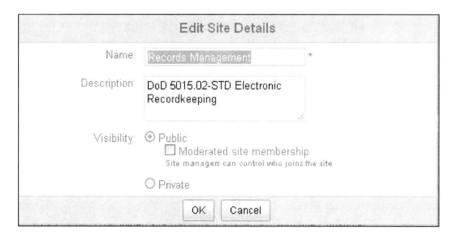

Here we have the option of either changing the site visibility to **Public**, but moderated, or to **Private**.

Requesting access to the moderated Records Management site

If we change the site from being wide open to the public to one being public but moderated, the Records Management site can still be found by users that are not members, but now, when users attempt to join the site, they instead see an option to **Request to Join** the site. They are no longer able to get immediate access to the site after joining. Their request to join the site must first be approved by the owner of the site:

After the user requests to join, the owner of the site will receive a notification of the request. Because we are the owners of the site, when we log back in as the user admin, we can see the request to join the site. It is located in the task list dashlet of the Share main dashboard. From the task list, we then have the option of either accepting or rejecting the request:

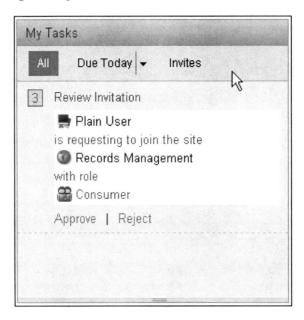

If the **My Tasks** dashlet is not available on the dashboard, it can be added to it from the **Customize Dashboard** screen.

After the user is approved, they will have full access to the Records Management site, but they will not have access to records in the File Plan until they are added as a member of one of the Records Management groups.

Access to a private Records Management site

The alternative to setting up the Records Management site as either a publicly moderated or publicly unmoderated site is to make the Records Management site private. We do this as shown above in the **Edit Site Details** dialog.

When the site is changed to private, the only way new members can be added to the site is for the site owner to send an invitation to them.

Invitations are sent from within the Records Management site. As Site Manager and owner of the site, we have an **Invite** button available from the homepage of the Records Management site. If we click on this, we will see a screen that lets us choose users that we would like to invite to the site:

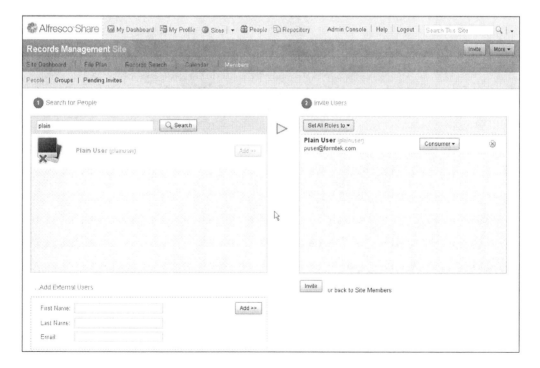

After searching for the user names, we add the names to the list of people we would like to invite and then set a site role for those users.

When we click on the **Invite** button, an e-mail invitation is sent to the selected users:

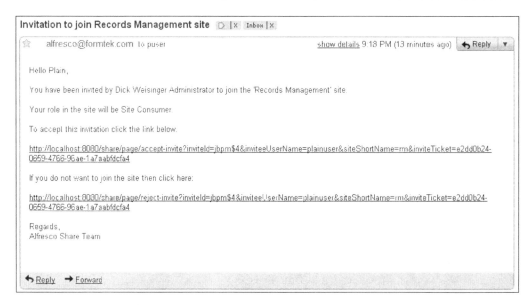

The FreeMarker template for the e-mail invitation sent out is located in the Alfresco repository and can be edited. The file can be found at `Repository/Data Dictionary/Email Templates/invite/invite-email.ftl`.

The user will also receive a new item in their task list, which they can see on the Share main dashboard:

The user then has the option to **Accept** or **Reject** the invitation for becoming a member.

Creating Records Management roles

A permission is the right that a user or group has to access a particular functionality in Alfresco.

Roles and permissions

In order to create very granular control over the types of functionality that users can access within the Records Management system, Alfresco has defined nearly 60 unique permissions.

A role for a user or group in the Records Management system is a collection of those privileges. The large number of granular permissions provides very detailed control over the way in which a role can be defined.

Access controls applied to the File Plan

For each of the five Records Management groups that we've already seen, there are a corresponding set of five roles, and there is a one-to-one mapping of each group to a role.

The top-level node of the Records Management File Plan, the `rm` site `documentLibrary` node, is secured by applying those roles as access control entries to the `documentLibrary` node. Children of this root node for the File Plan inherit the same access controls unless specifically overridden.

If we go to the Alfresco JSF Explorer client, we can see how the access controls are applied to the File Plan root node. In the client, we navigate to the space called **Company Home / Sites / rm / documentLibrary**.

From the **More Actions** drop-down, we can click on **Manage Space Users**. There we can see that the five groups have been associated with the appropriate roles and applied to the root node. Actually, what we're seeing in the **Roles** column of this page is a list of permissions (really `permissionGroups`) rather than the name of the Records Management roles:

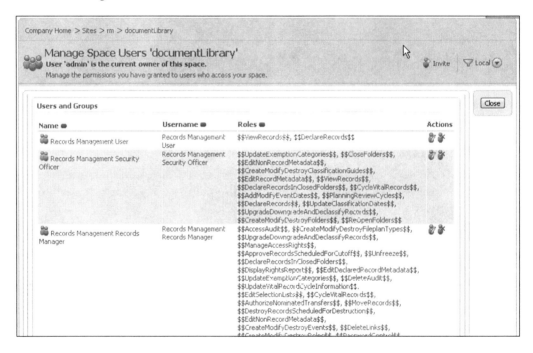

Unless a user belongs to one of the five Records Management role groups (or other role groups that may have been defined via the **Define Roles** tool), that user will not have the permissions to perform operations in any part of the File Plan.

In order to provide the flexibility of roles that can be easily edited from the user interface, Records Management roles are really a sort of super-role that consists of many individual roles or `permissionGroups`, most of which consist of only a single permission.

A similar view of the permissions that are associated with the **documentLibrary** node of the Share Records Management site is available through the Node Browser. A partial listing of all the permissions assigned to this node is shown in the screenshot below:

Viewing and editing the Records Management roles

Neither Share nor the Alfresco JSF Explorer client has a standard interface for editing roles. Roles are normally set up as permissionGroups and defined within an XML permission model file. For Records Management, the ability to edit roles with the ability to easily add or delete permissions to the role was added as a feature of the Management console.

 The roles tool for Records Management can't be used for editing any roles outside of Records Management.

Browsing role permissions

We can get to the Records Management **Define Roles** tool by going into the Management console and then clicking on the **Define Roles** entry in the left-hand navigation panel:

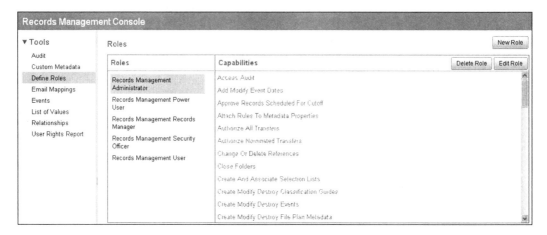

The **Define Roles** tool consists of a table with two columns. The entries in the first column show the available Records Management **Roles**. In this screenshot, we can see the five default roles. When one of the role entries in the first column is highlighted, then the second column, labeled **Capabilities**, shows the set of permissions that are enabled for that role.

In the next table, we can see a comparison of the default permissions that are available for each of the five Records Management roles.

We notice that the Records Management Administrator and Records Manager roles are very similar. The main distinction between the two is that the Administrator is able to manage access controls:

Capabilities

Records

		Administrator	Power User	Records Mgr	Security Officer	User
Declare Records	DeclareRecords	√		√	√	√
Move Records	MoveRecords	√		√		
Undeclare Records	UndeclareRecords	√		√		
View Records	ViewRecords	√	√	√	√	√

Folder Control

Close Folders	CloseFolders	√	√	√	√	
Create Modify Destroy Folders	CreateModify DestroyFolders	√	√	√	√	
Declare Records in Closed Folders	DeclareRecordsInClosed Folders	√	√	√	√	
Re-Open Folders	ReOpenFolders	√	√	√	√	

Metadata Control

Edit Declared Record Metadata	EditDeclared RecordMetadata	√		√		
Edit Non-Record Metadata	EditNonRecordMetadata	√	√	√	√	
Edit Record Metadata	EditRecordMetadata	√	√	√	√	

Vital Records

Cycle Vital Records	CycleVitalRecords	√	√	√	√	
Planning Review Cycles	PlanningReviewCycles	√	√	√	√	
Update Vital Record Cycle Information	UpdateVitalRecord CycleInformation	√		√		

References and Links

Change or Delete References	ChangeOrDeleteReferences	√		√		
Delete Links	DeleteLinks	√		√		

Events					
Add Modify Event Dates	`AddModifyEventDates`	√	√	√	√
Create Modify Destroy Events	`CreateModifyDestroyEvents`	√		√	
Cutoff					
Approve Records Scheduled for Cutoff	`ApproveRecords ScheduledForCutoff`	√		√	
Create Modify Destroy in Cutoff Folders	`CreateModifyRecords InCutoffFolders`	√		√	
Disposition and Transfers					
Authorize Nominated Transfers	`AuthorizeNominatedTransfers`	√		√	
Authorize All Transfers	`AuthorizeAllTransfers`	√		√	
Delete Records	`DeleteRecords`	√		√	
Destroy Records	`DestroyRecords`	√		√	
Destroy Records Scheduled for Destruction	`DestroyRecordsScheduled ForDestruction`	√		√	
Manually Change Disposition Dates	`ManuallyChange DispositionDates`	√		√	
Trigger An Event	`TriggerAnEvent`	√		√	
Update Trigger Dates	`UpdateTriggerDates`	√		√	
Hold Controls					
Extend Retention Period Or Freeze	`ExtendRetention PeriodOrFreeze`	√		√	
Unfreeze	`Unfreeze`	√		√	
View Update Reasons for Freeze	`ViewUpdateReasons ForFreeze`	√		√	
Audit					
Access Audit	`AccessAudit`	√		√	
Delete Audit	`DeleteAudit`	√		√	
Declare Audit As Record	`DeclareAuditAsRecord`	√		√	
Enable Disable Audit By Types	`EnableDisableAuditByTypes`	√		√	
Export Audit	`ExportAudit`	√		√	
Select Audit Metadata	`SelectAuditMetadata`	√		√	

Roles and Access Rights

Create Modify Destroy Roles	`CreateModifyDestroyRoles`	√	√	
Create Modify Destroy Users and Groups	`CreateModifyDestroy UsersAndGroups`	√	√	
Display Rights Report	`DisplayRightsReport`	√	√	
Manage Access Controls	`ManageAccessControls`	√		
Manage Access Rights	`ManageAccessRights`	√	√	
Password Control	`PasswordControl`	√	√	

File Plan Metadata, Lists, and E-mail

Attach Rules to Metadata Properties	`AttachRulesToMetadata Properties`	√	√	
Create and Associate Selection Lists	`CreateAndAssociate SelectionLists`	√	√	
Create Modify Destroy File Plan Metadata	`CreateModifyDestroy FileplanMetadata`	√	√	
Create Modify Destroy File Plan Types	`CreateModifyDestroy FileplanTypes`	√	√	
Create Modify Destroy Record Types	`CreateModifyDestroy RecordTypes`	√	√	
Create Modify Destroy Reference Types	`CreateModifyDestroy ReferenceTypes`	√	√	
Edit Selection Lists	`EditSelectionLists`	√	√	
Make Optional Parameters Mandatory	`MakeOptionalParameters Mandatory`	√	√	
Map E-mail Metadata	`MapEmailMetadata`	√	√	

Classified Records

Create Modify Destroy Classification Guides	`CreateModifyDestroy ClassificationGuides`	√	√	√
Create Modify Destroy Time Frames	`CreateModifyDestroy Timeframes`	√	√	
Map Classification Guide Metadata	`MapClassification GuideMetadata`	√	√	
Update Classification Dates	`UpdateClassificationDates`	√	√	√
Update Exemption Categories	`UpdateExemptionCategories`	√	√	√
Upgrade Downgrade and Declassify Records	`UpgradeDowngradeAnd DeclassifyRecords`	√	√	√

Editing role permissions

A role shown within the **Define Roles** tool can be edited by first highlighting the role name in the first column on the tool and then clicking on the **Edit Role** button.

On the **Edit Role** page, it is possible to edit the permissions that are assigned to the role. Because there are so many permissions, they have been grouped into related feature categories. It is possible to select all permissions of a feature category by selecting the **Select All** button to the upper-right of that group of entries.

After the new permission settings for the role is complete, we can then click on the **Save** button at the bottom of the page to update the settings.

Note that there is no user interface to create new permissions, only the ability to assign or remove permission settings for a given role:

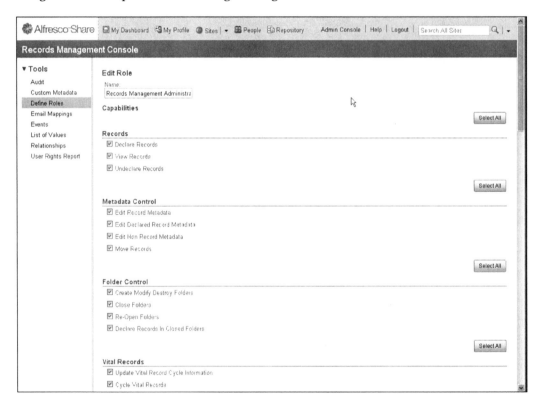

Creating a new role

A new role can be created by clicking on the **New Role** button in the Management Console. We note that the pages for creating and editing roles are very similar. When creating a new role, it is necessary to assign a unique name for the role and to then fill out the checkboxes for permissions that are to be assigned to the role.

When we're finished, we press the **Create** button. The new role will be created and added to the list of available roles. You might be wondering how do we then associate a group with this new role, and do we then need to manually create a group and associate it with the role? It turns out that we don't need to worry about any of that.

If, after creating a new role, we go to the Share Admin Console and navigate into the **Groups** area, we'll see that a new group has been created with the same name as the new role name that we just created. The group and role are automatically linked.

We can also go over to the Alfresco JSF Explorer client and look at the access controls that are set on that space after creating the new role. When we do that, we can verify that the access controls have automatically been applied to the File Plan root node.

Deleting a role

Existing roles can be deleted by clicking on the **Delete Role** button in the Management Console.

If we try deleting the new role that we just created, we get a popup message that the role was successfully deleted. If we then go back and look in the **Groups** tool in the Administration Console, we'll see that the group has also been removed. Similarly, if we go to the Explorer client and check the access control entries for the File Plan root node, we'll see that the entry for the new role that we created has now been removed.

So, we see that, behind the scenes, the Records Management console is automatically keeping the Records Management groups, roles, and access control entry information in sync for us.

Read and file permissions

There are two additional permissions that are not set using the **Define Roles** tool. These additional two permissions are:

- File a record
- Read a record

The permission to file a record is actually a superset of the permission to read a record. That is, if you can file a record, you can also read a record.

The Records Management administrator, by default, automatically has the permission to file a record included as part of the role for the administrator. This permission is not available for edit from the **Define Roles** tool, so it can't be removed from the administrator role, at least from the user interface.

Since the administrator role is applied at the root node of the File Plan, by default, all users in the administrator role will have complete rights to both file and read all parts of the File Plan. Because these permissions aren't exposed via the **Define Roles** tool, no other role can have these access control permissions automatically applied at the File Plan root.

Within the File Plan, it is possible to set read and file permissions. Users without these permissions, even if they are members of the Records Management site, will not be able to see any part of the File Plan.

The permission for a node within the File Plan is set by navigating to the record container or record on which the permissions are to be set, and then clicking on the **Manage Permissions** option for that item to specify the permissions:

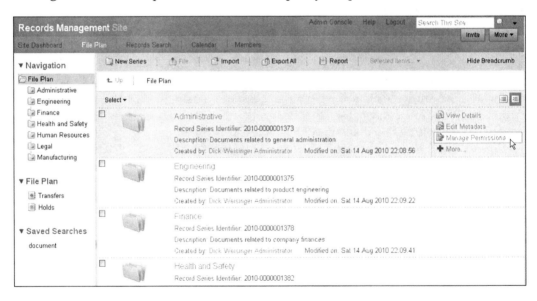

On the next screen, **Read** and **File** permissions can be managed for users and groups:

A user is added by clicking on the **Add User or Group** button. After doing that, a new row is added to the list of **Users and Groups**. By default, the new user will be added with the permission of **Read Only**. The drop-down list in the **Permissions** column for each row allows us to change the permission associated for that user or group.

Permissions are inherited by the child members of the node to which the permission was applied. For example, granting file and read access to a user at the record Series level will result in letting the user have file and read permission for all Categories, Folders, and records underneath the Series node.

If permissions to the user or group are not assigned at the top record Series level in the File Plan, the user will be able to see the parent containers in the File Plan that need to be navigated to get to the container to which the user has been granted access.

Consider, for example, adding access for a user at the Folder level in this path: `Administrative/Document Forms & Templates/Corporate Report Templates`.

If we grant read permission to a user for the Folder `Corporate Report Templates`, when accessing the File Plan, that user would first see a record Series called `Administrative`, and within that Series, there will be a record Category called `Document Forms & Templates`. However, no other Series, Category, or Folder containers would be visible to the user.

 Note that it's not possible to apply permissions directly at the record level.

The User Rights Report

From the Records Management Console, there is another tool that is useful for tracking permissions and role information. It provides a useful report that gives a quick summary of the distribution of users among the different Records Management roles. The tool is called the **User Rights Report**. In the list of tools on the Management Console, it is the last in the list of available tools:

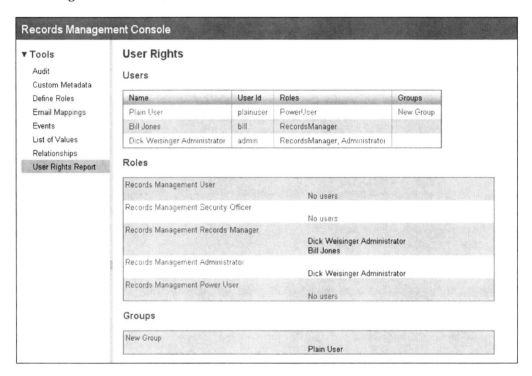

The **User Rights Report** is divided into three sections, showing information about **Users**, **Roles**, and **Groups**. The parts of the report labeled **Groups** refer to all groups other than the groups associated with Records Management roles. These **Groups** are the ones that have membership in the Share Records Management site, and users are marked as being site members as a result of belonging to a group that is a member of the site.

The first section of the report lists **Users** and their **Roles** and **Groups**. The second part of the report lists the information by **Roles** and shows the users in each of the roles. The final section lists **Groups** that are members of the Records Management site and the users that are in those groups.

The **User Rights Report** tool is a report and, as such, provides useful information, but it doesn't provide a way to edit or change any of the information. To do that, the **Define Roles** tool on this page should be used.

How does it work?

In this "How does it work?" section for this chapter on security, we will look primarily at how the data webscripts are used in the site webpages to retrieve information from the repository about users and roles. We'll also look at the permissions model for Records Management and at the file that is used to bootstrap the system with information about the five default Records Management roles.

Admin console—users

In the Administration console, the **Users** tool enables the management of users, allowing users to be created, user data to be edited, and users to be deleted.

On the **Users** page, there is a tool to search and view user information. User search in the **Users** admin tool is a bit frustrating because it isn't possible to see all the users in a single list. The field requires that at least one non-wildcard character be entered before the search is attempted.

The search operation on the **Users** page is made with a call to a repository webscript that accepts a filter, which can limit the users found. If we dig in a bit, we see that the limitation of a single character minimum length is enforced by the client, but it is not a limitation of the webscript.

The data webscript in the repository takes two parameters: `filter` and `maxResults`. The client-side JavaScript file, `tomcat\webapps\share\components\console\users.js`, builds the request URL and includes a filter based on the string entered in the search field. By testing the URL in the browser, we can find out that when the filter is omitted as a parameter in the webscript URL, all users will be returned in the results:

```
http://localhost:8080/share/proxy/alfresco/api/
people?filter=T&maxResults=100
```

Users in the repository

When a user is created in the repository, two types of objects are created for the user. A cm:person object is created to manage user profile information and a usr:user object is created to store information needed for Alfresco authentication. Internally, the AuthenticationService manages the usr:user objects and the PersonService handles the cm:person objects. usr:user objects are stored in the user://alfrescoUserStore and cm:person objects are stored in the workspace:// SpacesStore stores of the repository. In the following table, we see and compare how user metadata is divided between these two object types:

Data Store metadata properties	
usr:user object	**cm:person object**
(Stored in user:// alfrescoUserStore/system/ people/)	(Stored in workspace:// SpacesStore/system/people)
enabled	email
password	userName
username	owner
credentialsExpire	lastName
accountExpires	firstName
accountLocked	middleName
	homeFolder
	organizationId
	organization
	telephone
	mobile
	+ more...

The complete content model definition for the cm:person object can be found in the Alfresco file tomcat\webapps\alfresco\WEB-INF\ classes\alfresco\model\contentModel.xml. The content model for usr:user can be found in the file userModel.xml, as described in the next section.

Users as usr:users

The `usr:user` objects are used to hold authentication information for users when Alfresco authentication is used.

The object `usr:user` is defined in the user content model. The file for the content model is a little hard to find. It is located in `tomcat\webapps\alfresco\WEB-INF\lib\alfresco-repository-3.3.jar`. In that JAR file, the `userModel.xml` file can be found in the `org\alfresco\repo\security\authentication` directory:

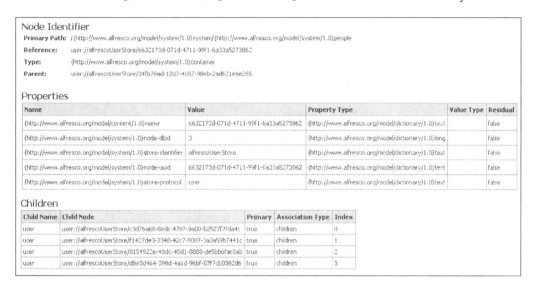

Users as cm:persons

When a new user is added, the user profile information is added to the `workspace://SpacesStore` store. We can check this by using the Node Browser tool in the Admin area of the Alfresco JSF Explorer client.

The profile information is added as the type `cm:person`. One entry of this type exists for every user in the system. We can find these objects by looking under the path `system/people` of the `SpacesStore` store. At that node in the repository, we see that the children are of type `cm:person` nodes and correspond to the users in the system:

Node Identifier

Primary Path: /{http://www.alfresco.org/model/system/1.0}system/{http://www.alfresco.org/model/system/1.0}people

Reference: workspace://SpacesStore/0a11e180-02f3-4de5-914c-f8ae701e0979

Type: {http://www.alfresco.org/model/system/1.0}container

Parent: workspace://SpacesStore/50609529-564d-4b3d-bfb2-ae5776633063

Properties

Name	Value	Property Type	Value Type	Residual
{http://www.alfresco.org/model/content/1.0}name	0a11e180-02f3-4de5-914c-f8ae701e0979	{http://www.alfresco.org/model/dictionary/1.0}text		false
{http://www.alfresco.org/model/system/1.0}node-dbid	26	{http://www.alfresco.org/model/dictionary/1.0}long		false
{http://www.alfresco.org/model/system/1.0}store-identifier	SpacesStore	{http://www.alfresco.org/model/dictionary/1.0}text		false
{http://www.alfresco.org/model/system/1.0}node-uuid	0a11e180-02f3-4de5-914c-f8ae701e0979	{http://www.alfresco.org/model/dictionary/1.0}text		false
{http://www.alfresco.org/model/system/1.0}store-protocol	workspace	{http://www.alfresco.org/model/dictionary/1.0}text		false

Children

Child Name	Child Node	Primary	Association Type	Index
admin	workspace://SpacesStore/dfc3fac9-ef9f-4eb6-bcc9-93b3b6508a5a	true	children	0
guest	workspace://SpacesStore/e1804d9c-6924-484d-9801-b214c33cb3ad	true	children	1
bill	workspace://SpacesStore/b69678df-8b18-4d9b-95fb-10b078c3e476	true	children	2
system	workspace://SpacesStore/aad36e49-8421-42f4-bfd5-5357fdeb8c26	true	children	3
plainuser	workspace://SpacesStore/4072b25b-a248-45c4-8aea-76c10aa1a442	true	children	4
tharold	workspace://SpacesStore/16722979-d2fd-47cf-90e0-9a0147c29d29	true	children	5

If we then click through into one of the child nodes corresponding to a user, we will then see the profile information stored for that user:

Node Identifier

Primary Path: /{http://www.alfresco.org/model/system/1.0}system/{http://www.alfresco.org/model/system/1.0}people/{http://www.alfresco.org/model/content/1.0}bill

Reference: workspace://SpacesStore/b69678df-8b18-4d9b-95fb-10b078c3e476

Type: {http://www.alfresco.org/model/content/1.0}person

Parent: workspace://SpacesStore/0a11e180-02f3-4de5-914c-f8ae701e0979

Properties

Name	Value	Property Type	Value Type	Residual
{http://www.alfresco.org/model/content/1.0}name	b69678df-8b18-4d9b-95fb-10b078c3e476	{http://www.alfresco.org/model/dictionary/1.0}text		false
{http://www.alfresco.org/model/system/1.0}node-dbid	567	{http://www.alfresco.org/model/dictionary/1.0}long		false
{http://www.alfresco.org/model/content/1.0}email	bjones@formtek.com	{http://www.alfresco.org/model/dictionary/1.0}text		false
{http://www.alfresco.org/model/system/1.0}store-identifier	SpacesStore	{http://www.alfresco.org/model/dictionary/1.0}text		false
{http://www.alfresco.org/model/content/1.0}sizeQuota	-1	{http://www.alfresco.org/model/dictionary/1.0}long		false
{http://www.alfresco.org/model/content/1.0}userName	bill	{http://www.alfresco.org/model/dictionary/1.0}text		false
{http://www.alfresco.org/model/content/1.0}sizeCurrent	661595	{http://www.alfresco.org/model/dictionary/1.0}long		false
{http://www.alfresco.org/model/content/1.0}owner	bill	{http://www.alfresco.org/model/dictionary/1.0}text		false
{http://www.alfresco.org/model/system/1.0}node-uuid	b69678df-8b18-4d9b-95fb-10b078c3e476	{http://www.alfresco.org/model/dictionary/1.0}text		false
{http://www.alfresco.org/model/content/1.0}lastName	Jones	{http://www.alfresco.org/model/dictionary/1.0}text		false
{http://www.alfresco.org/model/system/1.0}store-protocol	workspace	{http://www.alfresco.org/model/dictionary/1.0}text		false
{http://www.alfresco.org/model/content/1.0}homeFolder	workspace://SpacesStore/322c4132-335f-42a6-9ee6-3acc83a6224®	{http://www.alfresco.org/model/dictionary/1.0}noderef		false
{http://www.alfresco.org/model/content/1.0}firstName	Bill	{http://www.alfresco.org/model/dictionary/1.0}text		false

There is a lot of information on the page for the node. If we scroll to the bottom of the Node Browser page, we can see a section that shows the parent nodes of the child `cm:person` node that we've navigated into. You may have expected to see a single parent node listed there—the one corresponding to the `system/people` node from where we navigated. But there's more than just that one parent listed. That node is there, but we also see that there are quite a few other parent nodes in the list:

Parents

Child Name	Parent Node	Primary	Association Type
bill	workspace://SpacesStore/add3004a-ea05-46fc-9572-b0e1ad044a16	false	member
bill	workspace://SpacesStore/0a11e180-02f3-4de5-914c-f8ae701e0979	true	children
bill	workspace://SpacesStore/f55be5a6-794d-4ce9-bb2f-37b3411546d6	false	member
bill	workspace://SpacesStore/AUTH.ALF	false	inZone
bill	workspace://SpacesStore/04c8c3fd-2e36-4b8c-b89e-347efc5116b2	false	member
bill	workspace://SpacesStore/APP.DEFAULT	false	inZone

In this example, the `cm:person` node for the user bill has three types of parent-node **Association Type**s, as seen in the last column of the table, namely, **member**, **children**, and **inZone**. The association labeled **children** corresponds to the `system/person` node that we navigated from.

The three associations labeled as **member** have special interest to us with respect to security. By clicking through on these, we can find that the parent nodes for these entries correspond to the groups that this user belongs to:

Parent node	Authority name	Authority display name
workspace://SpacesStore/add3004a-ea05-46fc-9572-b0e1ad044a16	GROUP_site_rm_SiteConsumer	rm
workspace://SpacesStore/04c8c3fd-2e36-4b8c-b89e-347efc5116b2	GROUP_site_operations_SiteManager	operations
workspace://SpacesStore/f55be5a6-794d-4ce9-bb2f-37b3411546d6	GROUP_RecordsManager98c5a184-9901-4b7c-9e16-91522f2ccb2a	Records Management Records Manager

If we look up these parent nodes, we find that all three correspond to nodes of type `cm:authorityContainer`. Groups are thus represented as `cm:authorityContainers`.

We see from these groups that the user bill has site manager rights for the Share site called "operations". This gives him privileges to do things like manage the invitations to the "operations" site and to manage the contents that show up on the dashboard and the pages that will be available in the site for navigation.

User bill also has consumer rights for the Records Management site. In Records Management, bill doesn't have any control over things like managing the layout or controlling the members to the site. But the third group that bill belongs to above is the Records Manager group. This means that within the File Plan or Document Library area of this site, bill has all rights except for managing access controls.

Access to roles via webscripts

We next investigate to see how the Share pages for the Records Management site retrieve role information. The Management console page uses the JavaScript file `tomcat\webapps\share\components\console\rm-user-roles.js` for controlling the dynamics of the **Define Roles** tool.

Within the `onReady()` initialization method of the `Alfresco.admin.RMRoles` object, we can see that the URL for the webscript service call is created. The URL is in the form:

`http://localhost:8080/share/proxy/alfresco/api/rma/admin/rmroles/` (to return all roles),

or `http://localhost:8080/share/proxy/alfresco/api/rma/admin/rmroles/Administrator` (to limit the results returned to only the administrator).

For example, on a request for the user permissions of the role User, the following JSON packet is returned:

`http://localhost:8080/share/proxy/alfresco/api/rma/admin/rmroles/User`

```
{
  "data":
  {
  "name": "User",
  "displayLabel": "Records Management User",
  "capabilities" :
  [
    "ViewRecords",
    "DeclareRecords"
  ]
  }
}
```

Permissions

The permissions that are used to define Records Management roles are themselves defined in the file `tomcat\webapps\alfresco\WEB-INF\classes\module\org_ alfresco_dod5015\model\recordsPermissionModel.xml`. The definitions here bootstrap the creation of the default Records Management roles on installation. Remember that the settings in this file can be overridden by changes made to Records Management roles using the **Define Roles** tool.

The file defines the `permissionSet` that can be applied to objects that are associated with the `rma:filePlanComponent` aspect, which includes nearly all objects in the Records Management content model:

```
<permissionSet expose="select" type="rma:filePlanComponent">
```

Individual permissions are defined near the end of the `recordsPermissionModel. xml` file and then assigned to a `permissionGroup` that contains only that one permission, such as the following:

```
<permission name="_DeclareRecords" expose="false">
  <grantedToGroup permissionGroup="DeclareRecords"/>
</permission>
```

Near the top of the `permissionSet` are the main `permissionGroups` that aggregate the individual permissions into groups of permissions to be associated with the Records Management roles.

The following permission groups are defined in this way, each one corresponding to a role in Records Management:

- User
- PowerUser
- SecurityOfficer
- Records Manager
- Administrator

For example, the `permissionGroup` called `User` that corresponds to the Records Management User role is defined as follows:

```
<permissionGroup name="User" allowFullControl="false" expose="true">
  <includePermissionGroup type="rma:filePlanComponent"
    permissionGroup="DeclareRecords"/>
  <includePermissionGroup type="rma:filePlanComponent"
    permissionGroup="ViewRecords"/>
</permissionGroup>
```

Summary

In this chapter, we learned how role-based security is managed for the Alfresco Records Management site. Alfresco has a very rich and very granular permission structure, making it possible to create custom roles that can match the needs of most organizations.

We covered the following topics in this chapter:

- How to create Share users and groups
- How to add users to roles
- How to view the definition of a role, modify a role definition, and create a new role
- How to create a User Rights Report
- How to assign access controls to parts of the records File Plan

At the end of the chapter, in a "How does it work?" section, we looked in detail at how data webscripts are used to retrieve data from the Alfresco repository for users, groups, and roles. We also saw the definition of the permission model for Records Management and how the individual permissions are bundled into permissionGroups corresponding to the roles in Records Management.

In the next chapter, we will complete our discussion of Alfresco Records Management. In that last chapter, we'll discuss some additional areas of Records Management configuration. In particular, we will see how records and record containters of the Records Management content model can be extended using a tool within the Records Management console.

12
Configuring Records Management Parameters

This chapter looks in more detail at some of the configuration capabilities of the Records Management Console. In previous chapters, we touched on some of the things that can be done from the Management Console, such as the editing of roles and the auditing of system activity. In this chapter, we look more thoroughly at some of the other features that are available.

In this chapter, we will describe:

- How to create custom metadata properties associated with record object types
- How to map metadata extracted from e-mails to Records Management properties
- How to create and name custom events to use when building disposition schedules
- How to create custom mapping types to specify relationships between two records

At the end of this chapter, in a "How does it work?" section, we will discuss from a developer perspective some of the internals of how the Records Management Console works.

The construction of the Management Console is very similar to that of the Administration Console. We will look at some of the similarities between the two types of consoles and we will also look at how data dynamically configured and edited by the console tools are retrieved and stored.

The Records Management Console

We've already looked at parts of the Records Management Console in previous chapters. Recall that the Management Console is available from the **Records Management** dashlet found on the administrator's home page:

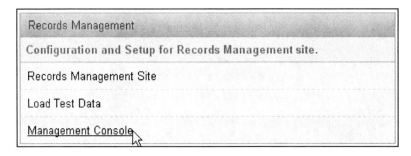

In *Chapter 9*, when we discussed Search and Auditing within Alfresco, we looked at how auditing capabilities are built into the Management Console. Then, later in *Chapter 11*, we discussed security and saw how role management is built into the Management Console. We also saw how the Console could be used to create roles for users of the Records Management site and how we could run a User Rights Report to show the relationships between users, groups, and Records Management roles.

Let's take a tour now of some of the remaining capabilities available in the Management Console that we have not yet discussed.

List of Values

From the list of available tools in the Tool list on the **Management Console** page, let's first discuss **List of Values**. Lists of values will later be referenced when we look at the **Custom Metadata** tool. We will look at how to create and manage a **List of Values**. To do that, we click on the **List of Values** link under the list of available **Tools**:

Out of the box, there are two **Lists** already defined: **Supplemental Markings** and **Transfer Locations**, although there are no entries defined for either of these. The Records application is actually already set up to use these two lists as we will see shortly. These two elements are described in the DoD 5015.2 specification.

Supplemental Markings

By clicking on the **Edit** button next to an existing list in the **List of Values** tool, we are able to modify the entries that are found in that list. For example, **Supplemental Markings** are security categories that are recommended by the DoD 5015.2 specification.

After installing the system, there are no default values for **Supplemental Markings**. We can edit the values now, and we will add the values recommended by the DoD.

Note that on the **Edit** window, after adding a value, you also need to assign which users or groups will be able to view the entry that you've added. This allows for very granular control over specifying which users will be able to see which entries. If no users or groups are specified for any of the new entries that we've added, any drop-down list that uses the list will not display any entries for anyone.

In this case, we will grant only the user **admin** the ability to see the security level set by the **Supplemental Markings**:

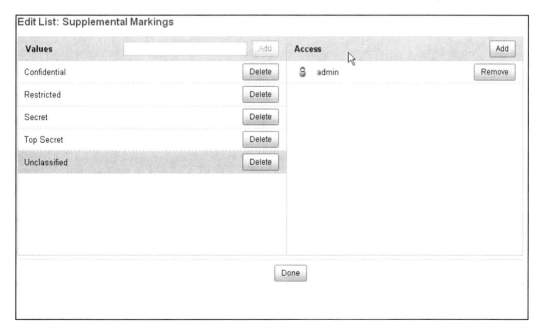

Now, for example, when authorized users (in this case, user **admin**) edit metadata for a record, they will see the following additional field on the edit form:

Transfer Locations

In a similar way, the **Transfer Location** information can be edited with the **List of Value** tool. For example, here we enter values for the names of the locations where the organization may house offsite storage facilities:

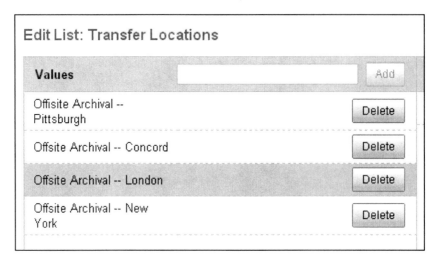

This **Transfer List** and the transfer values in it are used in the records application when specifying the transfer of records location for a step in the disposition that involves **Transfer**:

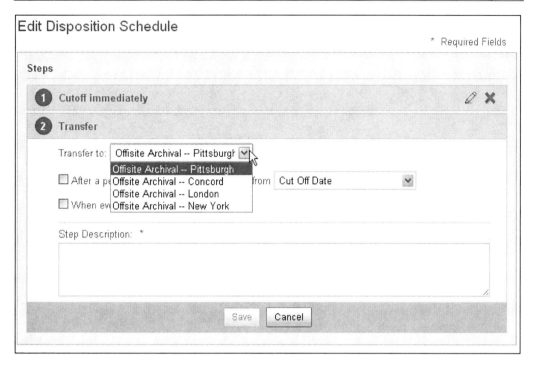

Creating a new List of Values

New lists can be created just as easily as existing lists can be edited. By clicking on the **New List** button of the tool, a pop-up is displayed that allows us to enter the **Name** of the new list that we create:

By entering a new **Name** and clicking on **OK**, we create a new list that is initialized to have no entries. After the new list is created, the screen shows us the available lists that we have. In the same way that we edited **Supplemental Markings** and **Transfer Locations**, we click on the **Edit** button for this new list. In this way, we can add new entries to the new list:

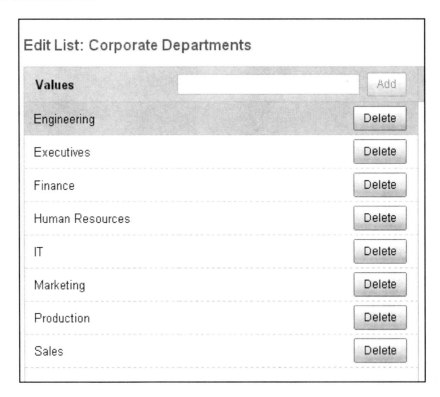

Deleting the List of Values

There is no way from the user interface to delete lists once you have created them. It is possible to delete the individual entries in a list and a list can be renamed; so in effect, a list might not be deleted, but it can be transformed into a totally different list.

Custom Metadata

Next, let's look at the **Custom Metadata** tool. The Alfresco content model framework is extremely flexible and allows for the properties associated with objects to be expanded at runtime by applying aspects. However, that still means that developers need to be involved in writing the configuration code that sets up the available aspects.

The **Custom Metadata** area for Records Management allows non-developers to expand on the available metadata properties that are associated with the type definitions for record objects.

By clicking on the **Custom Metadata** link under the **Tools** section of the page, we can see the screen that lets us add new properties to record objects:

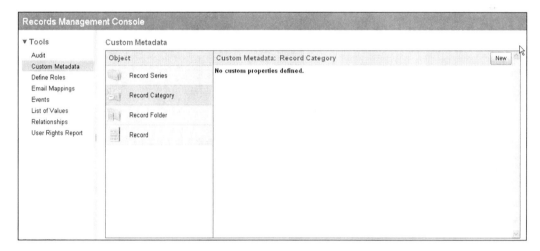

On the left-hand side of the tool, we see a list of the four available types of record objects to which new properties can be attached: record Series, record Categories, record Folders, and records.

For a record Category, we then click on the **New** button and we are presented with a screen for defining a new property. As an example, consider adding a new property to a record Category called **Department Authority**. The property will be of data type **Text** and will be selectable from a drop-down list by the user.

If we click on the **Use selection list** field, we can see a list of the available user-defined **List of Values** in the drop-down list. The second entry in this drop-down list is the **Corporate Departments** entry that we added in the last section:

The data types that are available for the user-defined property are: **Text**, **Boolean**, and **Date**.

We also have the option on this screen to specify whether or not the new property that we are creating should be **Mandatory** or not. For this particular example, we choose not to check it.

After clicking on the **Create** button, the new property is created and available to be used with the record Categories. The new property will be available just like any standard property for the Category:

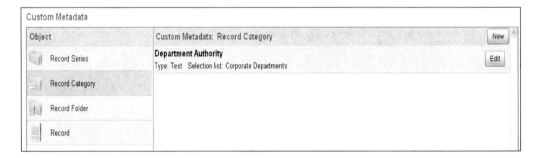

We can see this change in action by going into the File Plan and creating a new Category. On the pop-up form to create the new Category, there is now an entry called **Department** with the values that we defined from the **List of Values**.

The new property becomes available and viewable on the **Details** page for the Category and it is also available and editable on the page to edit metadata for the Category:

E-mail Mappings

We've seen earlier when we discussed the many ways to file data into Alfresco that e-mail messages could be filed into the repository by using inbound e-mail or by mounting the Alfresco repository as an IMAP folder within an e-mail client.

We've also discussed how, within Alfresco, metadata extractors can be built to capture metadata stored in a document from the file header of an uploaded document. Alfresco has a metadata extractor that can capture the metadata fields from e-mail headers on upload into the repository.

E-mail metadata

The format of e-mail messages is universally standard to allow the exchange of information between any e-mail systems. RFC 822 specifies the process for exchanging e-mail messages. That specification defines 25 metadata values that may be included in the header of an e-mail. E-mail vendors may also include metadata that is proprietary and has meaning only within their system.

 More information about RFC 822, which defines the format for an ARPA Internet text message, can be found here at `http://www.faqs.org/rfcs/rfc822.html`.

The **Email Mappings** tool provides a user interface to allow the metadata fields of an incoming e-mail message to be automatically mapped within the captured metadata that will be associated with the record and then managed within the Alfresco repository:

Incoming e-mail metadata field	Alfresco repository metadata
messageSubject	cm:subjectline
messageSubject	imap:messageSubject
messageSent	rma:publicationDate
messageSubject	cm:description
messageSubject	cm:title
messageTo	rma:address
messageFrom	imap:messageFrom
messageFrom	cm:originator
Thread-Index	imap:threadIndex
messageCc	rma:otherAddress
messageFrom	rma:originator
Date	rma:dateReceived
Date	imap:dateReceived
Message-ID	imap:messageId
messageTo	imap:messageTo
messageSent	cm:sentdate
messageSent	imap:dateSent
messageCc	imap:messageCc

From the table, we see that it is possible to map the value of an incoming metadata property to any number of properties for the node in the repository. For example, the e-mail metadata property `messageFrom` maps to `imap:messageFrom`, `cm:originator`, and `rma:originatory`.

Creating an e-mail mapping

To create a new e-mail mapping, we can simply fill in the e-mail property name in the field and then select from the appropriate repository property for the node that the data will be mapped to:

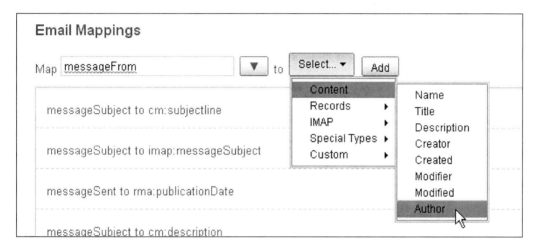

In this example, we show how a mapping can be set up between the e-mail property **messageFrom** and the repository property cm:author. After the repository property is selected, we then click on the **Add** button to add the mapping to the list.

Events

We saw when creating disposition schedules that the steps of the disposition can use either time-based or event-based triggers. As we've seen, events can be triggered manually by clicking buttons at either the Folder or record level detail page, depending on how the disposition was configured.

The Events tool in the Management Console provides a way to be able to enter user-defined events that can be used when building dispositions.

We see that while most of the events are simple, there are four possible types:

- Simple
- Obsoleted
- Cross Referenced Record Transferred
- Superseded

The next table shows the events and their types that are defined by default:

Abolished	Simple Event
All Allowances Granted Are Terminated	Simple Event
Case Closed	Simple Event
Case Complete	Simple Event
No longer needed	Simple Event
Obsolete	Obsoleted Event
Redesignated	Simple Event
Related Record Transferred To Inactive Storage	Cross Referenced Record Transferred
Separation	Simple Event
Study Complete	Simple Event
Superseded	Superseded Event
Training Complete	Simple Event
WGI Action Complete	Simple Event

Superseded events occur when an item becomes out of date and is to be replaced with a record that is current. **Obsoleted events** occur when an item becomes invalid or out of date and is typically not replaced with another record. Optionally, similar to superseded items, obsoleted items can be replaced with another record.

Obsoleted, superseded, and cross-referenced items often need to maintain a relationship with one or more other records. We've seen earlier that these types of relationships can be set up at the record level with the References option available from a record's details page. We can see how this is done on a record in the next screenshot:

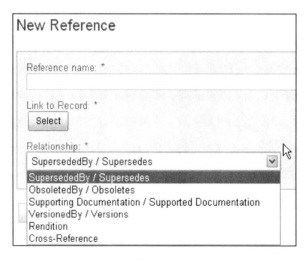

New user-defined events can be created by clicking on the **New Event** button in the **Events** tool. On the page to create the event, we can enter a text **Label** for the new event, specify its **Type**, and then click on **Save**. After doing that, the event then becomes available for use when defining event-based triggers in the disposition:

Once an event is defined, it can be edited by clicking on the **Edit** button near the end of the row in the list of events of the **Events** tool main page. From the **Edit** page, it is possible to change the label or type of the event.

An event can be deleted by clicking on the **Delete** button at the end of the row for the event in the list.

Relationships

The last tool in the Management Console that we will discuss is **Relationships**:

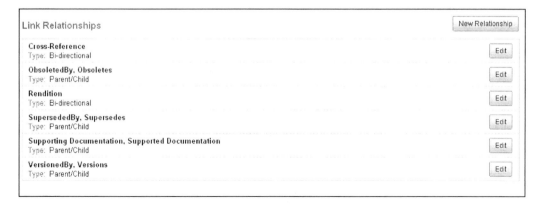

We just saw how relationships can be established between records from the References option on the records details page. The items in that drop-down list correspond to the link relationships that are created in this **Relationships** tool.

There are only two types of link relationships that can be created:

- Bi-directional (a relationship that can be traversed in both directions)
- Parent/Child (a container relationship in which the child cannot exist without its parent)

The labels that are applied to the nodes are what make the relationships unique and assign meaning to them. For example, in a parent/child relationship, the parent node might be labeled as "Versioned by" and the child node is labeled as "versions".

The following table summarizes the types of relationships that are available out of the box:

Cross-Reference	Bi-directional
ObsoletedBy, Obsoletes	Parent/Child
Rendition	Bi-directional
SupersededBy, Supersedes	Parent/Child
Supporting Documentation, Supported Documentation	Parent/Child
VersionedBy, Versions	Parent/Child

Clicking on the **New Relationship** button brings up the screen for defining a **New Relationship**. For a **Bi-directional** relationship, a single label is defined. For a **Parent/Child** relationship, a label to be associated with the **Source** node and a label to be applied to the **Target** node must be entered:

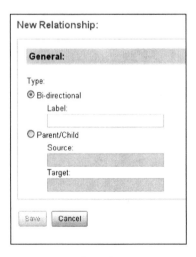

How does it work?

From the perspective of how the Share application is built on Spring-Surf, the Records Management Console presents an interesting study. Maybe it's not too surprising, but the console re-uses much of the same framework code that is also used in the Administration Console for managing Users, Groups, and Application parameters.

The Management Console page

Clicking on the link in the Records Management Console dashlet causes the following page URL to be displayed: `http://localhost:8080/share/page/console/rm-console/`. One thing to note with this URL is that it does not reference the `rm` site as part of it.

The URL format for a Console page is defined in the `tomcat\webapps\share\WEB-INF\classes\alfresco\share-config.xml` file:

```
<uri-templates>
  <uri-template id="sitedashboardpage">/site/{site}/dashboard</uri-
    template>
  <uri-template id="sitepage">/site/{site}/{pageid}</uri-template>
  <uri-template id="userdashboardpage">/user/{userid}/dashboard</uri-
    template>
  <uri-template id="userpage">/user/{userid}/{pageid}</uri-template>
  <uri-template id="userprofilepage">/user/{userid}/profile</uri-
    template>
  <uri-template id="consolepage">/console/{pageid}/{toolid}</uri-
    template>
</uri-templates>
```

Here we see that the `uri-template` ID called `consolepage` is defined and that it matches the signature of the URL page for the Records Management Console.

In this case, the `pageid` corresponds to `rm-console`. Armed with that information, we can find the page descriptor file `tomcat\webapps\share\WEB-INF\classes\alfresco\site-data\pages\rm-console.xml`:

```
<page>
  <title>Records Management Console</title>
  <title-id>page.rmConsole.title</title-id>
  <description>Records Management Administration
    Console</description>
  <description-id>page.rmConsole.description</description-id>
  <template-instance>console</template-instance>
  <authentication>user</authentication>
</page>
```

Here's where we see some interesting information. The `template-instance` used by the Records Management Console is `console`, the same as what is used for the Administration Console. In the case of the URL used for the Administration Console, the `pageid` is `admin-console`.

Rendering of Management Console tools

When the Management Console page is rendered, there is a list of eight tools that display in the left navigation area.

The Console JavaScript file `tomcat\webapps\share\WEB-INF\classes\templates\org\alfresco\console.js` collects the information about the available tools for the page and saves the information into the set of known page context data.

The Records Management Console family of components can all be found in the directory `tomcat\webapps\share\WEB-INF\classes\alfresco\site-webscripts\org\alfresco\components\console`. Components for the Administration Console are also located in that same directory:

Tool	Tool ID	Descriptor file name	Unique URL identifer
Audit	`rm-audit`	`rm-audit.get.desc.xml`	`/components/console/rm-audit`
Custom Metadata	`rm-custom-metadata`	`rm-custom-metadata.get.desc.xml`	`/components/console/rm-custom-metadata`
Define Roles	`rm-define-roles`	`rm-define-roles.get.desc.xml`	`/components/console/rm-define-roles`
Email Mappings	`rm-email-mappings`	`rm-email-mappings.get.desc.xml`	`/components/console/rm-email-mappings`
Events	`rm-events`	`rm-events.get.desc.xml`	`/components/console/rm-events`
List of Values	`rm-list-of-values`	`rm-list-of-values.get.desc.xml`	`/components/console/rm-list-of-values`
Relationships	`rm-references`	`rm-references.get.desc.xml`	`/components/console/rm-references`
User Rights Report	`rm-userrights`	`rm-userrights.get.desc.xml`	`/components/console/rm-userrights`

Each of the descriptor files identifies the component as belonging to the `rm-console` family. The unique URL identifier for the component is also listed. The unique URLs are shown in the last column of the table above.

For example, consider the descriptor file for the **Custom Metadata** component. This file includes the name, description, URL, and family identifier. The descriptor files for the other `rm-console` components provide similar information:

```
<webscript>
  <shortname>Admin Console User Rights Report</shortname>
  <description>Administration Console - User Rights Report
    Tool</description>
  <url>/components/console/rm-userrights</url>
  <family>rm-console</family>
</webscript>
```

The Console page layout

Now let's briefly look at the layout of the Management Console page. Since both the Administration and Records Management share the same template-instances, the layout of the page is the same for both of these.

The FreeMarker template layout file is `tomcat\webapps\share\WEB-INF\classes\alfresco\templates\org\alfresco\console.ftl`:

```
<@templateBody>
  <div id="alf-hd">
    <@region id="header" scope="global" protected="true" />
    <@region id="title" scope="page" protected="true" />
  </div>

  <div id="bd">
    <div class="yui-t1" id="divConsoleWrapper">
      <div id="yui-main">
        <div class="yui-b" id="divConsoleMain">
          <@region id="tool" scope="page" protected="true" />
        </div>
      </div>
      <div class="yui-b" id="divConsoleTools">
        <@region id="tools" scope="template" protected="true" />
      </div>
    </div>
  </div>
</@>

<@templateFooter>
```

```
    <div id="alf-ft">
      <@region id="footer" scope="global" protected="true" />
    </div>
  </@>
```

Here we see the standard `header` and `title` regions at the top and `footer` at the bottom that we've seen for web pages that we've analyzed in earlier chapters. Note that the scope of the `tools` region is for the template, which means that it will be common across all Records Management Console pages, no matter which tool is being viewed, whereas, the scope of the `tool` region is just for a single page.

The next screenshot shows the **Management Console** with the names of the regions superimposed over it. As you can see, the layout is quite simple. The **tool** region is occupied by a single component that specializes in performing a single administrative task:

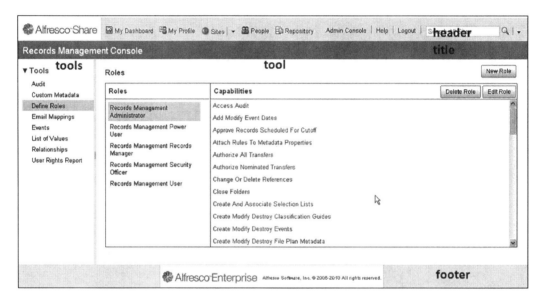

The tools navigation region

We saw above that left-most on the **Management Console** page is the region called **tools**, which is used for navigating to the administrative tool that will be displayed in the central **tool** region of the page.

The files that describe the workings of the **tools** component are stored here: `tomcat\webapps\share\WEB-INF\classes\alfresco\site-webscripts\org\alfresco\components\console\console-tools.*`.

The **tools** component is quite simple. The list of available tools was queried from the `sitedata` root-scoped object in the `console.js` file when preparing the context information for the page. This information is then passed along to the JavaScript controller file for this component, `console-tools.get.js`, which extracted the information and put it into an array as part of the model.

The FreeMarker layout file `console-tools.get.html.ftl` for the tools component simply formats the list of available tools for display:

```
<div id="${args.htmlid}-body" class="tool tools-link">
  <h2>${msg("header.tools")}</h2>
  <ul class="toolLink">
    <#list tools as tool>
    <li class="<#if tool_index=0>first-link</#if><#if tool.selected>
      selected</#if>">
        <span>
          <a href="${tool.id}" class="tool-link"
             title="${tool.description?html}">${tool.label?html}</a>
        </span>
    </li>
    </#list>
  </ul>
</div>
```

Custom Records Management metadata

We've seen with the **Custom Metadata** tool that it is possible to add user-defined metadata properties for record objects. In *Chapter 4*, we looked at the content model and saw how properties can be defined by and associated with aspects and types.

You may wonder how Alfresco manages to keep track of these custom metadata definitions. In the same way that the script files can be stored in the repository and activated immediately after editing the script, the custom metadata definitions are also stored in the repository.

The node reference value for the **Custom Metadata** definitions is `workspace://`
`SpacesStore/records_management_custom_model`. By using the **Node Browser** in
the JSF Explorer client, we can look up this definition file:

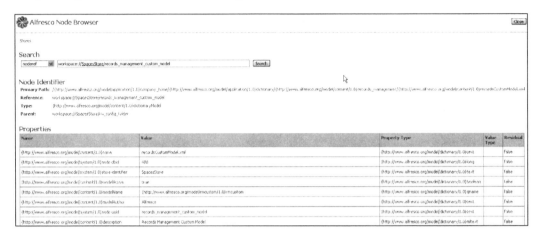

From the **Primary Path** information displayed in the **Node Browser**, we see that the
location for this file is `Company Home/Data Dictionary/Records Management/`
`recordsCustomModel.xml`.

The content of this file follows the standard format for an Alfresco content model file.
There is imported information from various other namespaces, the namespace for
the contents of this file is declared, and `data-types`, `constraints`, and `aspects` are
defined.

Custom Records Management namespace

The file defines the information contained in it with the prefix identifier `rmc` to
signify the Records Management custom metadata that it defines:

```
<namespaces>
  <namespace uri="http://www.alfresco.org/model/rmcustom/1.0"
    prefix="rmc"/>
</namespaces>
```

Custom aspects for record objects

We can see from this file that the standard Records Management object types are
extended by custom aspects defined in the `recordsCustomModel.xml` file:

```
<aspect name="rmc:customRecordSeriesProperties">
  <title>Properties for DOD5015 Custom Record Series</title>
  <properties>
```

```
    <property name="rmc:MyLabel">
      <title>Custom Metadata Field</title>
      <type>d:text</type>
      <mandatory>false</mandatory>
      <index enabled="true">
        <atomic>true</atomic>
        <stored>false</stored>
        <tokenised>FALSE</tokenised>
      </index>
    </property>
  </properties>
  <associations/>
  <overrides/>
  <mandatory-aspects/>
</aspect>
<aspect name="rmc:customRecordCategoryProperties">
  <title>Properties for DOD5015 Custom Record Category</title>
  <properties/>
  <associations/>
  <overrides/>
  <mandatory-aspects/>
</aspect>
<aspect name="rmc:customRecordFolderProperties">
  <title>Properties for Custom Record Folder</title>
  <properties/>
  <associations/>
  <overrides/>
  <mandatory-aspects/>
</aspect>
<aspect name="rmc:customRecordProperties">
  <title>Properties for Custom Record</title>
  <properties/>
  <associations/>
  <overrides/>
  <mandatory-aspects/>
</aspect>
```

After creating a new record Series with the custom metadata field `MyLabel` attached, we can see the property included in the node property list like any other property when browsing using the Node Browser. We would also be able to see in the Node Browser, although not shown here, that the aspect {`http://www.alfresco.org/ model/rmcustom/1.0`}`customRecordSeriesProperties` has been applied to the node for the **New Series**.

Properties

Name	Value
{http://www.alfresco.org/model/content/1.0}name	New Series
{http://www.alfresco.org/model/system/1.0}node-dbid	2220
{http://www.alfresco.org/model/system/1.0}store-identifier	SpacesStore
{http://www.alfresco.org/model/recordsmanagement/1.0}identifier	2010-0000002220
{http://www.alfresco.org/model/rmcustom/1.0}MyLabel	Data for my field
{http://www.alfresco.org/model/content/1.0}title	
{http://www.alfresco.org/model/system/1.0}node-uuid	83326a8d-6c07-42c6-b785-eb8e8b09e77a
{http://www.alfresco.org/model/content/1.0}modified	Sat Sep 18 12:54:29 PDT 2010
{http://www.alfresco.org/model/content/1.0}created	Sat Sep 18 12:54:29 PDT 2010
{http://www.alfresco.org/model/system/1.0}store-protocol	workspace
{http://www.alfresco.org/model/content/1.0}description	
{http://www.alfresco.org/model/content/1.0}creator	admin
{http://www.alfresco.org/model/content/1.0}modifier	admin

List of Values

As lists are created in the **List of Value** tool, the list and entry values are also stored dynamically in the repository file `Home/Data Dictionary/Records Management/ recordsCustomModel.xml`.

For example, the `Corporate Departments` list that we defined earlier is represented in the Records Management Custom content model as the following:

```
<constraint name="rmc:d7a13bb2-0999-4928-89d3-b8040d725663"
  type="org.alfresco.module.org_alfresco_module_dod5015.
  caveat.RMListOfValuesConstraint">
  <title>Corporate Departments</title>
  <parameter name="caseSensitive">
    <value>true</value>
```

```
    </parameter>
    <parameter name="matchLogic">
      <value>AND</value>
    </parameter>
    <parameter name="allowedValues">
      <list>
        <value>Engineering</value>
        <value>Executives</value>
        <value>Human Resources</value>
        <value>IT</value>
        <value>Marketing</value>
        <value>Production</value>
        <value>Sales</value>
        <value>Finance</value>
      </list>
    </parameter>
  </constraint>
```

In the example that we saw earlier, this list for Corporate Departments was assigned to a new custom property for a record Category.

The controller JavaScript file for the Custom Metadata component calls back to the repository to query the custom metadata for each of the record object types. After assigning this new property, we can make the following webscript call to find the custom properties returned in JSON format:

```
http://localhost:8080/share/proxy/alfresco/api/rma/admin/customproper
tydefinitions?element=recordCategory
```

```
{
  "data":
  {
    "customProperties":
    {
      "rmc:Department_Authority":
      {
        "dataType": "d:text",
        "label": "Department Authority",
        "description": "",
        "mandatory": false,
        "multiValued": false,
        "defaultValue": "",
        "protected": false,
        "propId": "Department_Authority",
        "constraintRefs":
```

```
[
  {
    "name": "rmc:d7a13bb2-0999-4928-89d3-b8040d725663",
    "title": "Corporate Departments",
    "type": "LIST",
    "parameters":
    {
      "caseSensitive": true,
      "listOfValues" :
      [

        "Executives","Sales","Engineering","Finance",
        "Production","Marketing","IT","Human Resources"
      ]
    }
  }
]
  }
 }
}
}
```

Events

Custom event data is also persisted to the repository to allow dynamic assignment and editing. The event data is stored in the repository file: Company Home/ Dictionary Data/Records Management/rm_event_config.json. The node reference for this file is workspace://SpacesStore/rm_event_config.

The event data is persisted in the JSON format. The contents of the file look like the following:

```
{"events":[{"eventDisplayLabel":"Training
  Complete","eventName":"training_complete",
  "eventType":"rmEventType.simple"},
{"eventDisplayLabel":"Case
  Complete","eventName":"case_complete",
  "eventType":"rmEventType.simple"},
{"eventDisplayLabel":"Obsolete","eventName":"obsolete",
  "eventType":"rmEventType.obsolete"},
{"eventDisplayLabel":"Separation","eventName":"separation",
  "eventType":"rmEventType.simple"},
{"eventDisplayLabel":"Case Closed","eventName":"case_closed",
  "eventType":"rmEventType.simple"},
{"eventDisplayLabel":"Redesignated","eventName":"re_designated",
  "eventType":"rmEventType.simple"},
```

```
{"eventDisplayLabel":"Employee Terminates
  Company","eventName":"1eeacddf-6452-48f1-bb7c-
  e3acbdd54488","eventType":"rmEventType.simple"},
{"eventDisplayLabel":"Study Complete","eventName":"study_complete",
  "eventType":"rmEventType.simple"},
{"eventDisplayLabel":"WGI action complete","eventName":"WGI_action_
complete",
  "eventType":"rmEventType.simple"},
{"eventDisplayLabel":"Superseded","eventName":"superseded",
  "eventType":"rmEventType.superseded"},
{"eventDisplayLabel":"All Allowances Granted Are
  Terminated","eventName":"all_allowances_granted_are_terminated",
  "eventType":"rmEventType.simple"},
{"eventDisplayLabel":"No longer
  needed","eventName":"no_longer_needed",
  "eventType":"rmEventType.simple"},
{"eventDisplayLabel":"Related Record Transfered To Inactive
  Storage","eventName":"related_record_trasfered_inactive_storage",
  "eventType":"rmEventType.crossReferencedRecordTransfered"},
{"eventDisplayLabel":"Abolished","eventName":"abolished",
  "eventType":"rmEventType.simple"}]}
```

WebScript calls for Management Console information

Much of the information that is edited by the Management Console is retrieved from and stored back to the repository when editing is completed.

The following table summarizes some of the calls made for retrieving the information for display. All calls have the base URL of:

`http://localhost:8080/share/proxy/alfresco/api/rma/admin/`. For example, we saw the results of the URL `http://localhost:8080/share/proxy/alfresco/api/rma/admin/custompropertydefinitions?element=recordCategory` listed above.

Parameters for the base URL webscript	Information retrieved
rmauditlog	Retrieve the auditlog.
custompropertydefinitions?element=record	Retrieve custom properties for records.
custompropertydefinitions?element=recordFolder	Retrieve custom properties for record Folders.
custompropertydefinitions?element=recordCategory	Retrieve custom properties for record Categories.

Parameters for the base URL webscript	Information retrieved
`custompropertydefinitions?element=recordSeries`	Retrieve custom properties for record Series.
`emailmap`	Retrieves a list of e-mail mappings.
`rmeventtypes`	Retrieves the types of events.
`rmevents`	Retrieves the events.
`rmconstraints`	Retrieves List of Value information.
`customreferencedefinitions`	Retrieve a list of custom reference definitions.
`rmroles`	Retrieve a list of all Records Management roles.
`rmroles/{roleID}` , like `rmroles/Adminstrator`	Retrieves a list of capabilities for a specific Records Management role.

Summary

In this chapter, we covered the following topics:

- How to build custom **List of Value** lists to be used as drop-down selections for custom properties
- How to add custom metadata properties to record object types;
- How to define custom events for event-driven triggers in disposition instructions
- How to map e-mail metadata fields to properties of the content node for the uploaded message that is stored in the repository
- How to create custom types of relationships between two records

At the end of this chapter in a "How does it work?" section, we included a detailed discussion about how the Records Management Console works. Much of the same framework code for the Management Console and the Administration Console is shared.

We saw how dynamically created properties are stored in the Records Management Custom (`rmc`) namespace, and we saw that the file where this data is persisted is in the `Data Dictionary` of the repository. The **List of Values** data is also stored in the same custom content model file. Custom event data is persisted in a similar way in a document stored under the `Data Dictionary` folder that allows the data to be dynamically applied.

This is the last chapter of this book on Alfresco Records Management. In this book, we've taken a complete tour of the features and capabilities of the Alfresco Records Management system from a user's perspective. We've also taken some deep dives into looking at Alfresco internals, and some of that information should come in handy as a starting point for additional development or customization projects that you may plan.

At the beginning of this book, we started by discussing the importance of Records Management. Despite the fact that the bulk of the material covered in this book focused on the mechanics of implementation of the Alfresco system, we noted early on that much of the success of a records program has nothing at all to do with software.

Success of a project is often very closely tied to the people, culture, and having an understanding of what your organization really needs to accomplish. Only after you have that part of the project under control should you jump into the details of the software.

Once you are ready for implementation, the software is the most important tool that will help you realize your Records Management goals, and Alfresco Records Management is a great selection as a software tool to help you to do just that.

Index

F

Federal Rules of Civil Procedure. *See* **FRCP**
File Plan
  about 344, 345
  Alfresco example File Plan 170, 171
  benefits 170
  components 168
  container, copying 181
  container metadata 179
  container, moving 181
  creating, best practices 172
  data, exporting to 230, 231
  data, importing from 229
  defining 168
  disposition schedule 207
  Search 353
  transfer items, finding 347, 348
  transfer items, rendering 346
  transfer pages, linking 346
  working 182
File Plan, components
  about 169
  categories 168
  folders 169
  series 168
File Plan, creating
  Containers, adding to 175
  steps 174
File Plan Document List
  Document List controller file 197
File Plan page, Records Management site
  about 86, 87
  File Plan toolbar 87-89
  left navigation panel 90, 91
File Plan report 334
File Plan toolbar
  about 87
  Export All button 88
  file button 88
  import button 88
  new containers 88
  Report button 88
  Selected Items button 90
File Plan, working
  Document Library FreeMarker
    presentation 191

  Document Library JavaScript controller
    file 184, 185
  documentlibrary page behavior 183, 184
  File Plan page setup, by preset 182, 183
filing records
  electronic file upload, internals 275-281
  non-electronic file upload, internals 281-284
  working 275
filter parameter 346
Filters.getFilterParams() method 348
folder
  closing 321
FRCP 17
FreeMarker template, Details page
  events component 312, 314
  FreeMarker components 303-306
  imported files 301, 302
  metadata component 312
  RecordsDocumentDetails object,
    initializing 302
  references component 314
  web preview component 307
from parameter 394
FTS-Alfresco query language
  about 364
  Booleans, testing 369
  conjunctive search 365
  date searching 370
  disjunctive search 365
  elements, grouping 369
  item, searching 364
  KEYWORDS 367, 368
  mandatory elements 372
  non-QNames, escaping 369
  operator precedence, hierarchy 372
  optional elements 372
  phrase, searching 365
  properties, searching 366
  property ranges, searching 370, 371
  proximity search 371
  QNames, escaping 368
  special fields 367
  terms, negating 366
  wildcard search 365

M

mandatory metadata
rma:originatingOrganization property 319
rma:originator property 319
rma:publicationDate property 319
specifying 318
method
Filters.getFilterParams() 348
setFilterIds() 345
model file, implementing
about 141
aspects 146
constraints 143
model file header 141, 142
model, installing 146
model namespace 142
types 143-145
model, installing
bootstrap deployment 147, 148
dynamic deployment 148, 149
Model-View-Controller. *See* **MVC**
MVC
about 55
advantage 56
web framework flow 56

N

NARA 325
National Archive and Records
    Administration. *See* **NARA**
new Content Model exposing, from Share
    user interface
metadata, editing 156-161
type information, verifying 154
Types, adding to Change Type action
    152-154
Types, adding to site upload form 150, 151
viewing forms, customizing 156-161
new model, creating
designing 139-141
model file, implementing 141
new Content Model exposing, from Share
    user interface 150

non-electronic record, Share
about 10
filing 251, 252

O

OCR 273
onActionXXX methods
onActionCopyTo 349
onActionMoveTo 349
onCreateSite method 66, 68
onFileUpload method 276
onNewContainer() method 284
onOK function 351
onReady() method 241, 279, 394
operator precedence, hierarchy 372
( ) 372
[ ] < > 372
+ | - 372
AND 372
NOT 372
OR 372
Optical Character Recognition. *See* **OCR**
Outlook 2007
IMAP, configuring 262-265

P

parameters, base URL webscript
customreferencedefinitions 456
rmauditlog 455, 456
rmconstraints 456
rmevents 456
rmeventtypes 456
rmroles 456
permissions
about 420, 421
File a record 420
managing 421
Read a record 420
presets.xml file 109
property file label
label.create-site 62
label.display-site 62
label.load-test-data 62

label.rm-console 62
label.summary 62
label.title 62

Q

Q2 records 214
QNAME field, special field 367
Quartz
    URL 336

R

record
    declaring 319
    freezing 329-331
    holding 329
    hold request, responding 330
    lifecycle 317
    locating, on Hold area 331, 332
    metadata packages, exporting 333
    on Hold, releasing 334
    package, exporting 332
    Release Hold action 334
    reviewing 320
record filing, CIFS used
    about 253
    configuring 255, 256
    steps 254
    troubleshooting, problems 256
record filing, IMAP used
    about 259
    configuring 260
    steps 260
record lifecycle
    about 11, 12, 208
    accession 211
    cutoff 209
    destruction 210
    retention 210
    transfer 210
    transfer, examples 211
record lifecycle, working
    background jobs 336
    File Plan component 344, 345
    notifications, reviewing 337
    report generation, triggering 349-352
    tracking 342

unique record ID 335, 336
records
    about 9, 10
    examples 10
    filing 246
    lifecycle 11, 12
    records management 11
    types 10
Records Details page
    about 288
    Alfresco Flash previewer 289
    Details screen 288
    Download action 292
    Events 297, 298
    Record actions 292
    Record Metadata 290
    references 298
    references, displaying 300
    references, types 299
    references, working 300
    URL links 297
    working 300
RecordsDocumentList class 202
records, filing
    Alfresco, via FTP 266
    from another Share site 252, 253
    from CIFS mounted drive 253
    from e-mail client, IMAP used 259
    from electronic record 247-250
    from non-electronic record 251
    multiple ways 246
    options 274
    scanning method, using 272
Records Management
    about 11, 13
    audits 376
    benefits 15-27
    configuration 101
    Electronic Records Management (ERM)
        systems 11
    groups 401
    Management Console 432
    Records Management and Search 353
    roles, creating 411
    versus document management 13, 14
    webscript dashlet flow 57
Records Management AMP files 41

Thank you for buying
Alfresco 3 Records Management

About Packt Publishing

Packt, pronounced 'packed', published its first book "*Mastering phpMyAdmin for Effective MySQL Management*" in April 2004 and subsequently continued to specialize in publishing highly focused books on specific technologies and solutions.

Our books and publications share the experiences of your fellow IT professionals in adapting and customizing today's systems, applications, and frameworks. Our solution based books give you the knowledge and power to customize the software and technologies you're using to get the job done. Packt books are more specific and less general than the IT books you have seen in the past. Our unique business model allows us to bring you more focused information, giving you more of what you need to know, and less of what you don't.

Packt is a modern, yet unique publishing company, which focuses on producing quality, cutting-edge books for communities of developers, administrators, and newbies alike. For more information, please visit our website: www.packtpub.com.

About Packt Open Source

In 2010, Packt launched two new brands, Packt Open Source and Packt Enterprise, in order to continue its focus on specialization. This book is part of the Packt Open Source brand, home to books published on software built around Open Source licences, and offering information to anybody from advanced developers to budding web designers. The Open Source brand also runs Packt's Open Source Royalty Scheme, by which Packt gives a royalty to each Open Source project about whose software a book is sold.

Writing for Packt

We welcome all inquiries from people who are interested in authoring. Book proposals should be sent to author@packtpub.com. If your book idea is still at an early stage and you would like to discuss it first before writing a formal book proposal, contact us; one of our commissioning editors will get in touch with you.

We're not just looking for published authors; if you have strong technical skills but no writing experience, our experienced editors can help you develop a writing career, or simply get some additional reward for your expertise.

Alfresco Developer Guide

ISBN: 978-1-847193-11-7   Paperback: 556 pages

Customizing Alfresco with actions, web scripts, web forms, workflows, and more

1. Learn to customize the entire Alfresco platform, including both Document Management and Web Content Management

2. Jam-packed with real-world, step-by-step examples to jump start your development

3. Content modeling, custom actions, Java API, RESTful web scripts, advanced workflow

Alfresco 3 Web Content Management

ISBN: 978-1-847198-00-6   Paperback: 440 pages

Create an infrastructure to manage all your web content, and deploy it to various external production systems

1. A complete guide to Web Content Creation and Distribution

2. Understand the concepts and advantages of Publishing-style Web CMS

3. Leverage a single installation to manage multiple websites

4. Integrate Alfresco web applications with external systems

LaVergne, TN USA
19 January 2011
213164LV00003B/66/P